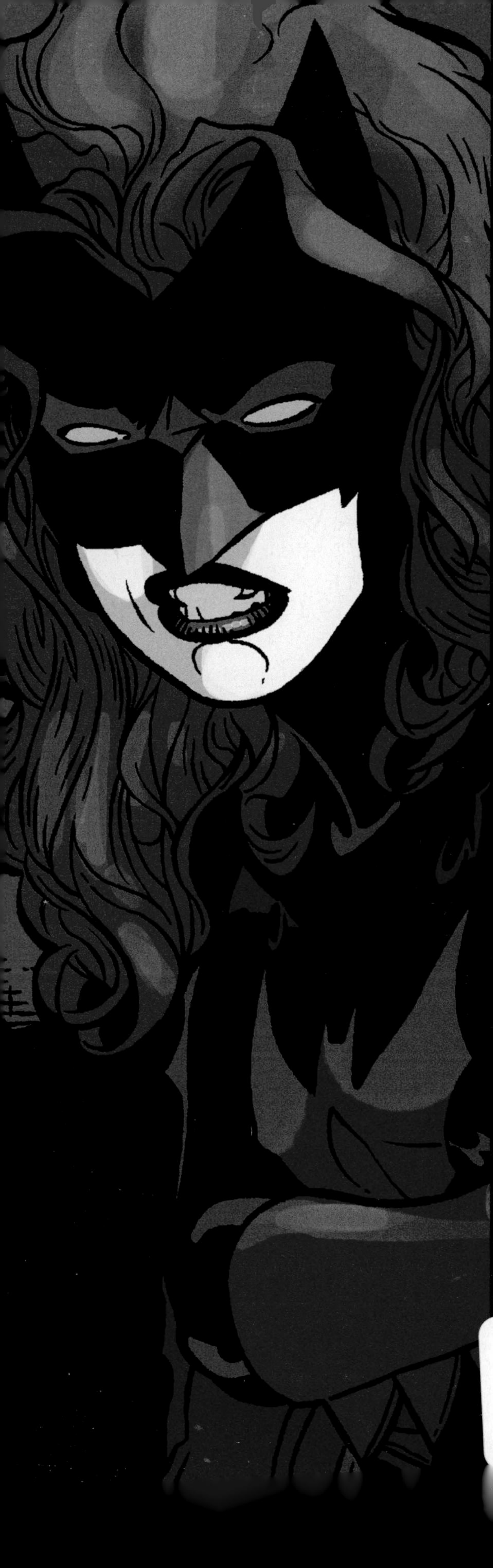

VOLUME 6
THE UNKNOWNS

BATWOMAN

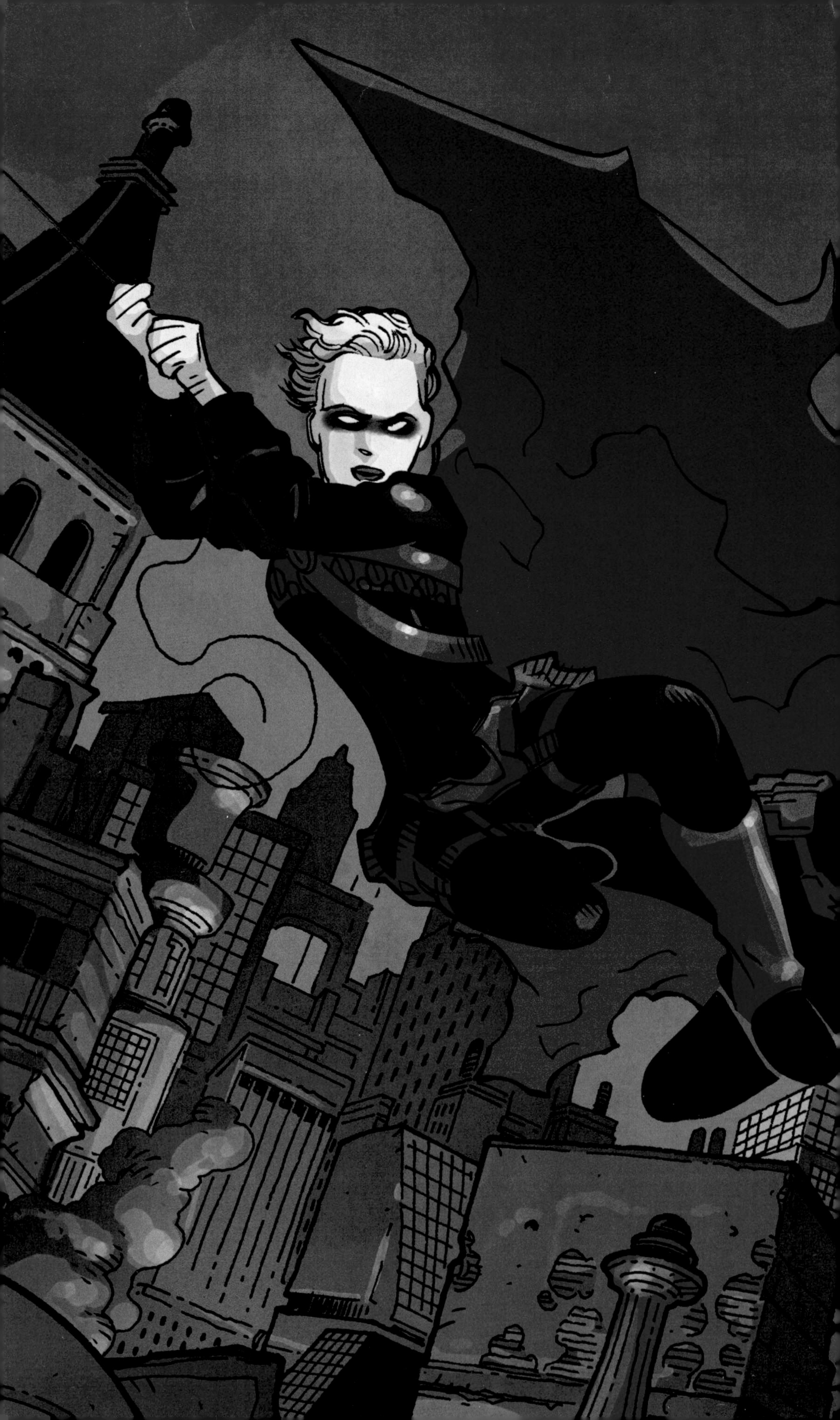

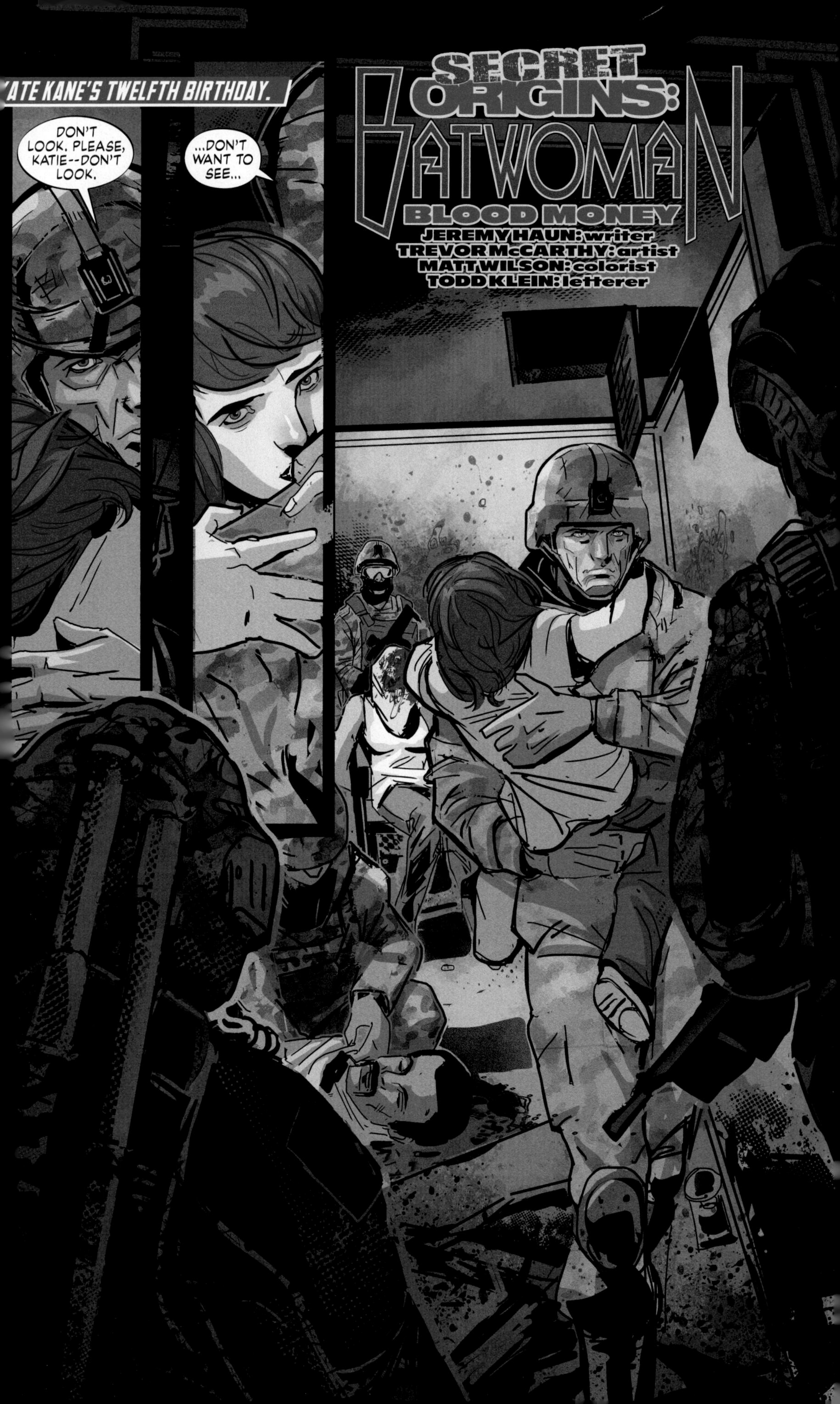

ATE KANE'S TWELFTH BIRTHDAY.
DON'T LOOK. PLEASE, KATIE--DON'T LOOK.
...DON'T WANT TO SEE...
SECRET ORIGINS: BATWOMAN
BLOOD MONEY
JEREMY HAUN: writer
TREVOR McCARTHY: artist
MATT WILSON: colorist
TODD KLEIN: letterer

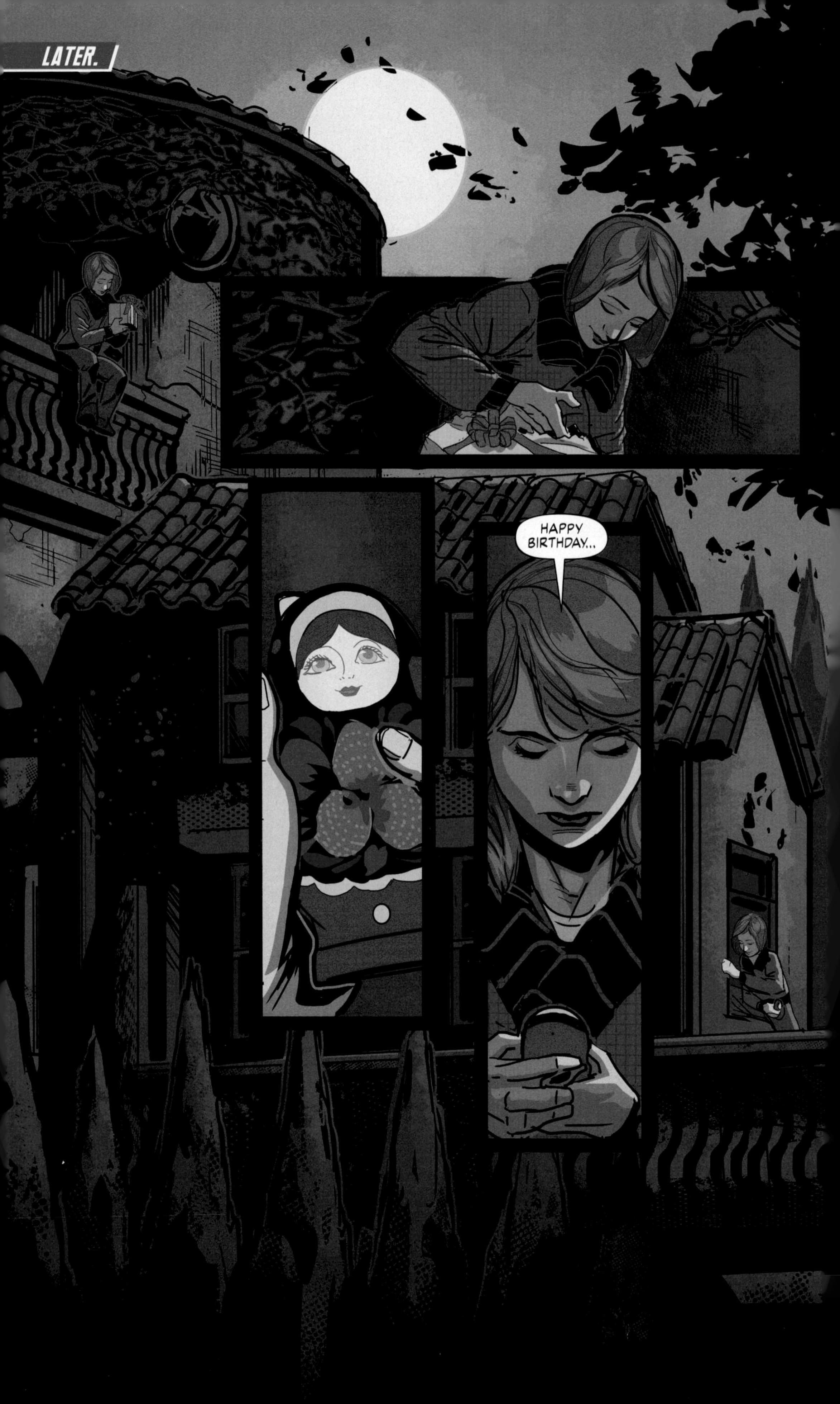
LATER.
HAPPY BIRTHDAY...

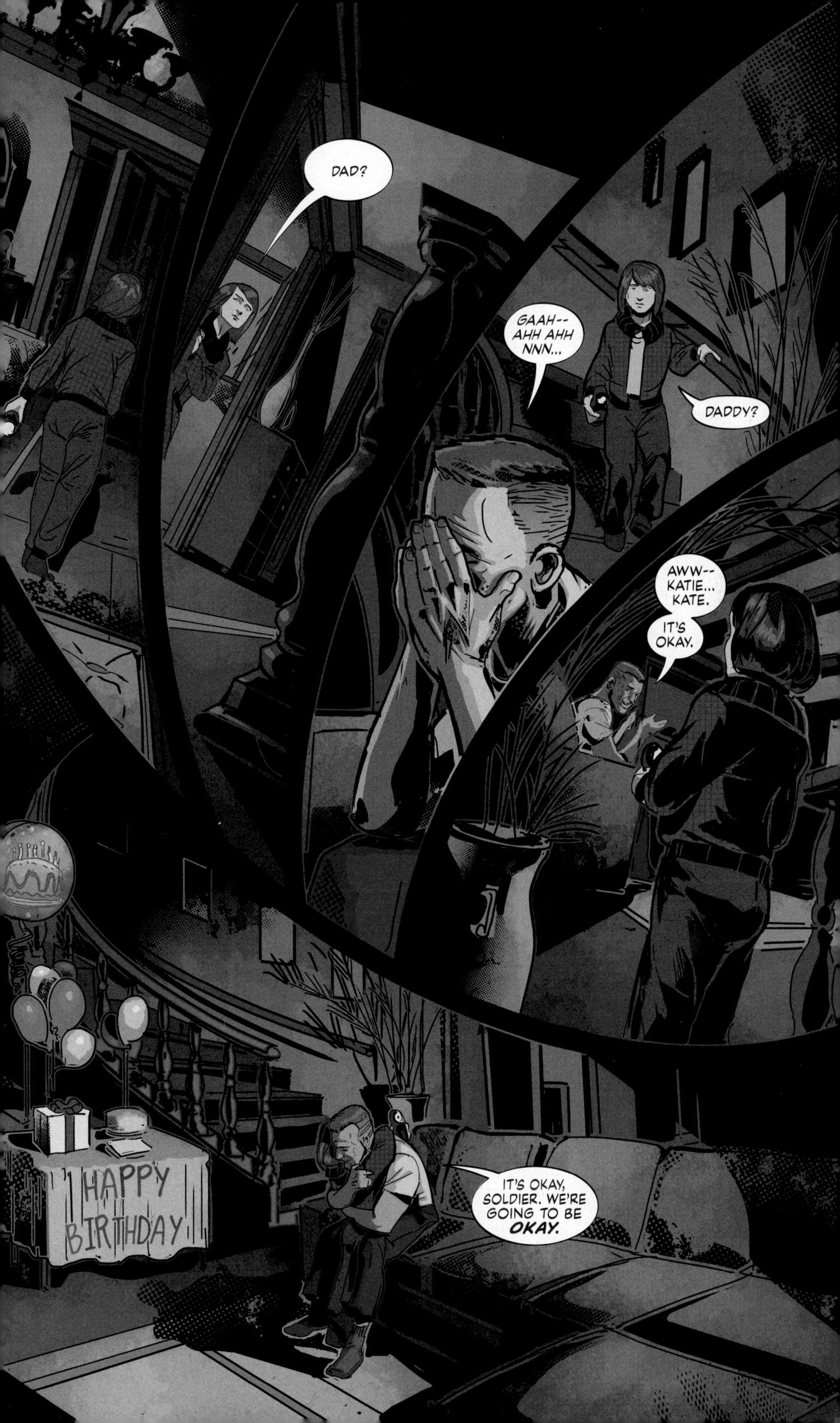
DAD?
GAAH-- AHH AHH NNN...
DADDY?
AWW-- KATIE... KATE.
IT'S OKAY.
HAPPY BIRTHDAY
IT'S OKAY, SOLDIER. WE'RE GOING TO BE ***OKAY.***

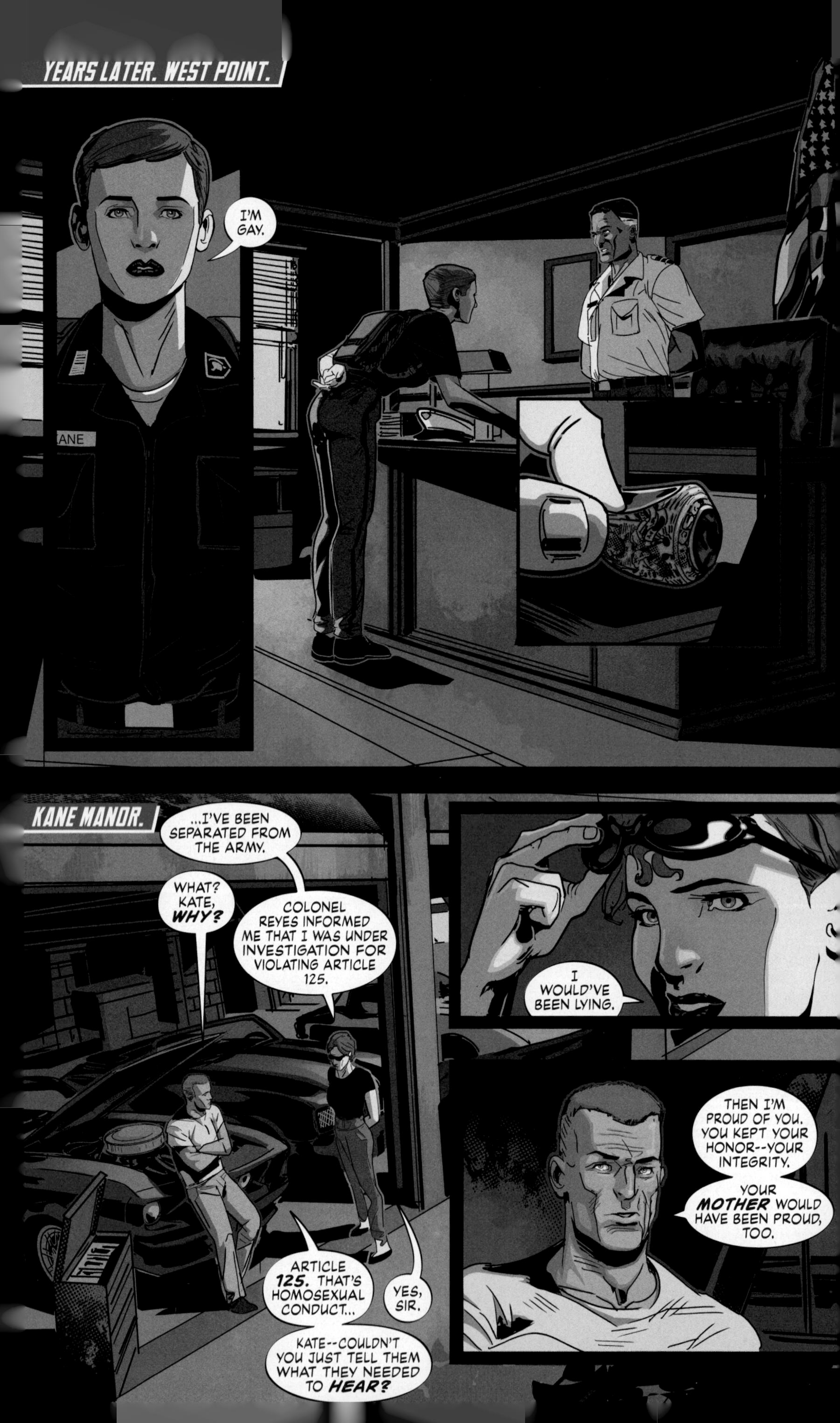
YEARS LATER. WEST POINT.
I'M GAY.
KANE
KANE MANOR.
...I'VE BEEN SEPARATED FROM THE ARMY.
WHAT? KATE, WHY?
COLONEL REYES INFORMED ME THAT I WAS UNDER INVESTIGATION FOR VIOLATING ARTICLE 125.
ARTICLE 125. THAT'S HOMOSEXUAL CONDUCT...
YES, SIR.
KATE--COULDN'T YOU JUST TELL THEM WHAT THEY NEEDED TO HEAR?
I WOULD'VE BEEN LYING.
THEN I'M PROUD OF YOU. YOU KEPT YOUR HONOR--YOUR INTEGRITY.
YOUR MOTHER WOULD HAVE BEEN PROUD, TOO.

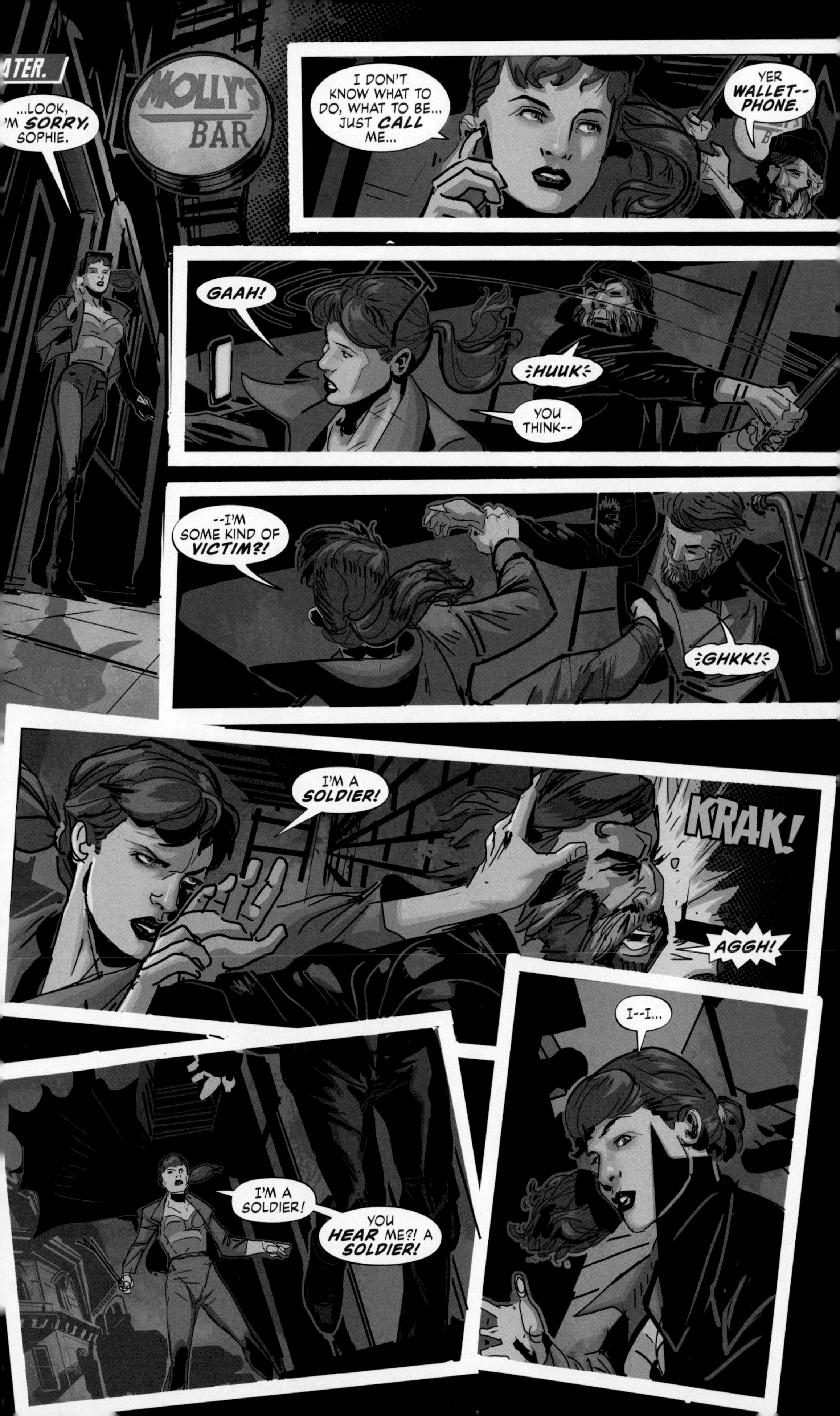

ATER.
...LOOK, 'M SORRY, SOPHIE.
MOLLY'S BAR
I DON'T KNOW WHAT TO DO, WHAT TO BE... JUST CALL ME...
YER WALLET--PHONE.
GAAH!
HUUK
YOU THINK--
--I'M SOME KIND OF VICTIM?!
GHKK!
I'M A SOLDIER!
KRAK!
AGGH!
I'M A SOLDIER!
YOU HEAR ME?! A SOLDIER!
I--I...

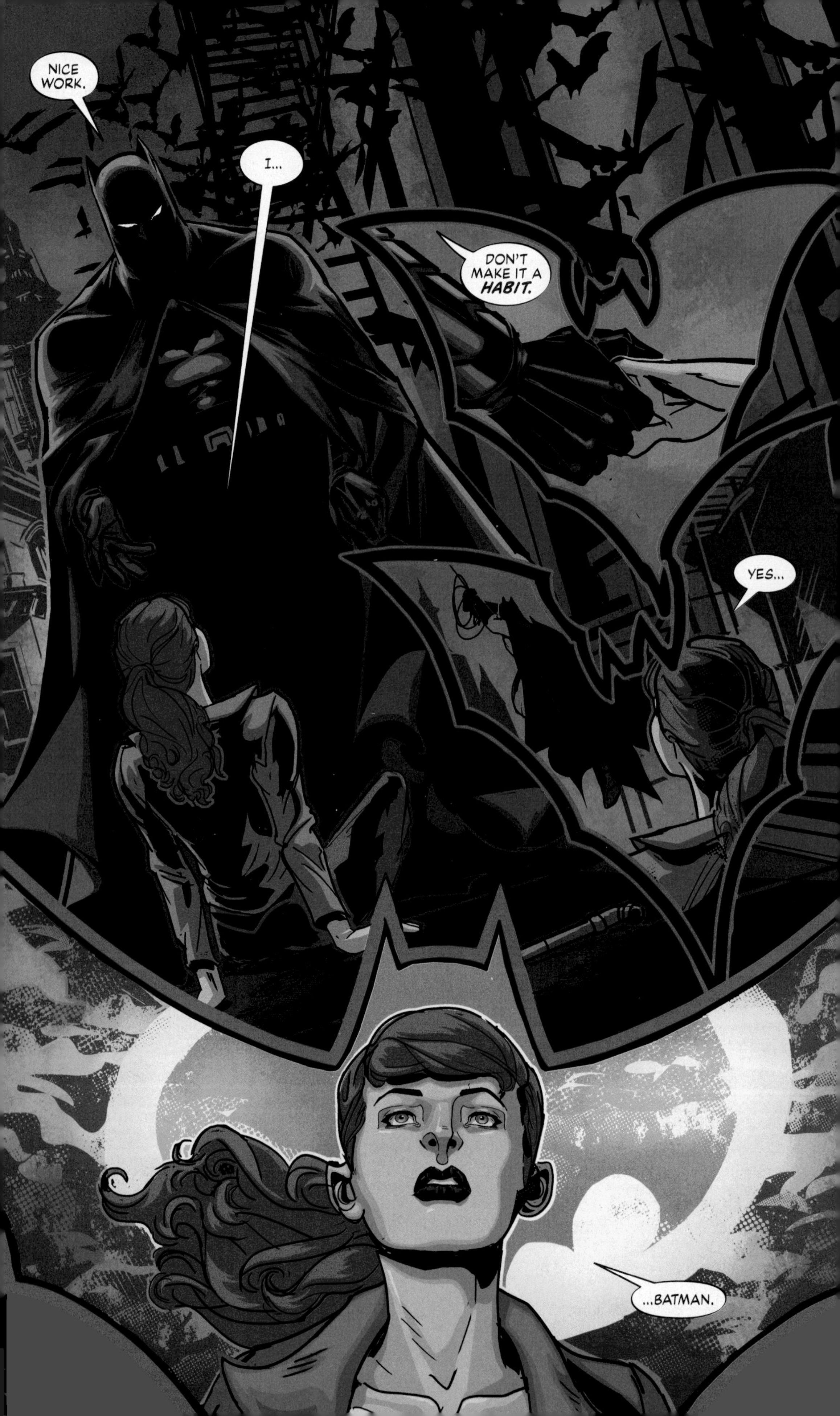
NICE WORK.
I...
DON'T MAKE IT A *HABIT.*
YES...
...BATMAN.

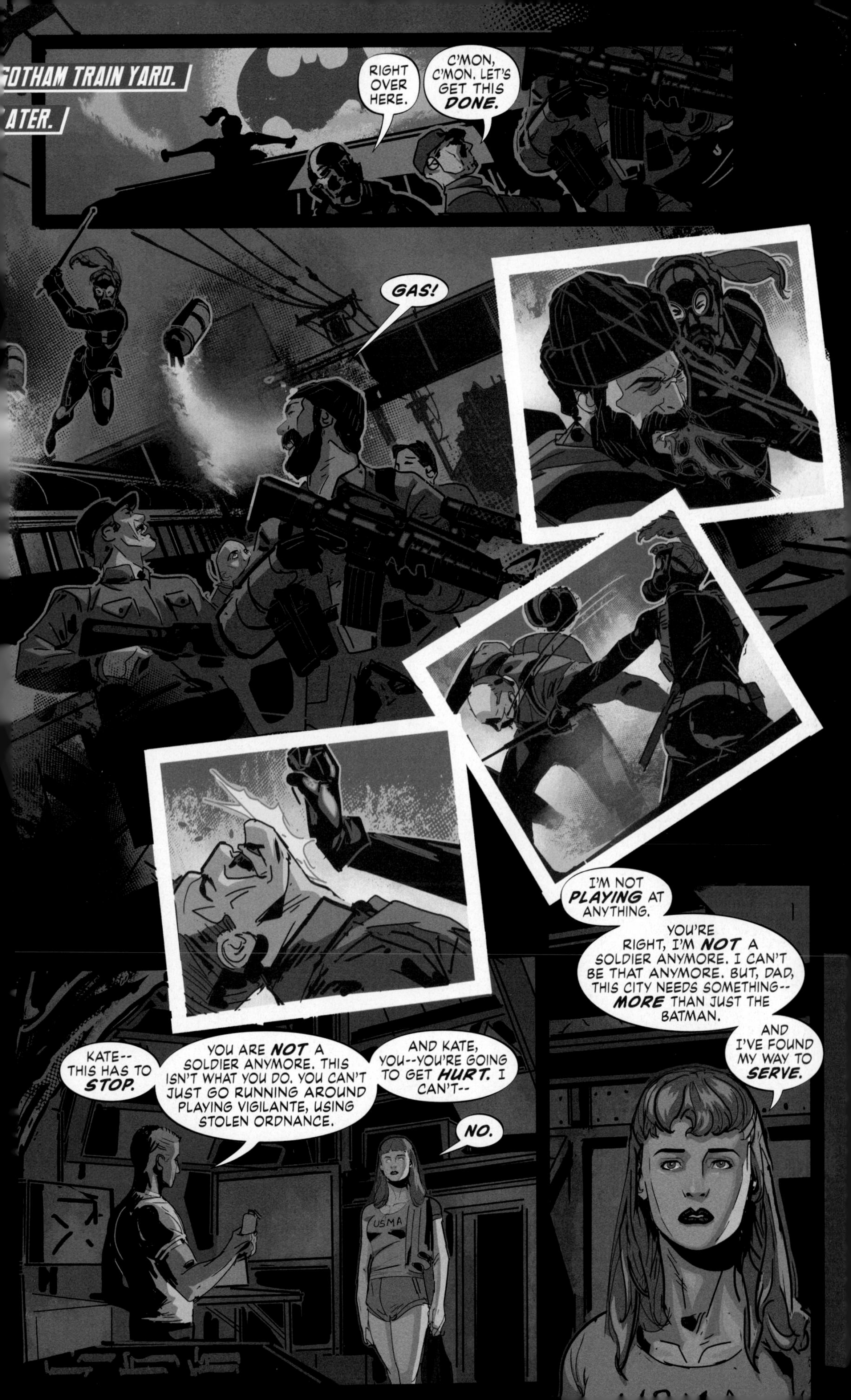
GOTHAM TRAIN YARD.
LATER.
RIGHT OVER HERE.
C'MON, C'MON. LET'S GET THIS DONE.
GAS!
I'M NOT PLAYING AT ANYTHING.
KATE-- THIS HAS TO STOP.
YOU ARE NOT A SOLDIER ANYMORE. THIS ISN'T WHAT YOU DO. YOU CAN'T JUST GO RUNNING AROUND PLAYING VIGILANTE, USING STOLEN ORDNANCE.
AND KATE, YOU--YOU'RE GOING TO GET HURT. I CAN'T--
NO.
YOU'RE RIGHT, I'M NOT A SOLDIER ANYMORE. I CAN'T BE THAT ANYMORE. BUT, DAD, THIS CITY NEEDS SOMETHING-- MORE THAN JUST THE BATMAN.
AND I'VE FOUND MY WAY TO SERVE.
USMA

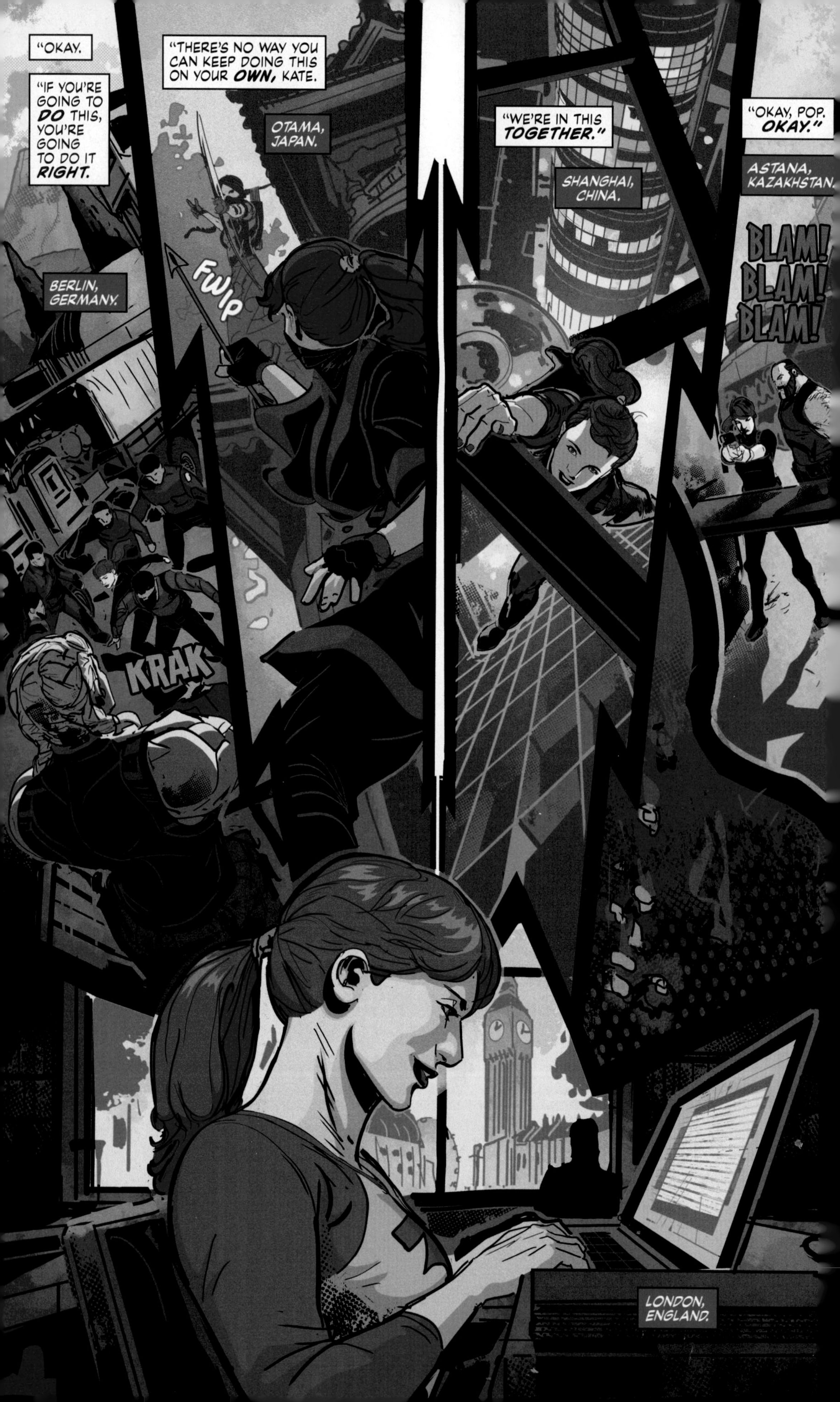
"OKAY.
"IF YOU'RE GOING TO DO THIS, YOU'RE GOING TO DO IT RIGHT.
BERLIN, GERMANY.
KRAK
"THERE'S NO WAY YOU CAN KEEP DOING THIS ON YOUR OWN, KATE.
OTAMA, JAPAN.
FWIP
"WE'RE IN THIS TOGETHER."
SHANGHAI, CHINA.
"OKAY, POP. OKAY."
ASTANA, KAZAKHSTAN.
BLAM! BLAM! BLAM!
LONDON, ENGLAND.

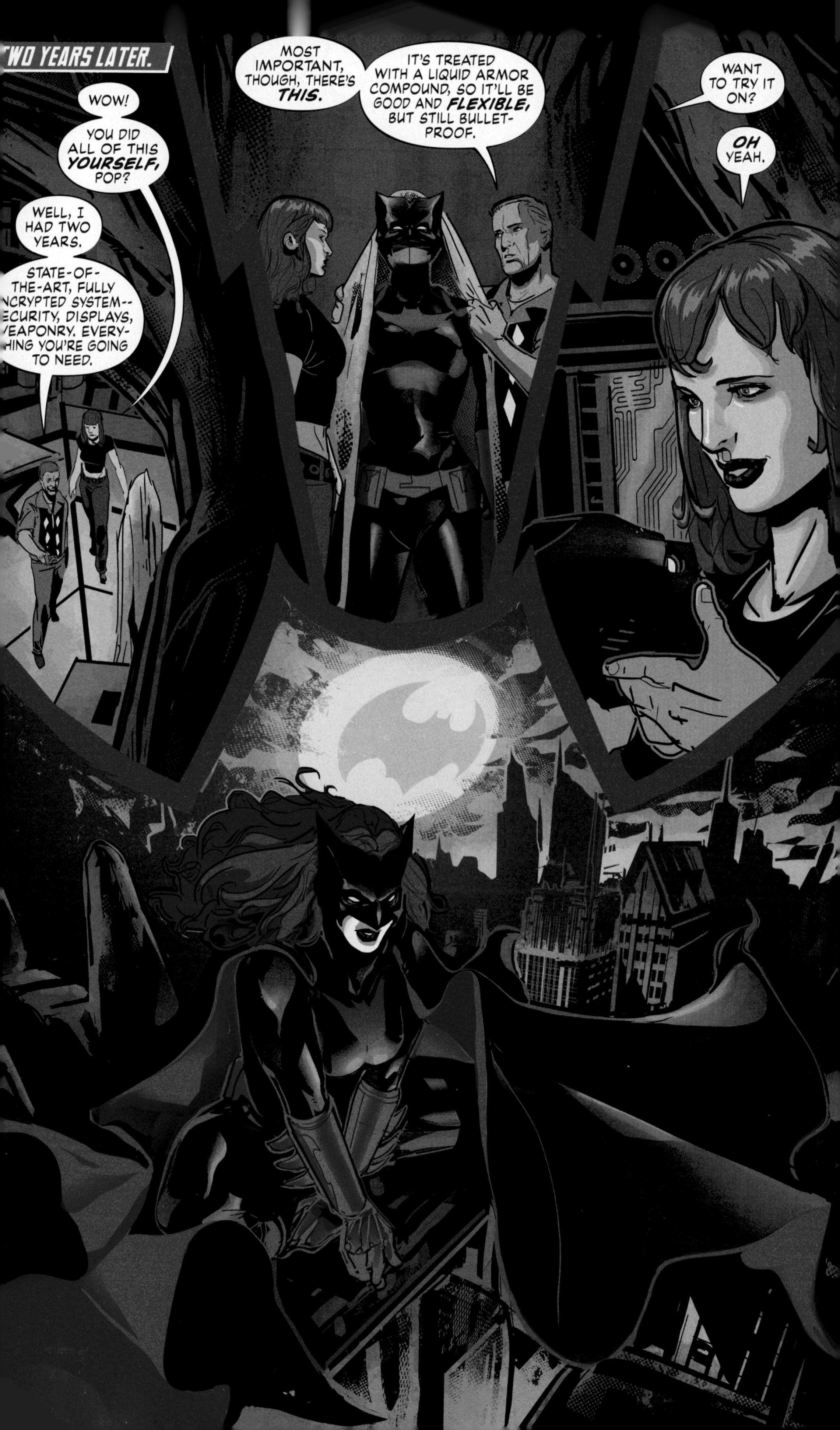
TWO YEARS LATER.
WOW!
YOU DID ALL OF THIS YOURSELF, POP?
WELL, I HAD TWO YEARS.
STATE-OF-THE-ART, FULLY ENCRYPTED SYSTEM--SECURITY, DISPLAYS, WEAPONRY. EVERYTHING YOU'RE GOING TO NEED.
MOST IMPORTANT, THOUGH, THERE'S THIS.
IT'S TREATED WITH A LIQUID ARMOR COMPOUND, SO IT'LL BE GOOD AND FLEXIBLE, BUT STILL BULLET-PROOF.
WANT TO TRY IT ON?
OH YEAH.

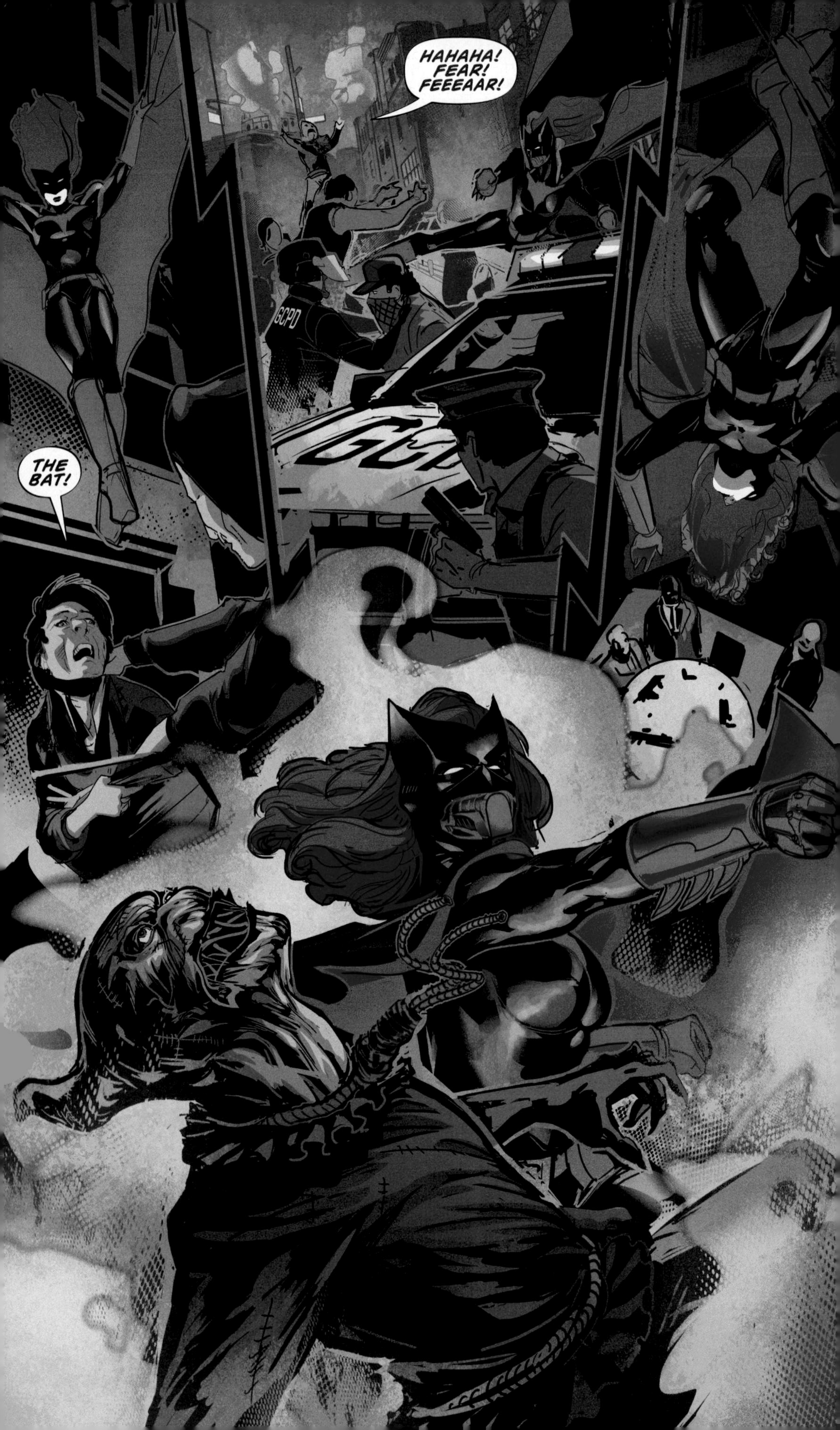
HAHAHA! FEAR! FEEEAAR!
THE BAT!

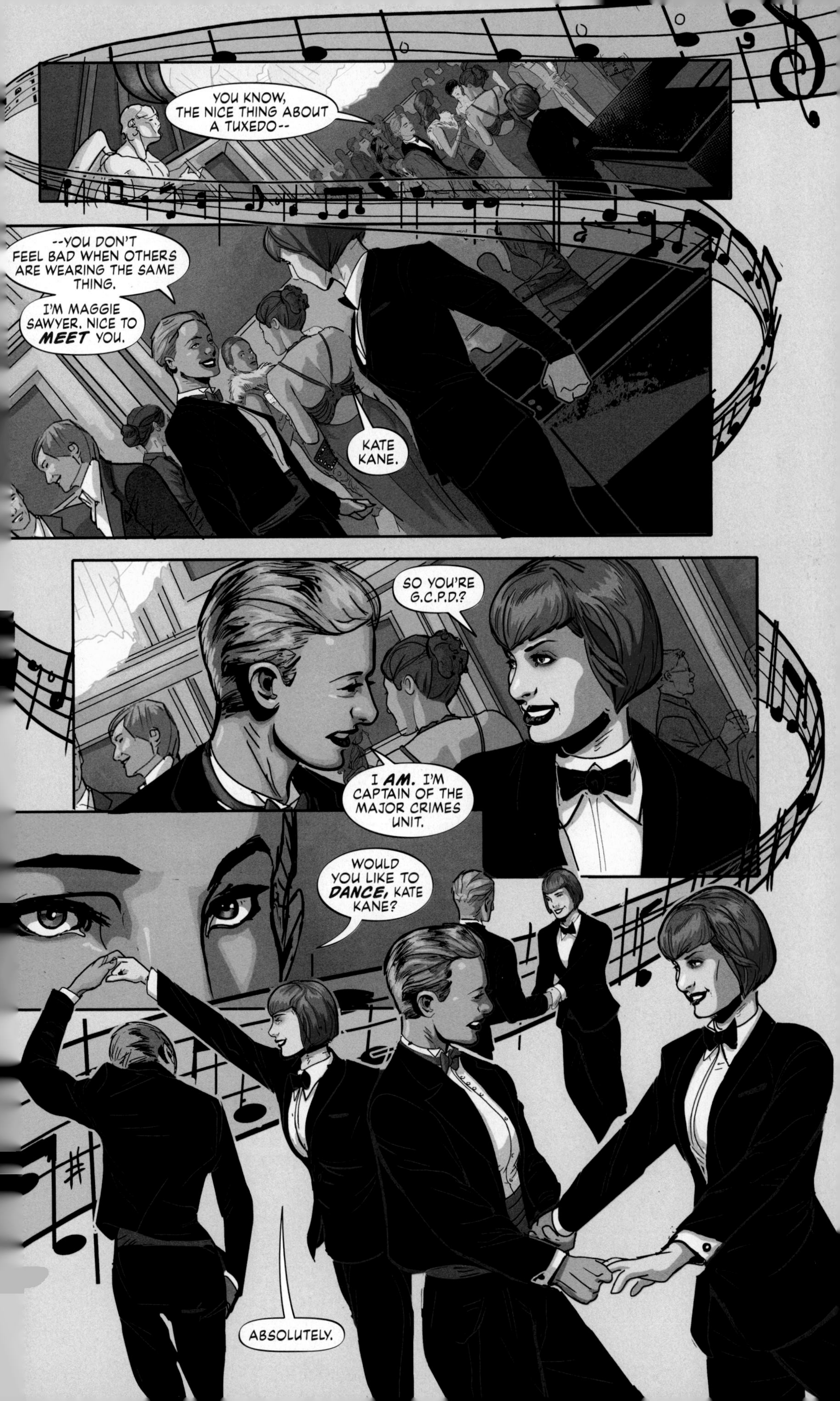
YOU KNOW, THE NICE THING ABOUT A TUXEDO--
--YOU DON'T FEEL BAD WHEN OTHERS ARE WEARING THE SAME THING.
I'M MAGGIE SAWYER. NICE TO MEET YOU.
KATE KANE.
SO YOU'RE G.C.P.D.?
I AM. I'M CAPTAIN OF THE MAJOR CRIMES UNIT.
WOULD YOU LIKE TO DANCE, KATE KANE?
ABSOLUTELY.

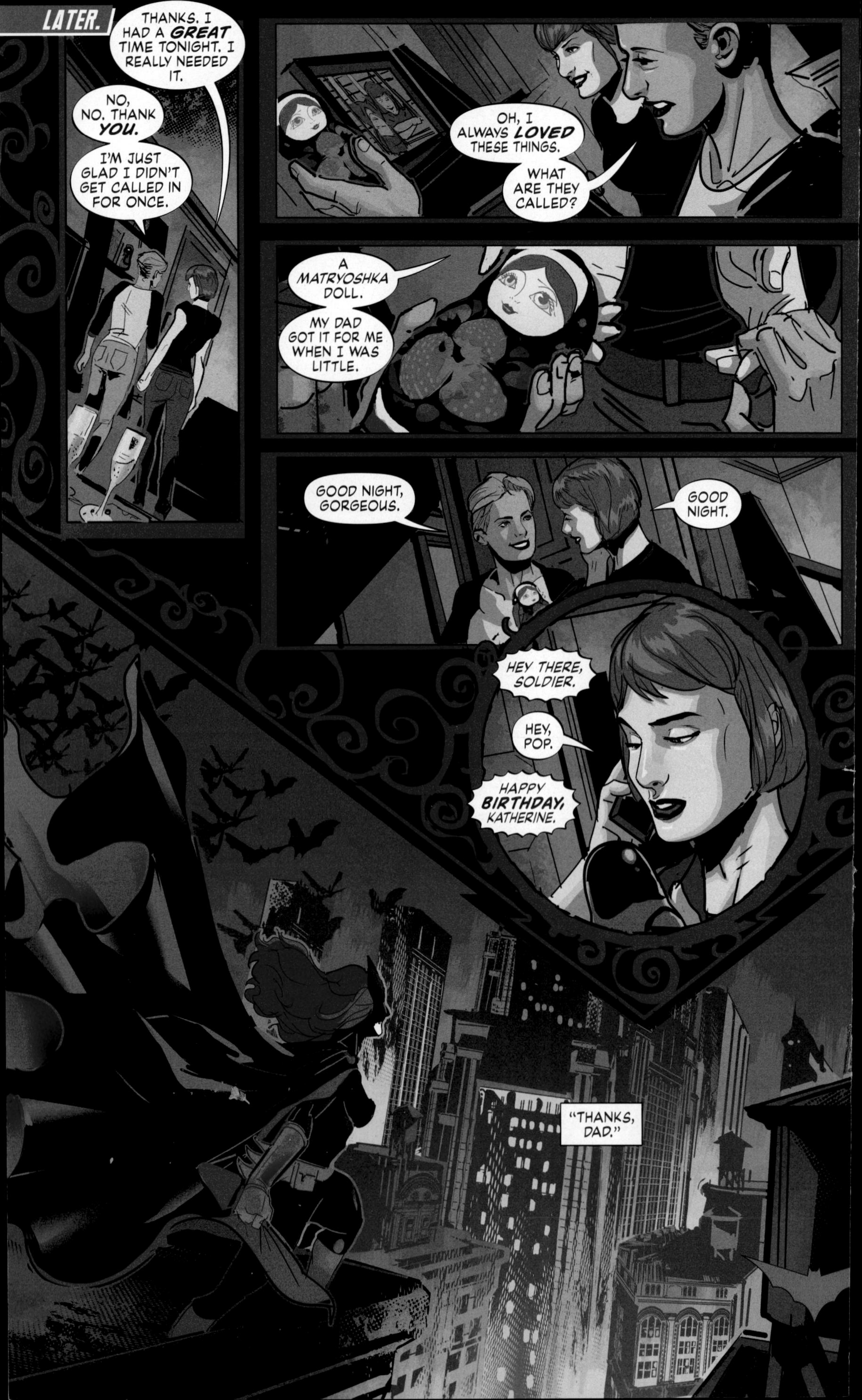
LATER.
THANKS. I HAD A GREAT TIME TONIGHT. I REALLY NEEDED IT.
NO, NO. THANK YOU.
I'M JUST GLAD I DIDN'T GET CALLED IN FOR ONCE.
OH, I ALWAYS LOVED THESE THINGS.
WHAT ARE THEY CALLED?
A MATRYOSHKA DOLL.
MY DAD GOT IT FOR ME WHEN I WAS LITTLE.
GOOD NIGHT, GORGEOUS.
GOOD NIGHT.
HEY THERE, SOLDIER.
HEY, POP.
HAPPY BIRTHDAY, KATHERINE.
"THANKS, DAD."

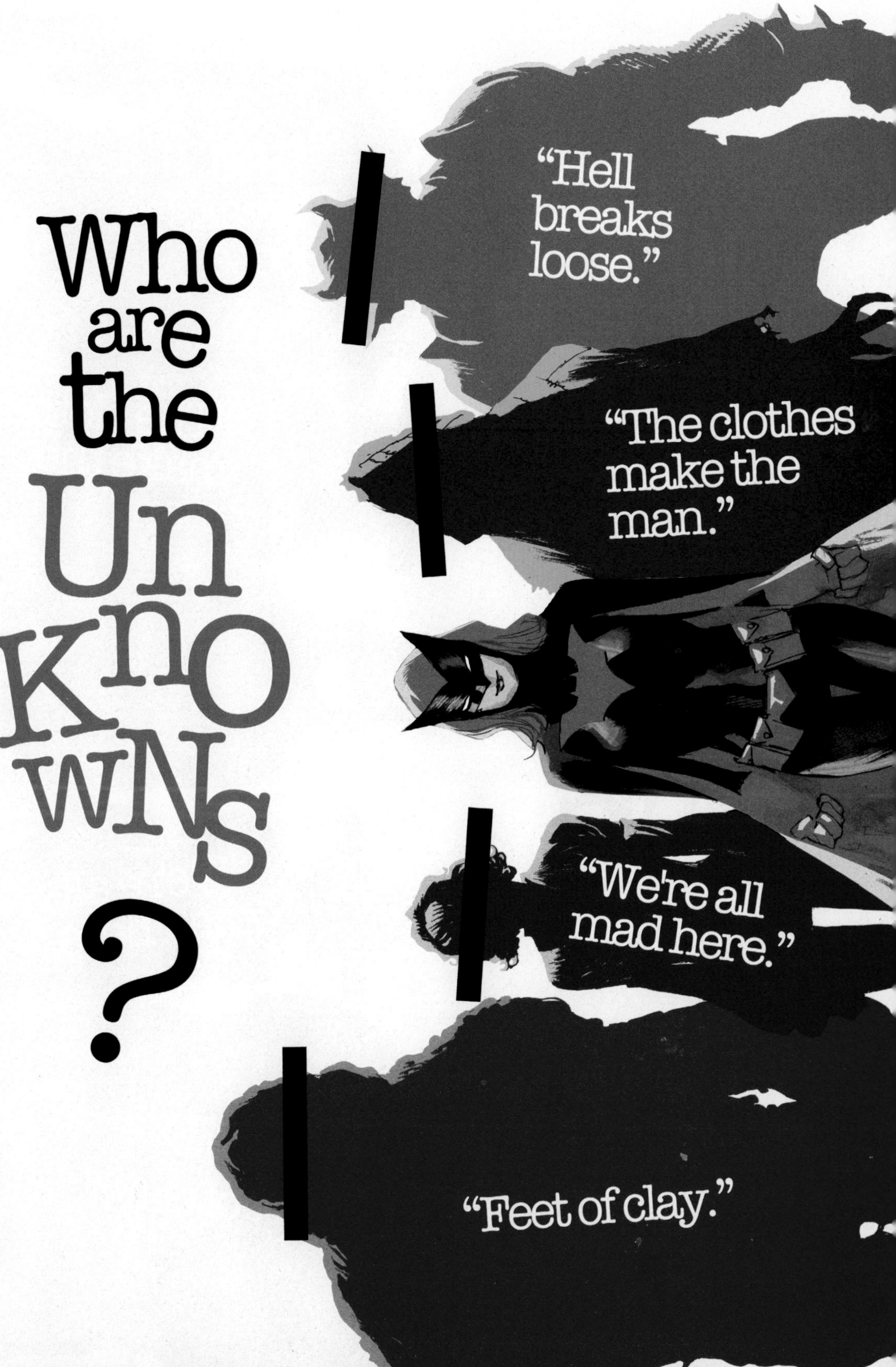
Who are the UnKnoWNs ?
"Hell breaks loose."
"The clothes make the man."
"We're all mad here."
"Feet of clay."

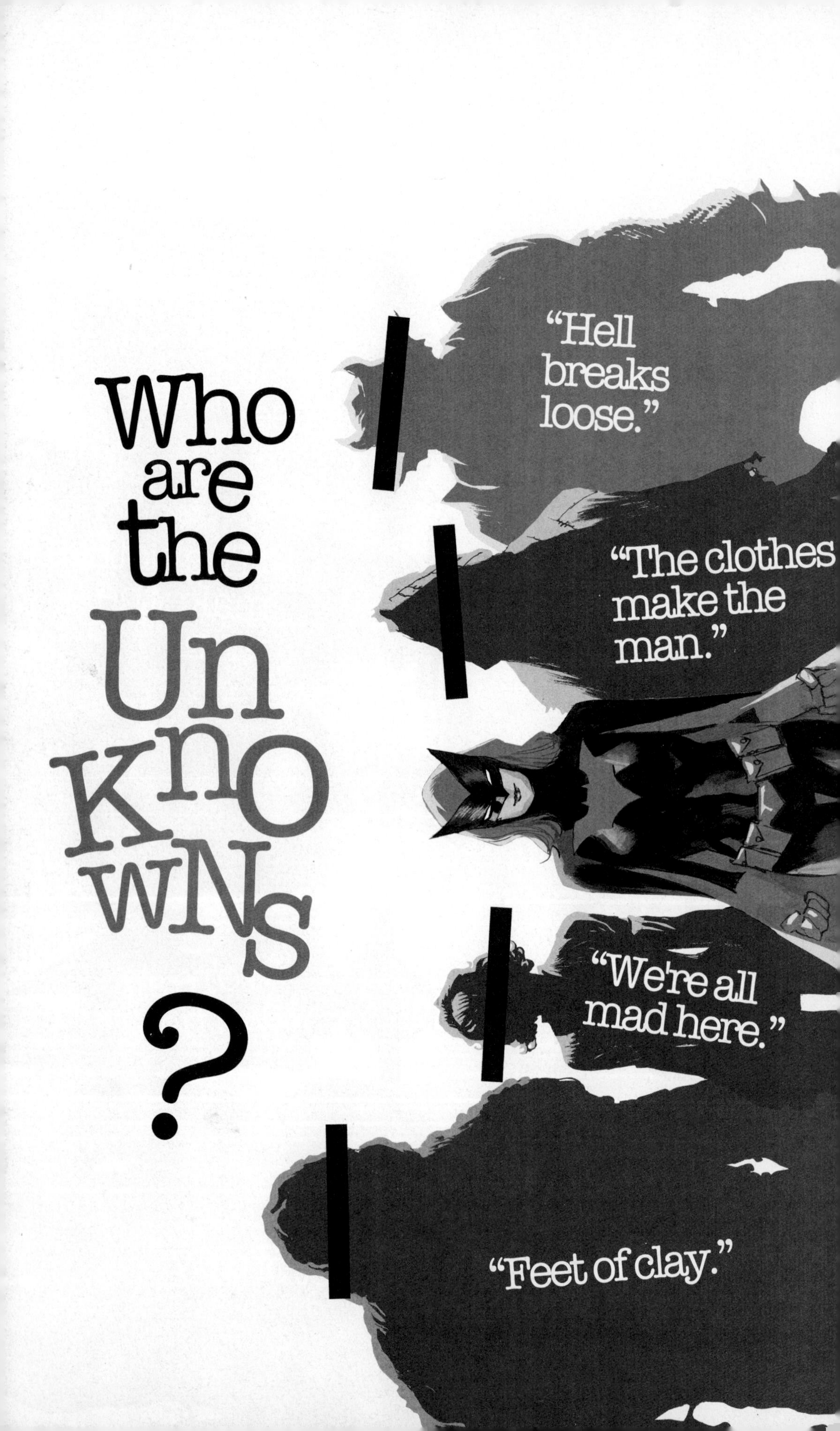
Who are the UnKnoWNs?
"Hell breaks loose."
"The clothes make the man."
"We're all mad here."
"Feet of clay."

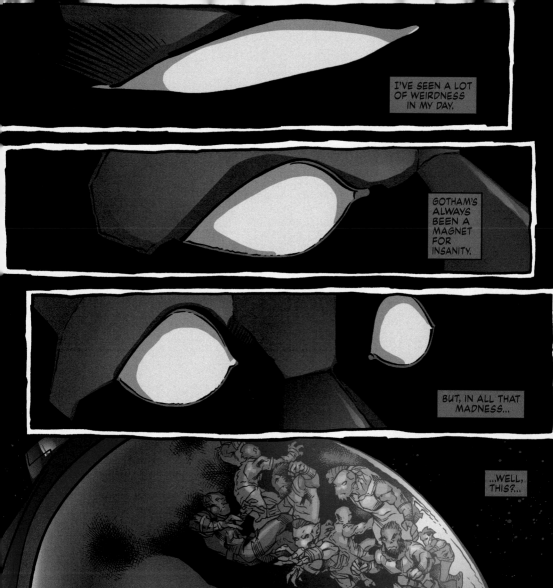

I'VE SEEN A LOT OF WEIRDNESS IN MY DAY.

GOTHAM'S ALWAYS BEEN A MAGNET FOR INSANITY.

BUT, IN ALL THAT MADNESS...

...WELL, THIS?...

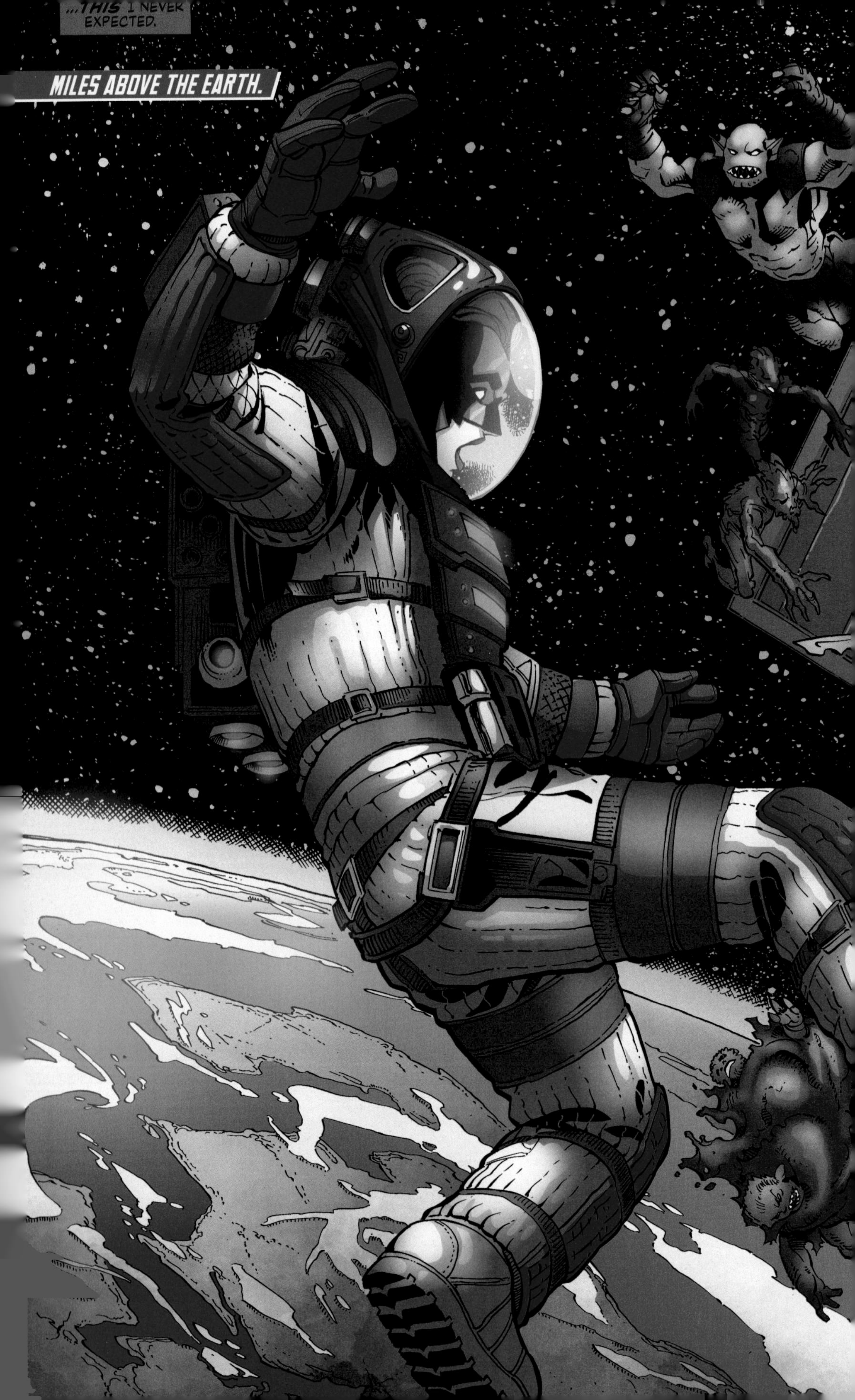

...THIS I NEVER EXPECTED.
MILES ABOVE THE EARTH.

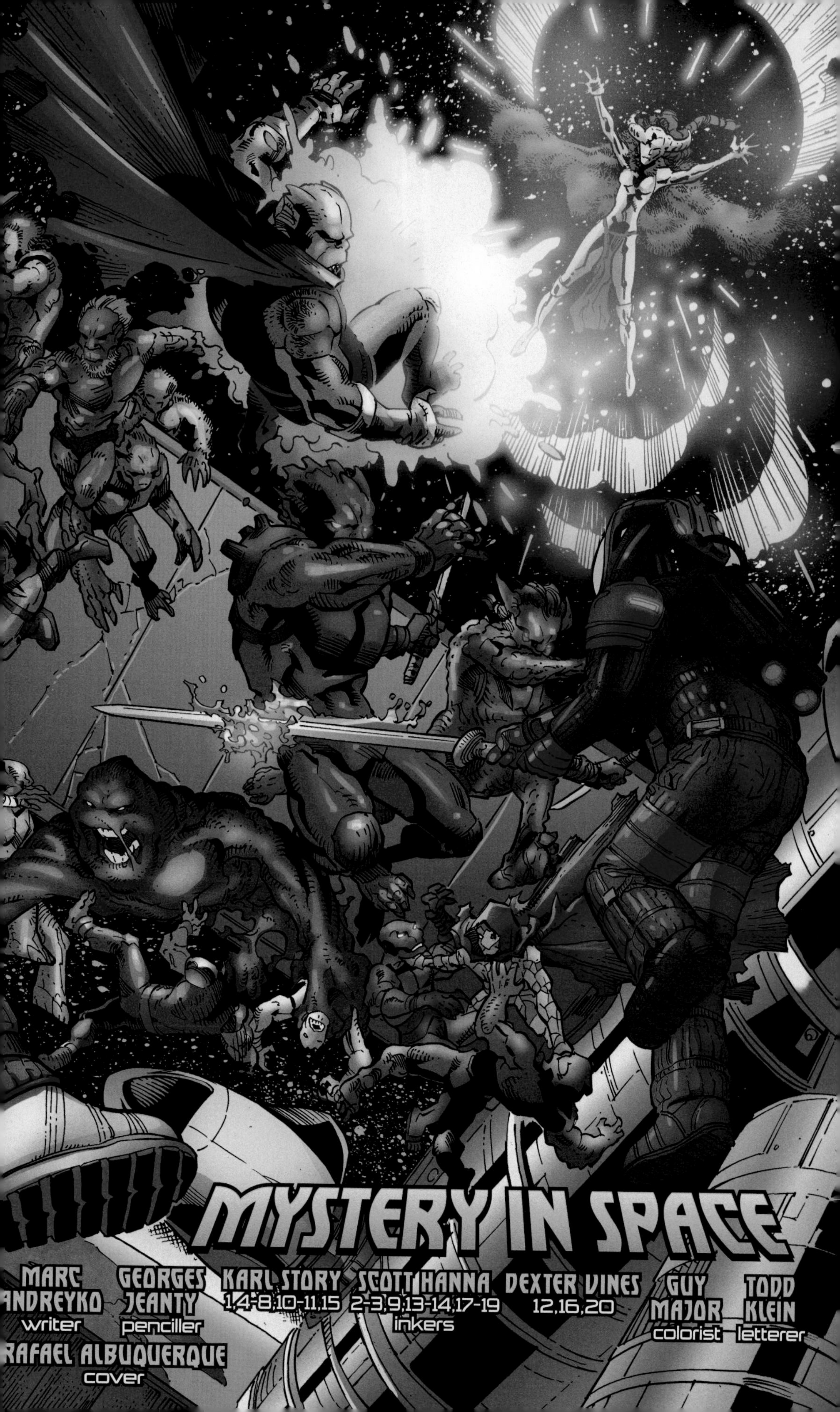
MYSTERY IN SPACE
MARC ANDREYKO writer
GEORGES JEANTY penciller
KARL STORY 1,4-8,10-11,15
SCOTT HANNA 2-3,9,13-14,17-19
DEXTER VINES 12,16,20
inkers
GUY MAJOR colorist
TODD KLEIN letterer
RAFAEL ALBUQUERQUE cover

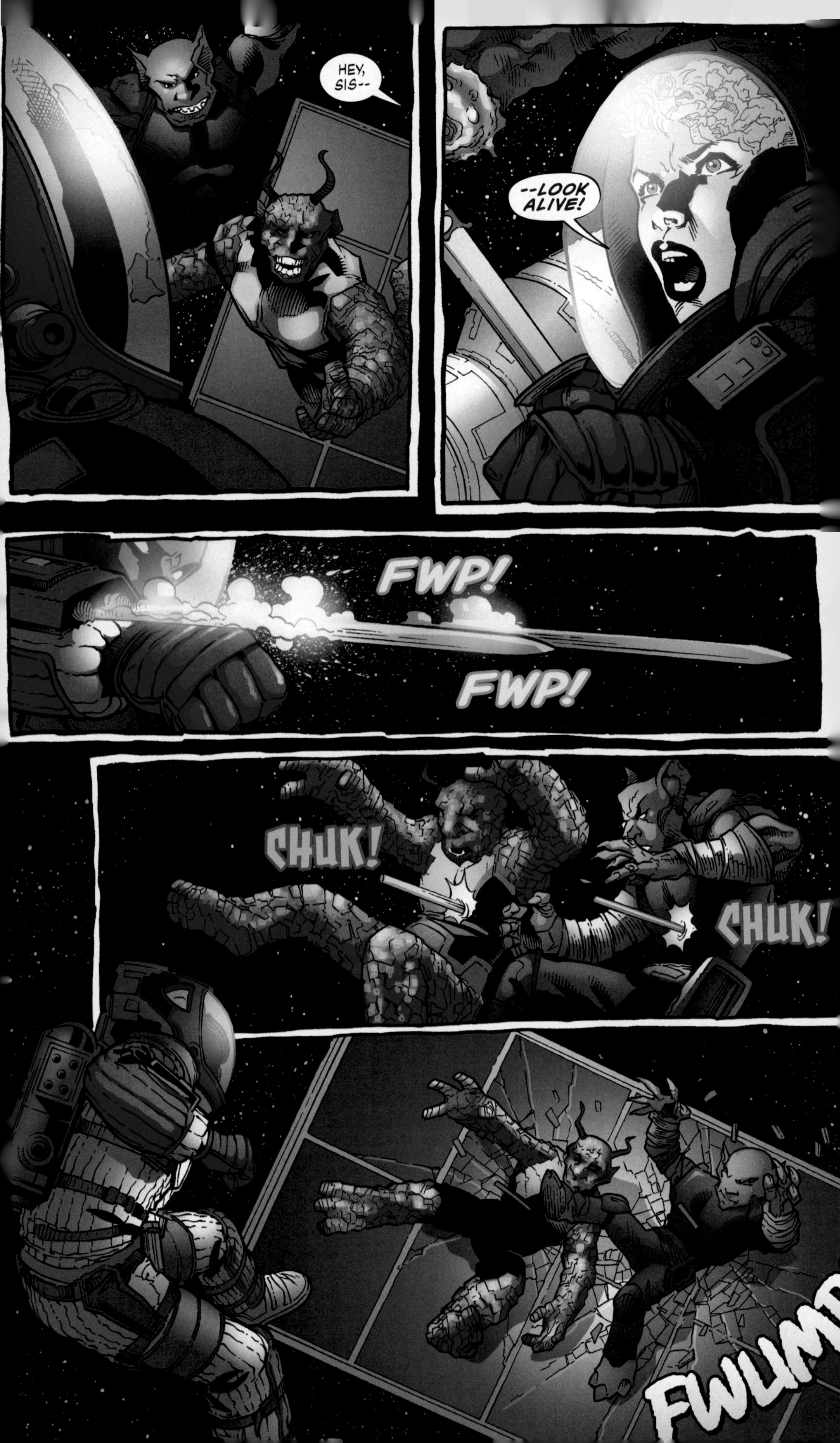
HEY, SIS--
--LOOK ALIVE!
FWP!
FWP!
CHUK!
CHUK!

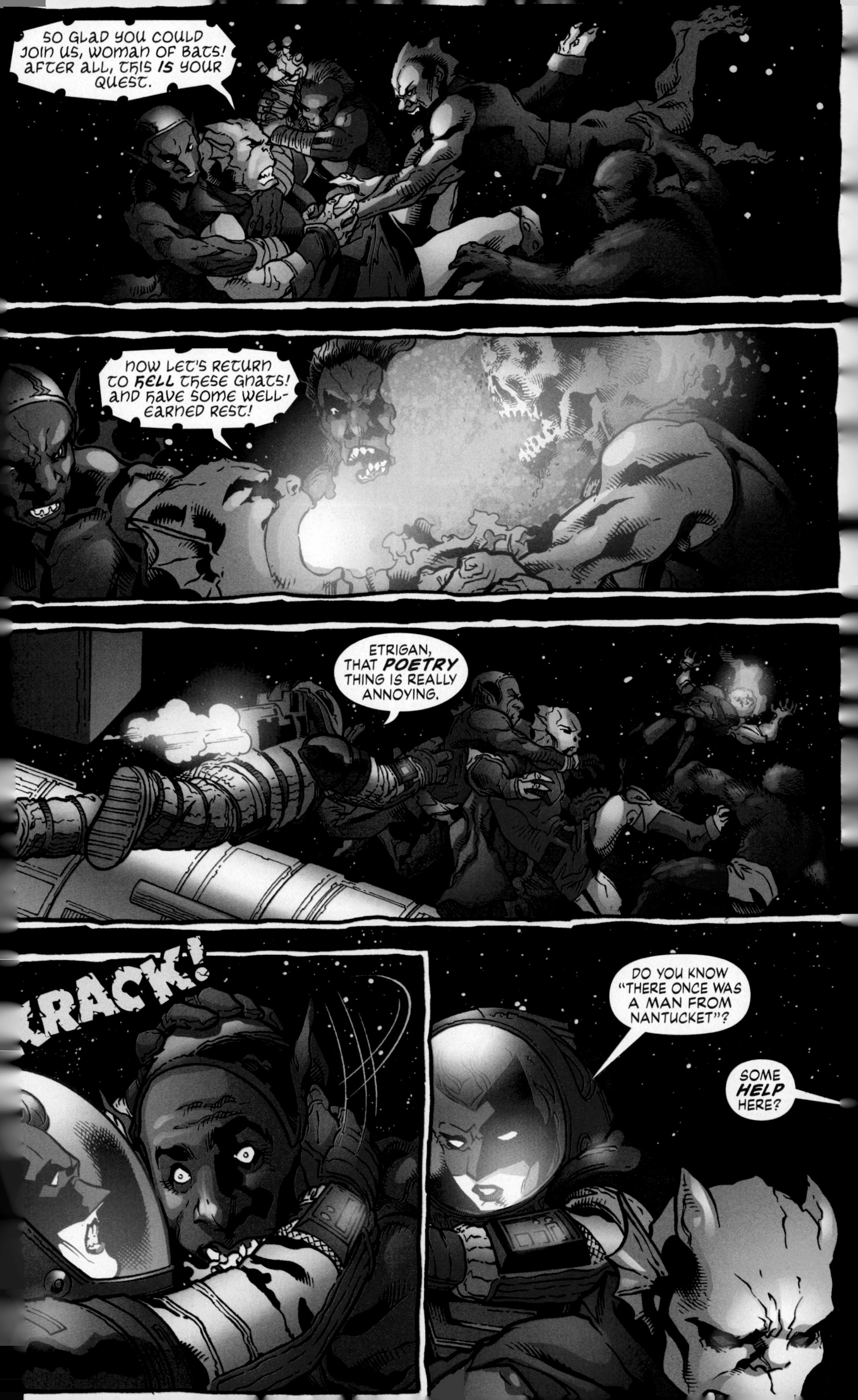
SO GLAD YOU COULD JOIN US, WOMAN OF BATS! AFTER ALL, THIS IS YOUR QUEST.
NOW LET'S RETURN TO HELL THESE GNATS! AND HAVE SOME WELL-EARNED REST!
ETRIGAN, THAT POETRY THING IS REALLY ANNOYING.
KRACK!
DO YOU KNOW "THERE ONCE WAS A MAN FROM NANTUCKET"?
SOME HELP HERE?

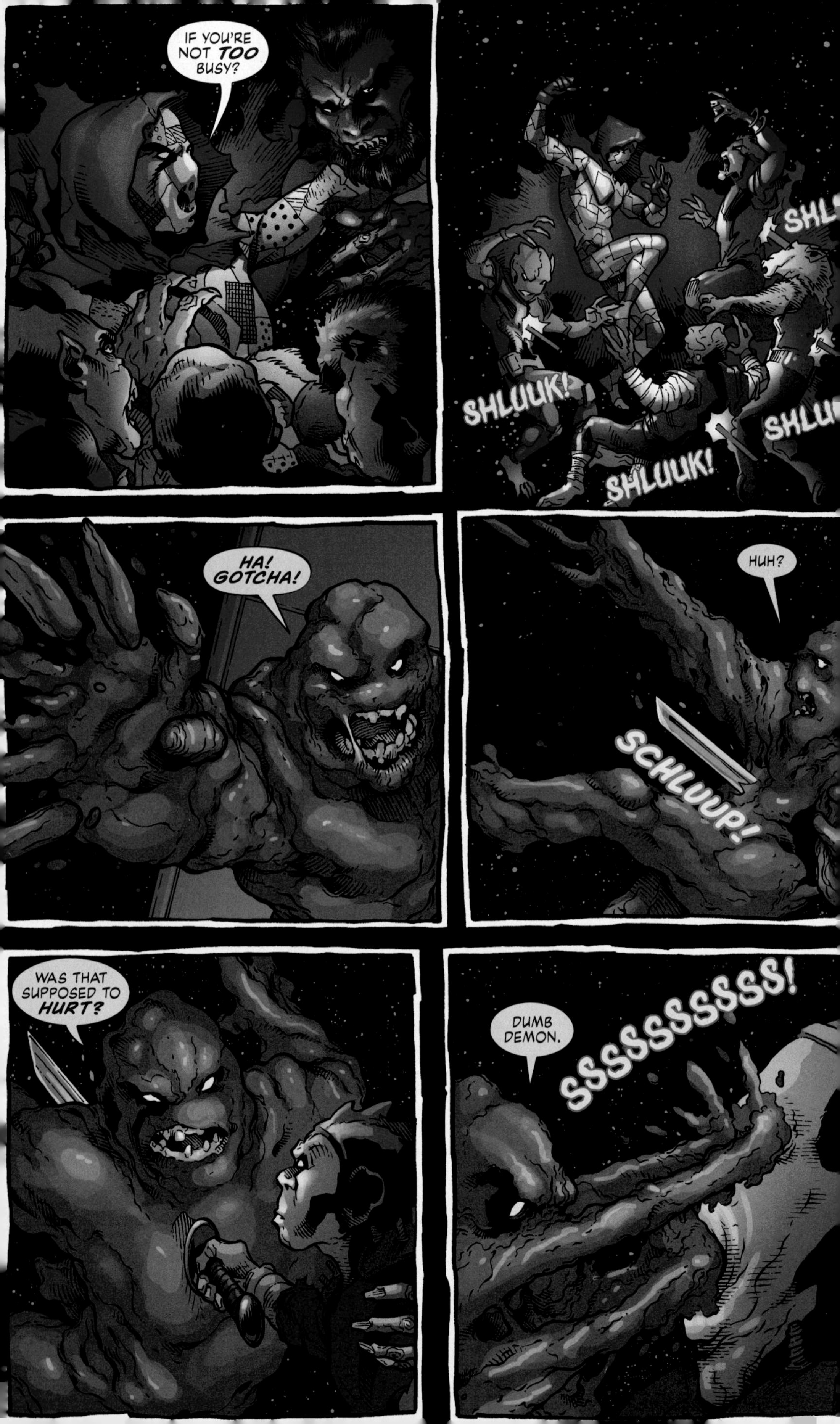
IF YOU'RE NOT *TOO* BUSY?
SHLUUK!
SHLUUK!
HA! GOTCHA!
HUH?
SCHLUUP!
WAS THAT SUPPOSED TO *HURT?*
SSSSSSSSSS!
DUMB DEMON.

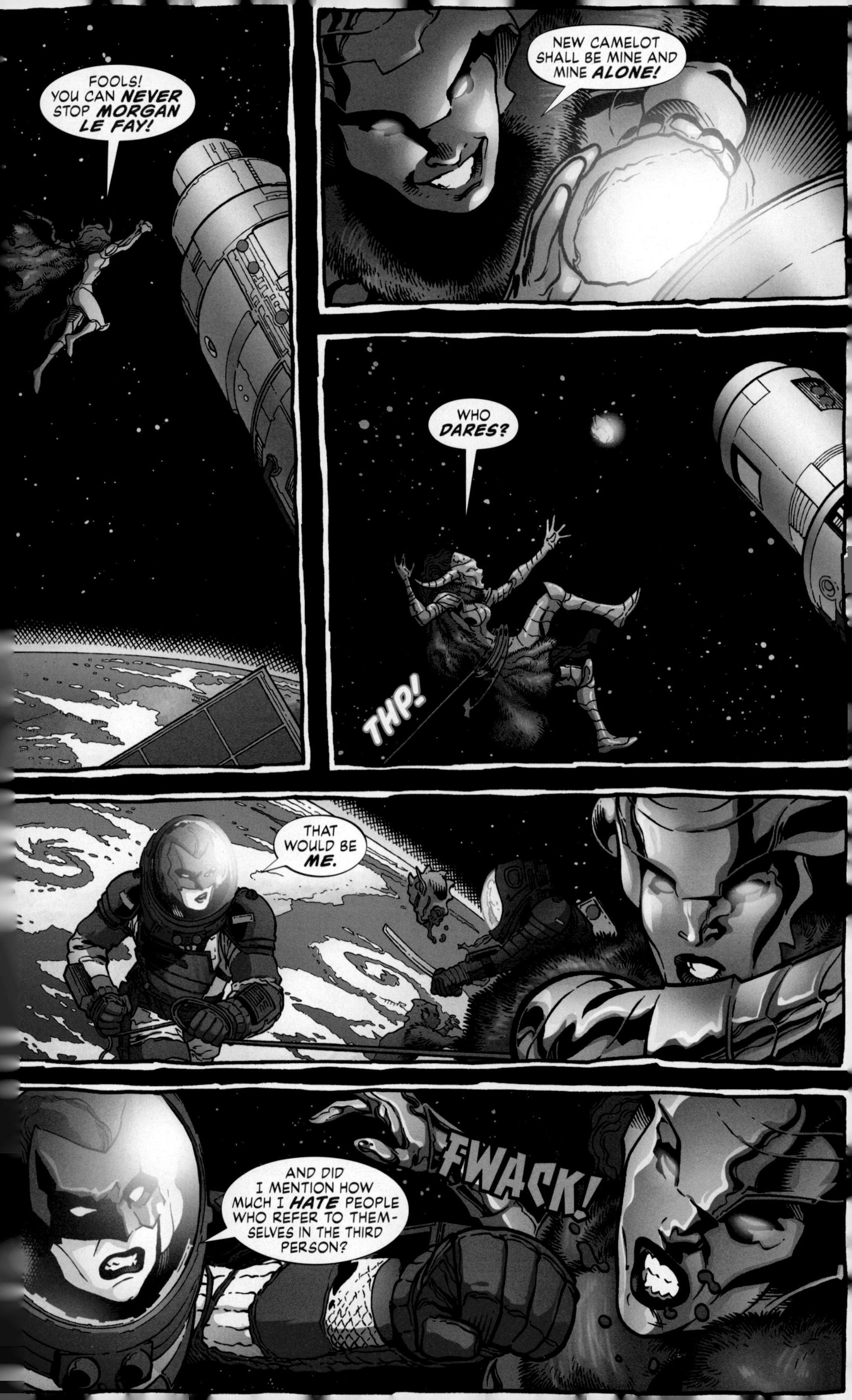
FOOLS! YOU CAN NEVER STOP MORGAN LE FAY!
NEW CAMELOT SHALL BE MINE AND MINE ALONE!
WHO DARES?
THP!
THAT WOULD BE ME.
AND DID I MENTION HOW MUCH I HATE PEOPLE WHO REFER TO THEM-SELVES IN THE THIRD PERSON?
FWACK!

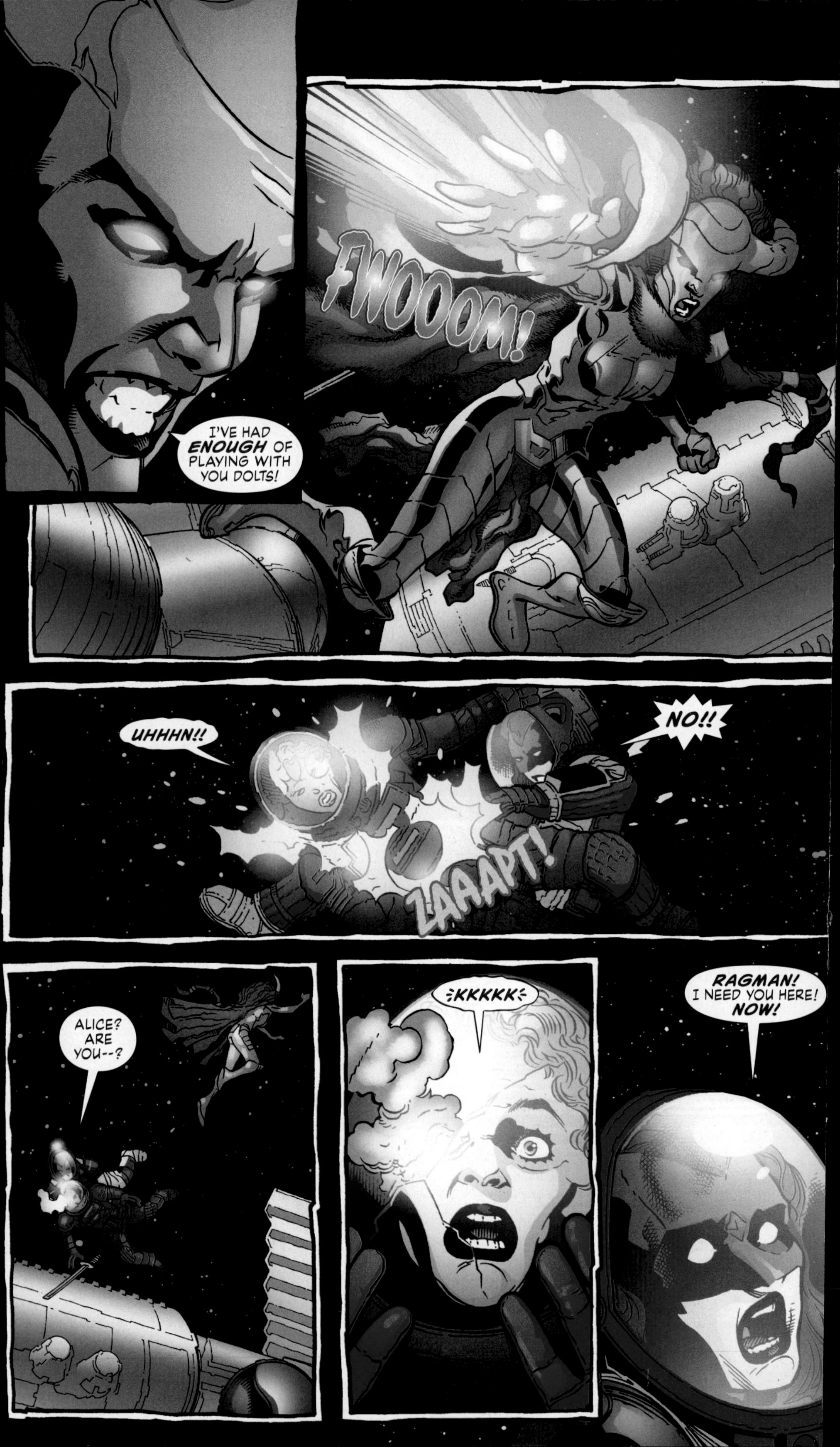
I'VE HAD ENOUGH OF PLAYING WITH YOU DOLTS!
FWOOOM!
UHHHN!!
NO!!
ZAAAPT!
ALICE? ARE YOU--?
KKKKK
RAGMAN! I NEED YOU HERE! NOW!

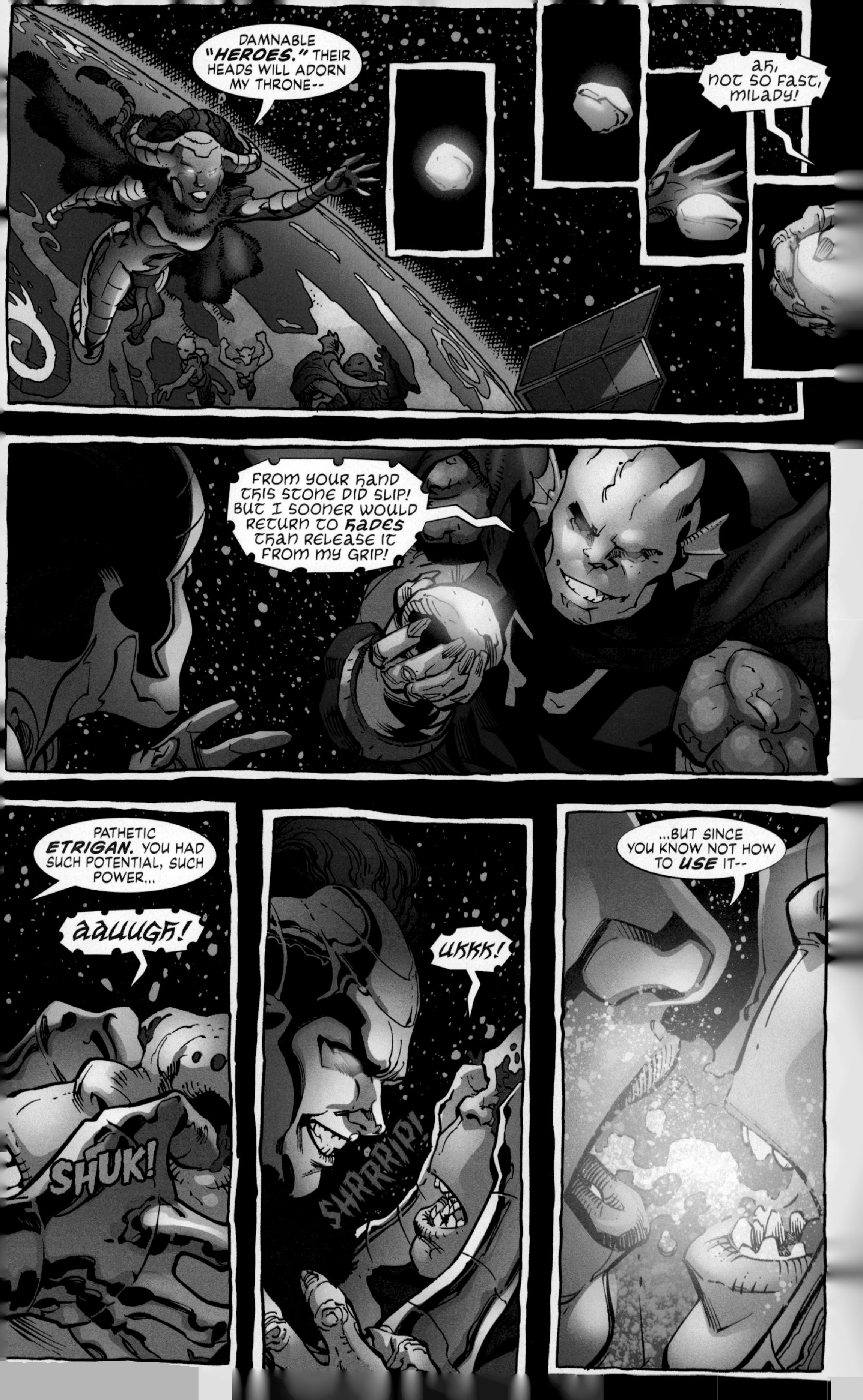
DAMNABLE "HEROES." THEIR HEADS WILL ADORN MY THRONE--
AH, NOT SO FAST, MILADY!
FROM YOUR HAND THIS STONE DID SLIP! BUT I SOONER WOULD RETURN TO HADES THAN RELEASE IT FROM MY GRIP!
PATHETIC ETRIGAN. YOU HAD SUCH POTENTIAL, SUCH POWER...
AAUUGH!
SHUK!
UKKK!
SHRRRIP!
...BUT SINCE YOU KNOW NOT HOW TO USE IT--

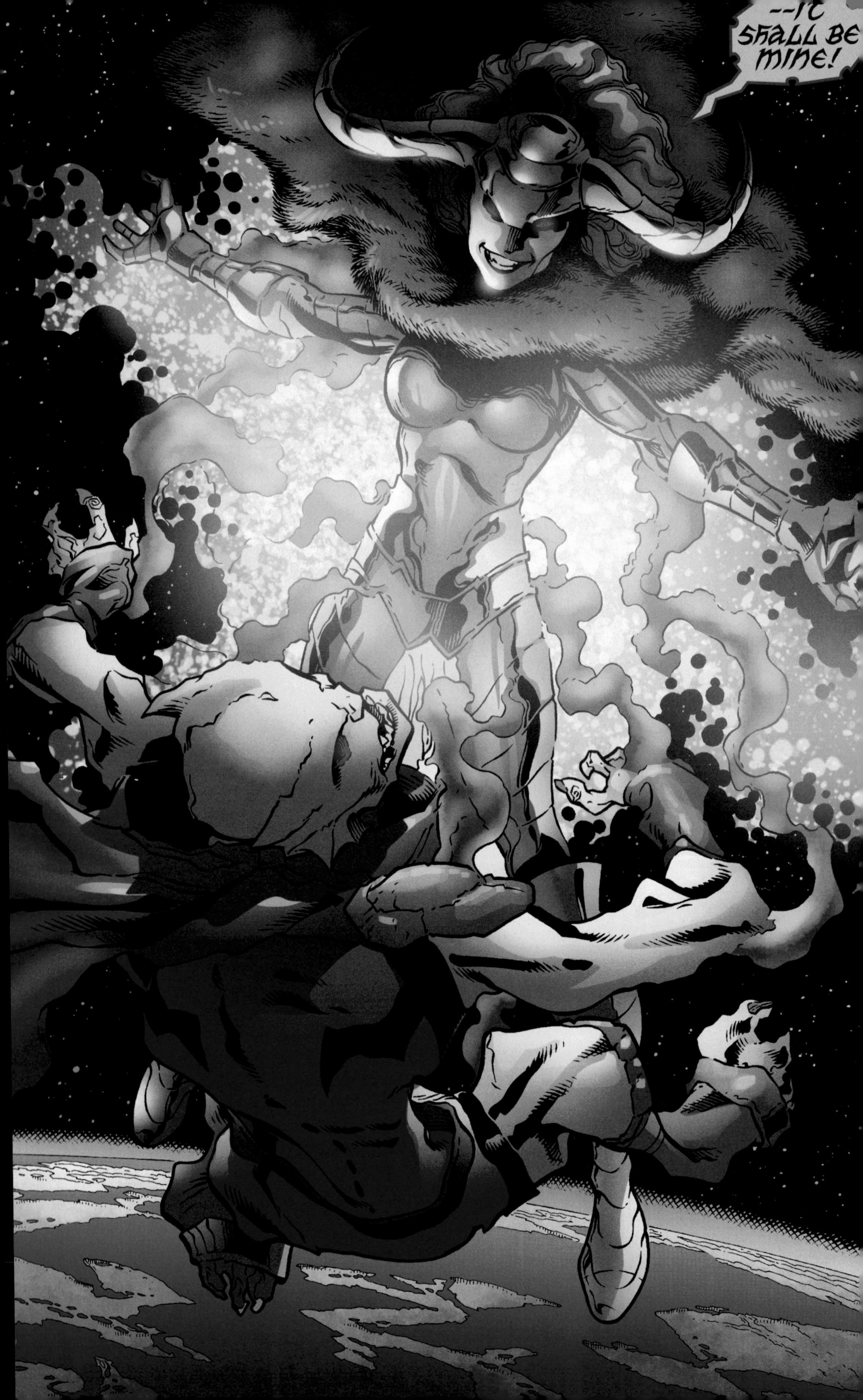
--IT SHALL BE MINE!

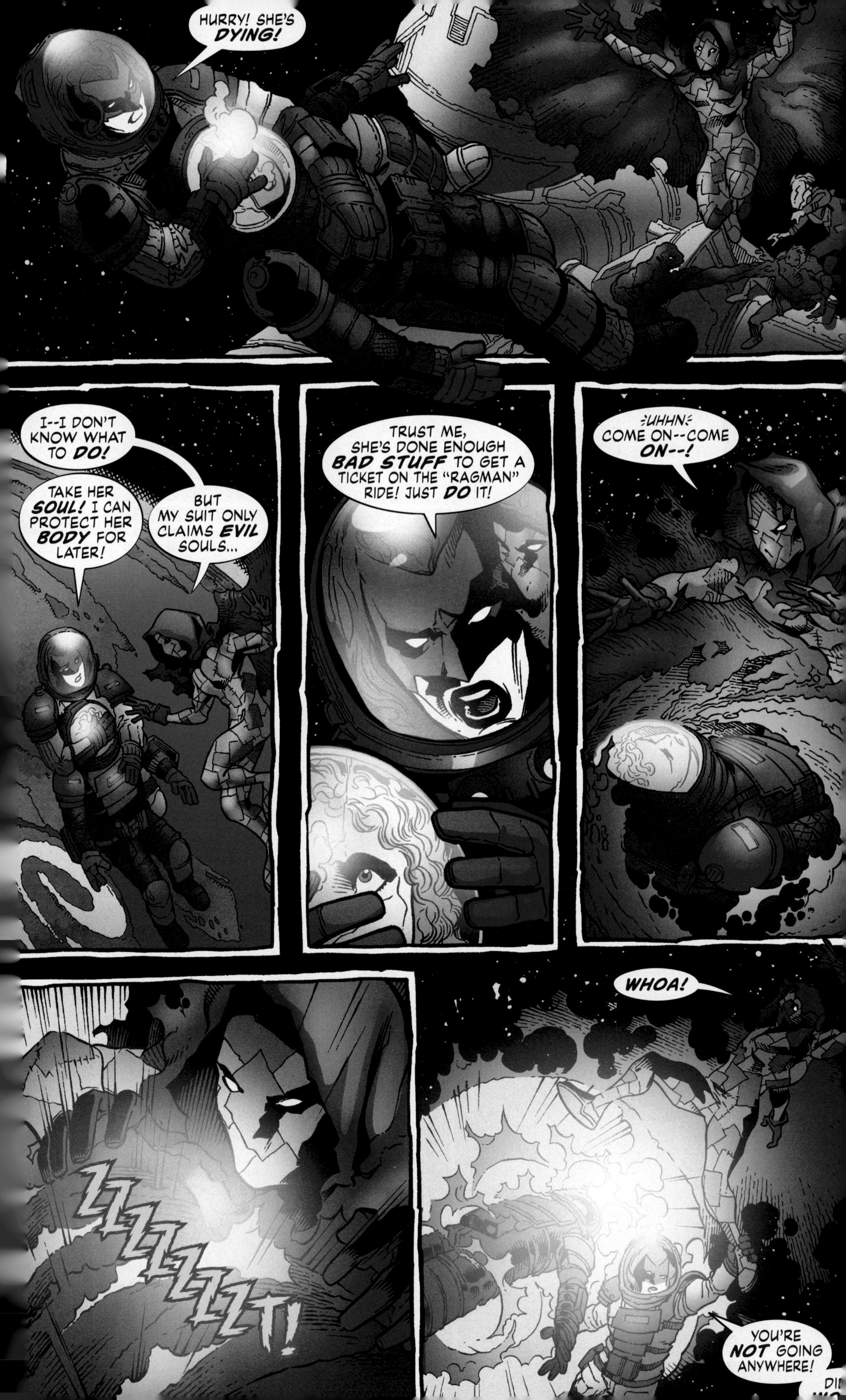
HURRY! SHE'S DYING!
I--I DON'T KNOW WHAT TO DO!
TAKE HER SOUL! I CAN PROTECT HER BODY FOR LATER!
BUT MY SUIT ONLY CLAIMS EVIL SOULS...
TRUST ME, SHE'S DONE ENOUGH BAD STUFF TO GET A TICKET ON THE "RAGMAN" RIDE! JUST DO IT!
UHHN
COME ON--COME ON--!
ZZZZZZZZZT!
WHOA!
YOU'RE NOT GOING ANYWHERE!

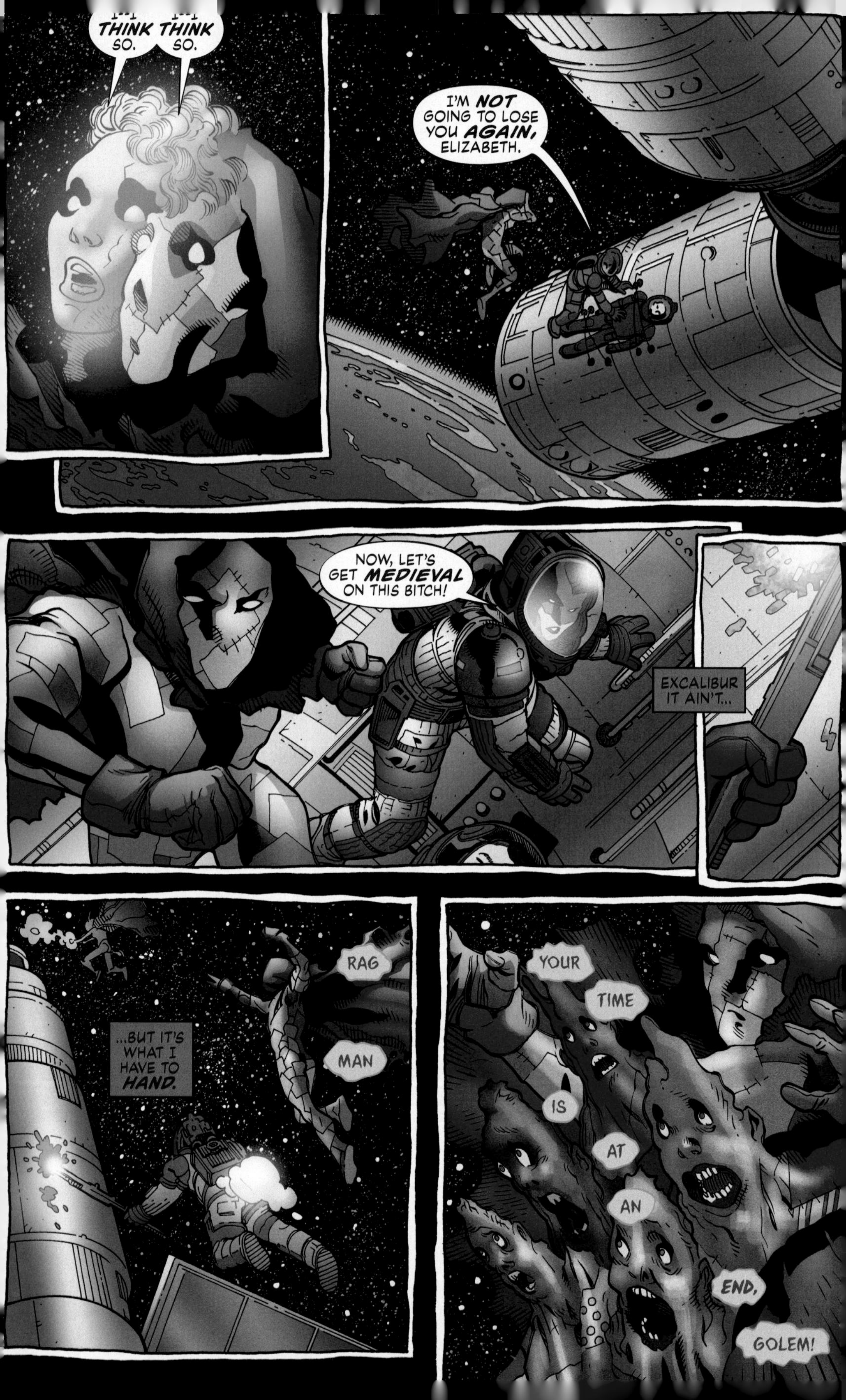

THINK SO.
THINK SO.
I'M NOT GOING TO LOSE YOU AGAIN, ELIZABETH.
NOW, LET'S GET MEDIEVAL ON THIS BITCH!
EXCALIBUR IT AIN'T...
...BUT IT'S WHAT I HAVE TO HAND.
RAG
MAN
YOUR
TIME
IS
AT
AN
END,
GOLEM!

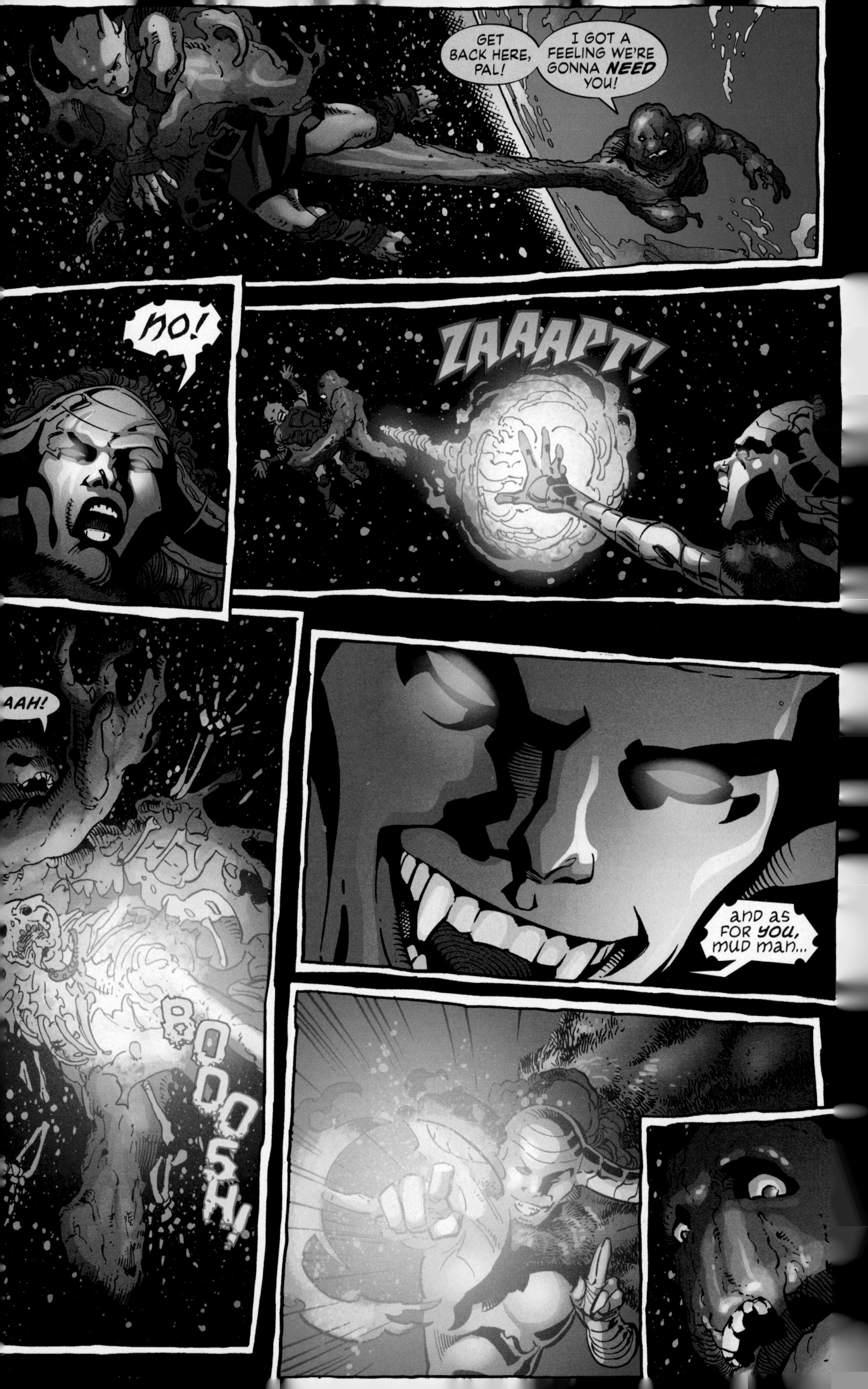
GET BACK HERE, PAL!
I GOT A FEELING WE'RE GONNA NEED YOU!
NO!
ZAAAPT!
AAH!
BOOOOSH!
and as FOR YOU, mud man...

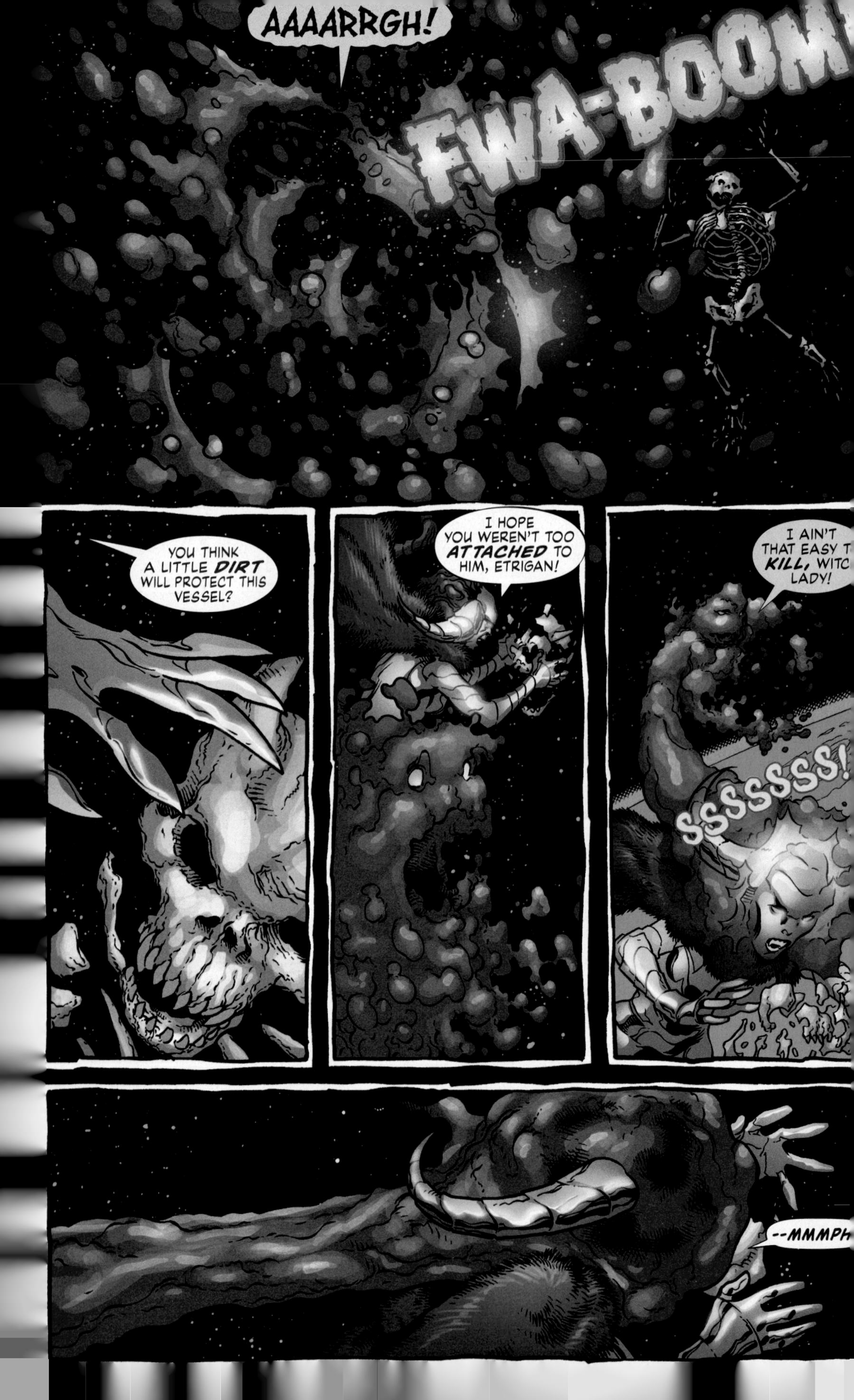
AAAARRGH!
FWA-BOOM!
YOU THINK A LITTLE DIRT WILL PROTECT THIS VESSEL?
I HOPE YOU WEREN'T TOO ATTACHED TO HIM, ETRIGAN!
I AIN'T THAT EASY TO KILL, WITCH LADY!
SSSSSSSSS!
--MMMPH

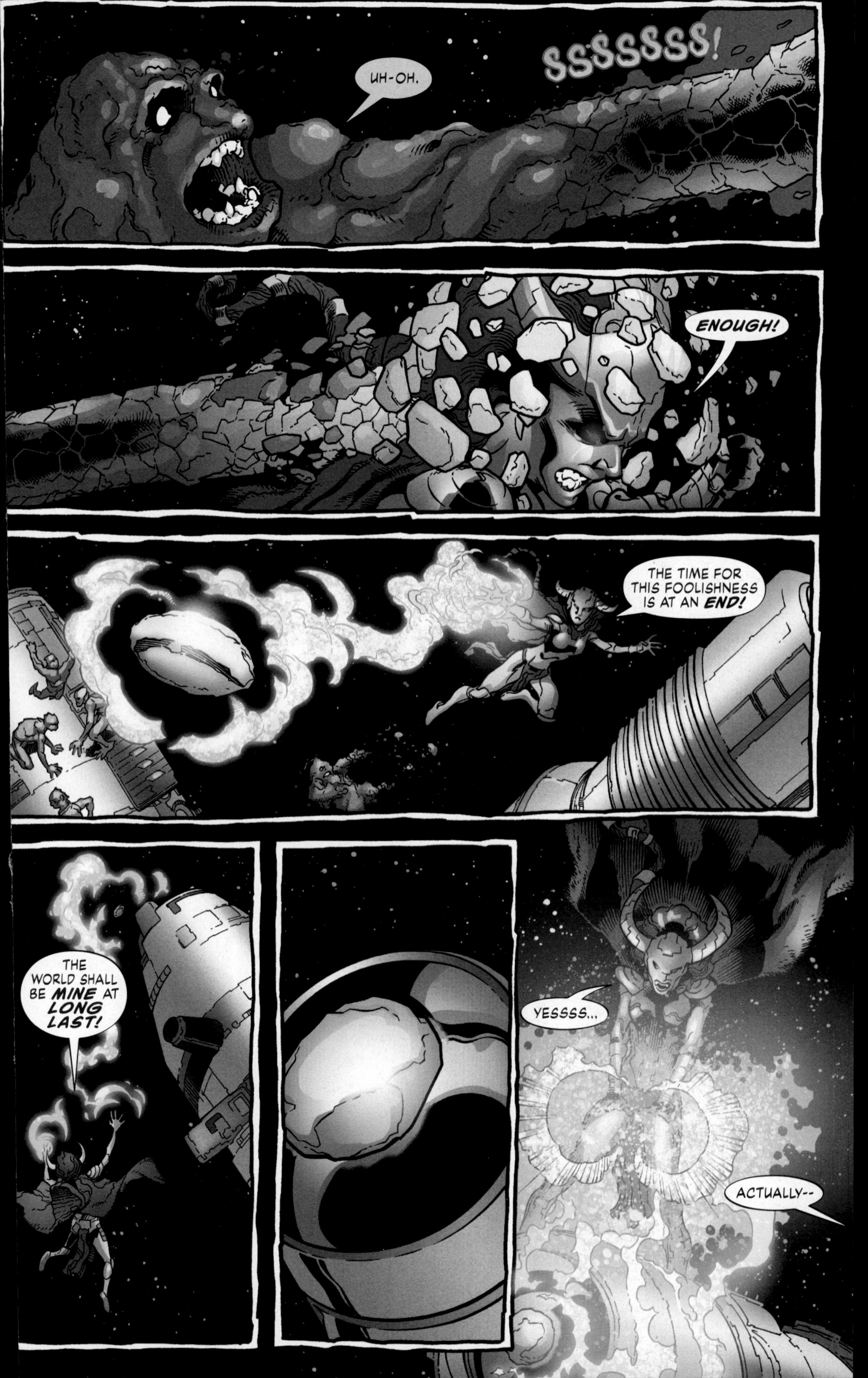
UH-OH.
SSSSSSS!
ENOUGH!
THE TIME FOR THIS FOOLISHNESS IS AT AN END!
THE WORLD SHALL BE MINE AT LONG LAST!
YESSSS...
ACTUALLY--

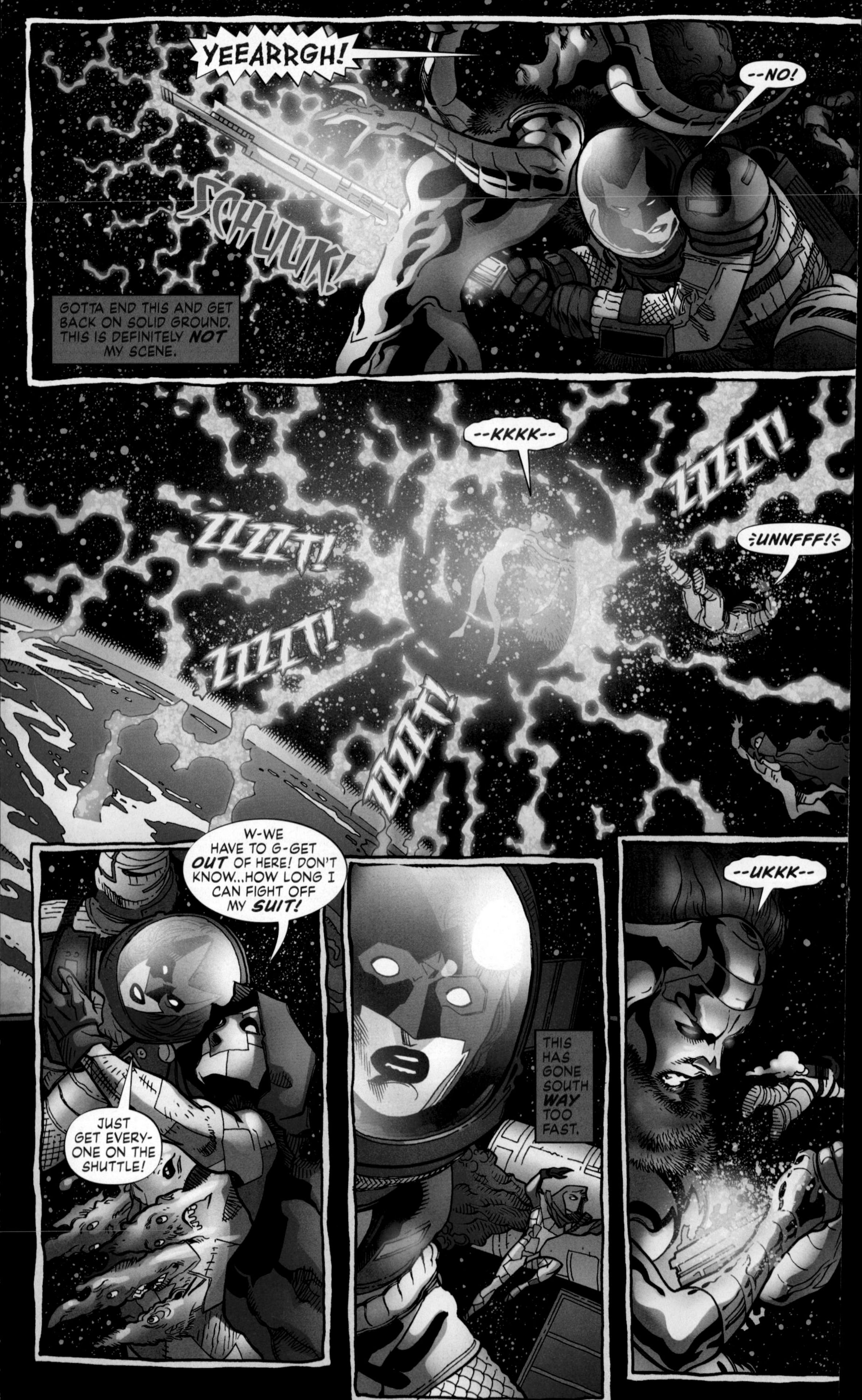

YEEARRGH!
--NO!
SCHUUK!
GOTTA END THIS AND GET BACK ON SOLID GROUND. THIS IS DEFINITELY NOT MY SCENE.
--KKKK--
ZZZZT!
ZZZZT!
ZZZZT!
UNNFFF!
ZZZZT!
W-WE HAVE TO G-GET OUT OF HERE! DON'T KNOW...HOW LONG I CAN FIGHT OFF MY SUIT!
JUST GET EVERY-ONE ON THE SHUTTLE!
THIS HAS GONE SOUTH WAY TOO FAST.
--UKKK--

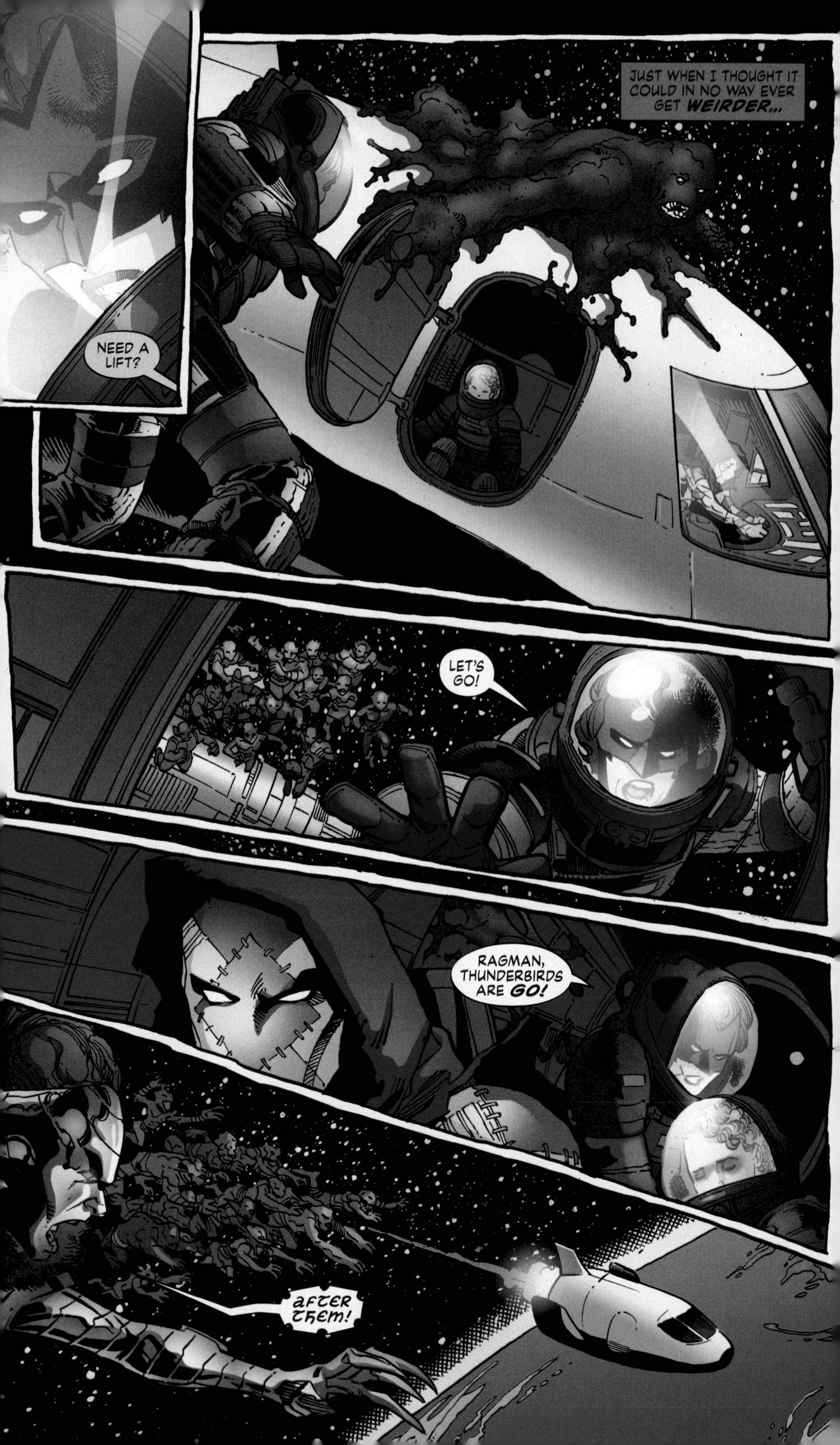
JUST WHEN I THOUGHT IT COULD IN NO WAY EVER GET WEIRDER...
NEED A LIFT?
LET'S GO!
RAGMAN, THUNDERBIRDS ARE GO!
AFTER THEM!

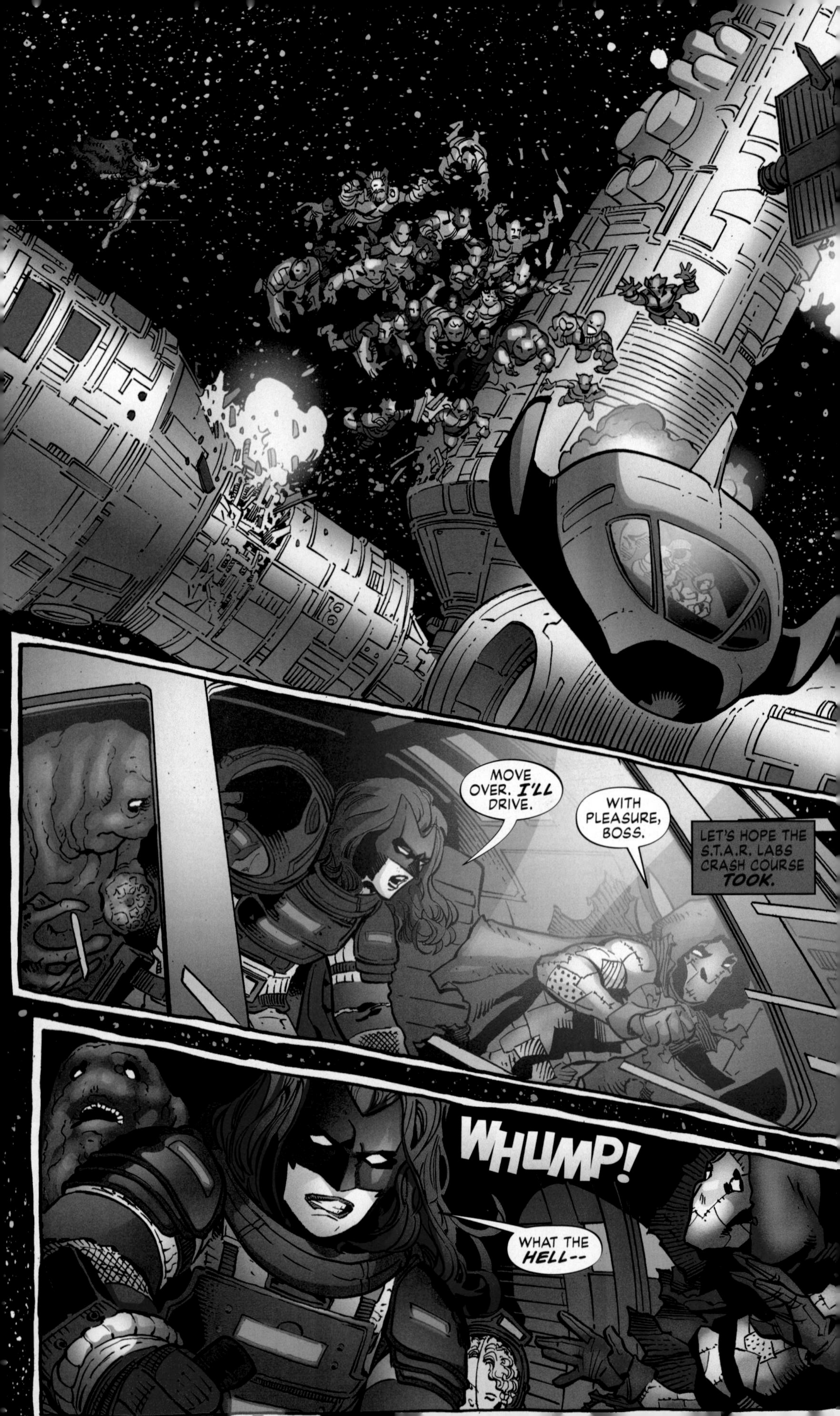
MOVE OVER. I'LL DRIVE.
WITH PLEASURE, BOSS.
LET'S HOPE THE S.T.A.R. LABS CRASH COURSE TOOK.
WHUMP!
WHAT THE HELL--

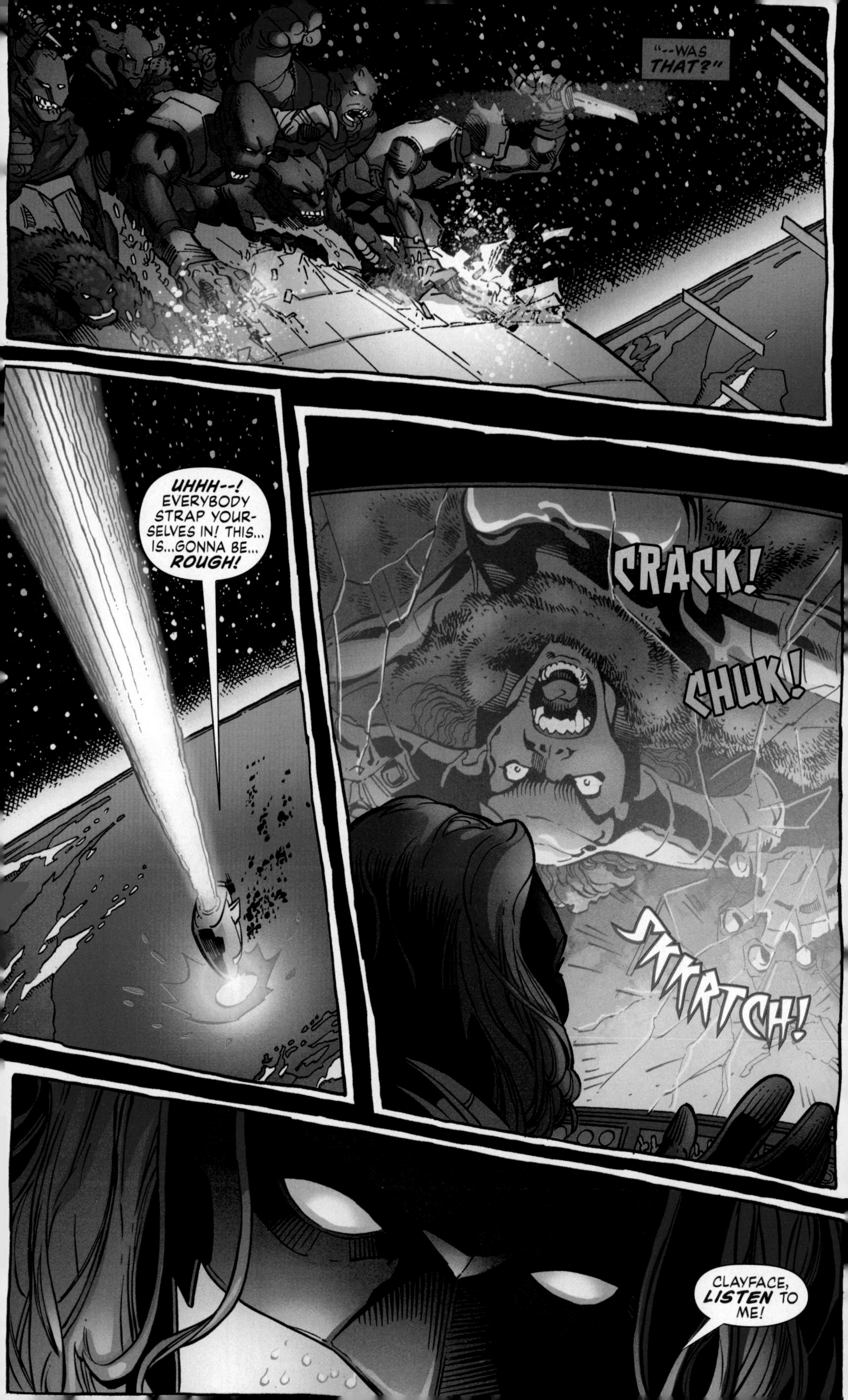
"--WAS THAT?"
UHHH--! EVERYBODY STRAP YOURSELVES IN! THIS... IS...GONNA BE... ROUGH!
CRACK!
CHUK!
SKKRTCH!
CLAYFACE, LISTEN TO ME!

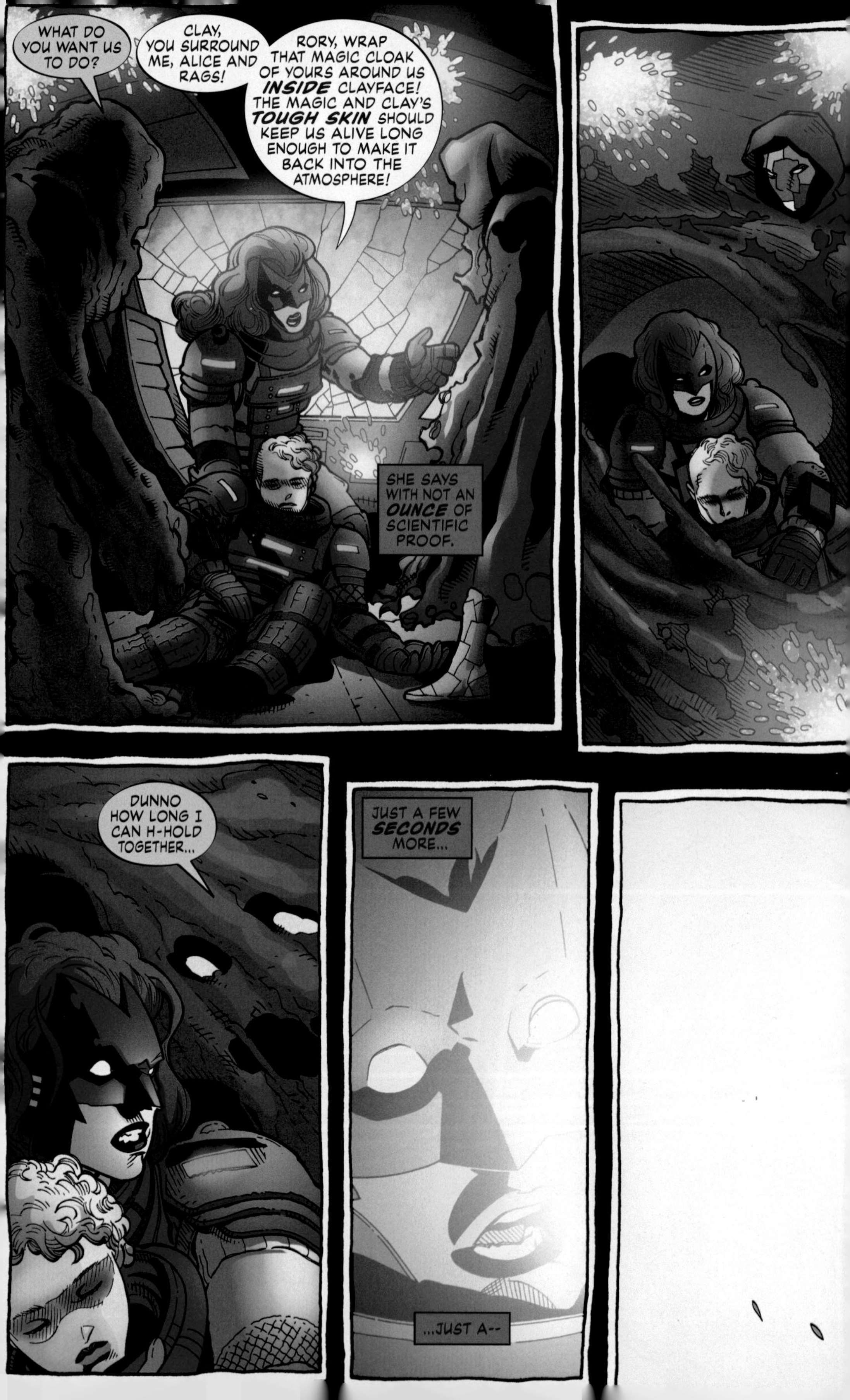
WHAT DO YOU WANT US TO DO?
CLAY, YOU SURROUND ME, ALICE AND RAGS!
RORY, WRAP THAT MAGIC CLOAK OF YOURS AROUND US INSIDE CLAYFACE! THE MAGIC AND CLAY'S TOUGH SKIN SHOULD KEEP US ALIVE LONG ENOUGH TO MAKE IT BACK INTO THE ATMOSPHERE!
SHE SAYS WITH NOT AN OUNCE OF SCIENTIFIC PROOF.
DUNNO HOW LONG I CAN H-HOLD TOGETHER...
JUST A FEW SECONDS MORE...
...JUST A--

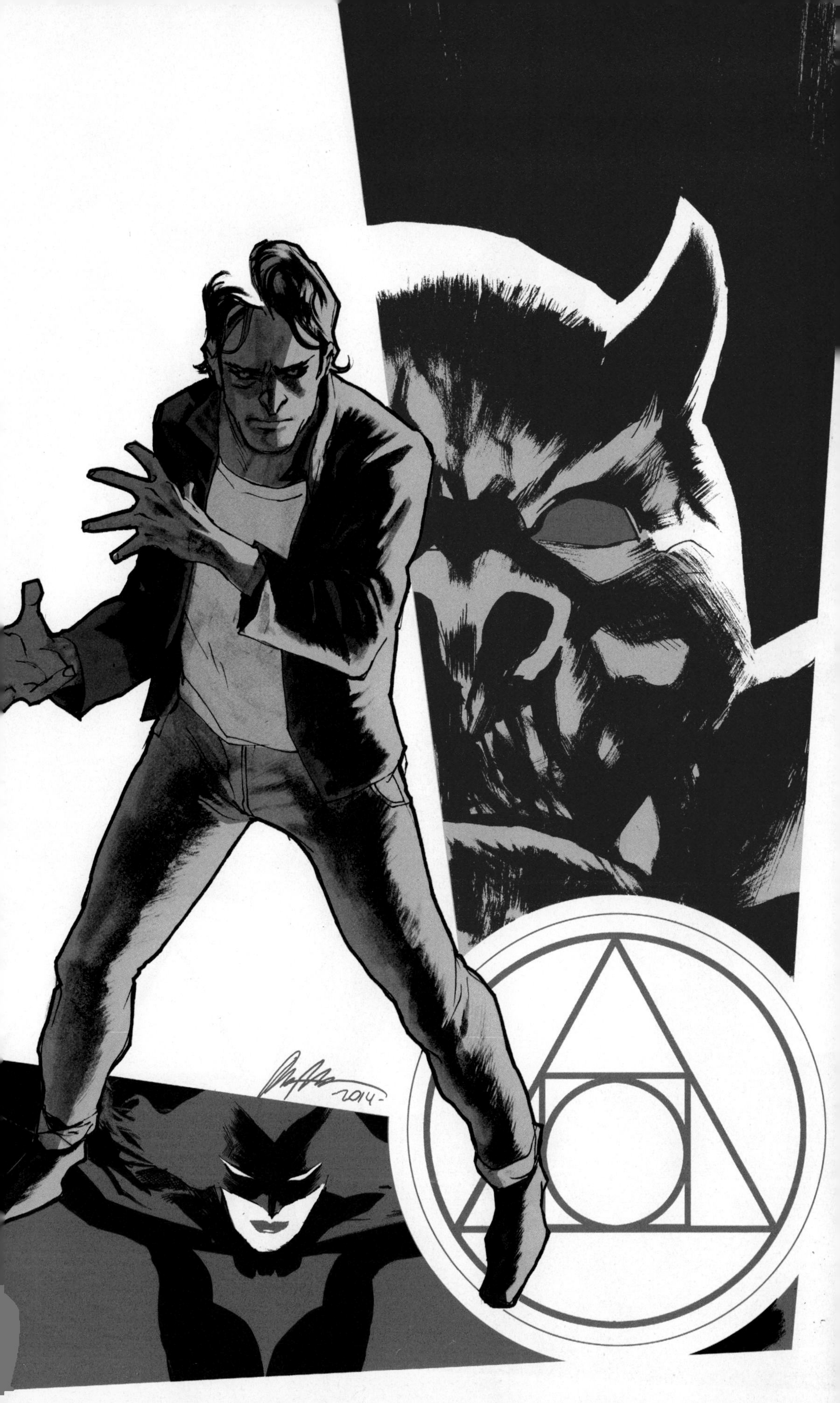

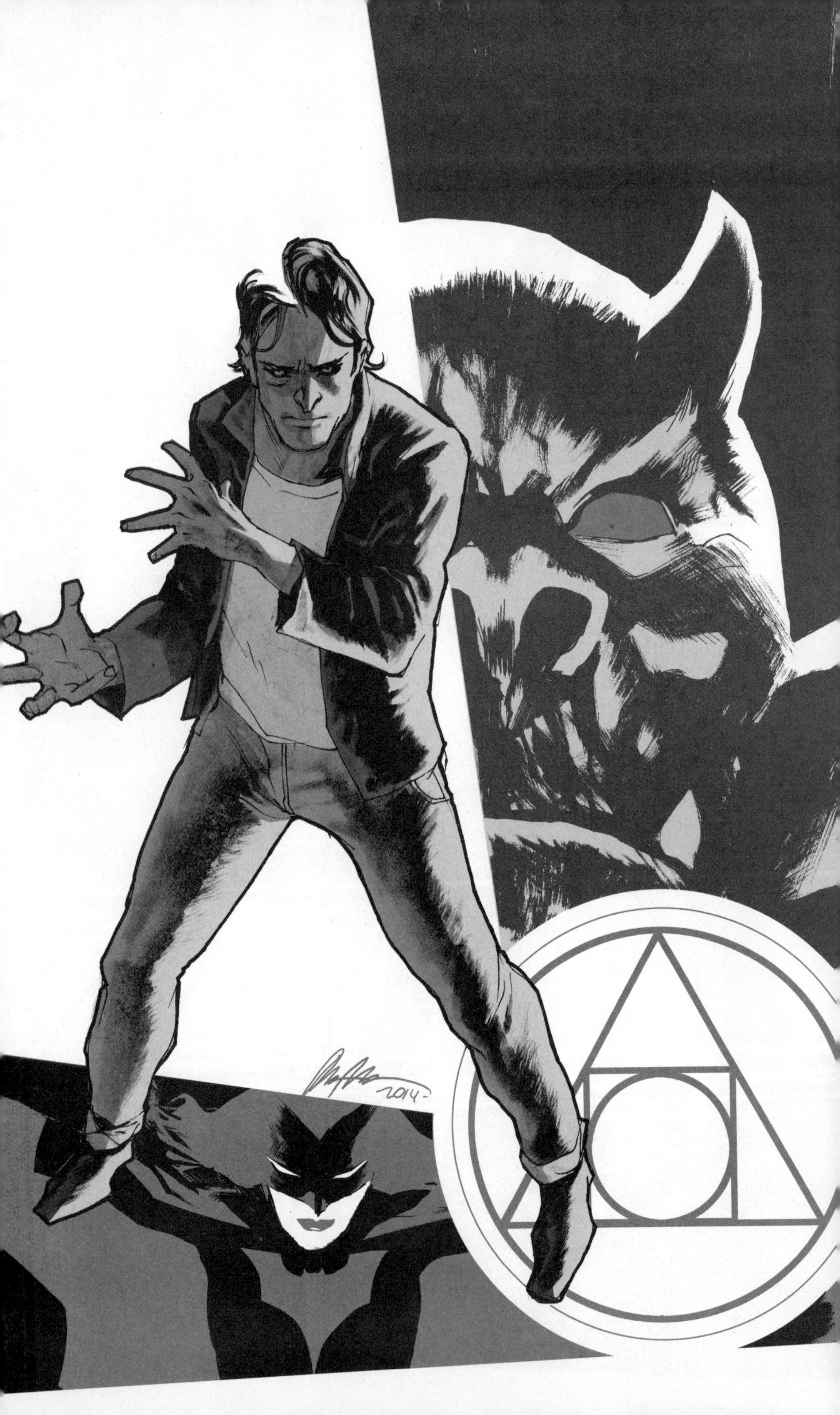

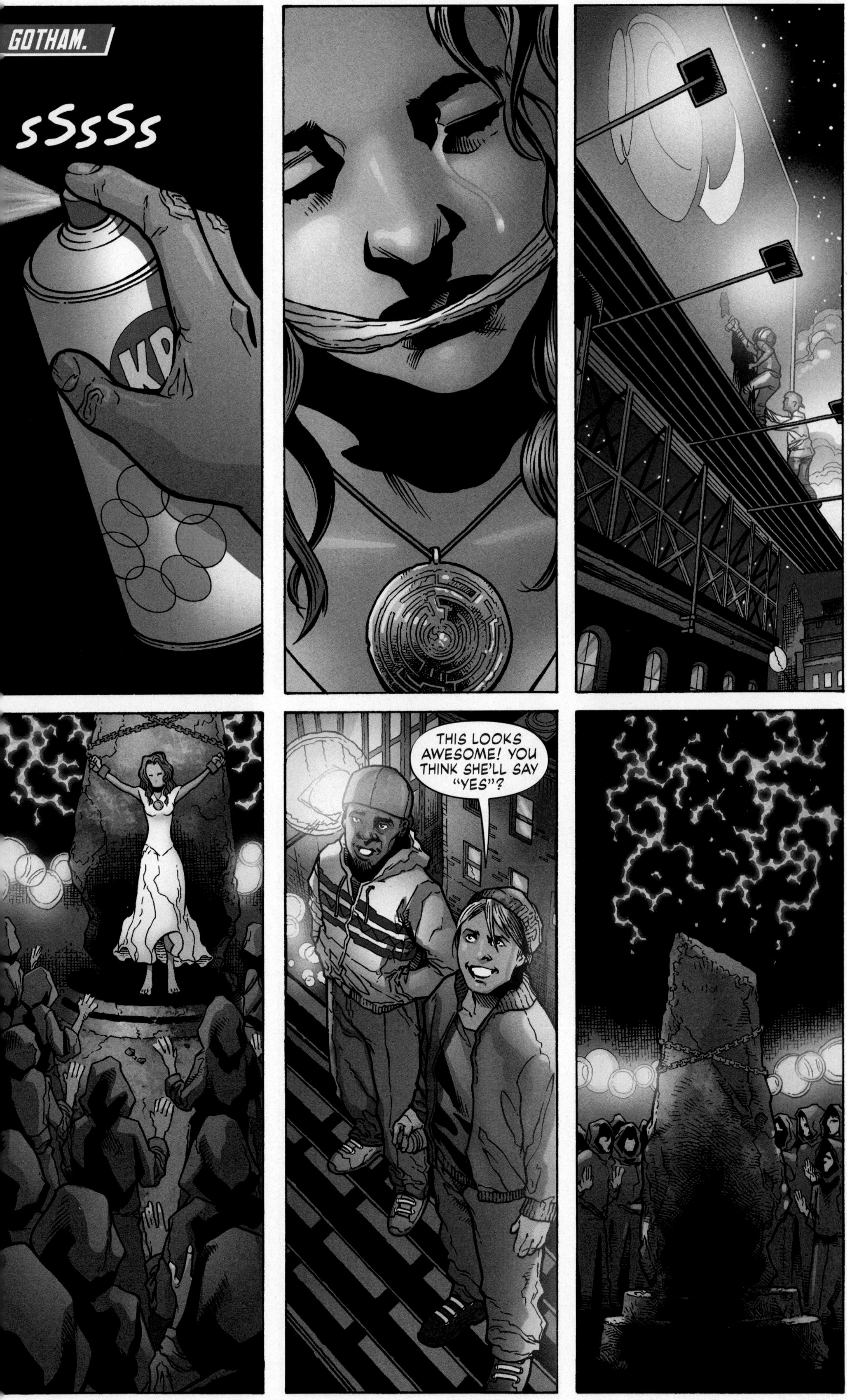
GOTHAM.
sSsSs
KP
THIS LOOKS AWESOME! YOU THINK SHE'LL SAY "YES"?

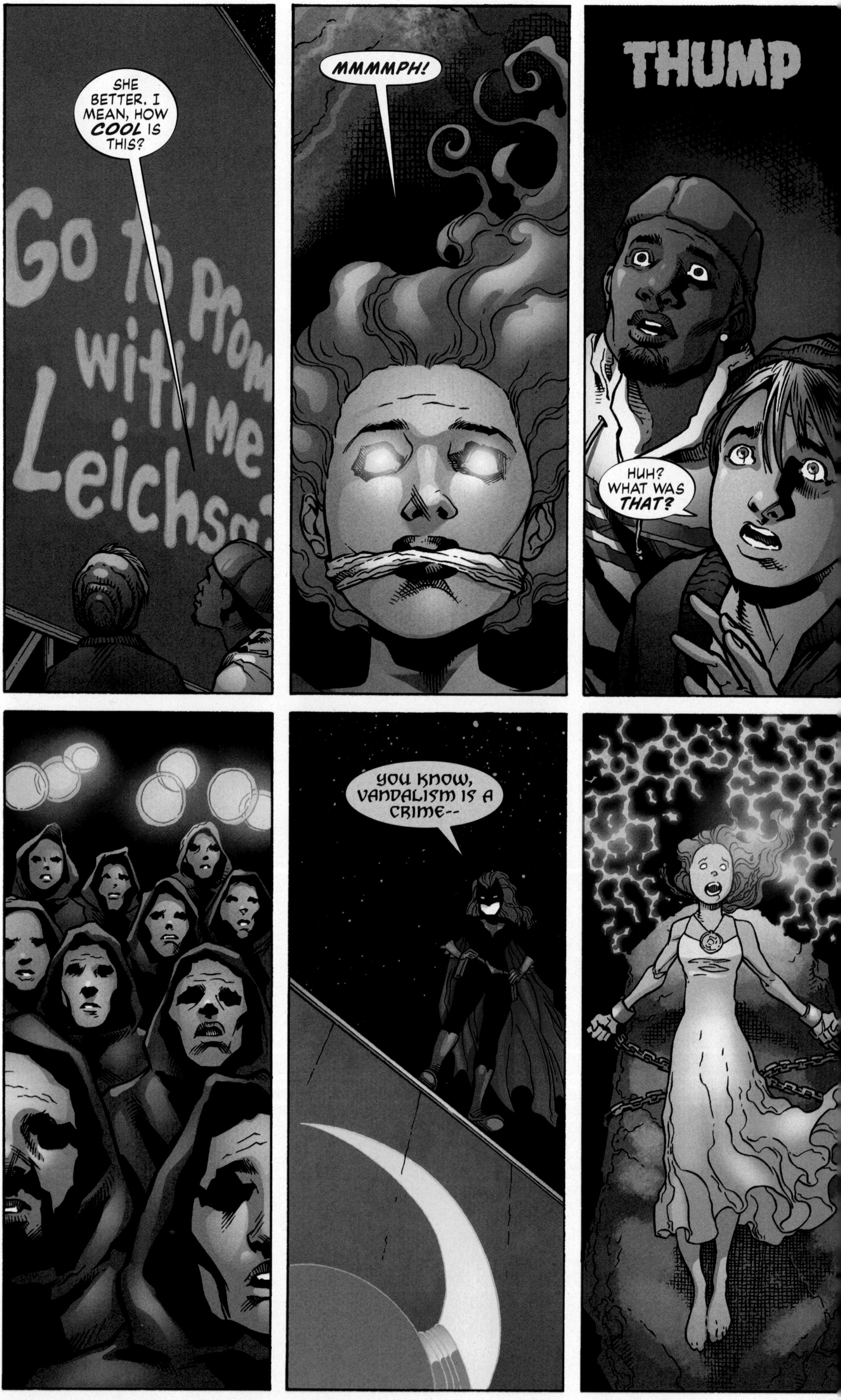
SHE BETTER. I MEAN, HOW COOL IS THIS?
Go to Prom with me Leichsa?
MMMMPH!
THUMP
HUH? WHAT WAS THAT?
YOU KNOW, VANDALISM IS A CRIME--

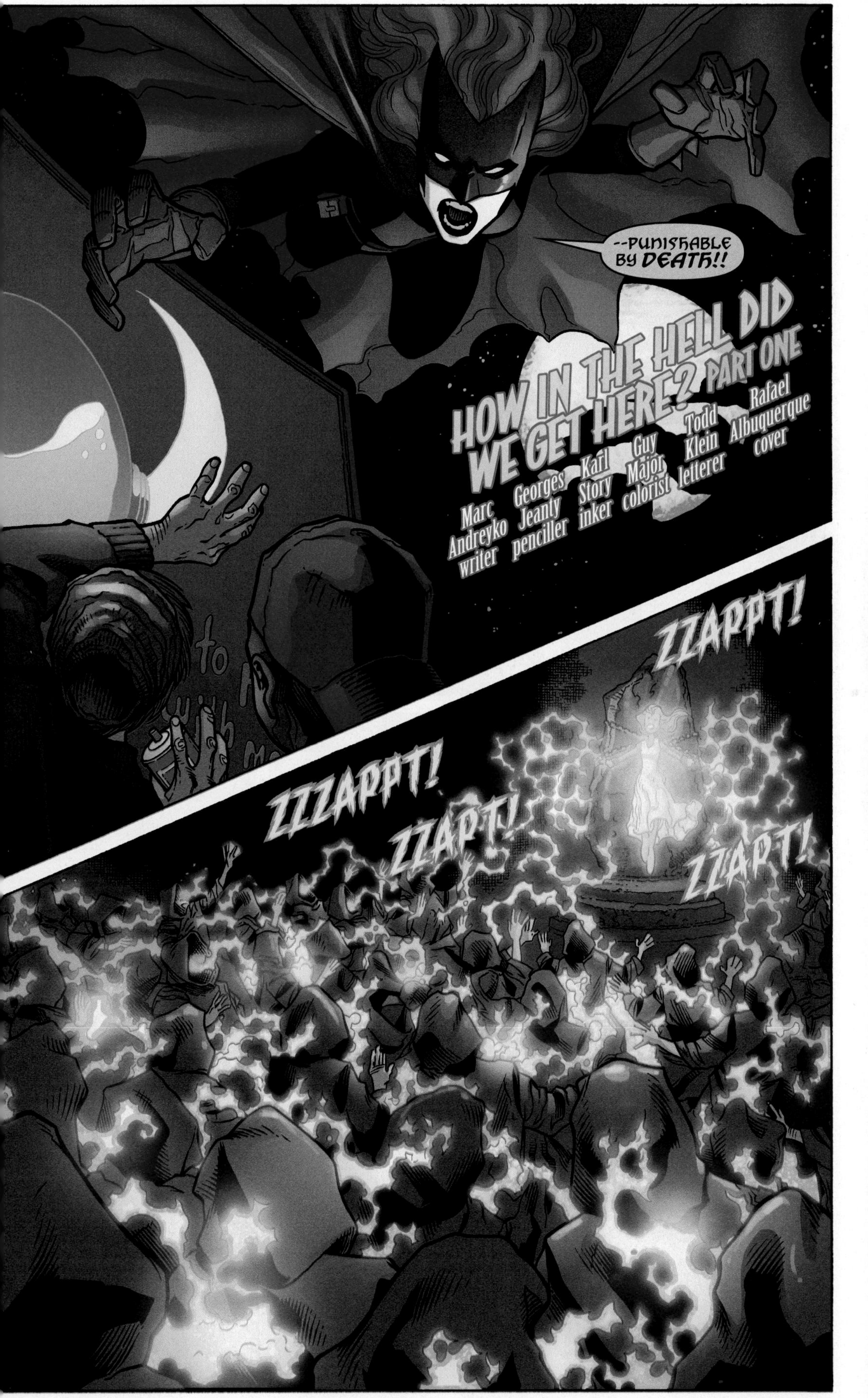
--PUNISHABLE BY DEATH!!
HOW IN THE HELL DID WE GET HERE? PART ONE
Marc Andreyko writer
Georges Jeanty penciller
Karl Story inker
Guy Major colorist
Todd Klein letterer
Rafael Albuquerque cover
ZZAPPT!
ZZZAPPT!
ZZAPT!
ZZAPT!

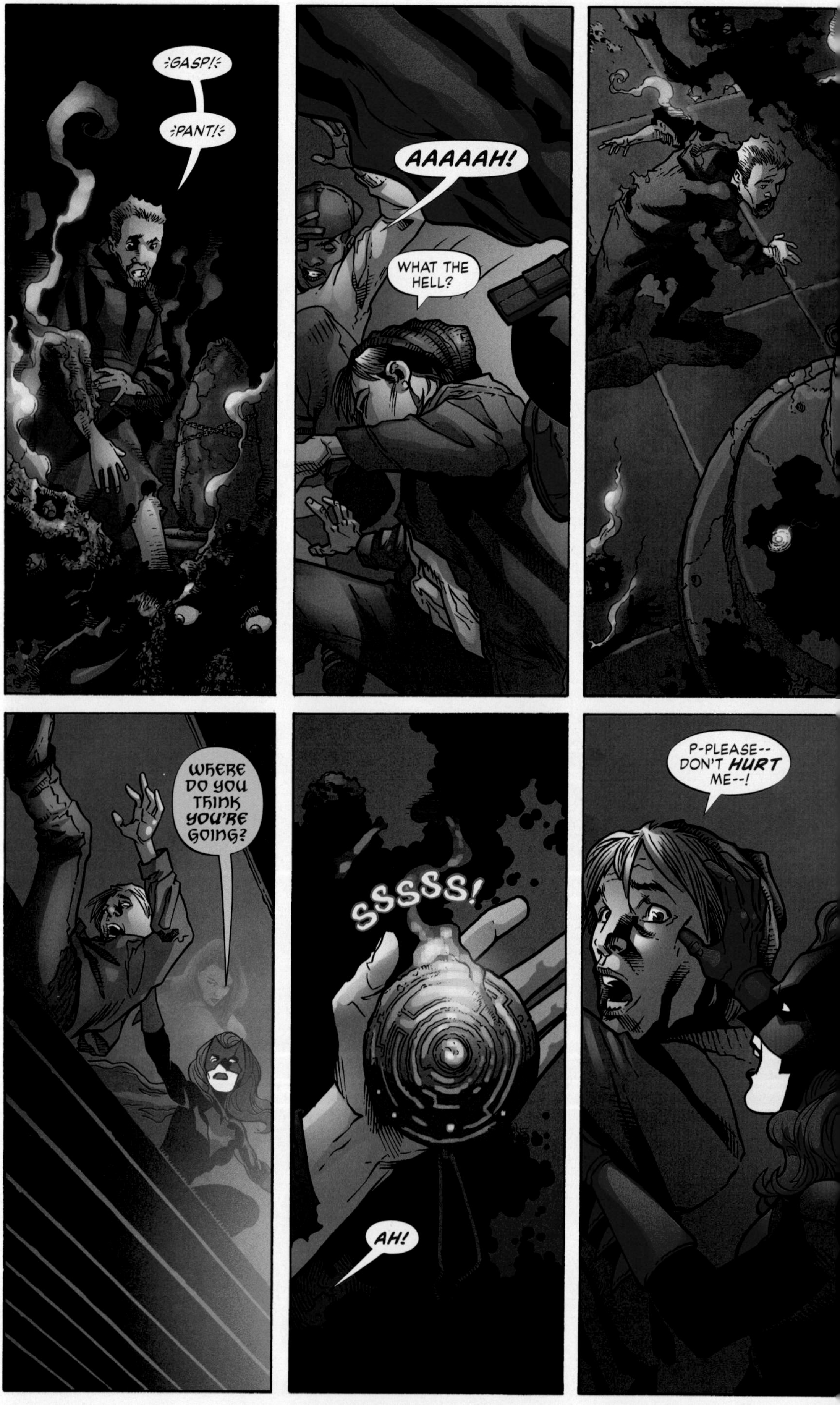
GASP!
PANT!
AAAAAH!
WHAT THE HELL?
WHERE DO YOU THINK YOU'RE GOING?
SSSSS!
AH!
P-PLEASE-- DON'T HURT ME--!

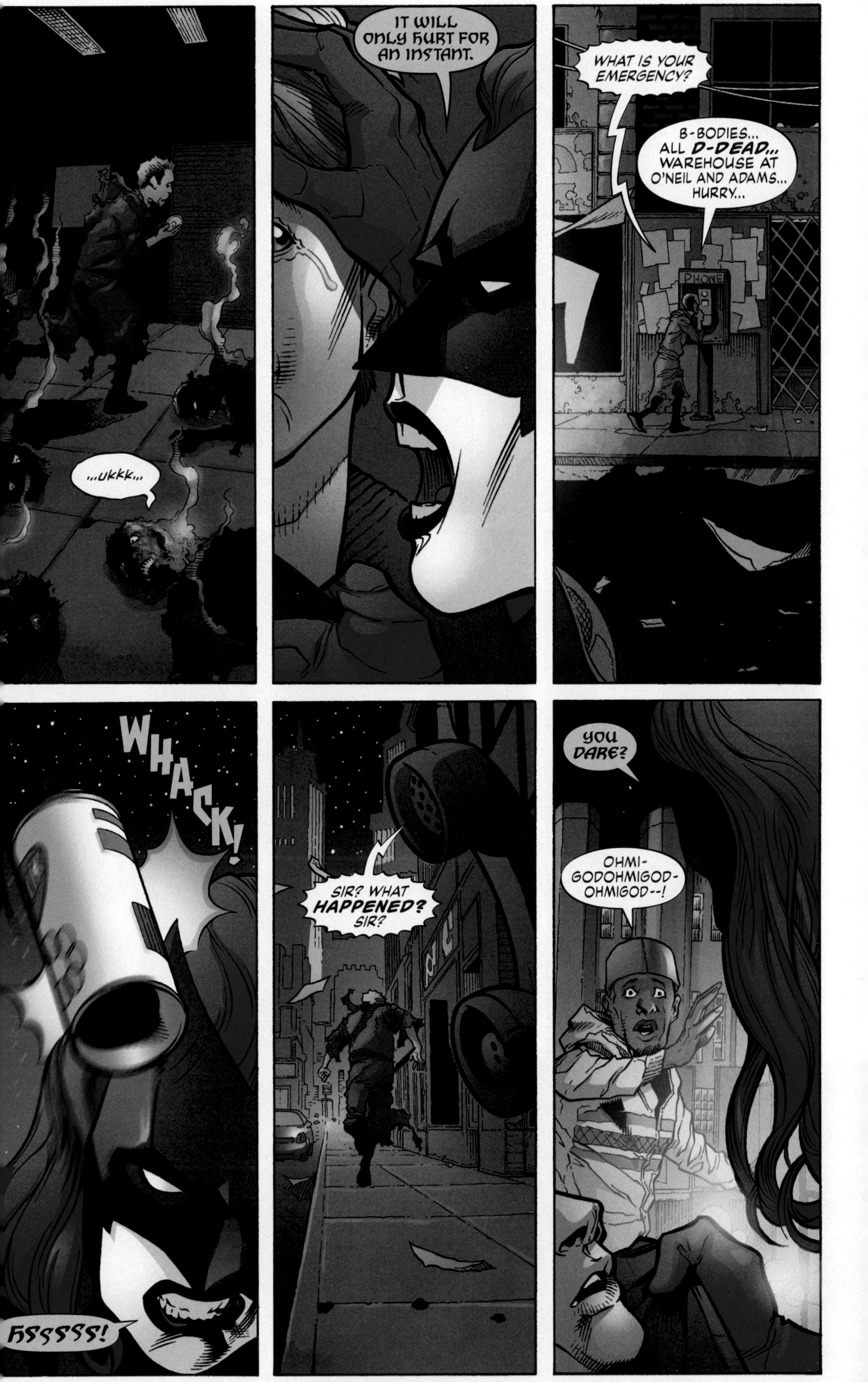
...UKKK...
IT WILL ONLY HURT FOR AN INSTANT.
WHAT IS YOUR EMERGENCY?
B-BODIES... ALL D-DEAD... WAREHOUSE AT O'NEIL AND ADAMS... HURRY...
PHONE
WHACK!
HSSSSS!
SIR? WHAT HAPPENED? SIR?
YOU DARE?
OHMI-GODOHMIGOD-OHMIGOD--!

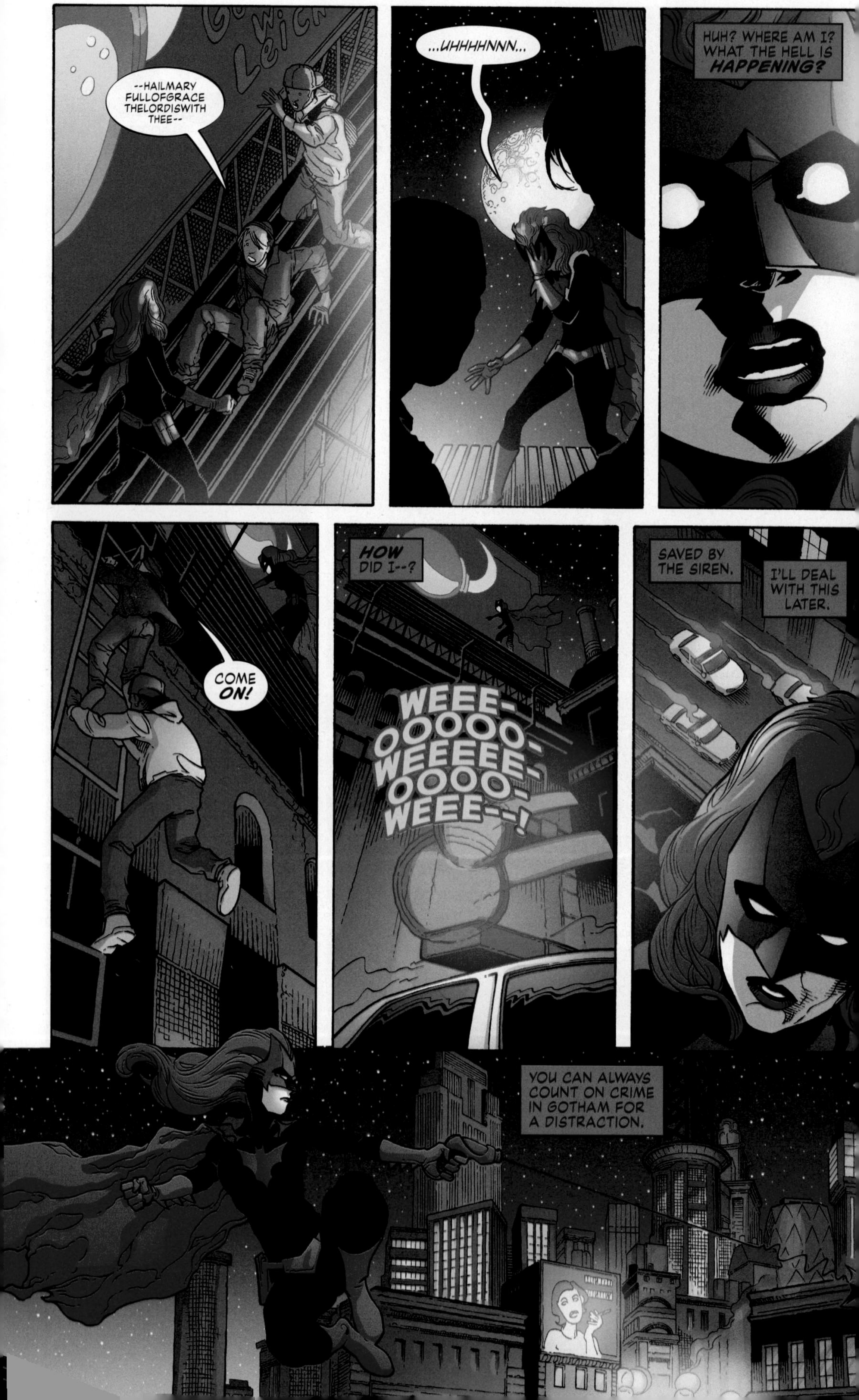
--HAILMARY FULLOFGRACE THELORDISWITH THEE--
...UHHHHNNN...
HUH? WHERE AM I? WHAT THE HELL IS HAPPENING?
COME ON!
HOW DID I--?
WEEE-OOOOO-WEEEEE-OOOO-WEEE--!
SAVED BY THE SIREN.
I'LL DEAL WITH THIS LATER.
YOU CAN ALWAYS COUNT ON CRIME IN GOTHAM FOR A DISTRACTION.

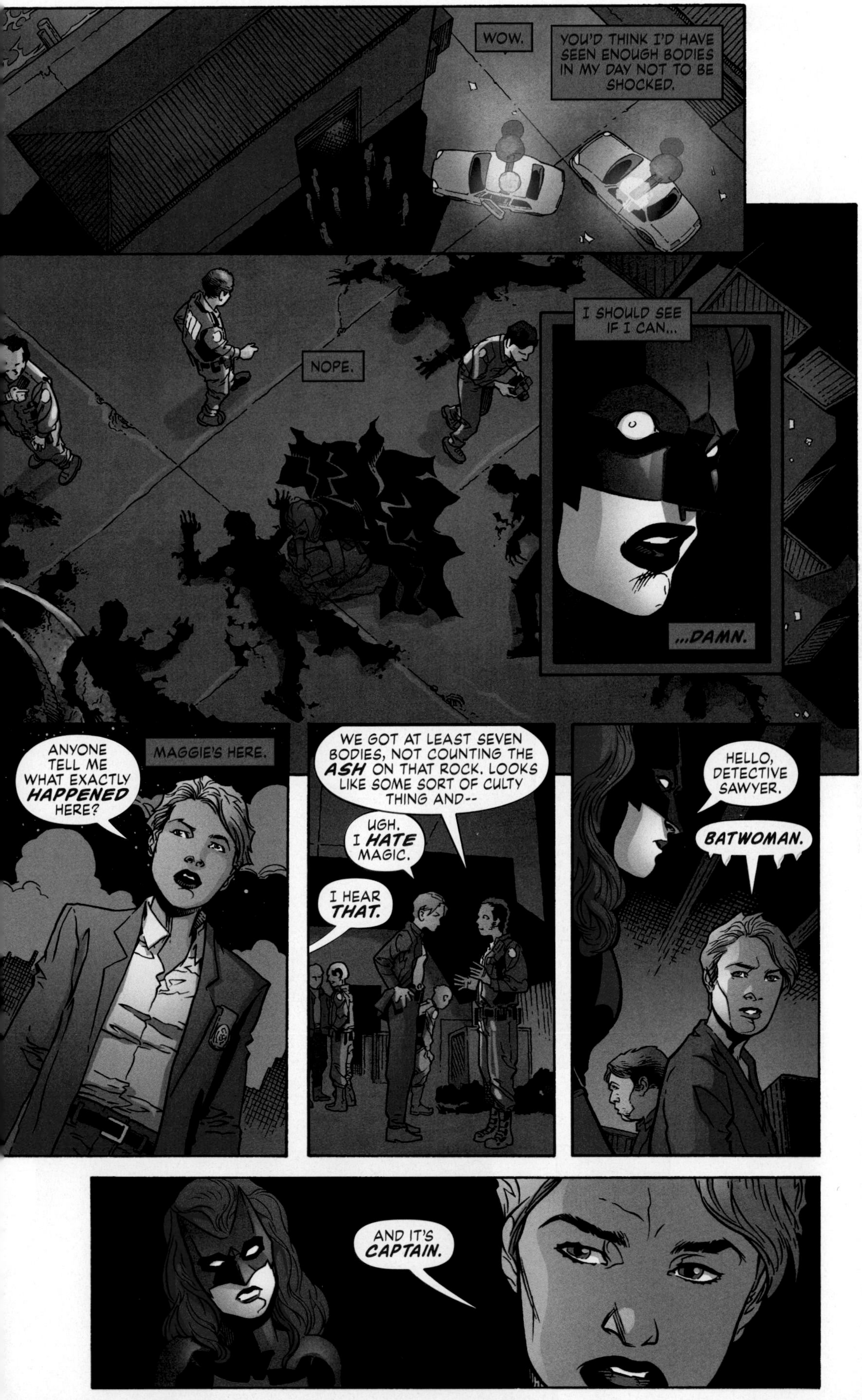

WOW.
YOU'D THINK I'D HAVE SEEN ENOUGH BODIES IN MY DAY NOT TO BE SHOCKED.
NOPE.
I SHOULD SEE IF I CAN...
...DAMN.
MAGGIE'S HERE.
ANYONE TELL ME WHAT EXACTLY HAPPENED HERE?
WE GOT AT LEAST SEVEN BODIES, NOT COUNTING THE ASH ON THAT ROCK. LOOKS LIKE SOME SORT OF CULTY THING AND--
UGH. I HATE MAGIC.
I HEAR THAT.
HELLO, DETECTIVE SAWYER.
BATWOMAN.
AND IT'S CAPTAIN.

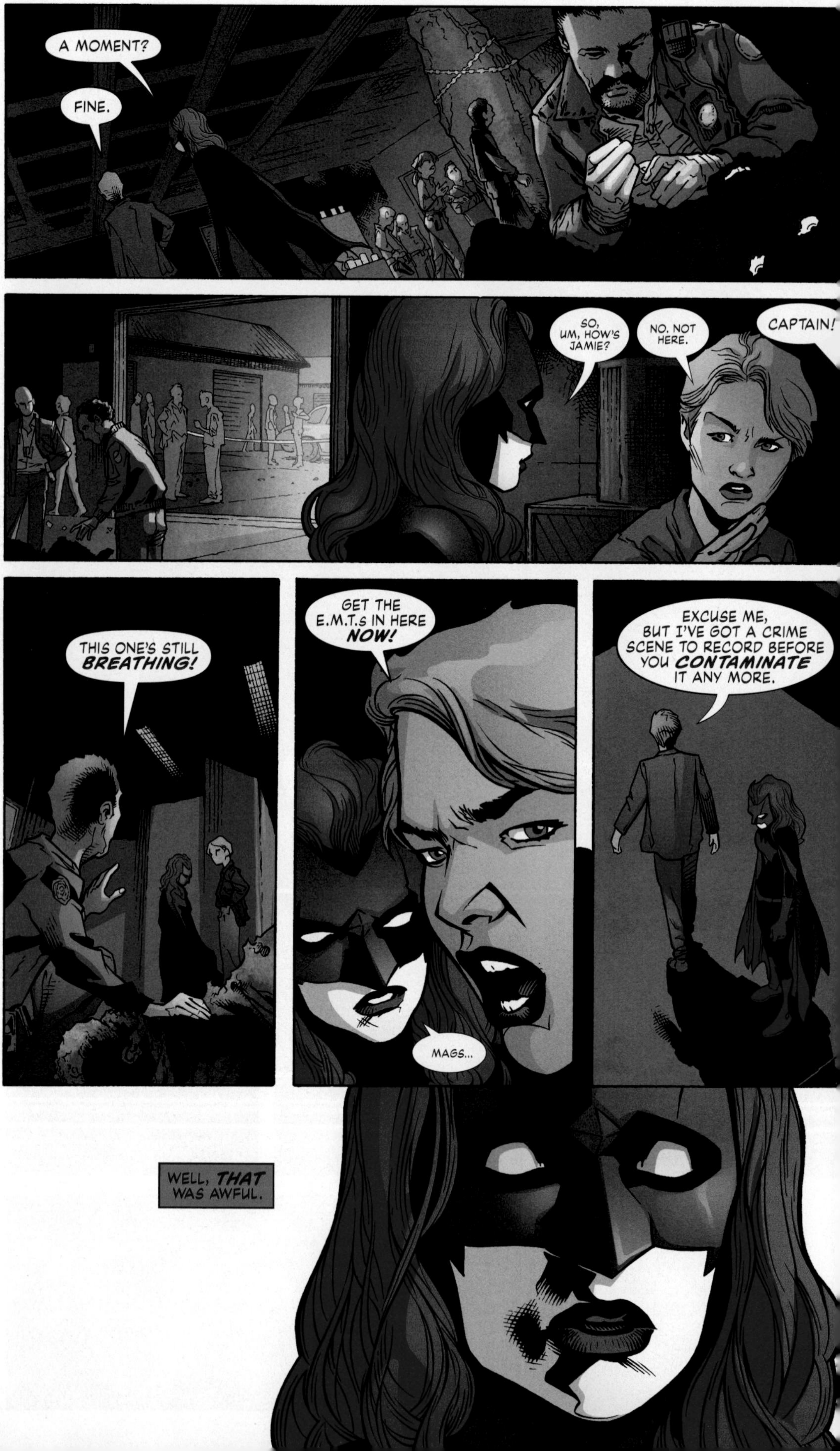

A MOMENT?
FINE.
SO, UM, HOW'S JAMIE?
NO. NOT HERE.
CAPTAIN!
THIS ONE'S STILL *BREATHING!*
GET THE E.M.T.s IN HERE *NOW!*
MAGS...
EXCUSE ME, BUT I'VE GOT A CRIME SCENE TO RECORD BEFORE YOU *CONTAMINATE* IT ANY MORE.
WELL, *THAT* WAS AWFUL.

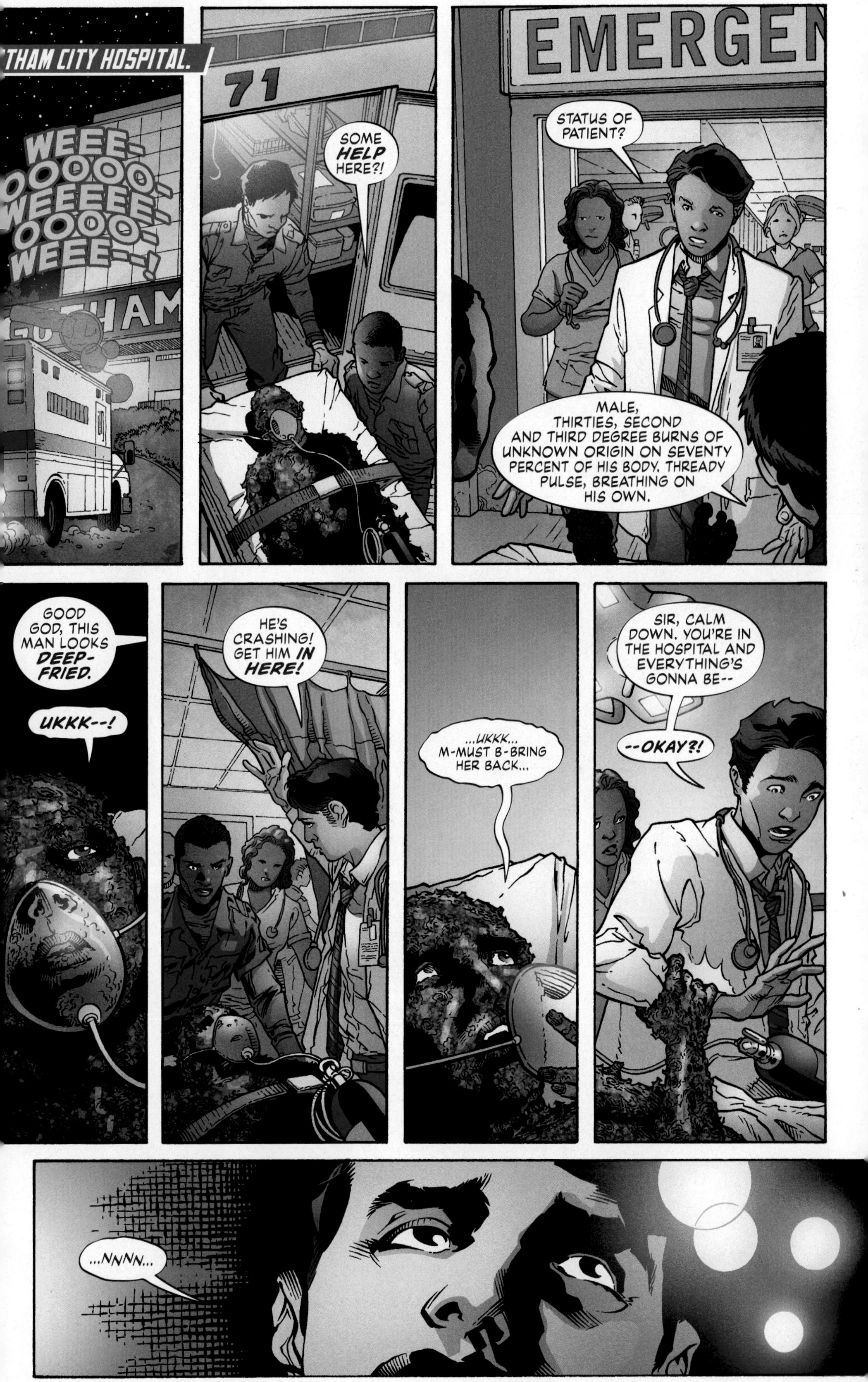
THAM CITY HOSPITAL.
WEEE-OOOOO-WEEEEE-OOOO-WEEE--!
GOTHAM
71
SOME HELP HERE?!
EMERGEN
STATUS OF PATIENT?
MALE, THIRTIES, SECOND AND THIRD DEGREE BURNS OF UNKNOWN ORIGIN ON SEVENTY PERCENT OF HIS BODY. THREADY PULSE, BREATHING ON HIS OWN.
GOOD GOD, THIS MAN LOOKS DEEP-FRIED.
UKKK--!
HE'S CRASHING! GET HIM IN HERE!
...UKKK... M-MUST B-BRING HER BACK...
SIR, CALM DOWN. YOU'RE IN THE HOSPITAL AND EVERYTHING'S GONNA BE--
--OKAY?!
...NNNN...

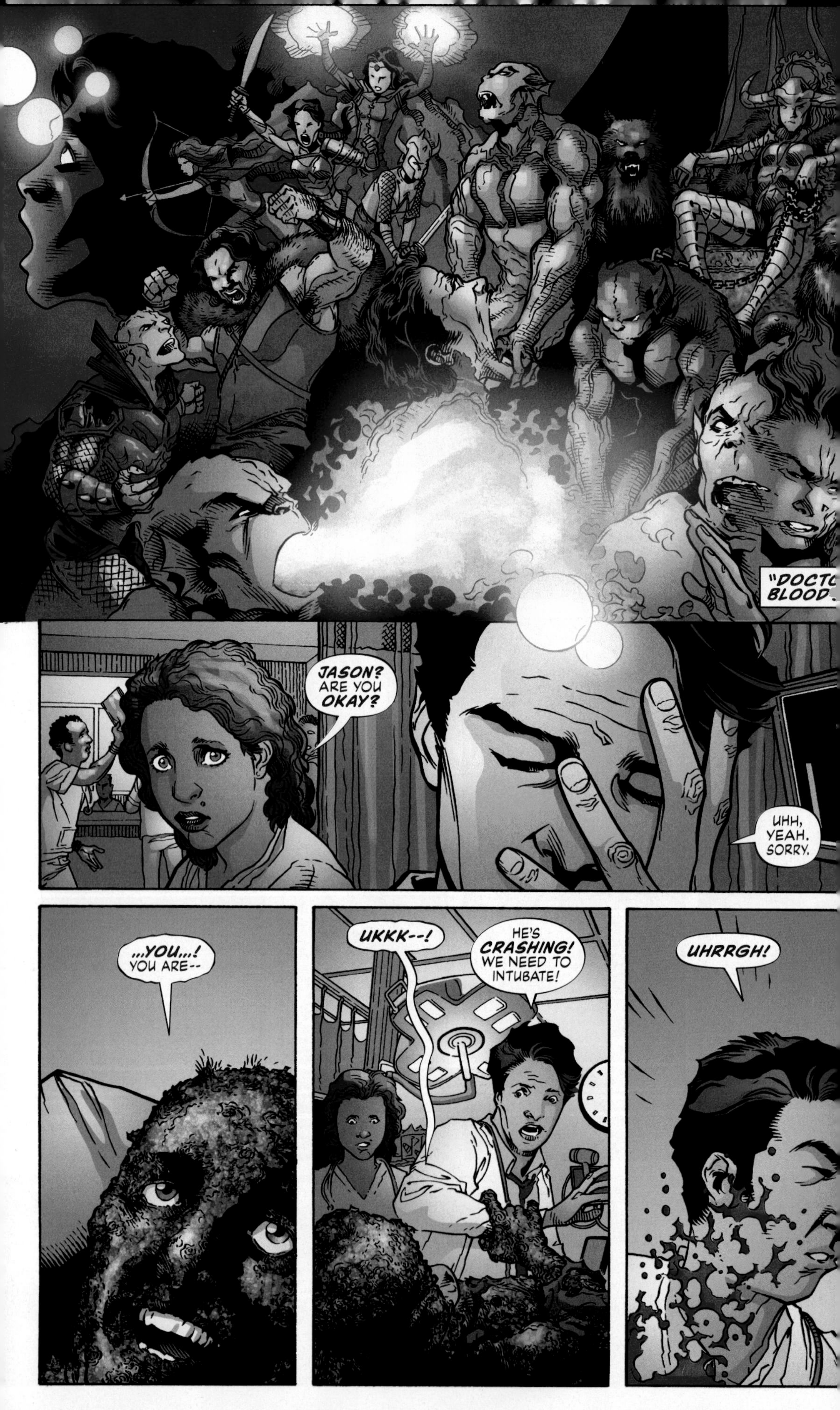
"DOCTO
BLOOD"
JASON? ARE YOU OKAY?
UHH, YEAH. SORRY.
...YOU...! YOU ARE--
UKKK--!
HE'S CRASHING! WE NEED TO INTUBATE!
UHRRGH!

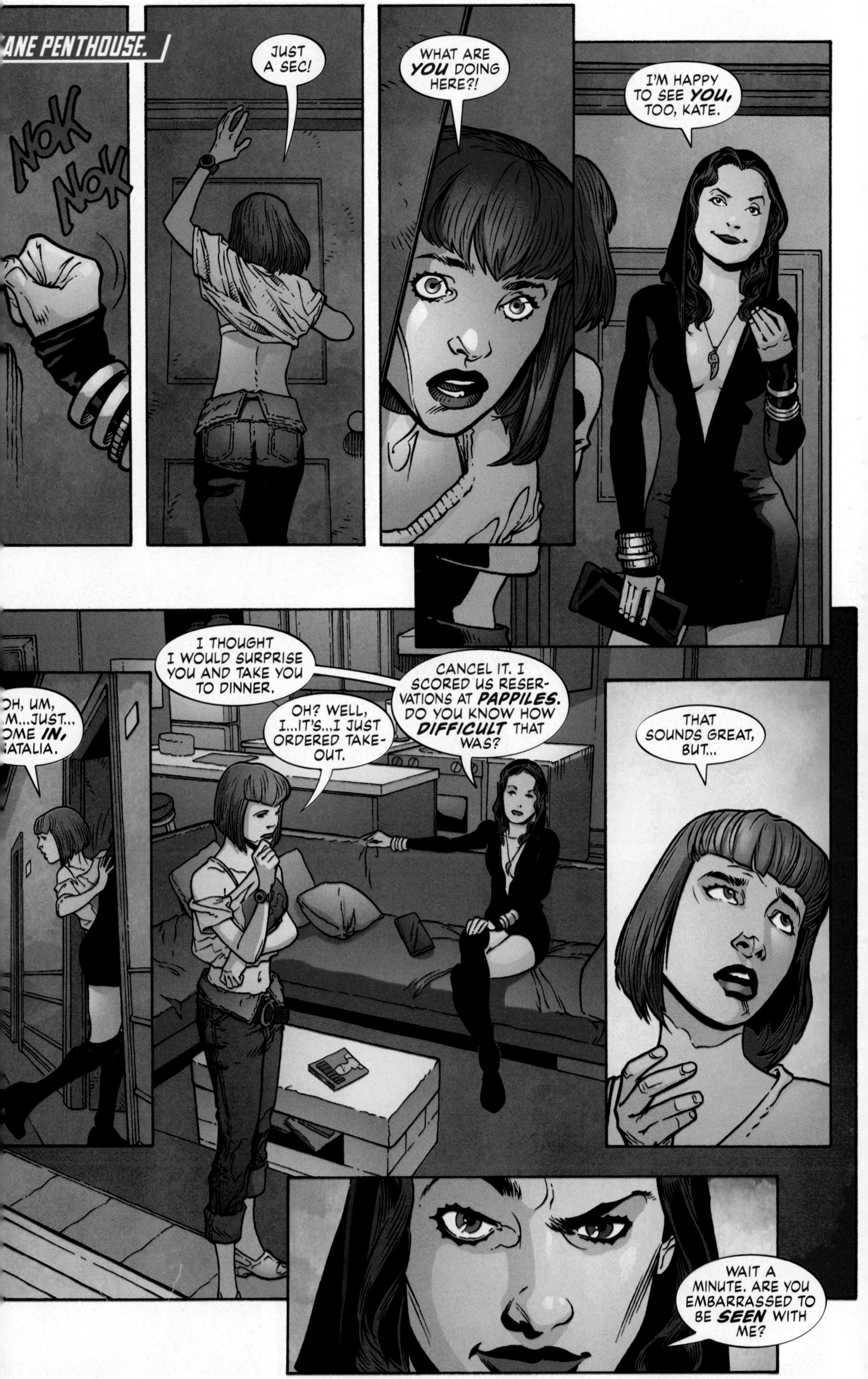

ANE PENTHOUSE.
NOK NOK
JUST A SEC!
WHAT ARE YOU DOING HERE?!
I'M HAPPY TO SEE YOU, TOO, KATE.
OH, UM, M...JUST... OME IN, ATALIA.
I THOUGHT I WOULD SURPRISE YOU AND TAKE YOU TO DINNER.
OH? WELL, I...IT'S...I JUST ORDERED TAKE-OUT.
CANCEL IT. I SCORED US RESER-VATIONS AT PAPPILES. DO YOU KNOW HOW DIFFICULT THAT WAS?
THAT SOUNDS GREAT, BUT...
WAIT A MINUTE. ARE YOU EMBARRASSED TO BE SEEN WITH ME?

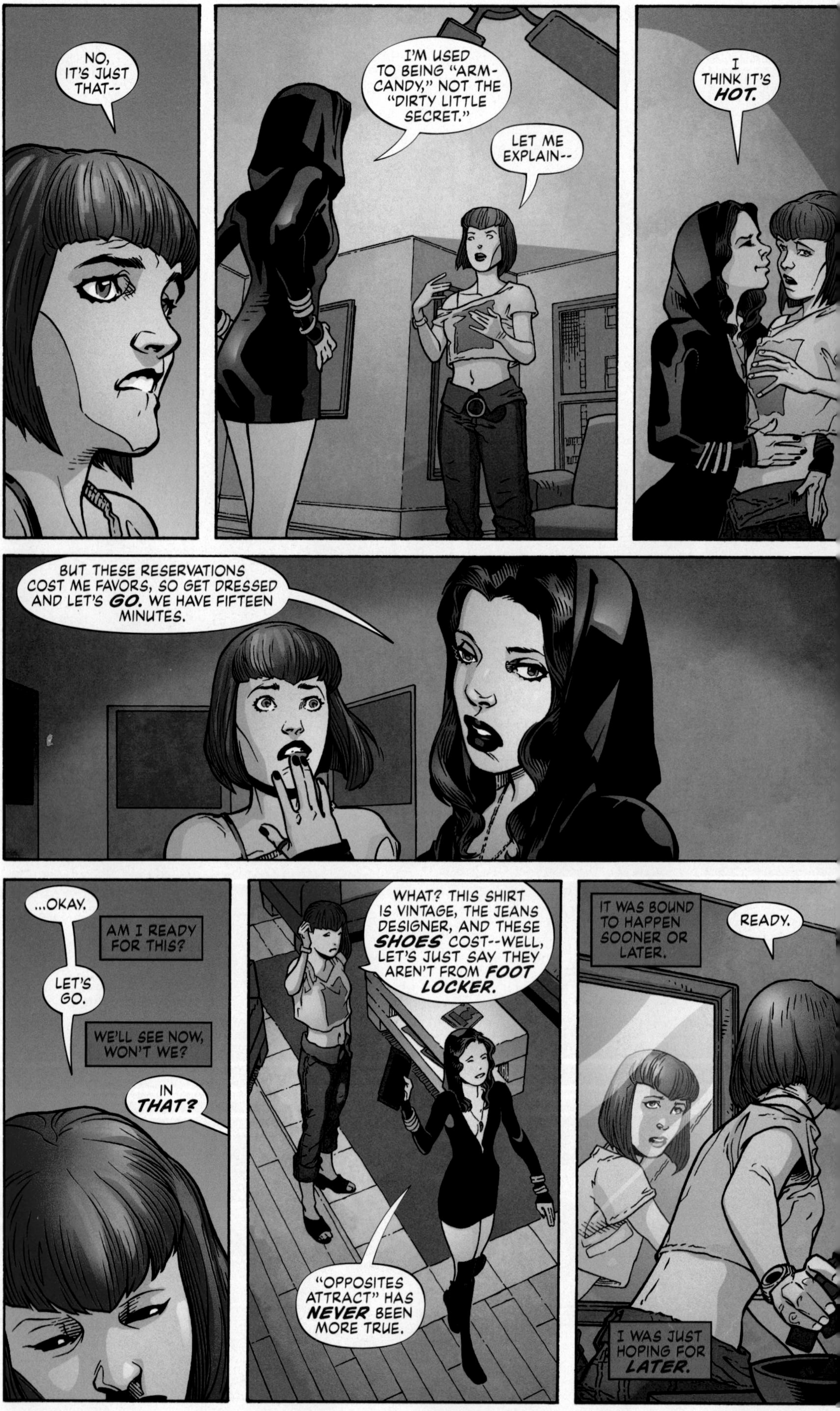
NO, IT'S JUST THAT--
I'M USED TO BEING "ARM-CANDY," NOT THE "DIRTY LITTLE SECRET."
LET ME EXPLAIN--
I THINK IT'S HOT.
BUT THESE RESERVATIONS COST ME FAVORS, SO GET DRESSED AND LET'S GO. WE HAVE FIFTEEN MINUTES.
...OKAY.
AM I READY FOR THIS?
LET'S GO.
WE'LL SEE NOW, WON'T WE?
IN THAT?
WHAT? THIS SHIRT IS VINTAGE, THE JEANS DESIGNER, AND THESE SHOES COST--WELL, LET'S JUST SAY THEY AREN'T FROM FOOT LOCKER.
"OPPOSITES ATTRACT" HAS NEVER BEEN MORE TRUE.
IT WAS BOUND TO HAPPEN SOONER OR LATER.
READY.
I WAS JUST HOPING FOR LATER.

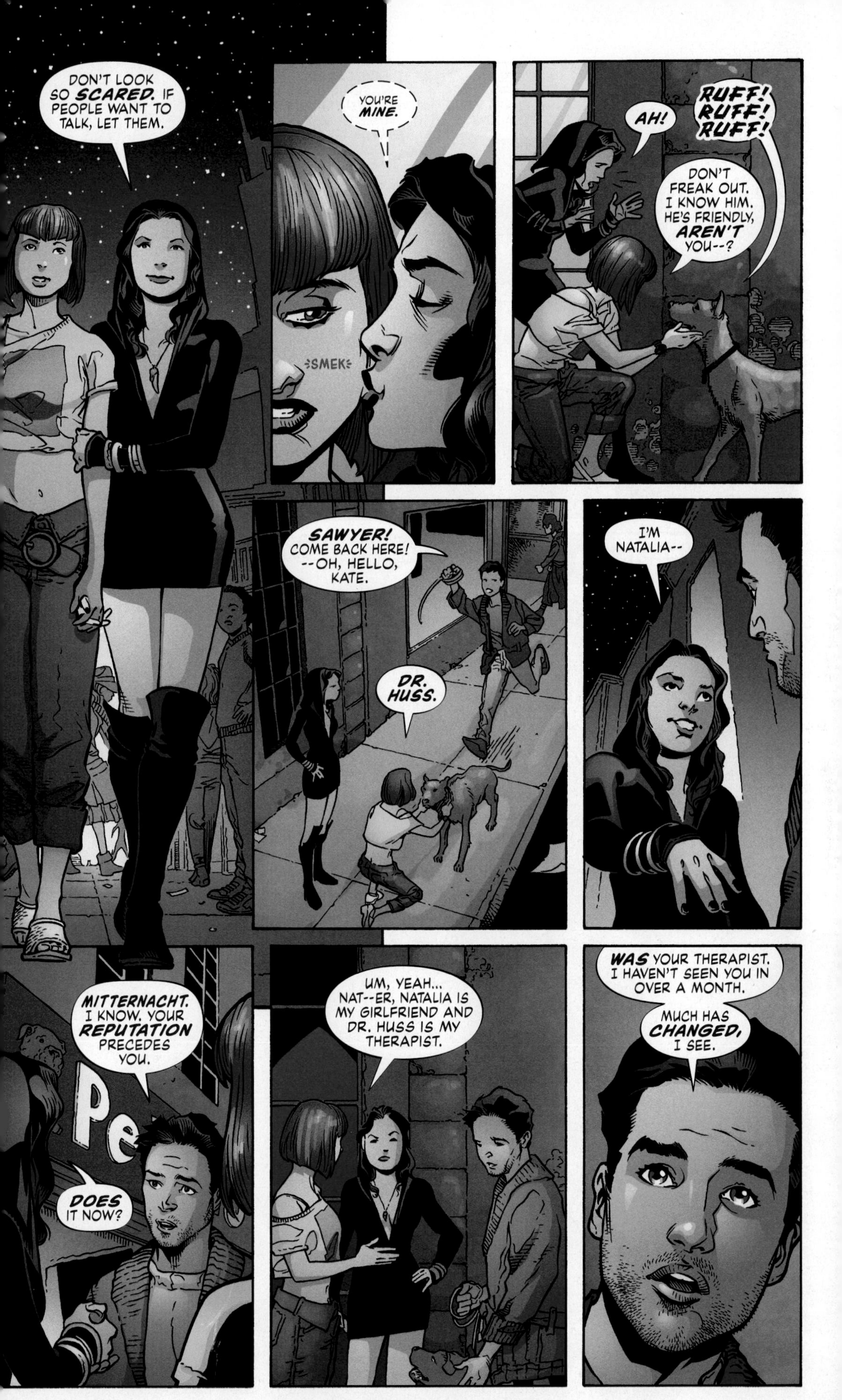
DON'T LOOK SO SCARED. IF PEOPLE WANT TO TALK, LET THEM.
YOU'RE MINE.
SMEK
AH!
RUFF! RUFF! RUFF!
DON'T FREAK OUT. I KNOW HIM. HE'S FRIENDLY, AREN'T YOU--?
SAWYER! COME BACK HERE! --OH, HELLO, KATE.
DR. HUSS.
I'M NATALIA--
MITTERNACHT. I KNOW. YOUR REPUTATION PRECEDES YOU.
DOES IT NOW?
UM, YEAH... NAT--ER, NATALIA IS MY GIRLFRIEND AND DR. HUSS IS MY THERAPIST.
WAS YOUR THERAPIST. I HAVEN'T SEEN YOU IN OVER A MONTH.
MUCH HAS CHANGED, I SEE.

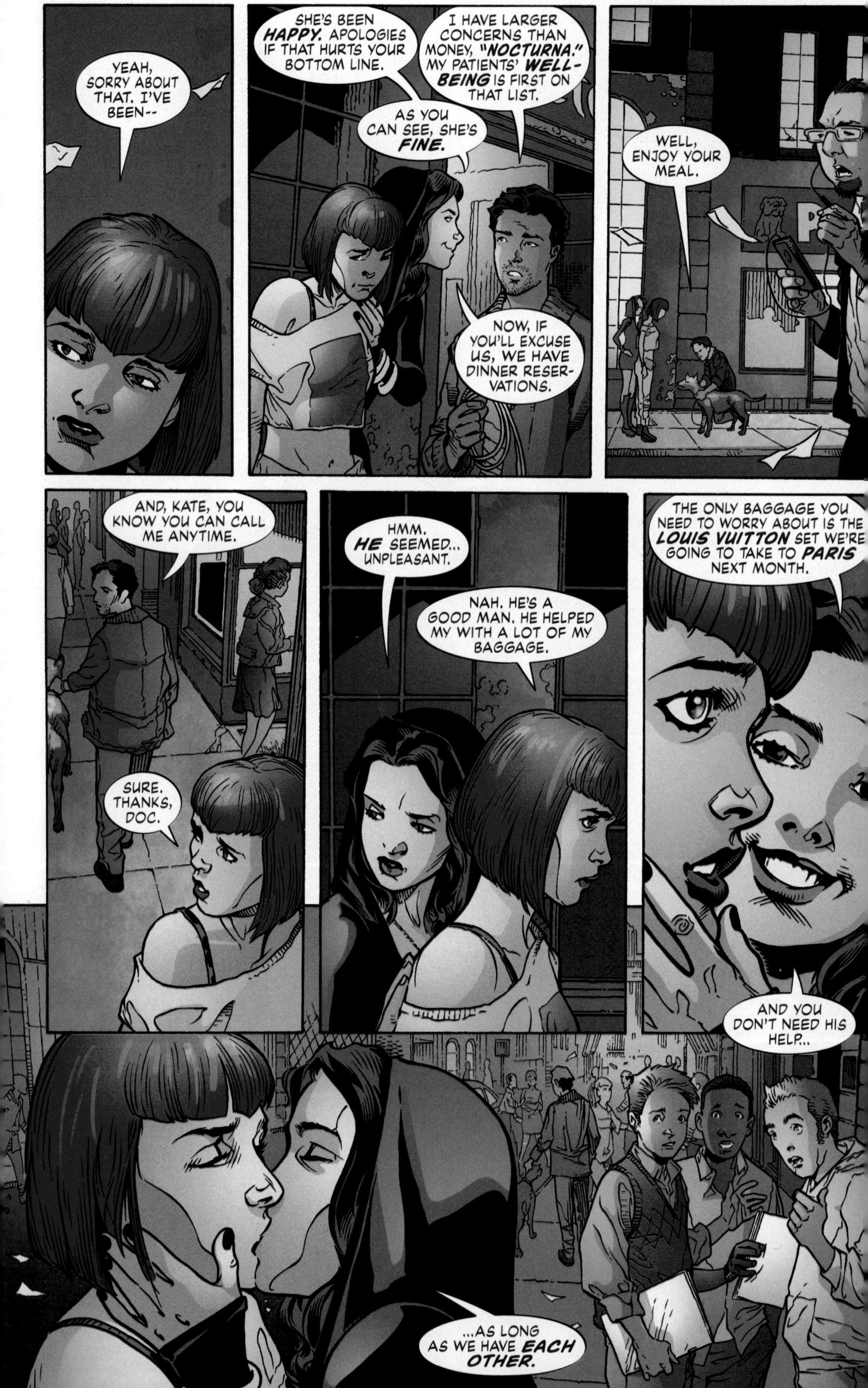
YEAH, SORRY ABOUT THAT. I'VE BEEN--
SHE'S BEEN HAPPY. APOLOGIES IF THAT HURTS YOUR BOTTOM LINE.
I HAVE LARGER CONCERNS THAN MONEY, "NOCTURNA." MY PATIENTS' WELL-BEING IS FIRST ON THAT LIST.
AS YOU CAN SEE, SHE'S FINE.
NOW, IF YOU'LL EXCUSE US, WE HAVE DINNER RESERVATIONS.
WELL, ENJOY YOUR MEAL.
AND, KATE, YOU KNOW YOU CAN CALL ME ANYTIME.
SURE. THANKS, DOC.
HMM. HE SEEMED... UNPLEASANT.
NAH. HE'S A GOOD MAN. HE HELPED MY WITH A LOT OF MY BAGGAGE.
THE ONLY BAGGAGE YOU NEED TO WORRY ABOUT IS THE LOUIS VUITTON SET WE'RE GOING TO TAKE TO PARIS NEXT MONTH.
AND YOU DON'T NEED HIS HELP...
...AS LONG AS WE HAVE EACH OTHER.

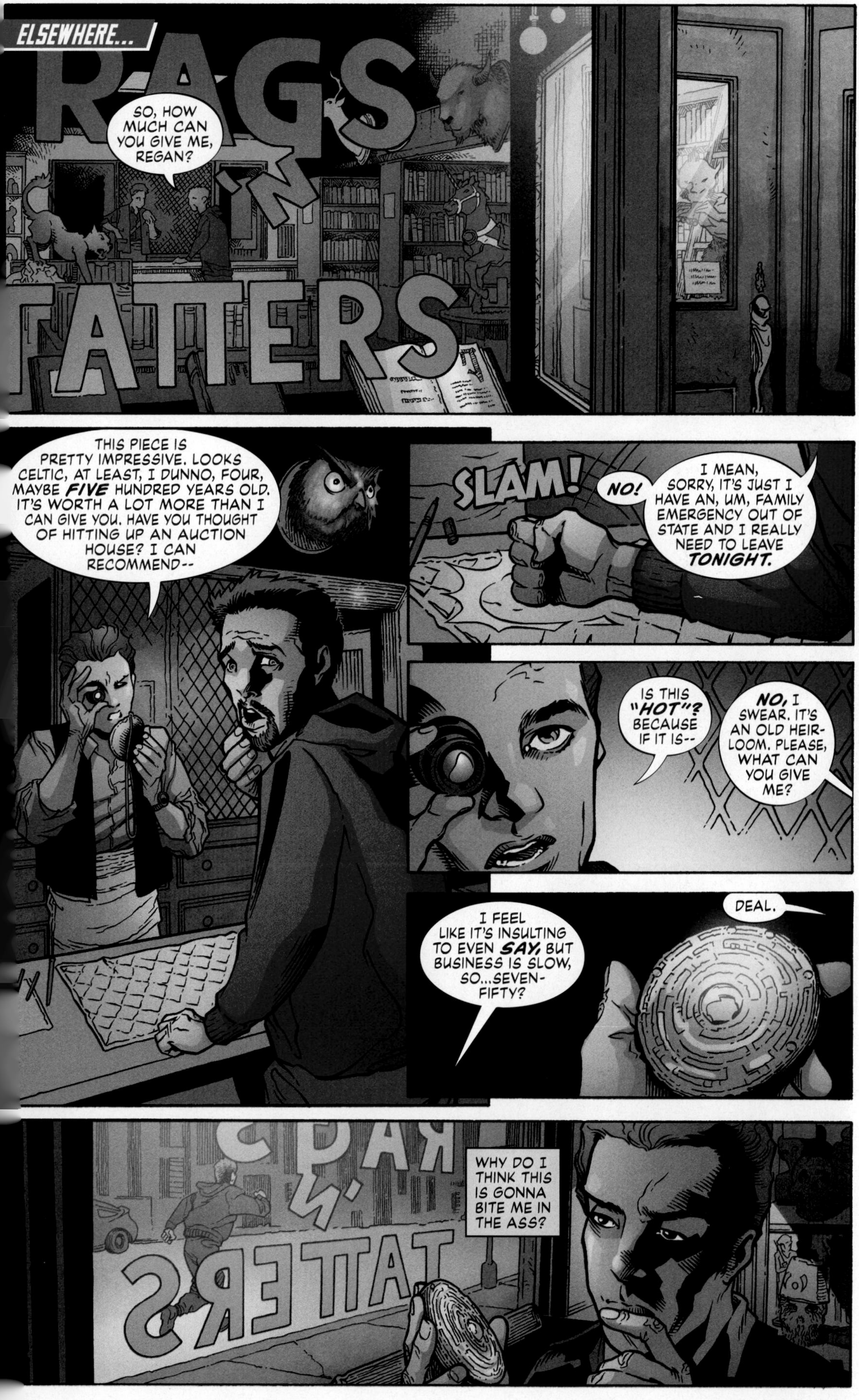
ELSEWHERE...
RAGS 'N' TATTERS
SO, HOW MUCH CAN YOU GIVE ME, REGAN?
THIS PIECE IS PRETTY IMPRESSIVE. LOOKS CELTIC, AT LEAST, I DUNNO, FOUR, MAYBE FIVE HUNDRED YEARS OLD. IT'S WORTH A LOT MORE THAN I CAN GIVE YOU. HAVE YOU THOUGHT OF HITTING UP AN AUCTION HOUSE? I CAN RECOMMEND--
SLAM!
NO!
I MEAN, SORRY, IT'S JUST I HAVE AN, UM, FAMILY EMERGENCY OUT OF STATE AND I REALLY NEED TO LEAVE TONIGHT.
IS THIS "HOT"? BECAUSE IF IT IS--
NO, I SWEAR. IT'S AN OLD HEIRLOOM. PLEASE, WHAT CAN YOU GIVE ME?
I FEEL LIKE IT'S INSULTING TO EVEN SAY, BUT BUSINESS IS SLOW, SO...SEVEN-FIFTY?
DEAL.
WHY DO I THINK THIS IS GONNA BITE ME IN THE ASS?

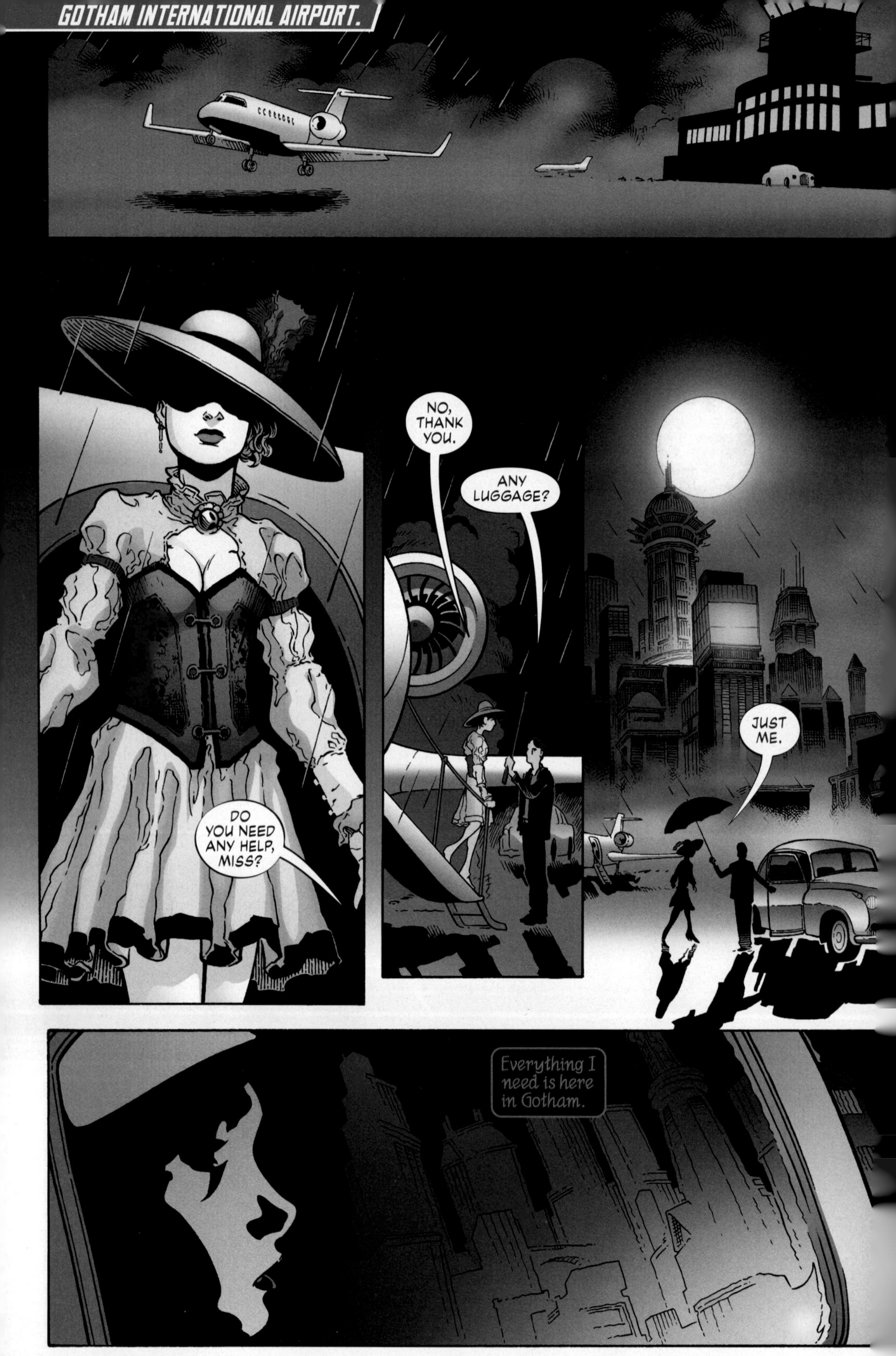
GOTHAM INTERNATIONAL AIRPORT.
DO YOU NEED ANY HELP, MISS?
NO, THANK YOU.
ANY LUGGAGE?
JUST ME.
Everything I need is here in Gotham.

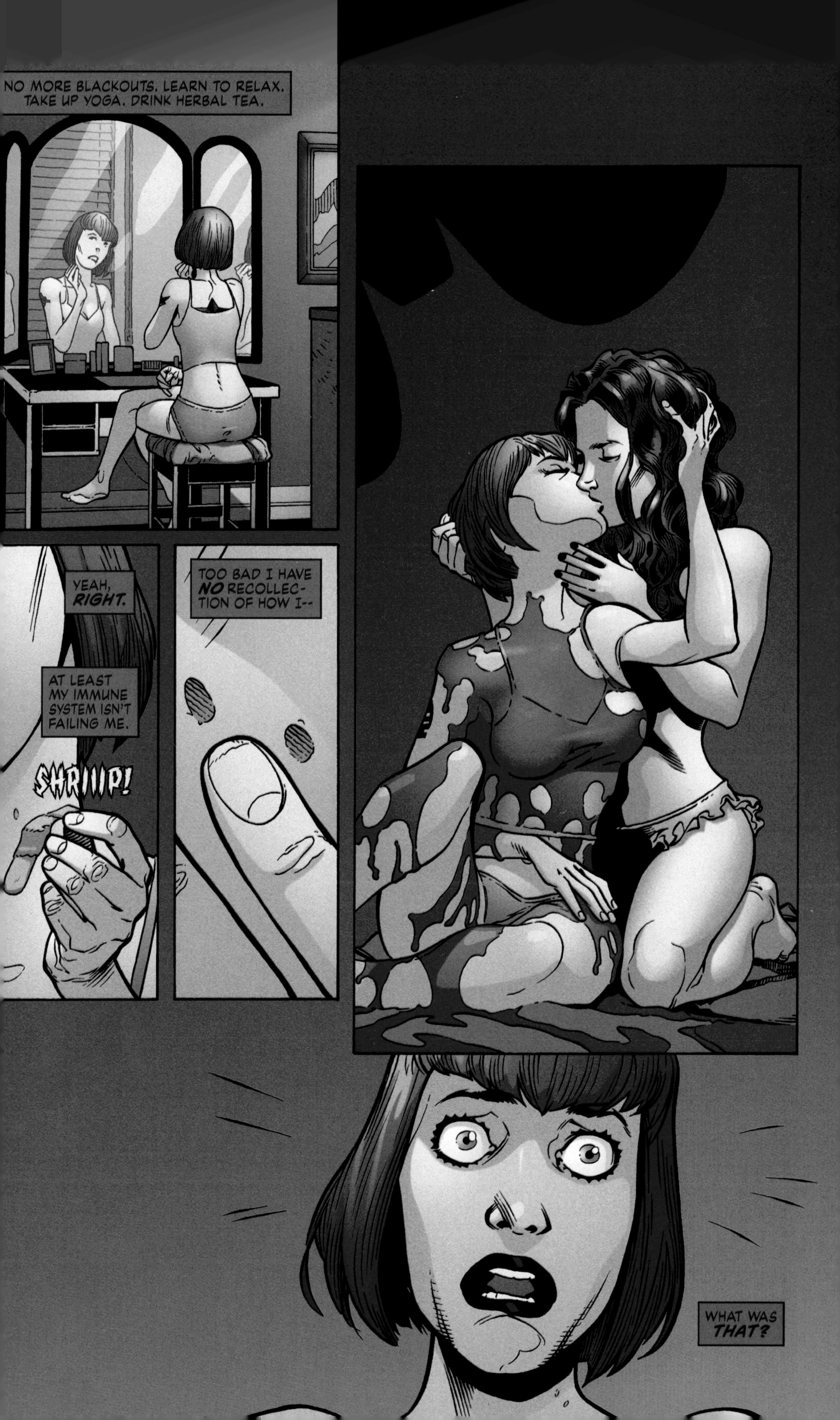
NO MORE BLACKOUTS. LEARN TO RELAX. TAKE UP YOGA. DRINK HERBAL TEA.
YEAH, RIGHT.
AT LEAST MY IMMUNE SYSTEM ISN'T FAILING ME.
SHRIIIP!
TOO BAD I HAVE NO RECOLLECTION OF HOW I--
WHAT WAS THAT?

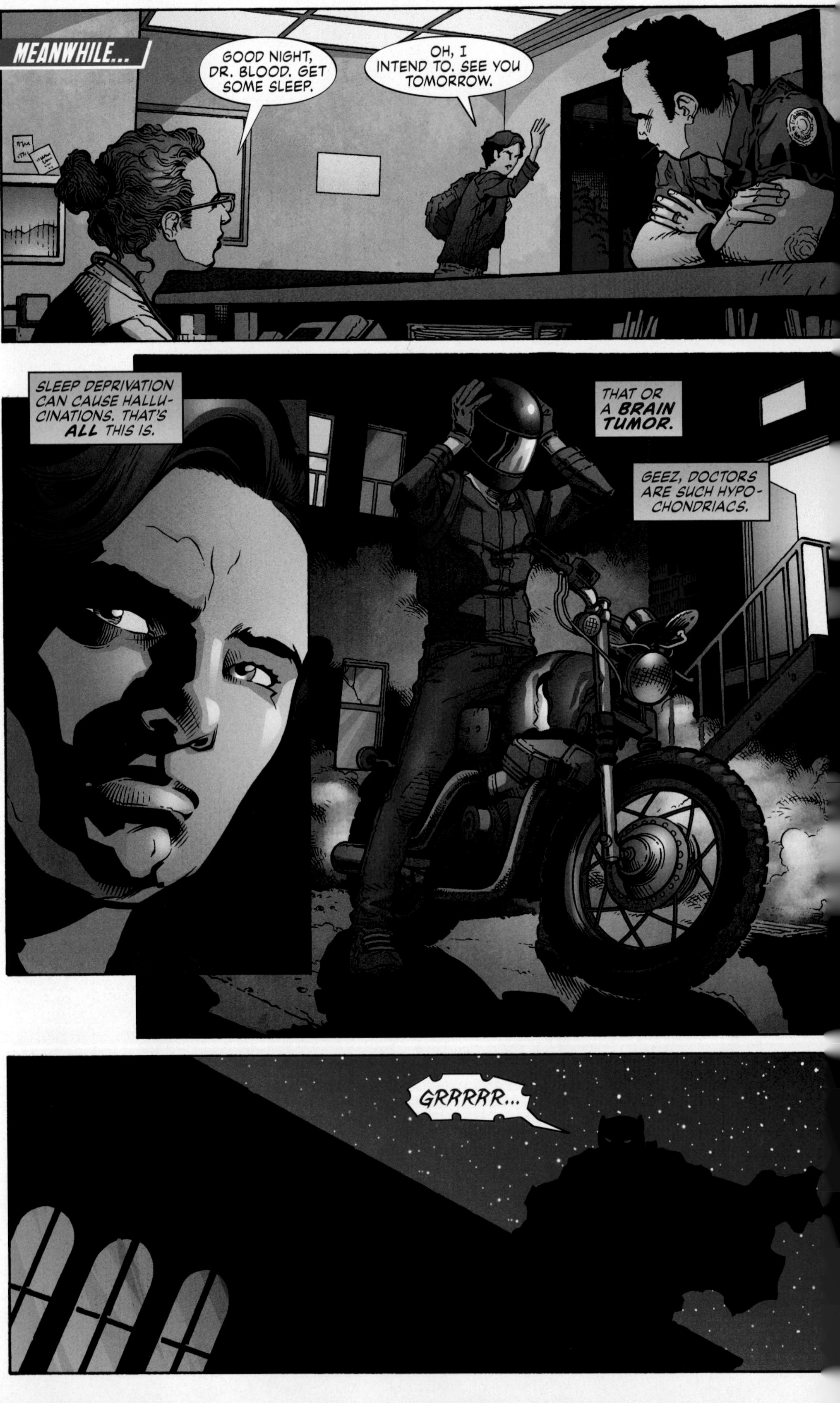
MEANWHILE...
GOOD NIGHT, DR. BLOOD. GET SOME SLEEP.
OH, I INTEND TO. SEE YOU TOMORROW.
SLEEP DEPRIVATION CAN CAUSE HALLUCINATIONS. THAT'S ALL THIS IS.
THAT OR A BRAIN TUMOR.
GEEZ, DOCTORS ARE SUCH HYPOCHONDRIACS.
GRRRRR...

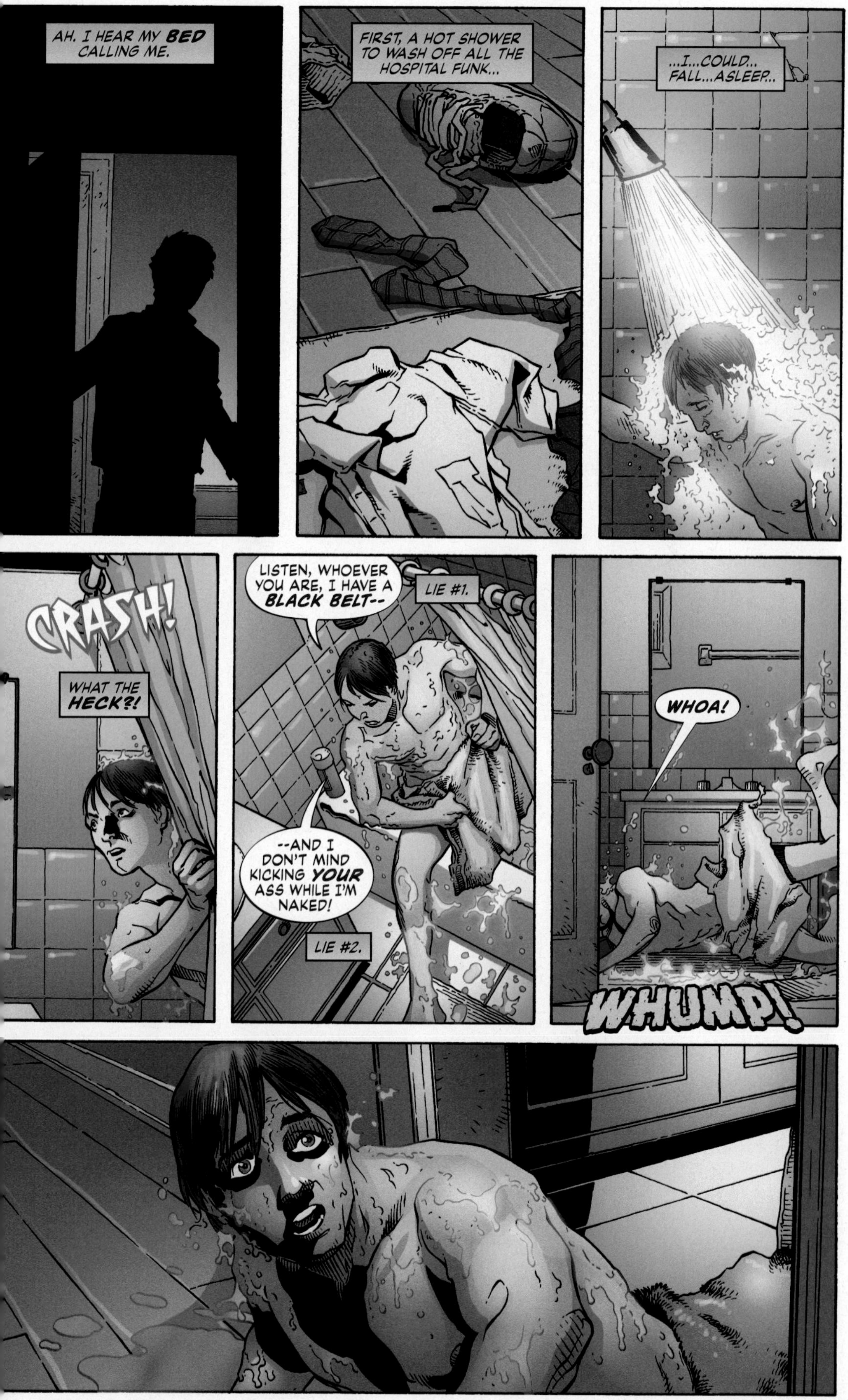

AH. I HEAR MY BED CALLING ME.
FIRST, A HOT SHOWER TO WASH OFF ALL THE HOSPITAL FUNK...
...I...COULD... FALL...ASLEEP...
CRASH!
WHAT THE HECK?!
LISTEN, WHOEVER YOU ARE, I HAVE A BLACK BELT--
LIE #1.
--AND I DON'T MIND KICKING YOUR ASS WHILE I'M NAKED!
LIE #2.
WHOA!
WHUMP!

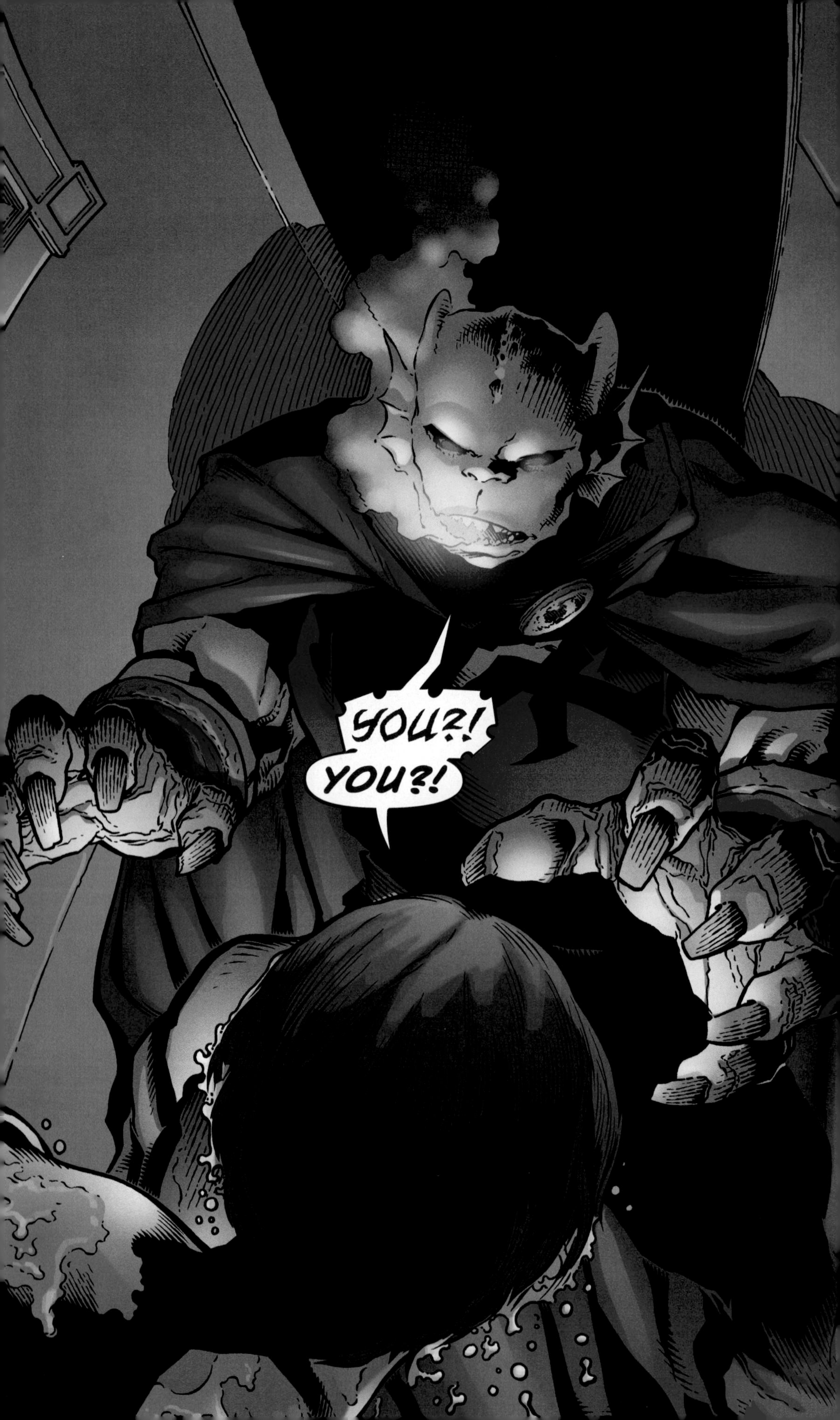
YOU?! YOU?!

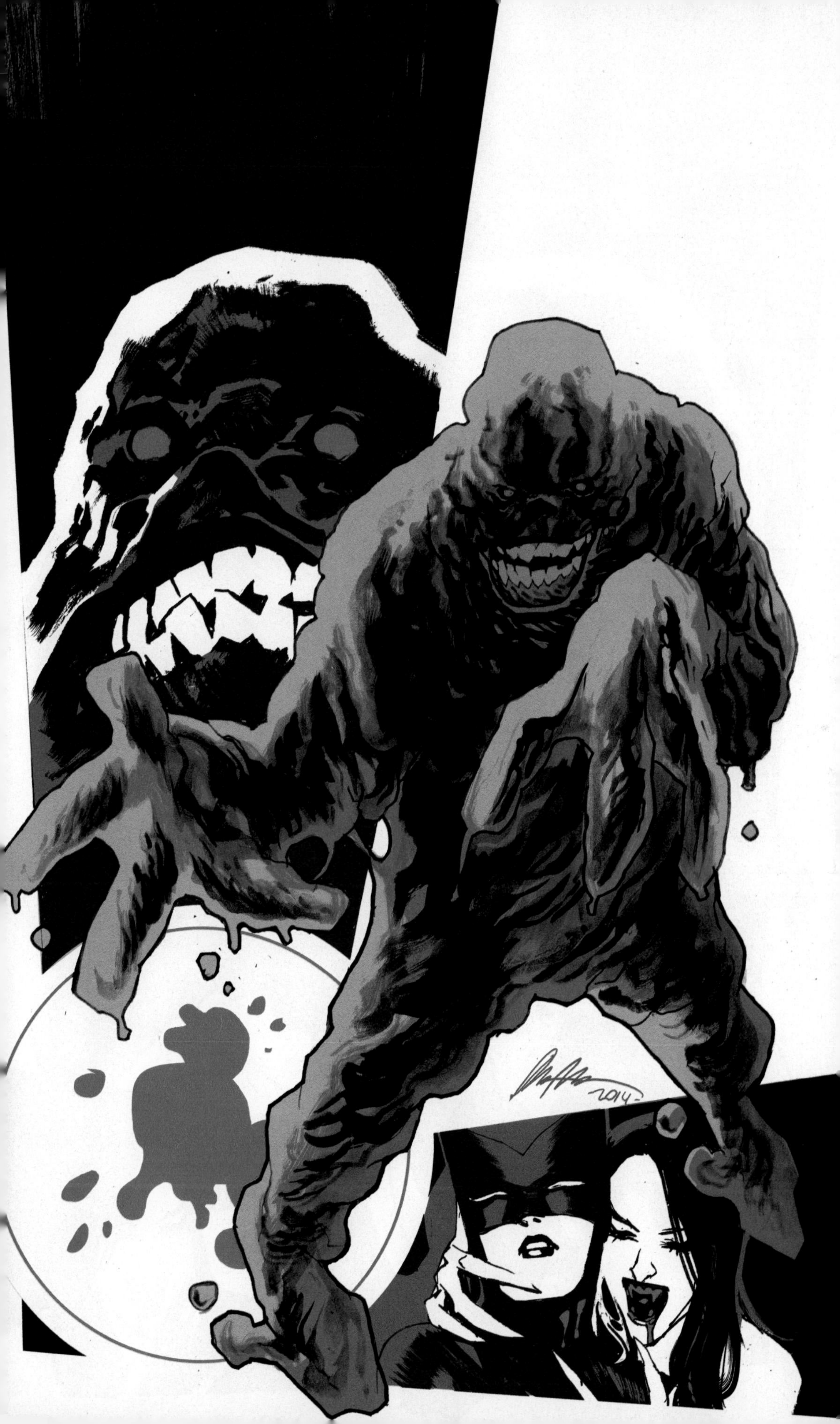

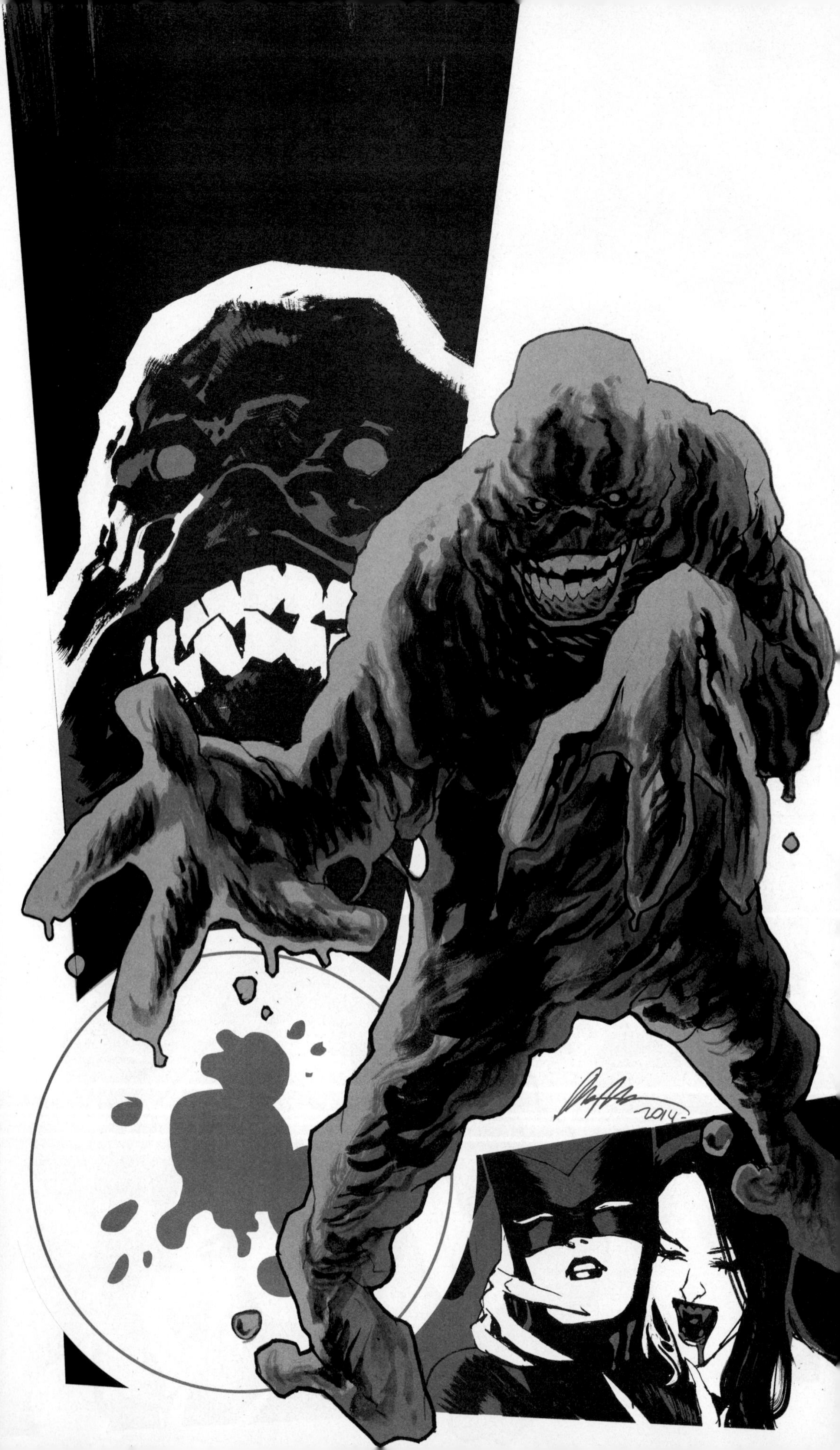

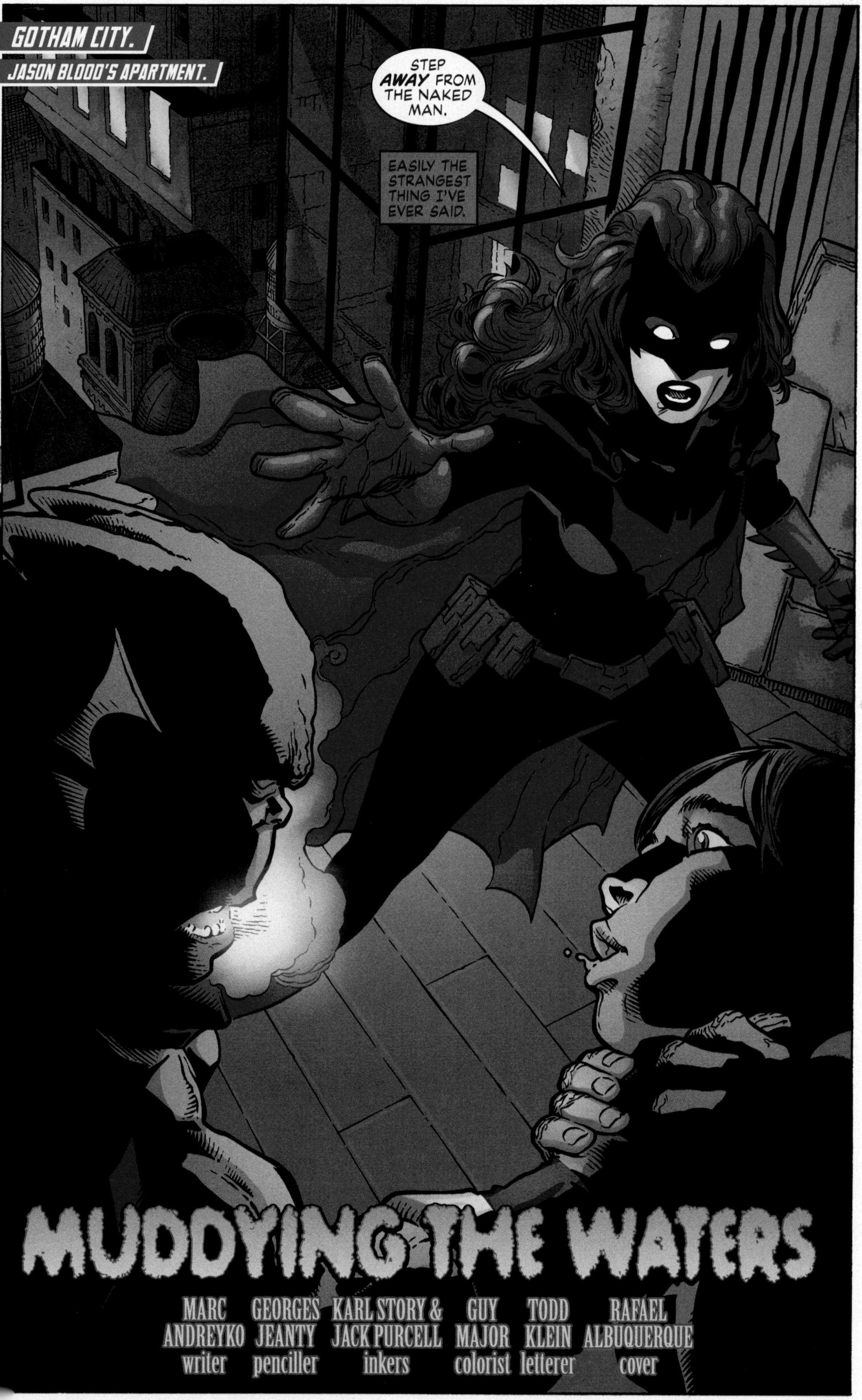
GOTHAM CITY.
JASON BLOOD'S APARTMENT.
STEP AWAY FROM THE NAKED MAN.
EASILY THE STRANGEST THING I'VE EVER SAID.
MUDDYING THE WATERS
MARC ANDREYKO writer
GEORGES JEANTY penciller
KARL STORY & JACK PURCELL inkers
GUY MAJOR colorist
TODD KLEIN letterer
RAFAEL ALBUQUERQUE cover

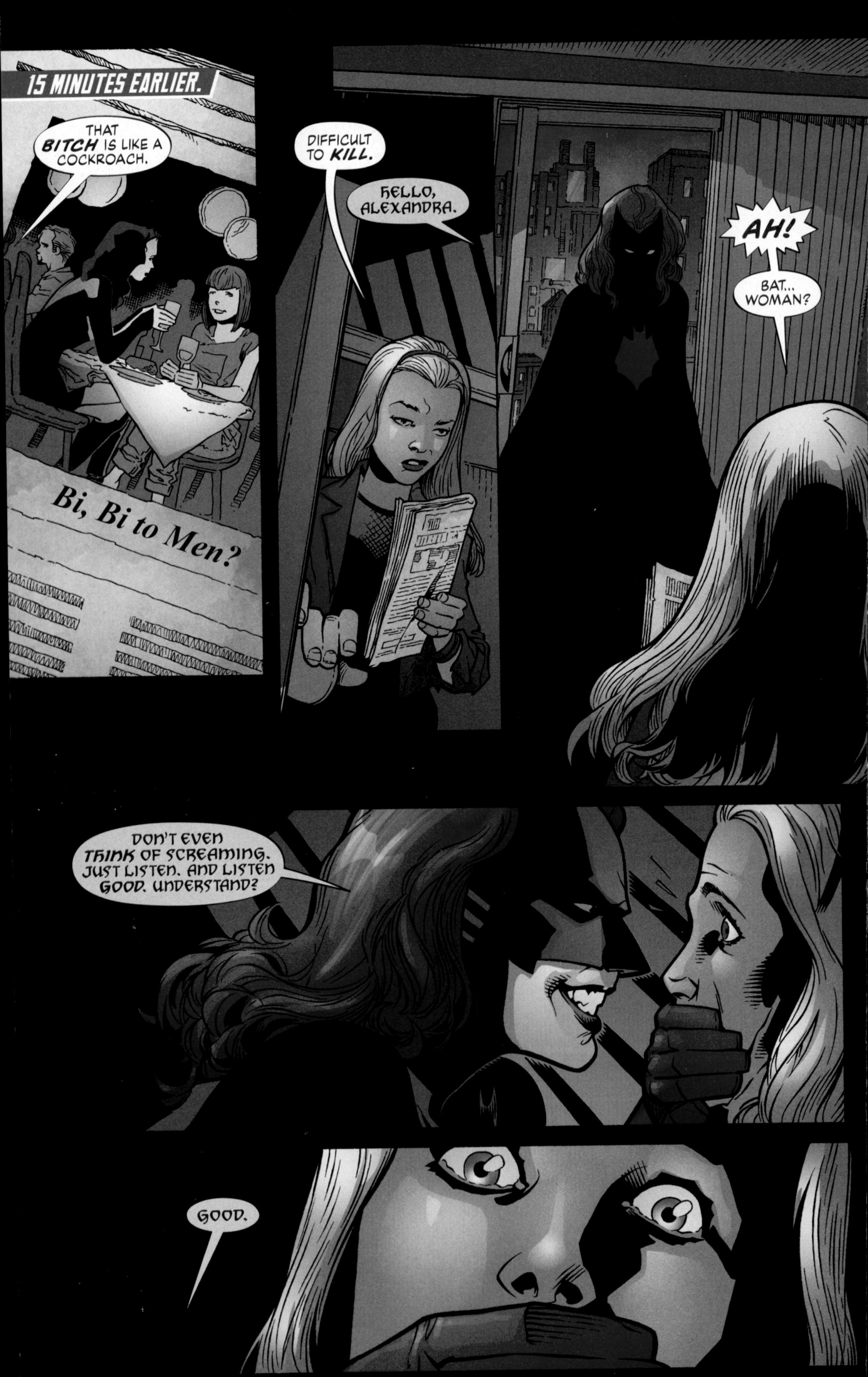
15 MINUTES EARLIER.
THAT BITCH IS LIKE A COCKROACH.
Bi, Bi to Men?
DIFFICULT TO KILL.
HELLO, ALEXANDRA.
AH!
BAT... WOMAN?
DON'T EVEN THINK OF SCREAMING. JUST LISTEN. AND LISTEN GOOD. UNDERSTAND?
GOOD.

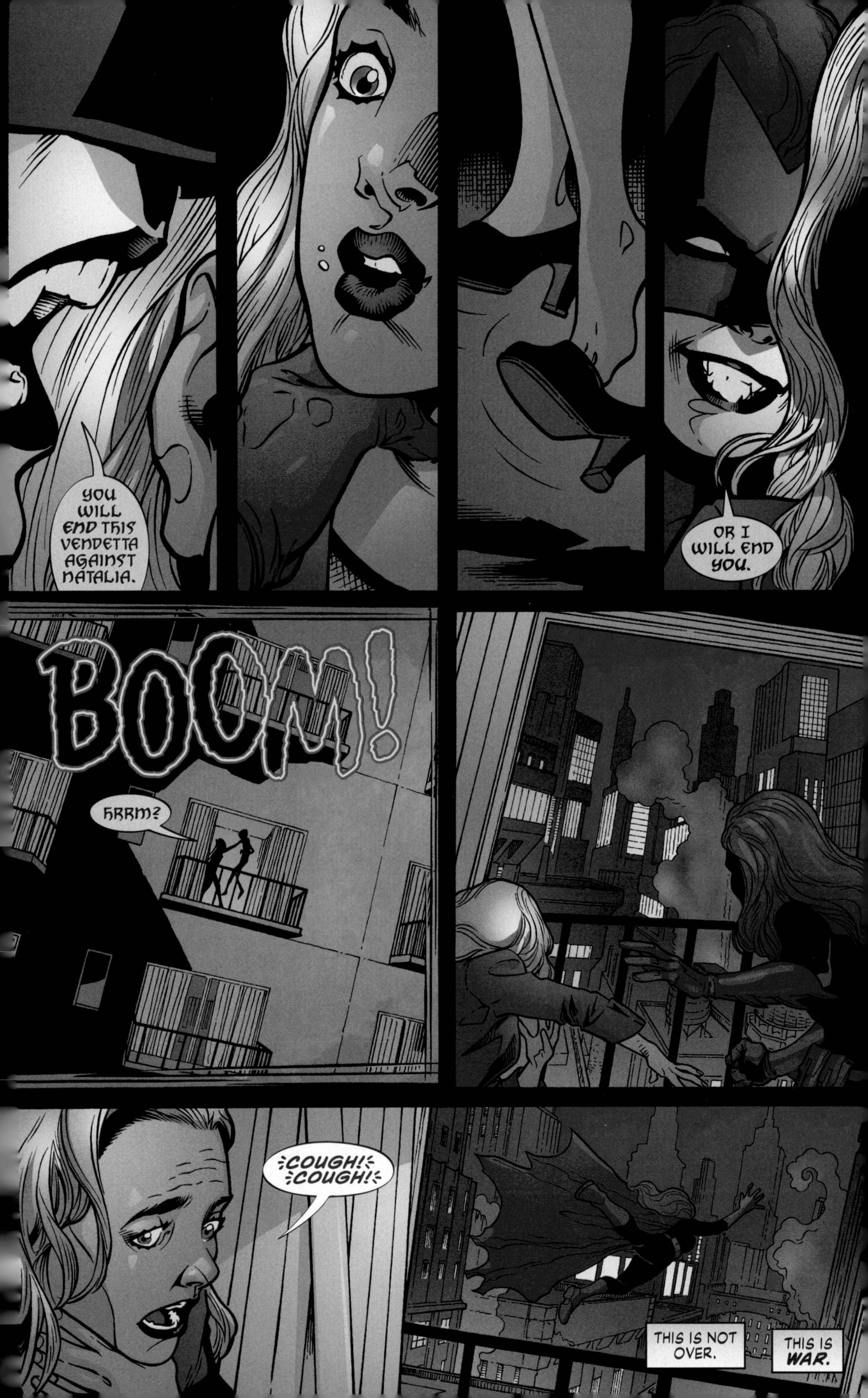
YOU WILL END THIS VENDETTA AGAINST NATALIA.
OR I WILL END YOU.
BOOM!
HRRM?
COUGH! COUGH!
THIS IS NOT OVER.
THIS IS WAR.

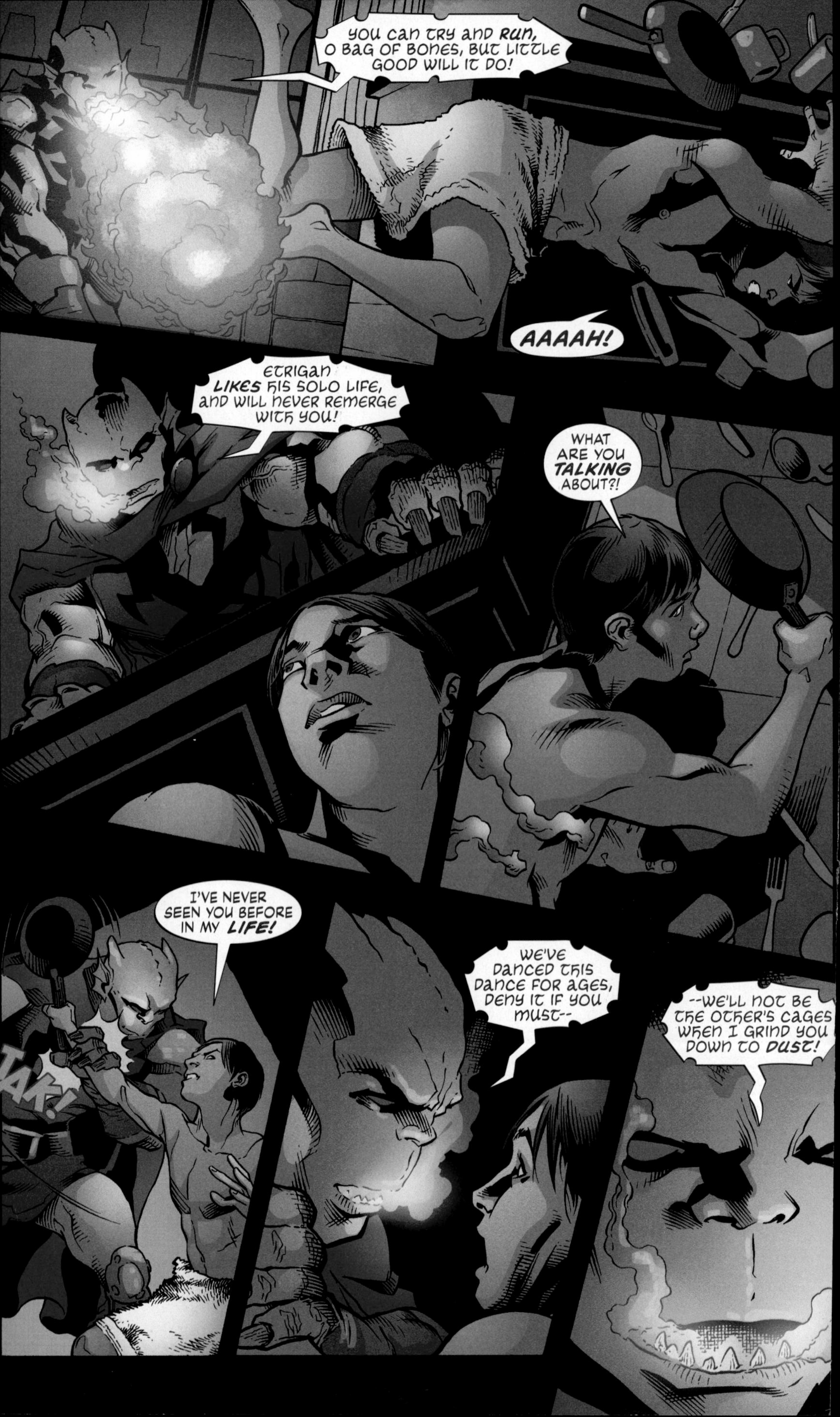
YOU CAN TRY AND RUN, O BAG OF BONES, BUT LITTLE GOOD WILL IT DO!
AAAAH!
ETRIGAN LIKES HIS SOLO LIFE, AND WILL NEVER REMERGE WITH YOU!
WHAT ARE YOU TALKING ABOUT?!
I'VE NEVER SEEN YOU BEFORE IN MY LIFE!
WE'VE DANCED THIS DANCE FOR AGES, DENY IT IF YOU MUST--
--WE'LL NOT BE THE OTHER'S CAGES WHEN I GRIND YOU DOWN TO DUST!

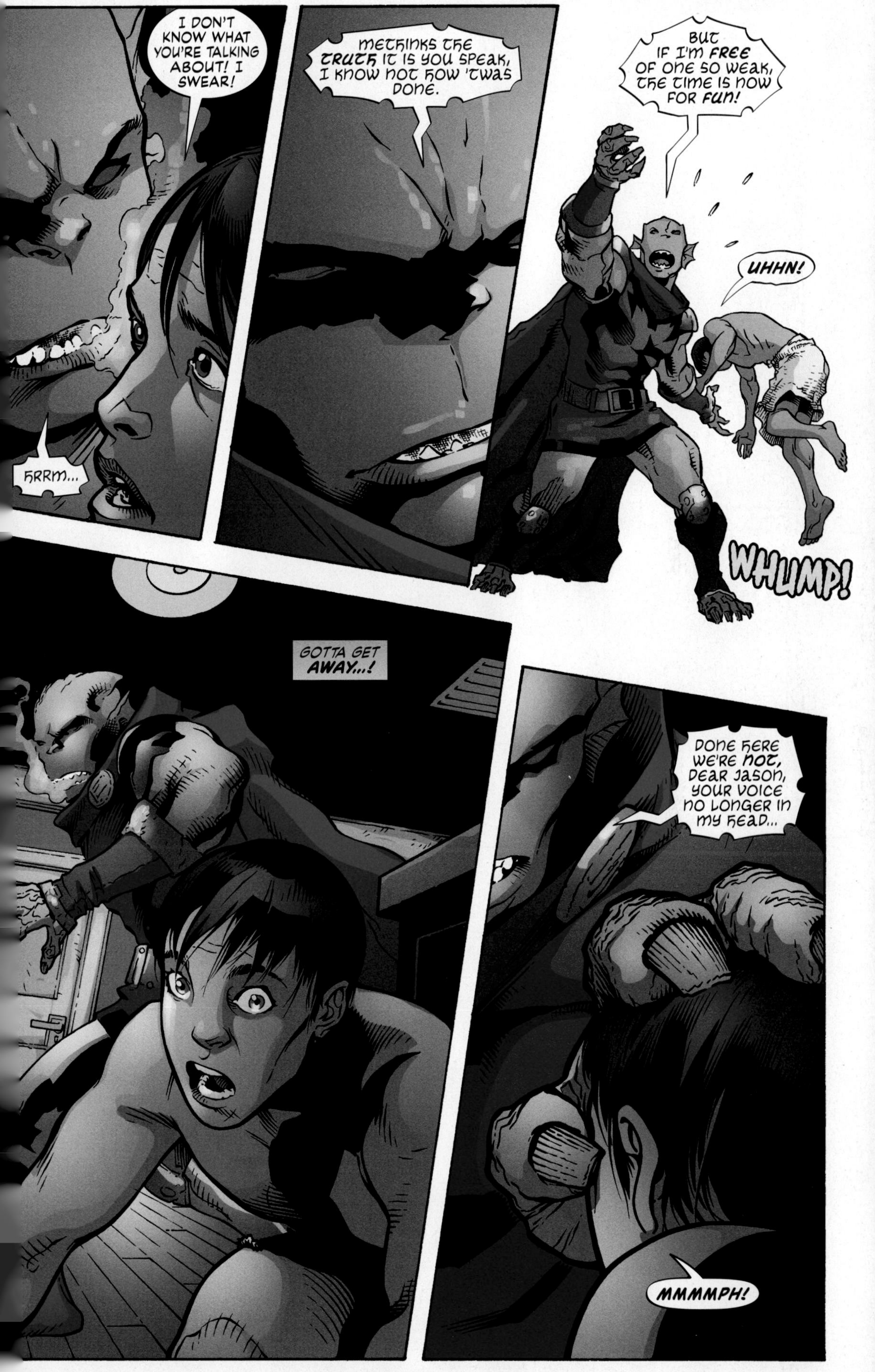
I DON'T KNOW WHAT YOU'RE TALKING ABOUT! I SWEAR!
HRRM...
METHINKS THE TRUTH IT IS YOU SPEAK, I KNOW NOT HOW 'TWAS DONE.
BUT IF I'M FREE OF ONE SO WEAK, THE TIME IS NOW FOR FUN!
UHHN!
WHUMP!
GOTTA GET AWAY...!
DONE HERE WE'RE NOT, DEAR JASON, YOUR VOICE NO LONGER IN MY HEAD...
MMMMPH!

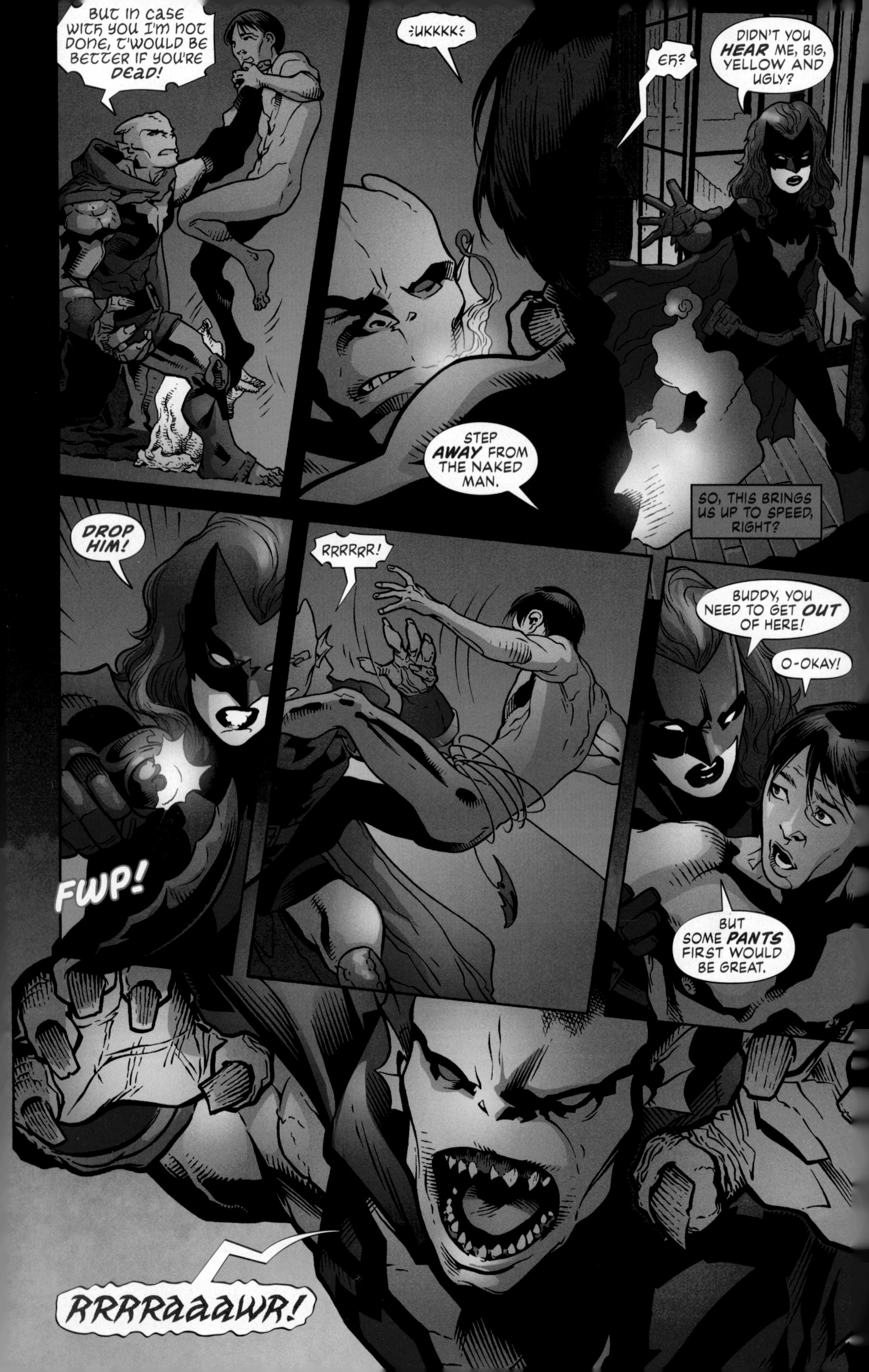
BUT IN CASE WITH YOU I'M NOT DONE, T'WOULD BE BETTER IF YOU'RE DEAD!
UKKKK
EH?
DIDN'T YOU HEAR ME, BIG, YELLOW AND UGLY?
STEP AWAY FROM THE NAKED MAN.
SO, THIS BRINGS US UP TO SPEED, RIGHT?
DROP HIM!
FWP!
RRRRRR!
BUDDY, YOU NEED TO GET OUT OF HERE!
O-OKAY!
BUT SOME PANTS FIRST WOULD BE GREAT.
RRRRAAAAWR!

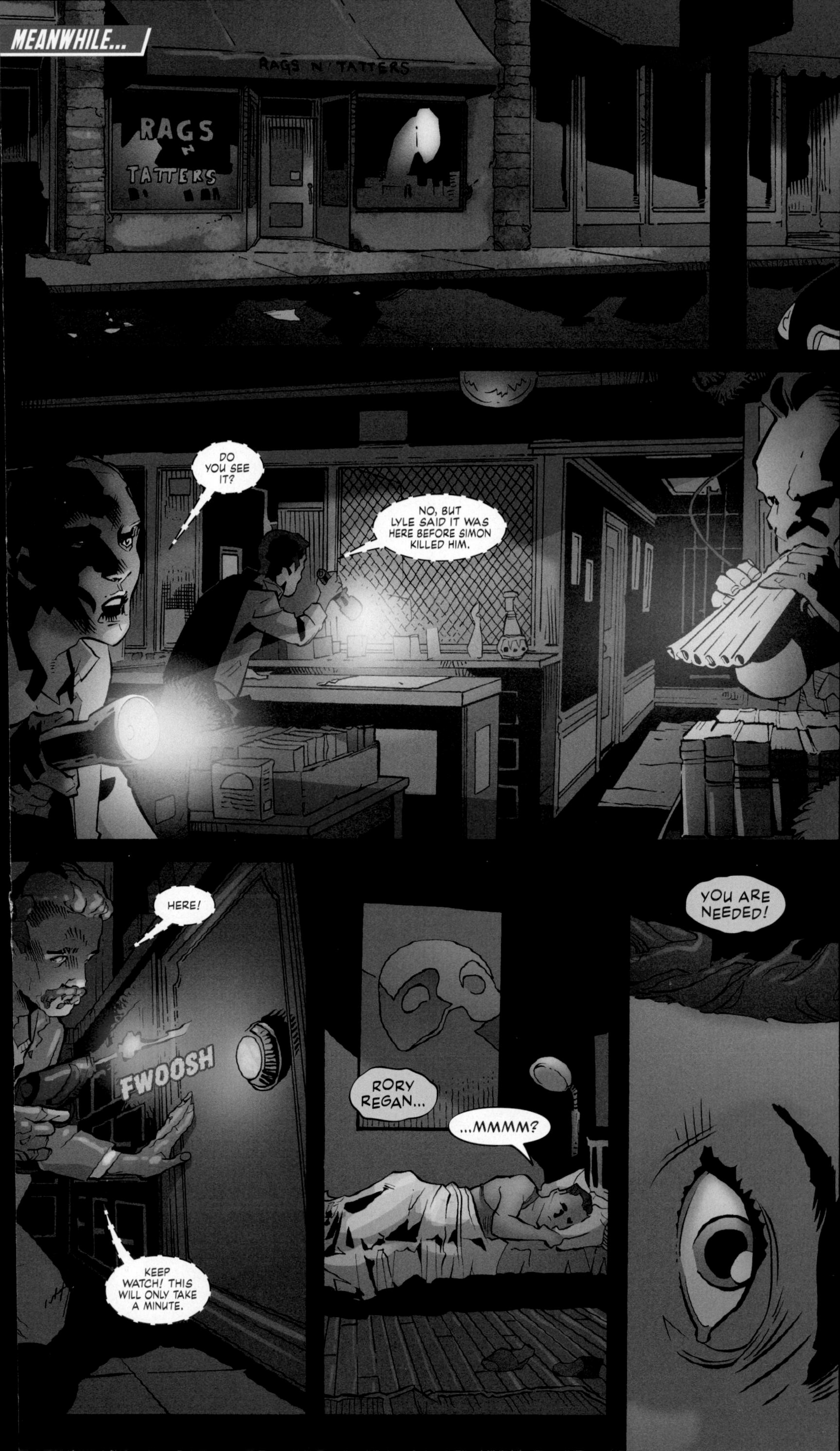
MEANWHILE...
RAGS N' TATTERS
RAGS N TATTERS
DO YOU SEE IT?
NO, BUT LYLE SAID IT WAS HERE BEFORE SIMON KILLED HIM.
HERE!
FWOOSH
KEEP WATCH! THIS WILL ONLY TAKE A MINUTE.
RORY REGAN...
...MMMM?
YOU ARE NEEDED!

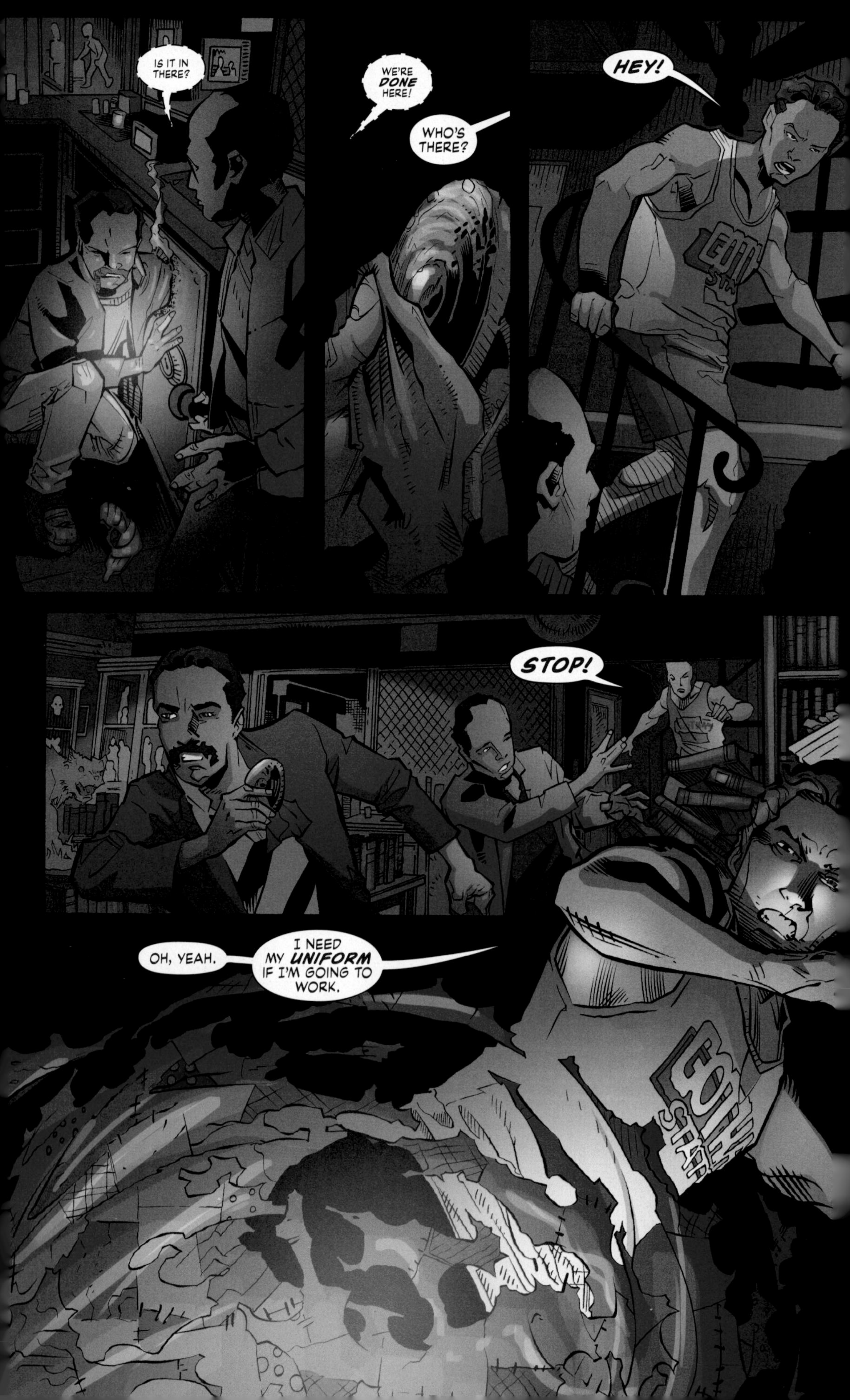
IS IT IN THERE?
WE'RE DONE HERE!
WHO'S THERE?
HEY!
STOP!
OH, YEAH.
I NEED MY UNIFORM IF I'M GOING TO WORK.

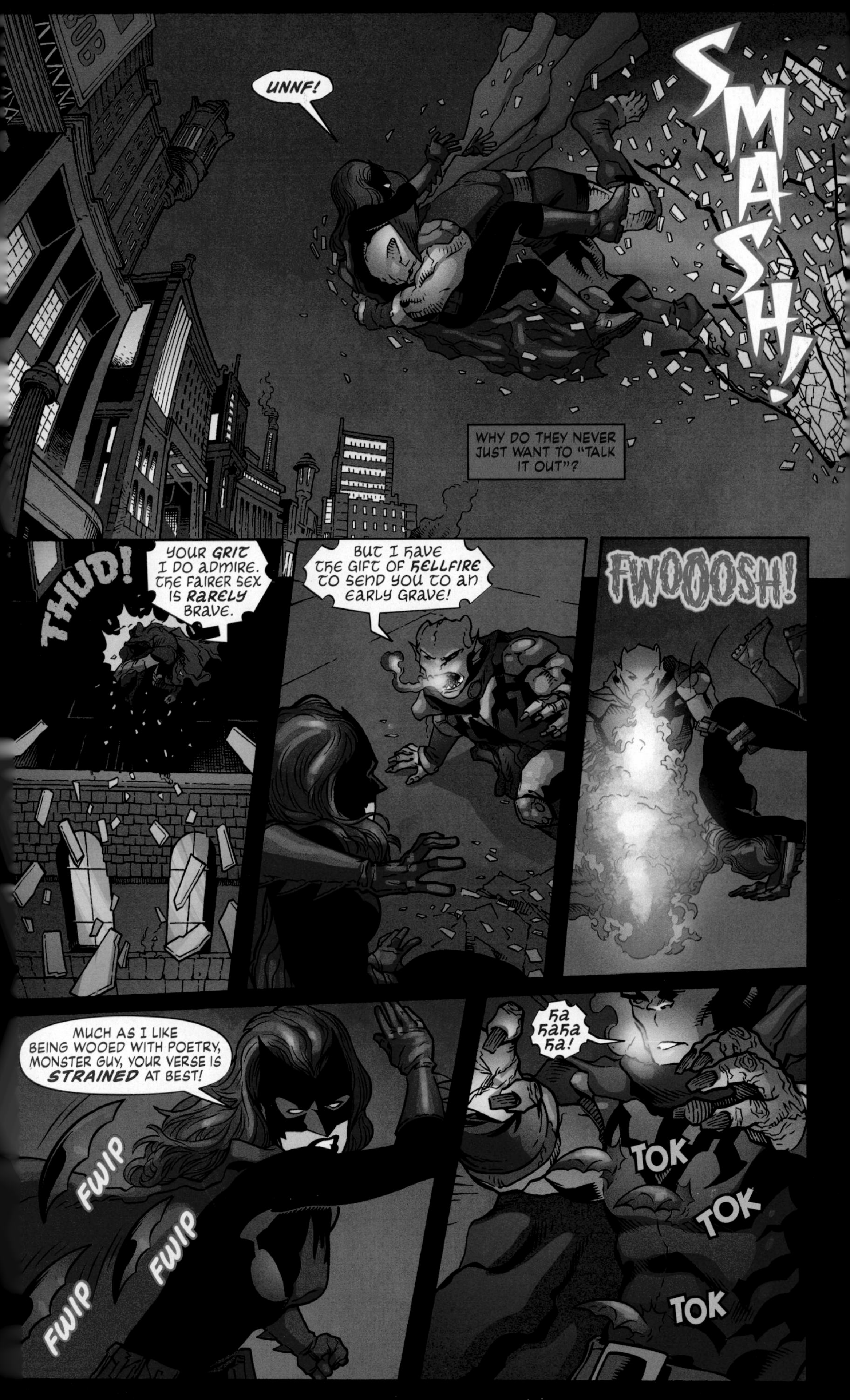

UNNF!
SMASH!
WHY DO THEY NEVER JUST WANT TO "TALK IT OUT"?
THUD!
YOUR GRIT I DO ADMIRE. THE FAIRER SEX IS RARELY BRAVE.
BUT I HAVE THE GIFT OF HELLFIRE TO SEND YOU TO AN EARLY GRAVE!
FWOOOSH!
MUCH AS I LIKE BEING WOOED WITH POETRY, MONSTER GUY, YOUR VERSE IS STRAINED AT BEST!
FWIP
FWIP
FWIP
HA HAHA HA!
TOK
TOK
TOK

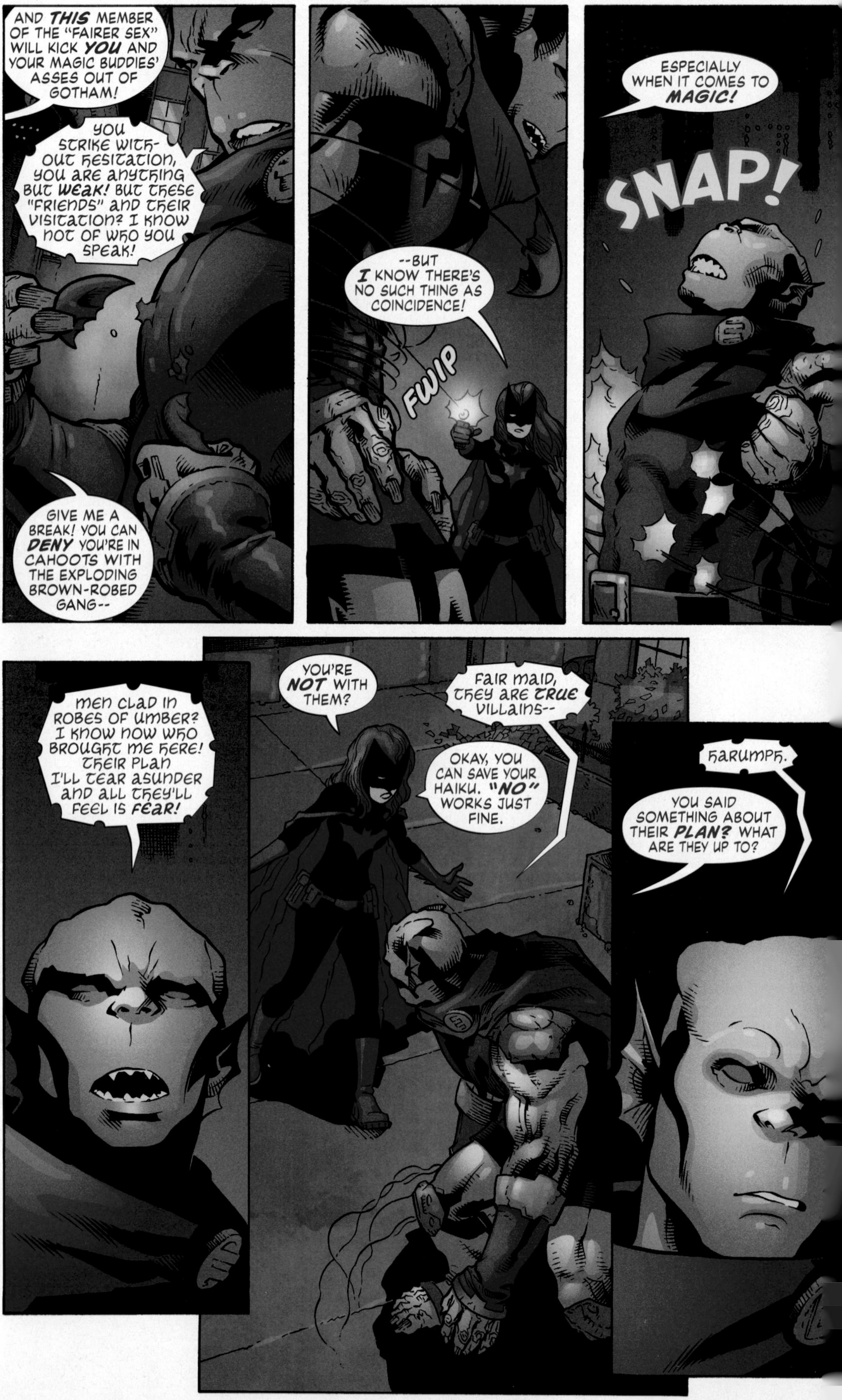
AND THIS MEMBER OF THE "FAIRER SEX" WILL KICK YOU AND YOUR MAGIC BUDDIES' ASSES OUT OF GOTHAM!
YOU STRIKE WITH-OUT HESITATION, YOU ARE ANYTHING BUT WEAK! BUT THESE "FRIENDS" AND THEIR VISITATION? I KNOW NOT OF WHO YOU SPEAK!
GIVE ME A BREAK! YOU CAN DENY YOU'RE IN CAHOOTS WITH THE EXPLODING BROWN-ROBED GANG--
--BUT I KNOW THERE'S NO SUCH THING AS COINCIDENCE!
FWIP
ESPECIALLY WHEN IT COMES TO MAGIC!
SNAP!
MEN CLAD IN ROBES OF UMBER? I KNOW NOW WHO BROUGHT ME HERE! THEIR PLAN I'LL TEAR ASUNDER AND ALL THEY'LL FEEL IS FEAR!
YOU'RE NOT WITH THEM?
FAIR MAID, THEY ARE TRUE VILLAINS--
OKAY, YOU CAN SAVE YOUR HAIKU. "NO" WORKS JUST FINE.
HARUMPH.
YOU SAID SOMETHING ABOUT THEIR PLAN? WHAT ARE THEY UP TO?

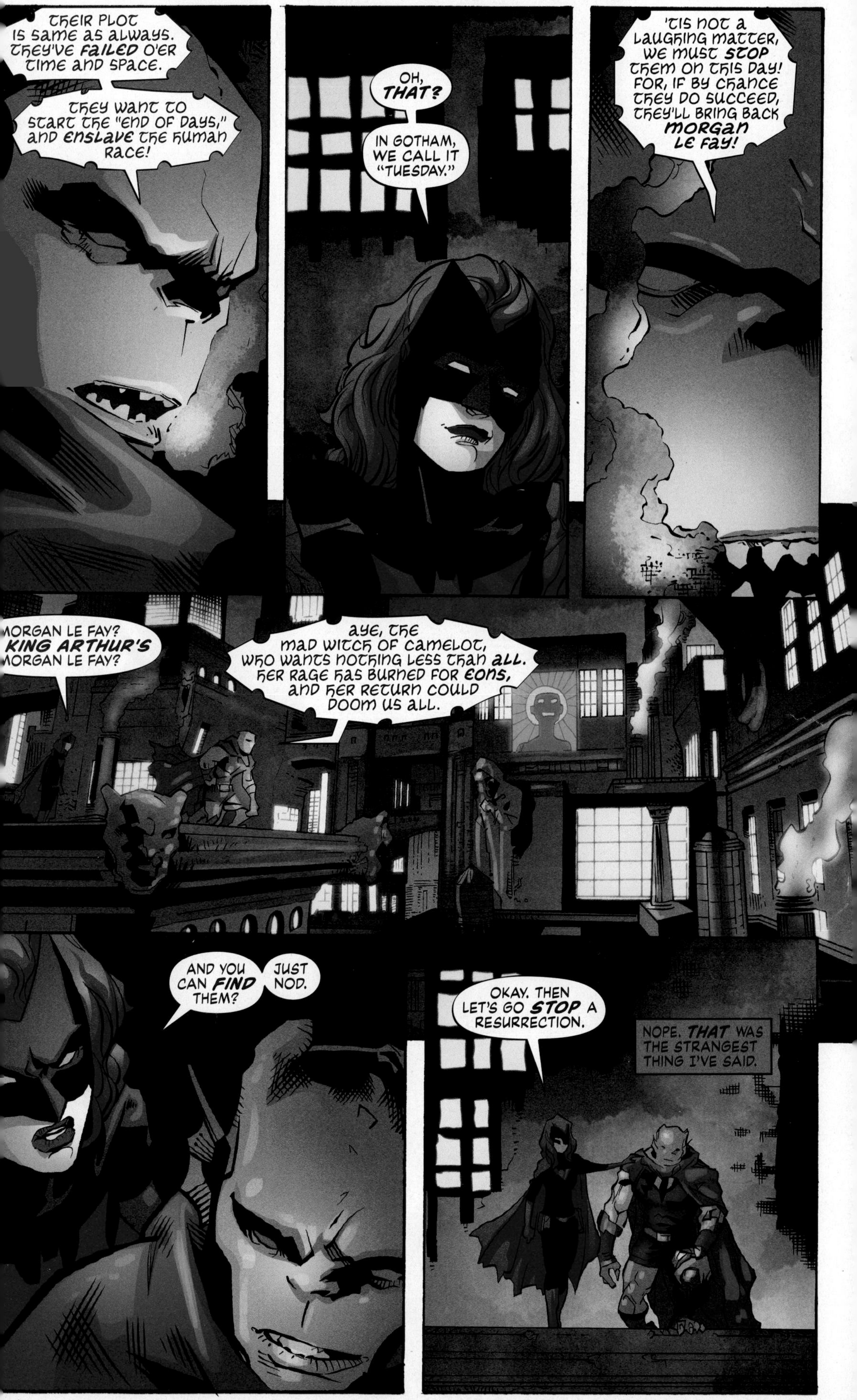
THEIR PLOT IS SAME AS ALWAYS. THEY'VE FAILED O'ER TIME AND SPACE.
THEY WANT TO START THE "END OF DAYS," AND ENSLAVE THE HUMAN RACE!
OH, THAT?
IN GOTHAM, WE CALL IT "TUESDAY."
'TIS NOT A LAUGHING MATTER, WE MUST STOP THEM ON THIS DAY! FOR, IF BY CHANCE THEY DO SUCCEED, THEY'LL BRING BACK MORGAN LE FAY!
MORGAN LE FAY? KING ARTHUR'S MORGAN LE FAY?
AYE, THE MAD WITCH OF CAMELOT, WHO WANTS NOTHING LESS THAN ALL. HER RAGE HAS BURNED FOR EONS, AND HER RETURN COULD DOOM US ALL.
AND YOU CAN FIND THEM?
JUST NOD.
OKAY. THEN LET'S GO STOP A RESURRECTION.
NOPE. THAT WAS THE STRANGEST THING I'VE SAID.

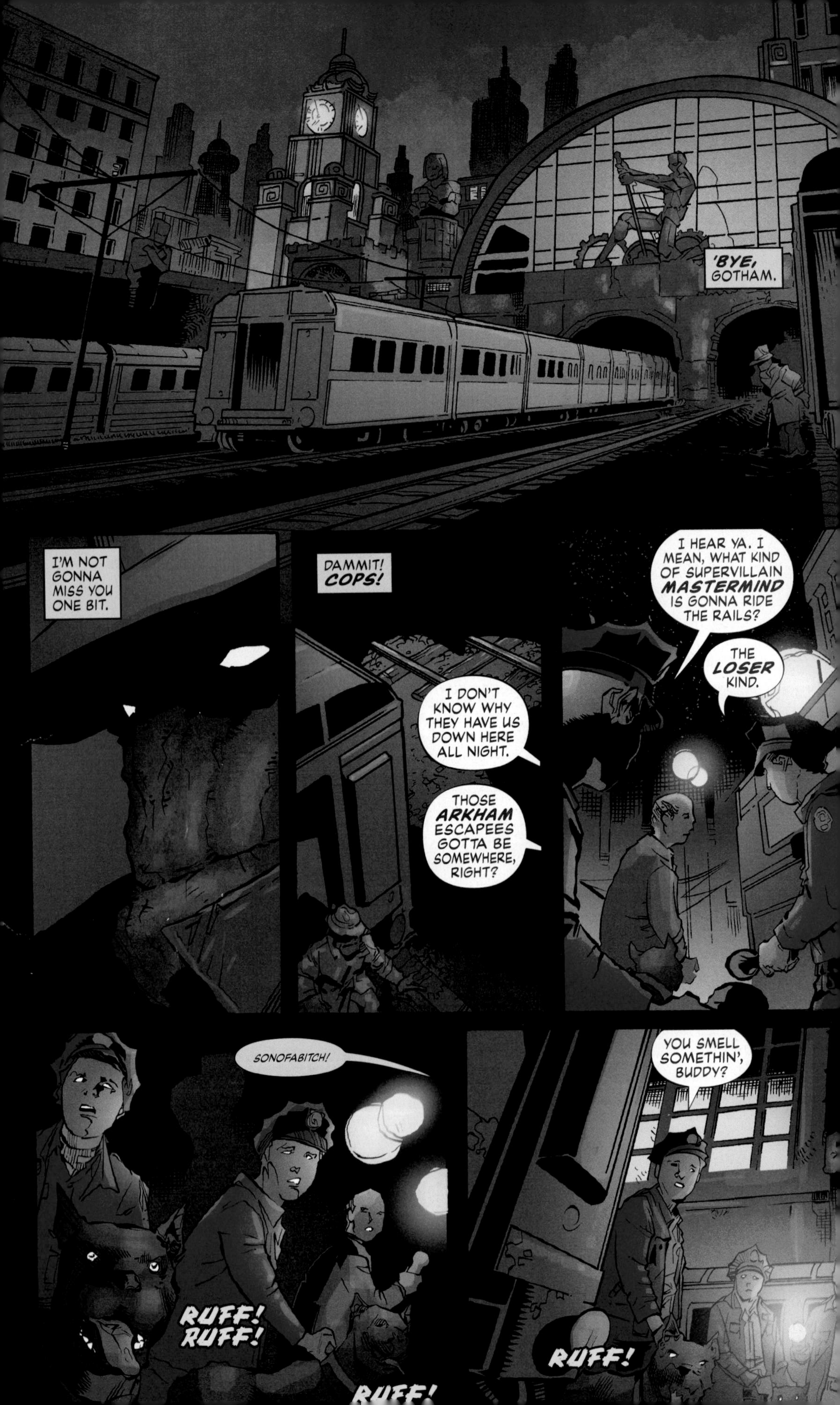
'BYE, GOTHAM.
I'M NOT GONNA MISS YOU ONE BIT.
DAMMIT! COPS!
I DON'T KNOW WHY THEY HAVE US DOWN HERE ALL NIGHT.
THOSE ARKHAM ESCAPEES GOTTA BE SOMEWHERE, RIGHT?
I HEAR YA. I MEAN, WHAT KIND OF SUPERVILLAIN MASTERMIND IS GONNA RIDE THE RAILS?
THE LOSER KIND.
SONOFABITCH!
RUFF! RUFF!
RUFF!
YOU SMELL SOMETHIN', BUDDY?
RUFF!

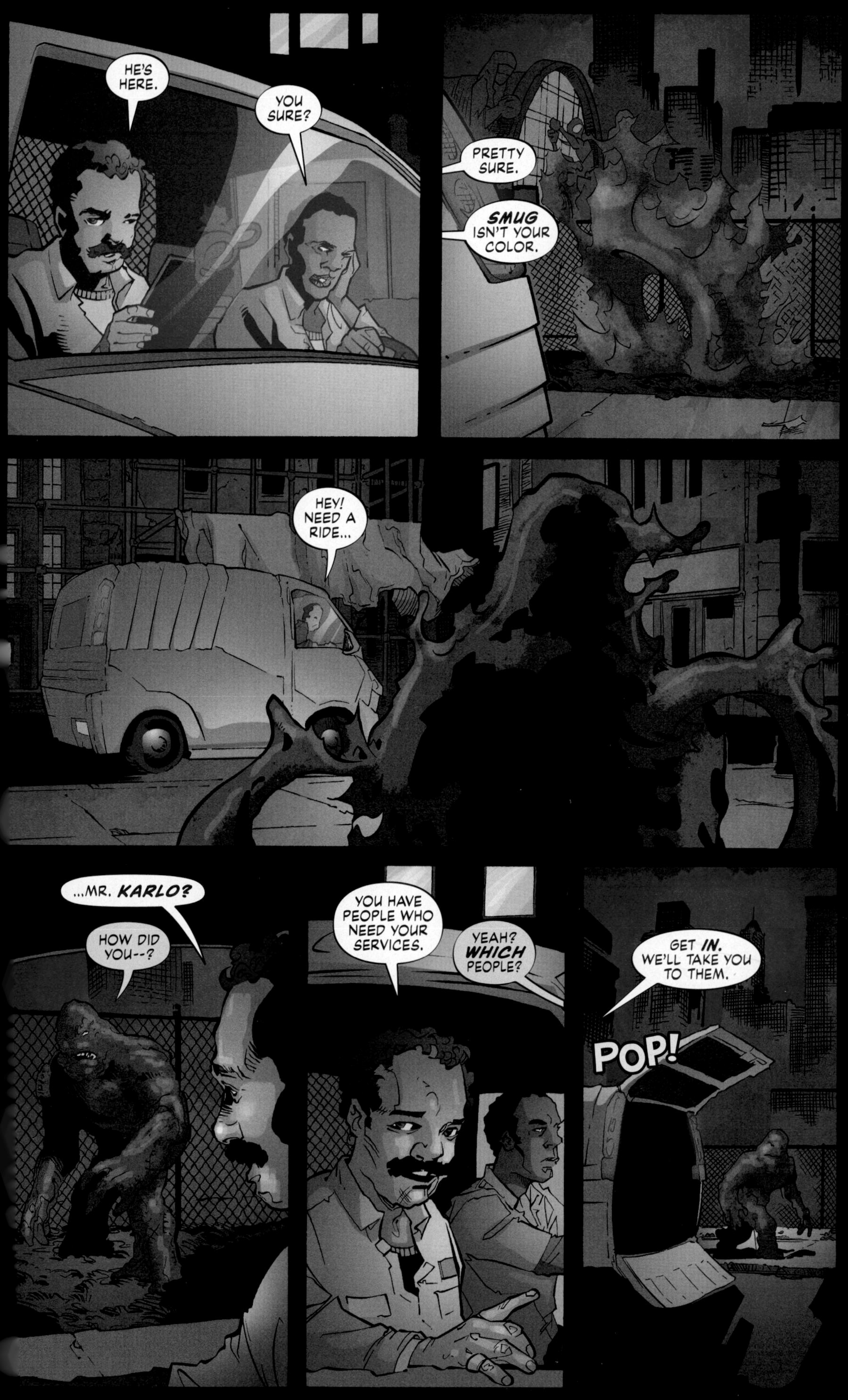
HE'S HERE.
YOU SURE?
PRETTY SURE.
SMUG ISN'T YOUR COLOR.
HEY! NEED A RIDE...
...MR. KARLO?
HOW DID YOU--?
YOU HAVE PEOPLE WHO NEED YOUR SERVICES.
YEAH? WHICH PEOPLE?
GET IN. WE'LL TAKE YOU TO THEM.
POP!

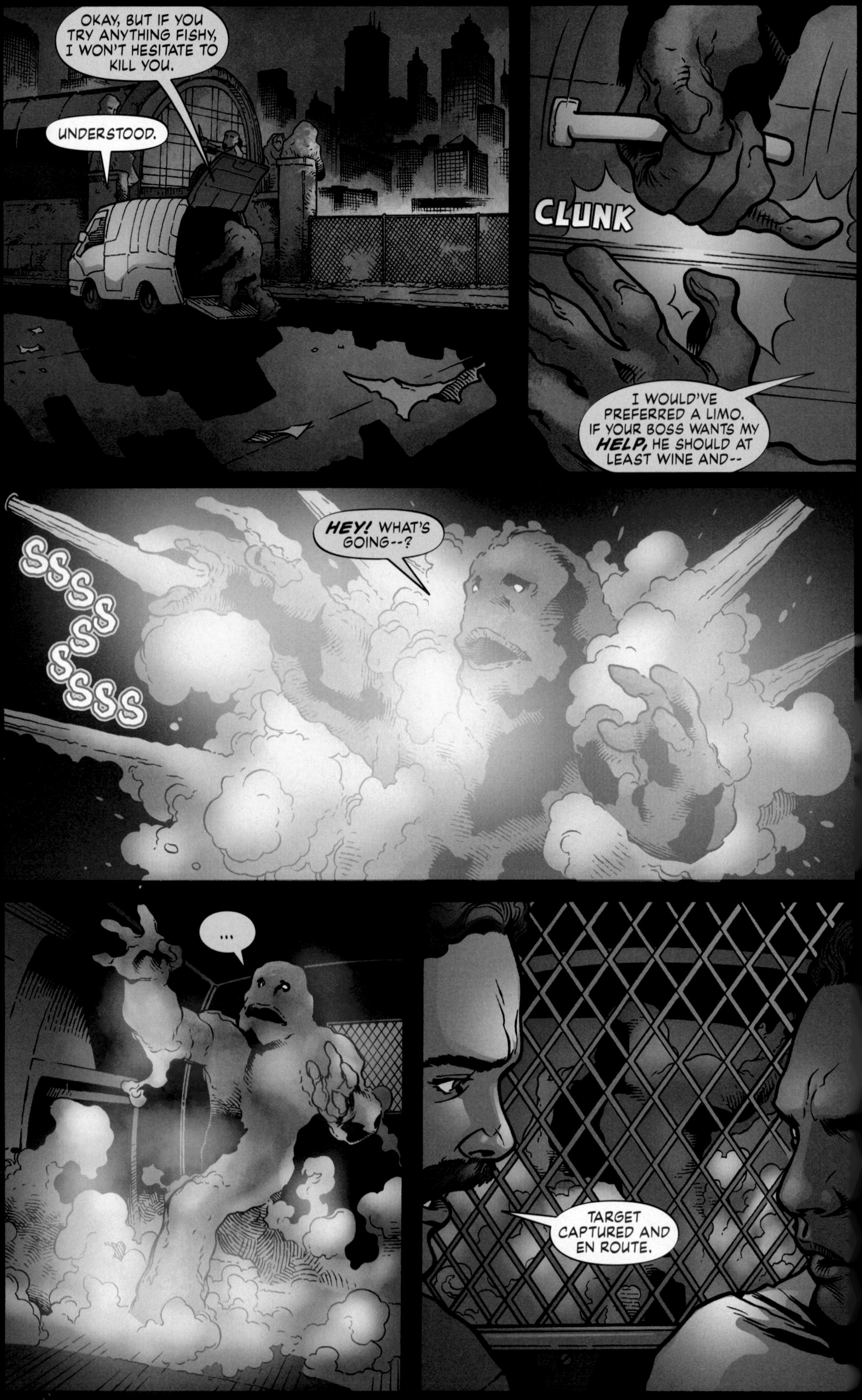
OKAY, BUT IF YOU TRY ANYTHING FISHY, I WON'T HESITATE TO KILL YOU.
UNDERSTOOD.
CLUNK
I WOULD'VE PREFERRED A LIMO. IF YOUR BOSS WANTS MY *HELP,* HE SHOULD AT LEAST WINE AND--
SSSSSSSSSSS
HEY! WHAT'S GOING--?
...
TARGET CAPTURED AND EN ROUTE.

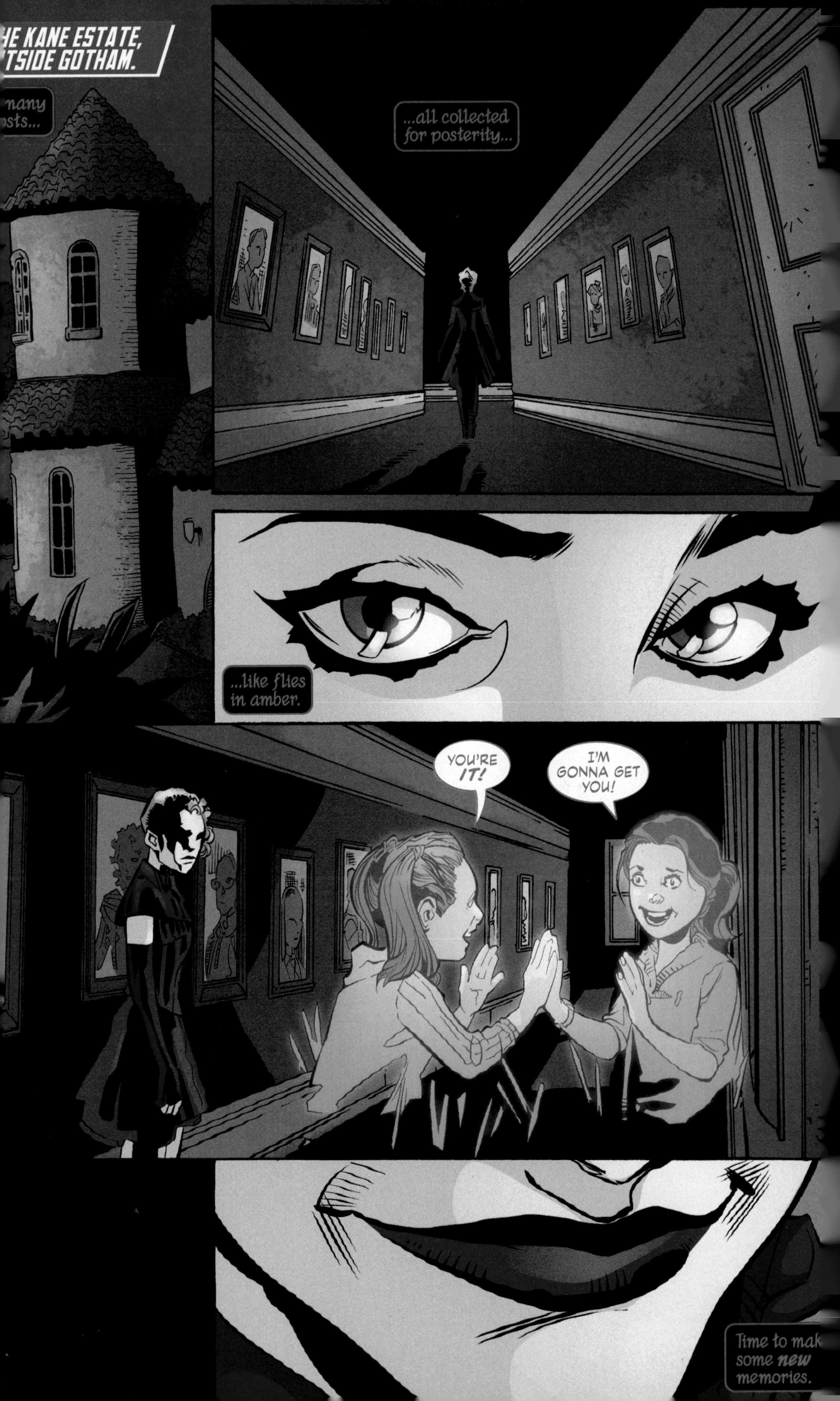
HE KANE ESTATE,
TSIDE GOTHAM.
many
sts...
...all collected
for posterity...
...like flies
in amber.
YOU'RE
IT!
I'M
GONNA GET
YOU!
Time to mak
some new
memories.

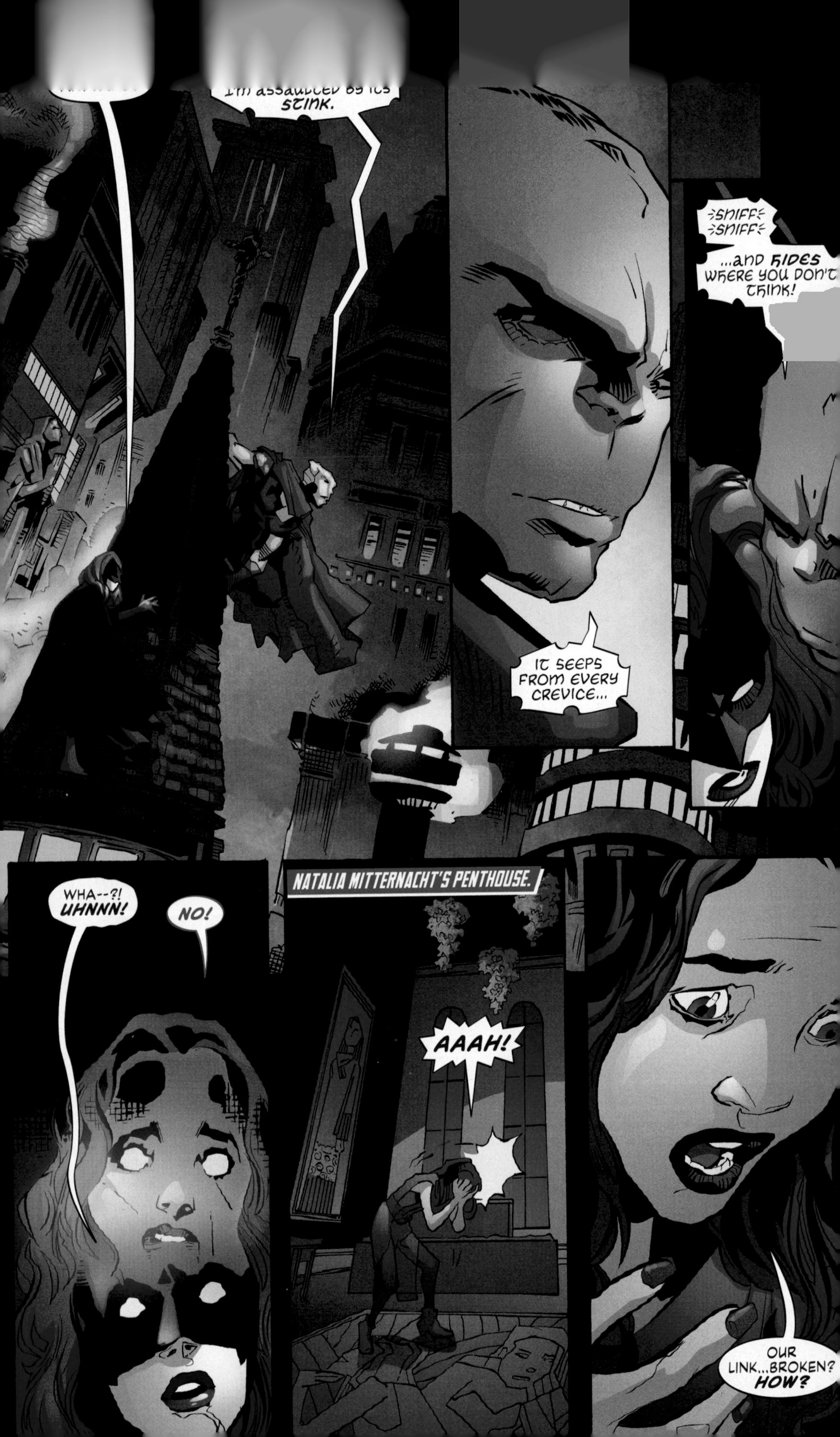
I'm assaulted by its STINK.
IT SEEPS FROM EVERY CREVICE...
SNIFF SNIFF
...and HIDES WHERE YOU DON'T THINK!
WHA--?! UHNNN!
NO!
NATALIA MITTERNACHT'S PENTHOUSE.
AAAH!
OUR LINK...BROKEN? HOW?

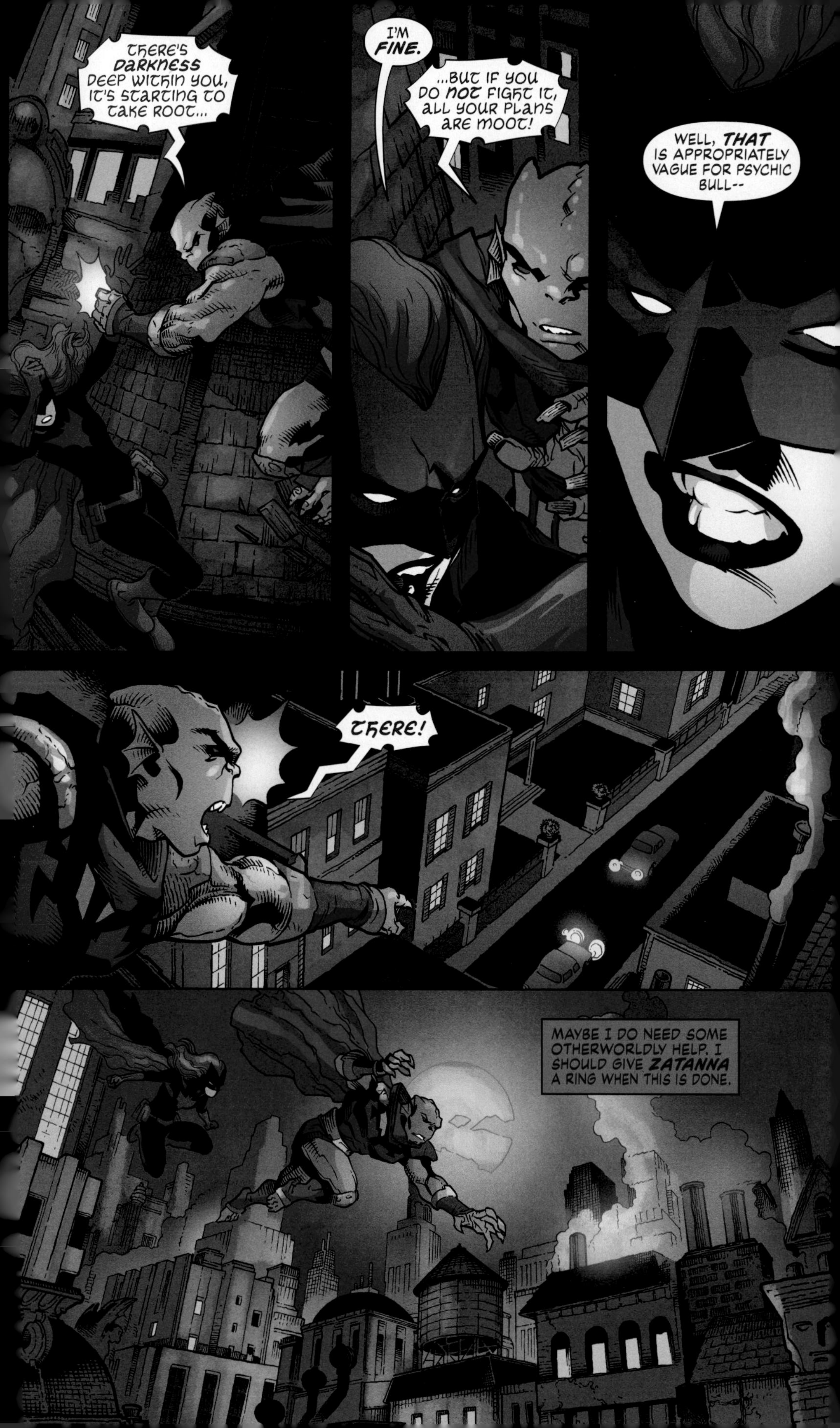
THERE'S DARKNESS DEEP WITHIN YOU, IT'S STARTING TO TAKE ROOT...
I'M FINE.
...BUT IF YOU DO NOT FIGHT IT, ALL YOUR PLANS ARE MOOT!
WELL, THAT IS APPROPRIATELY VAGUE FOR PSYCHIC BULL--
THERE!
MAYBE I DO NEED SOME OTHERWORLDLY HELP. I SHOULD GIVE ZATANNA A RING WHEN THIS IS DONE.

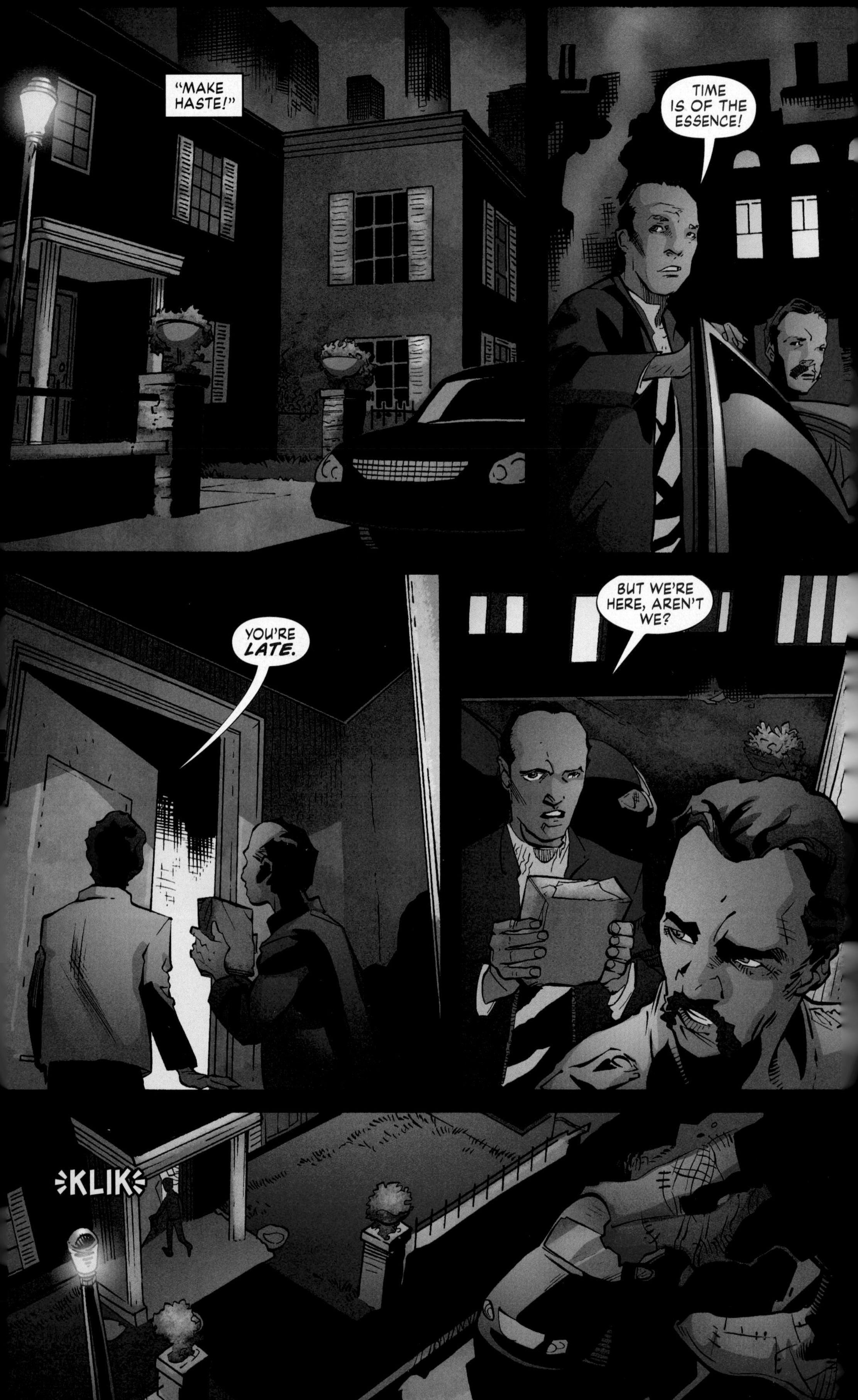
"MAKE HASTE!"
TIME IS OF THE ESSENCE!
YOU'RE *LATE.*
BUT WE'RE HERE, AREN'T WE?
KLIK

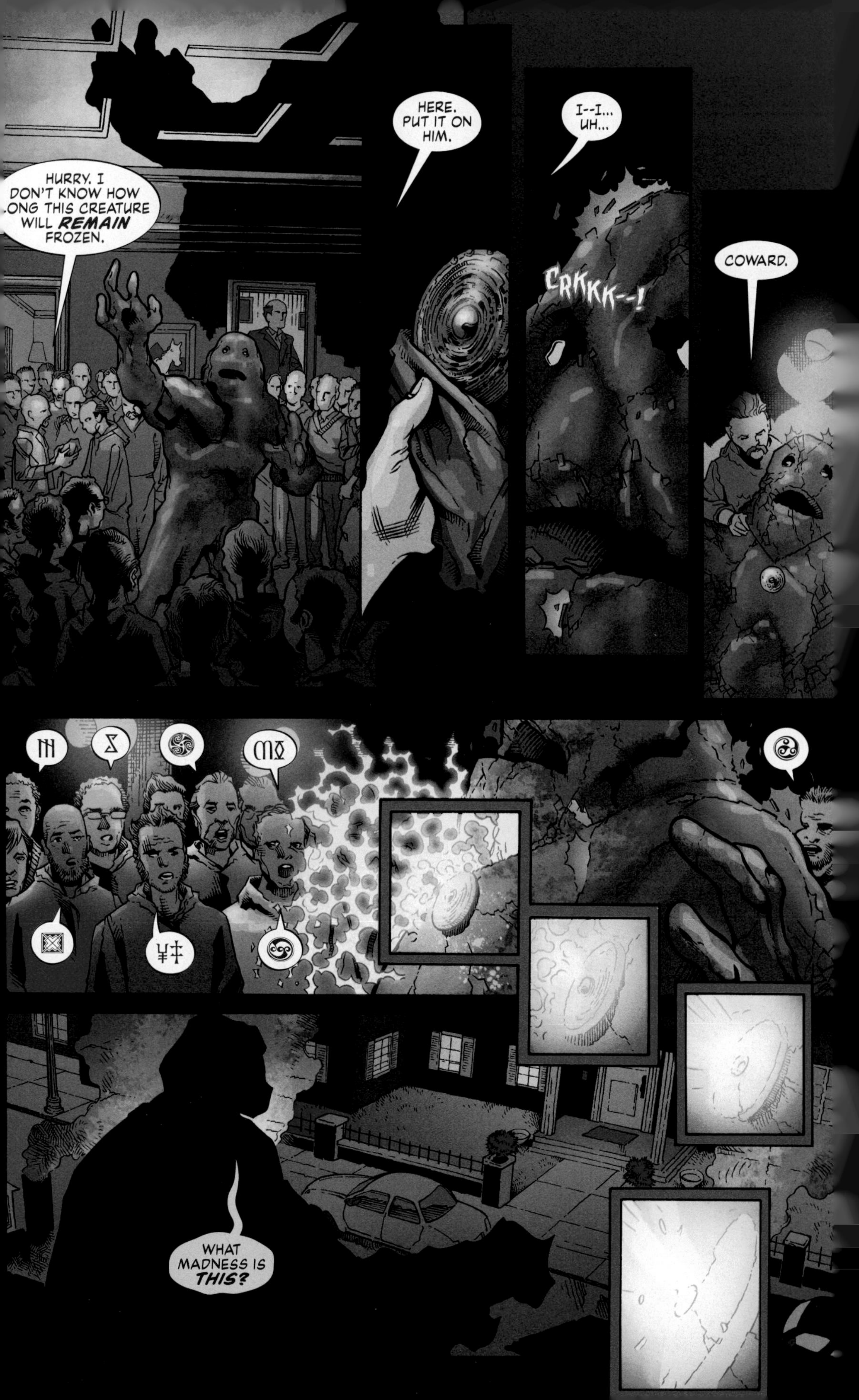
HURRY. I DON'T KNOW HOW .ONG THIS CREATURE WILL **REMAIN** FROZEN.
HERE. PUT IT ON HIM.
I--I... UH...
CRKKK--!
COWARD.
WHAT MADNESS IS **THIS?**

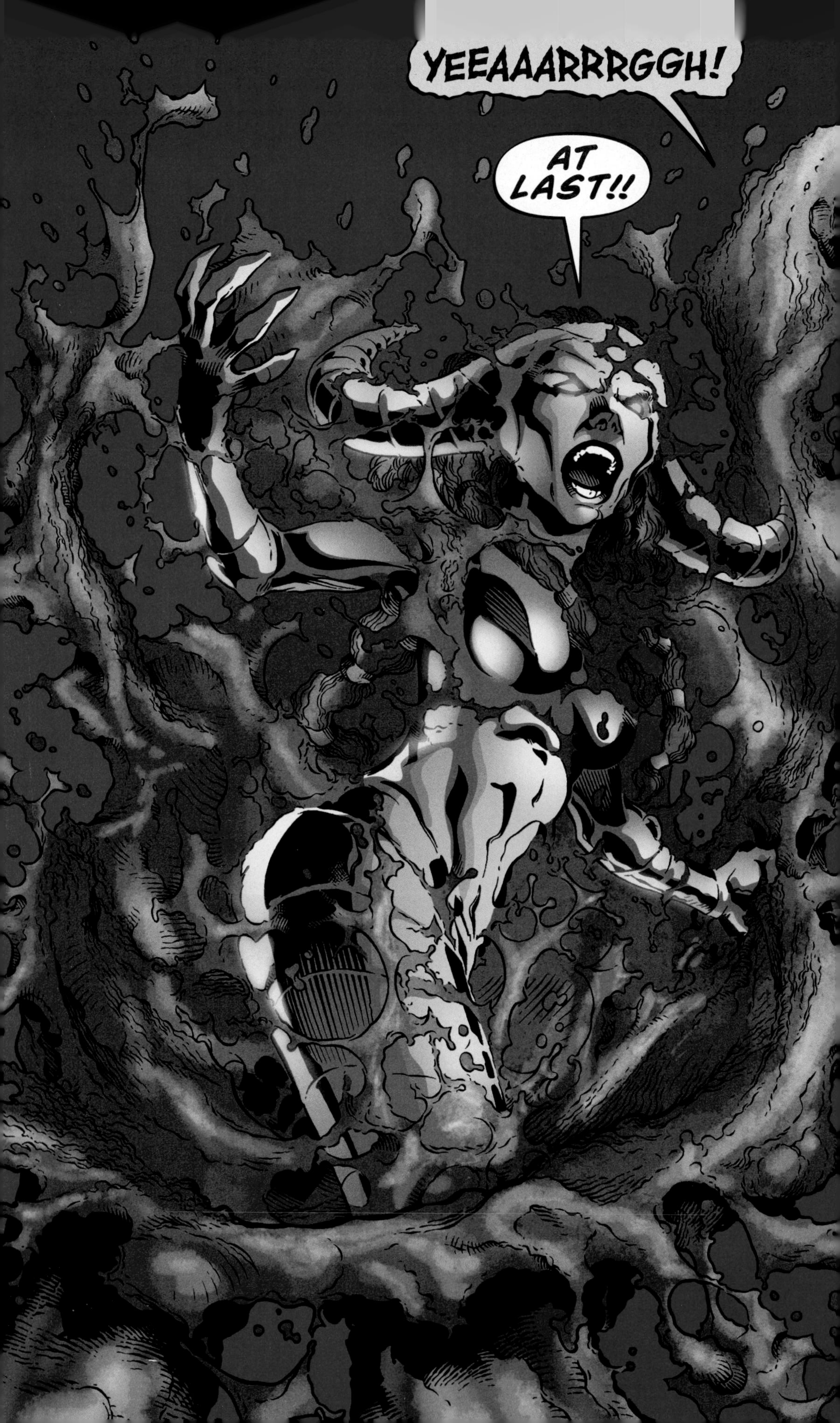
YEEAAARRRGGH!
AT LAST!!

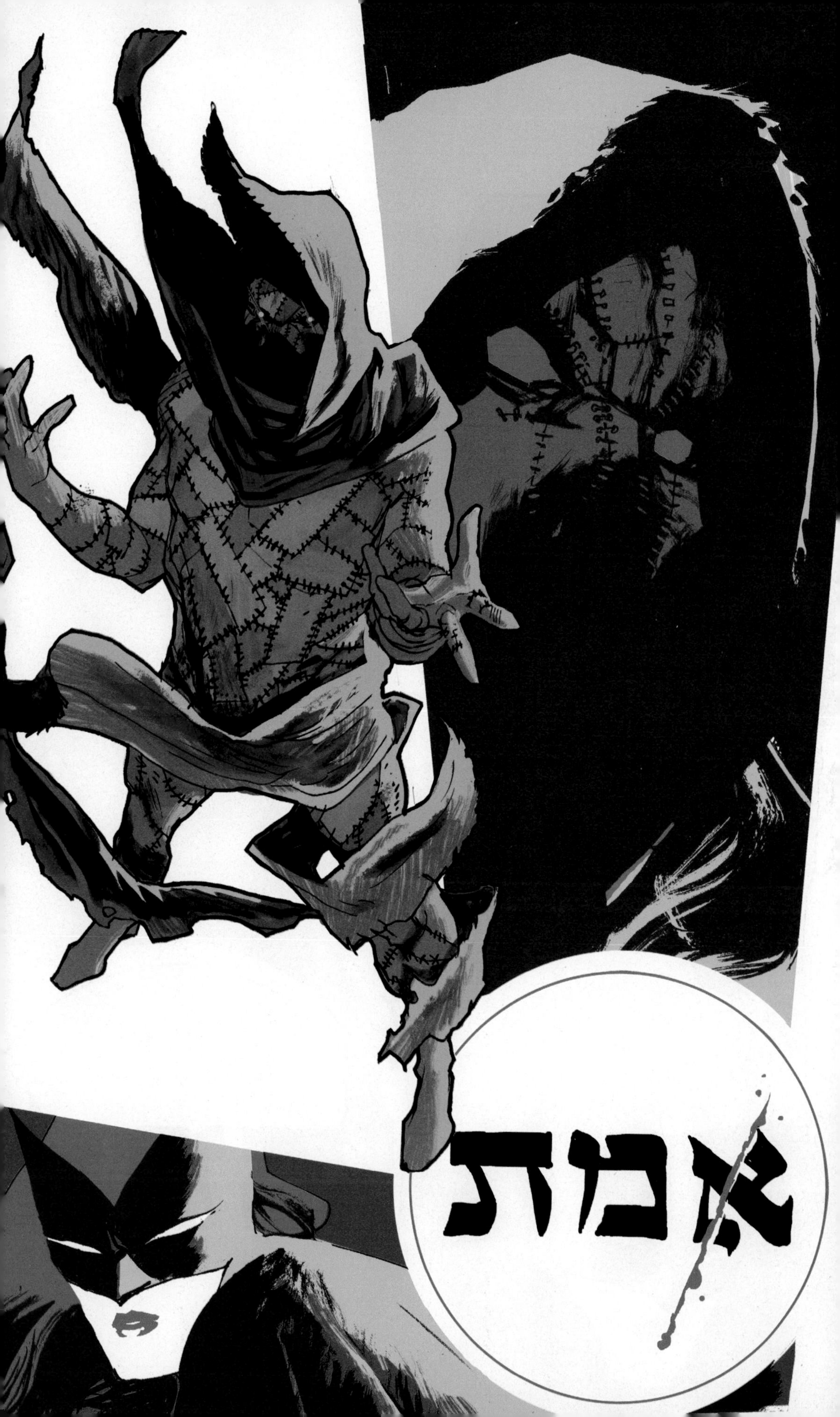

אמת

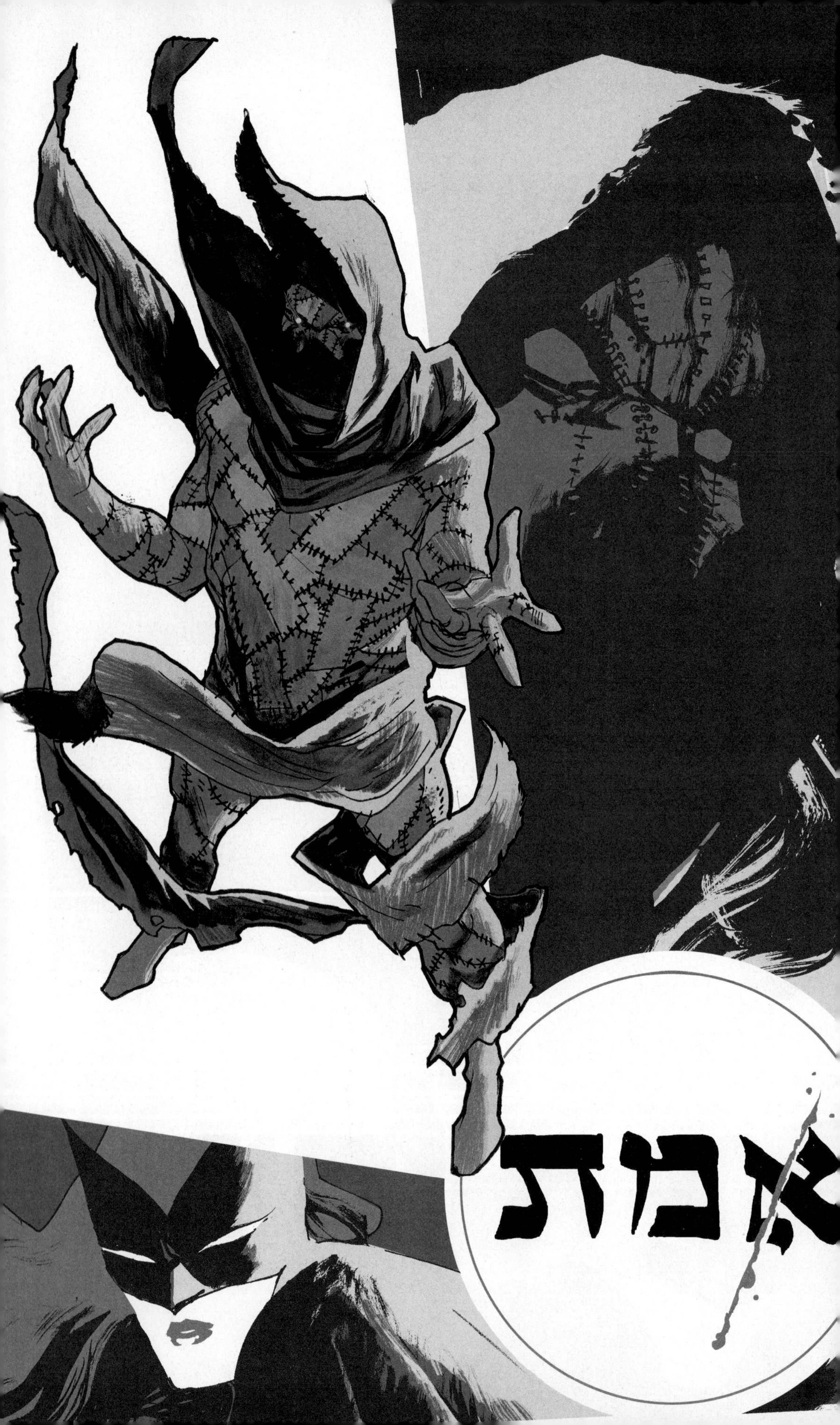
אמת

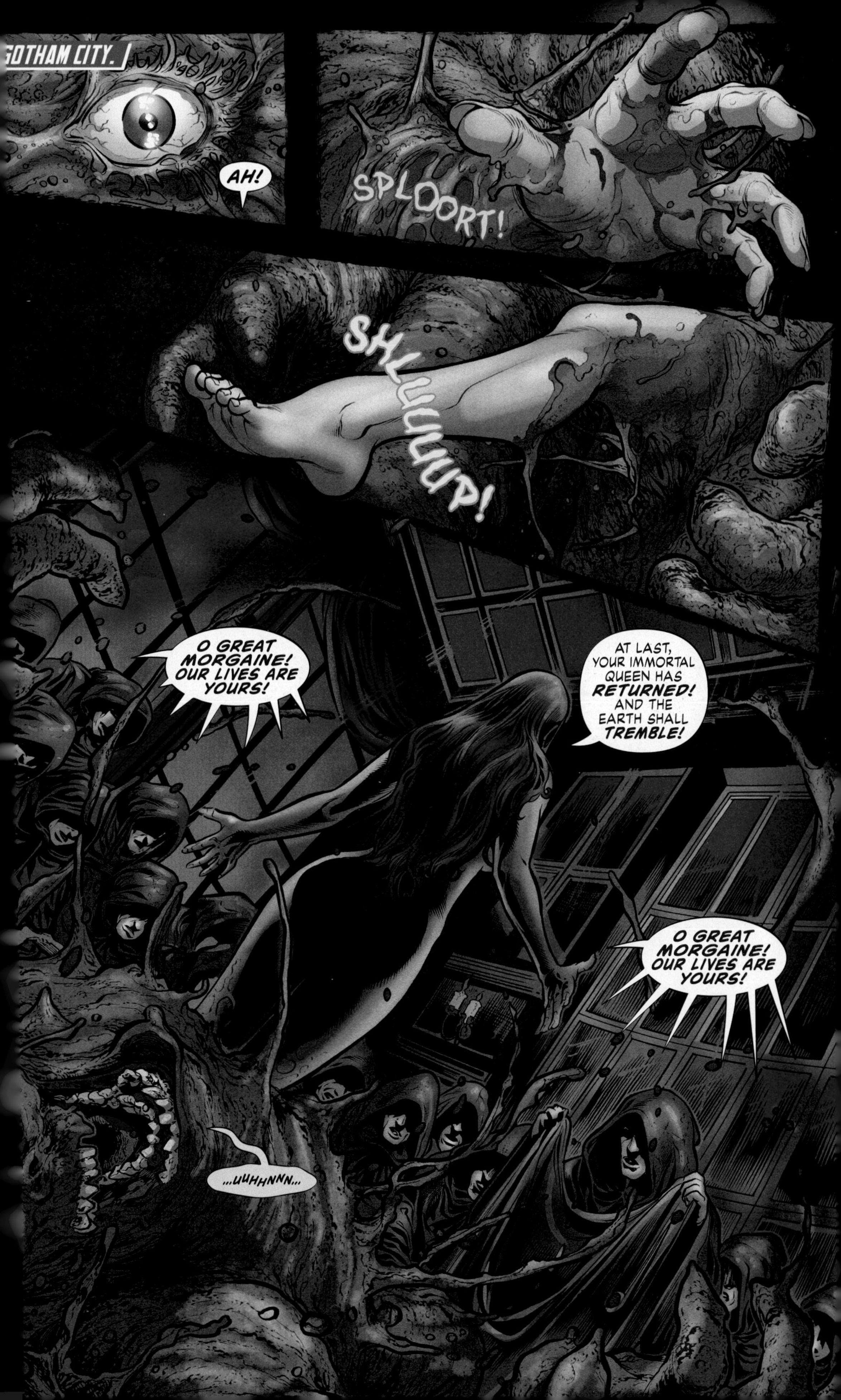

GOTHAM CITY.
AH!
SPLOORT!
SHLUUUP!
O GREAT MORGAINE! OUR LIVES ARE YOURS!
AT LAST, YOUR IMMORTAL QUEEN HAS RETURNED! AND THE EARTH SHALL TREMBLE!
O GREAT MORGAINE! OUR LIVES ARE YOURS!
...UUHHNNN...

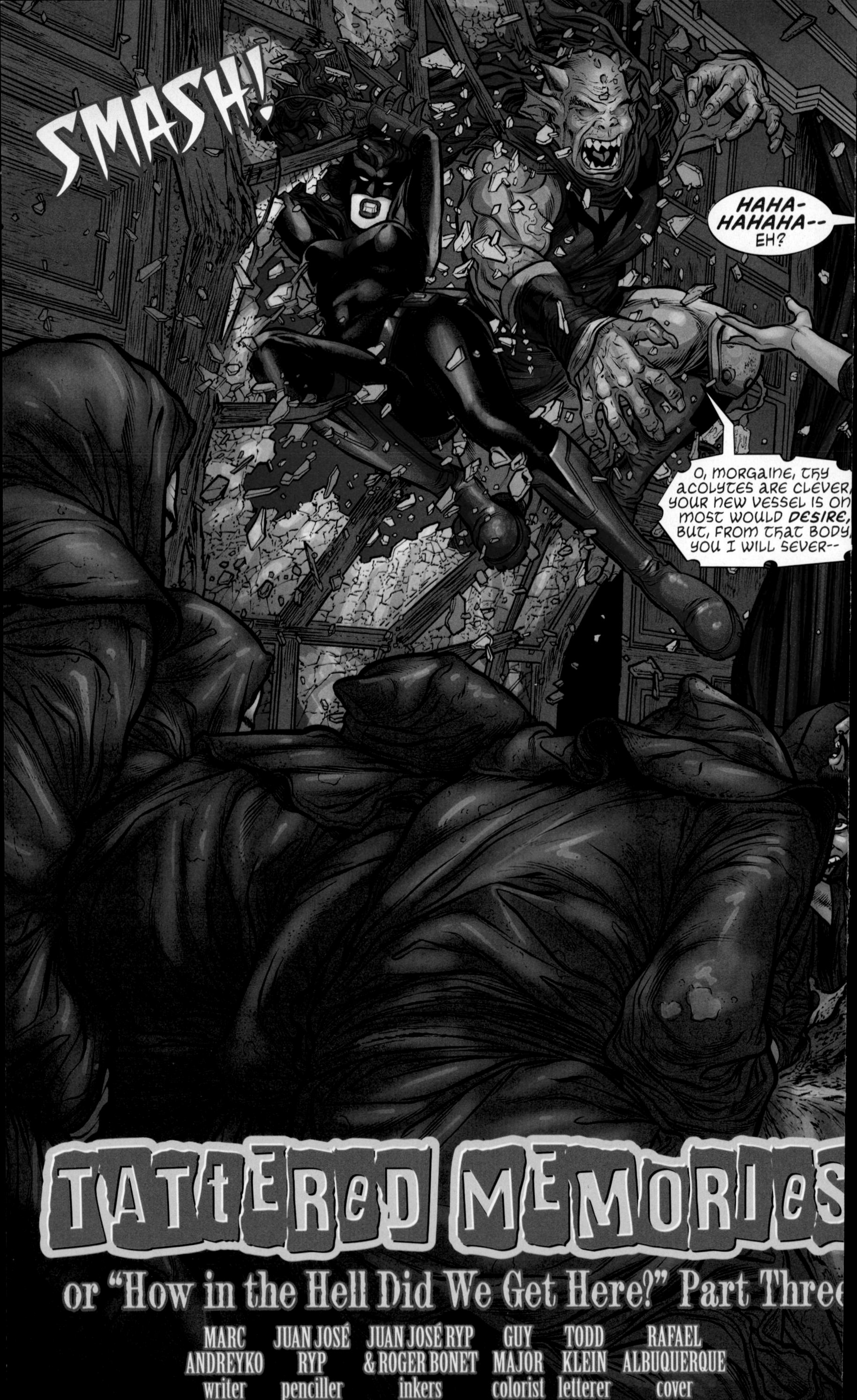
SMASH!
HAHA-HAHAHA--EH?
O, MORGAINE, THY ACOLYTES ARE CLEVER, YOUR NEW VESSEL IS ON MOST WOULD DESIRE, BUT, FROM THAT BODY, YOU I WILL SEVER--
TATTERED MEMORIES
or "How in the Hell Did We Get Here?" Part Three
MARC ANDREYKO writer
JUAN JOSÉ RYP penciller
JUAN JOSÉ RYP & ROGER BONET inkers
GUY MAJOR colorist
TODD KLEIN letterer
RAFAEL ALBUQUERQUE cover

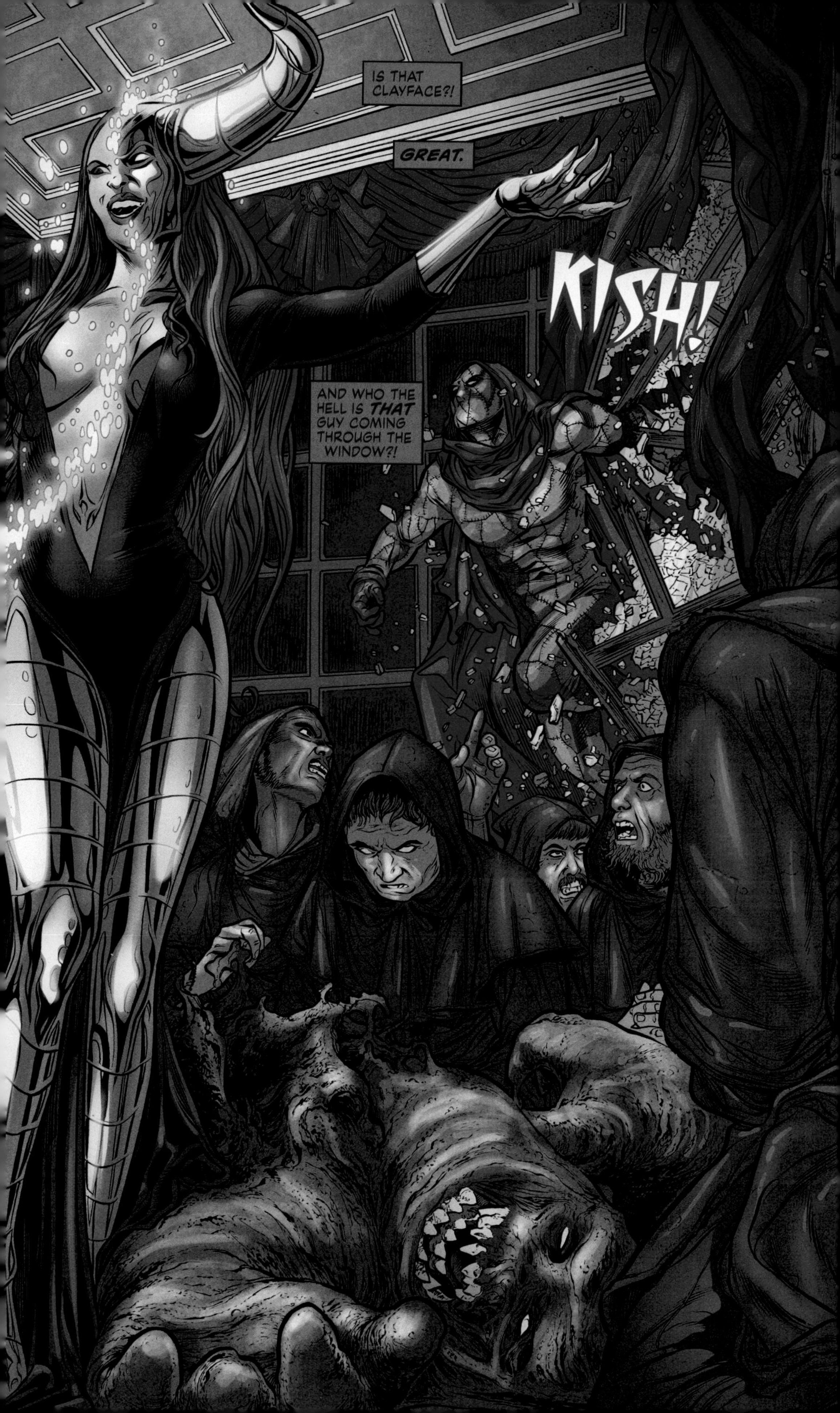
IS THAT CLAYFACE?!
GREAT.
KISH!
AND WHO THE HELL IS THAT GUY COMING THROUGH THE WINDOW?!

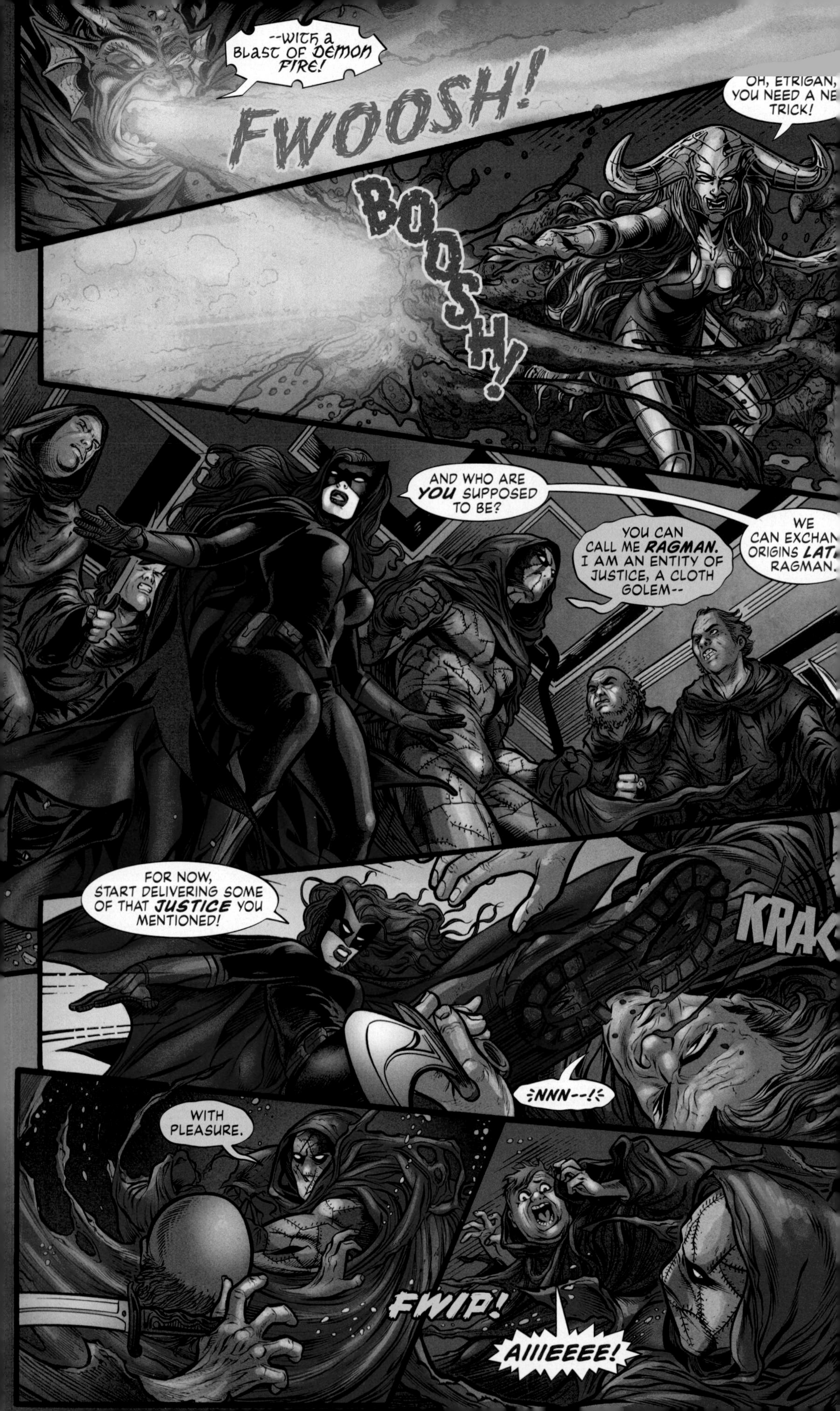
--WITH A BLAST OF DEMON FIRE!
FWOOSH!
OH, ETRIGAN, YOU NEED A NE
TRICK!
BOOSH!
AND WHO ARE YOU SUPPOSED TO BE?
YOU CAN CALL ME RAGMAN. I AM AN ENTITY OF JUSTICE, A CLOTH GOLEM--
WE CAN EXCHAN
ORIGINS LAT
RAGMAN.
FOR NOW, START DELIVERING SOME OF THAT JUSTICE YOU MENTIONED!
KRAK
NNN--!
WITH PLEASURE.
FWIP!
AIIIEEEE!

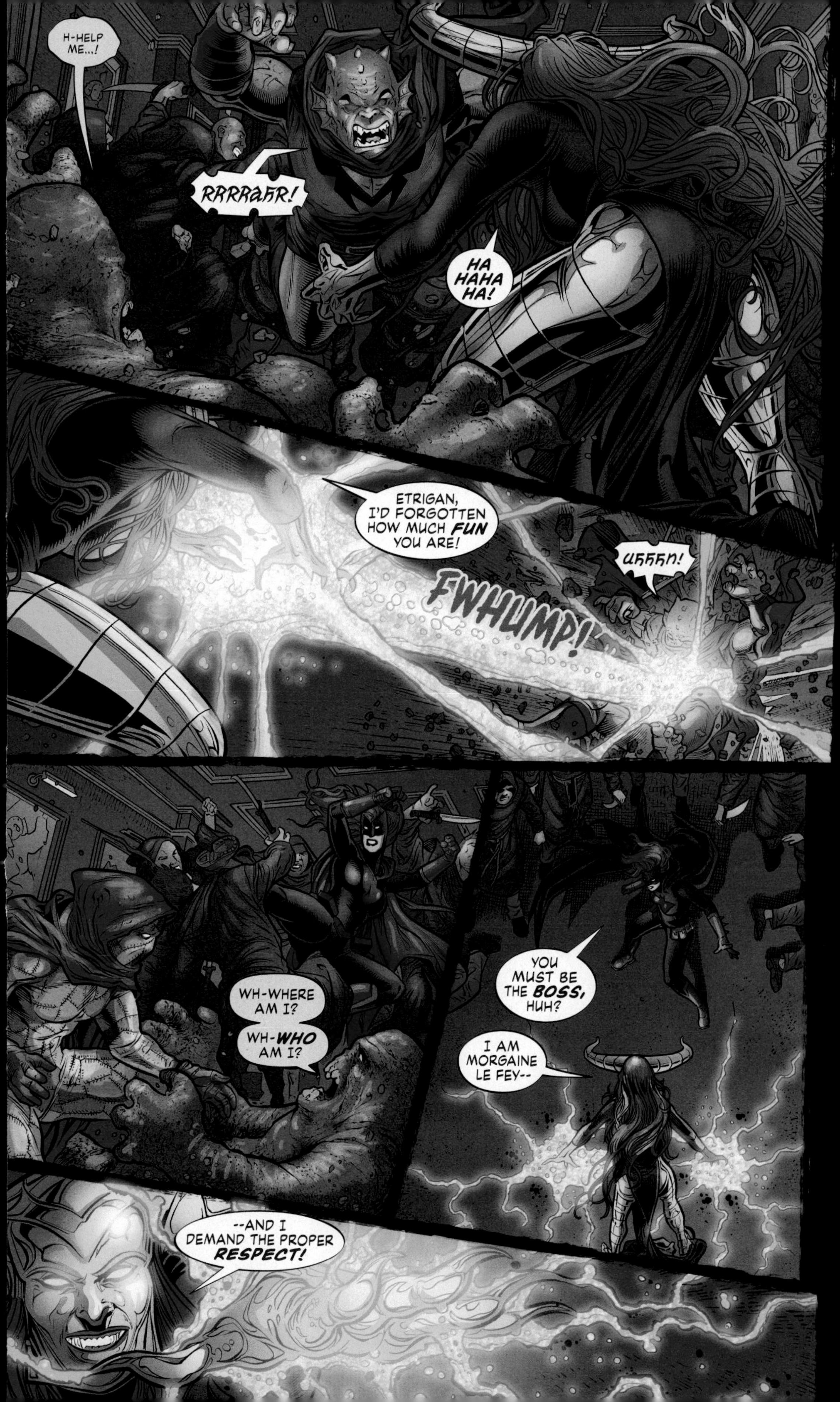
H-HELP ME...!
RRRRAHR!
HA HAHA HA!
ETRIGAN, I'D FORGOTTEN HOW MUCH FUN YOU ARE!
UHHHN!
FWHUMP!
WH-WHERE AM I?
WH-WHO AM I?
YOU MUST BE THE BOSS, HUH?
I AM MORGAINE LE FEY--
--AND I DEMAND THE PROPER RESPECT!

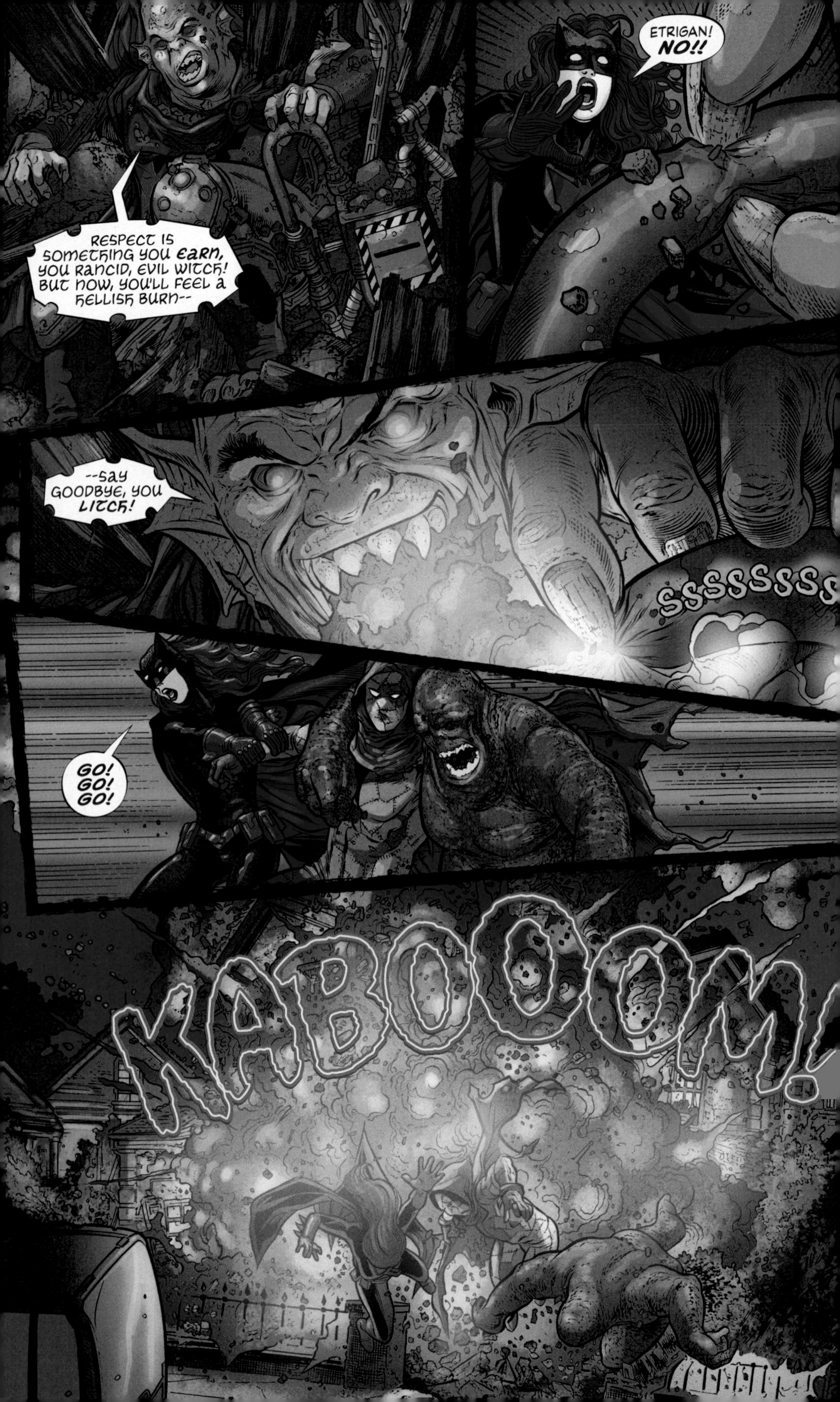
ETRIGAN! NO!!
RESPECT IS SOMETHING YOU EARN, YOU RANCID, EVIL WITCH! BUT NOW, YOU'LL FEEL A HELLISH BURN--
--SAY GOODBYE, YOU LITCH!
SSSSSSSS
GO! GO! GO!
KABOOOM!

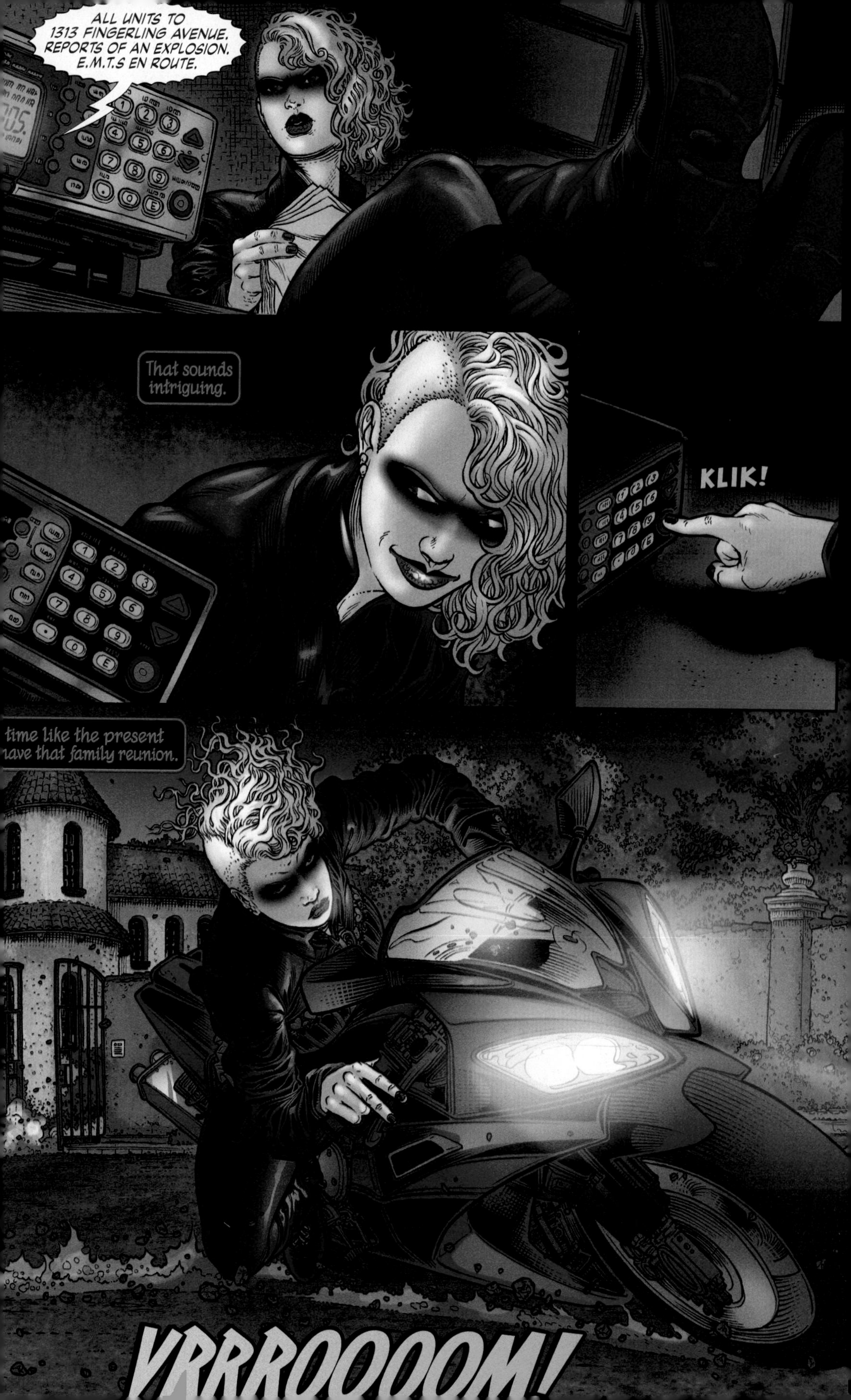
ALL UNITS TO 1313 FINGERLING AVENUE. REPORTS OF AN EXPLOSION. E.M.T.S EN ROUTE.
That sounds intriguing.
KLIK!
time like the present
ave that family reunion.
VRRROOOOM!

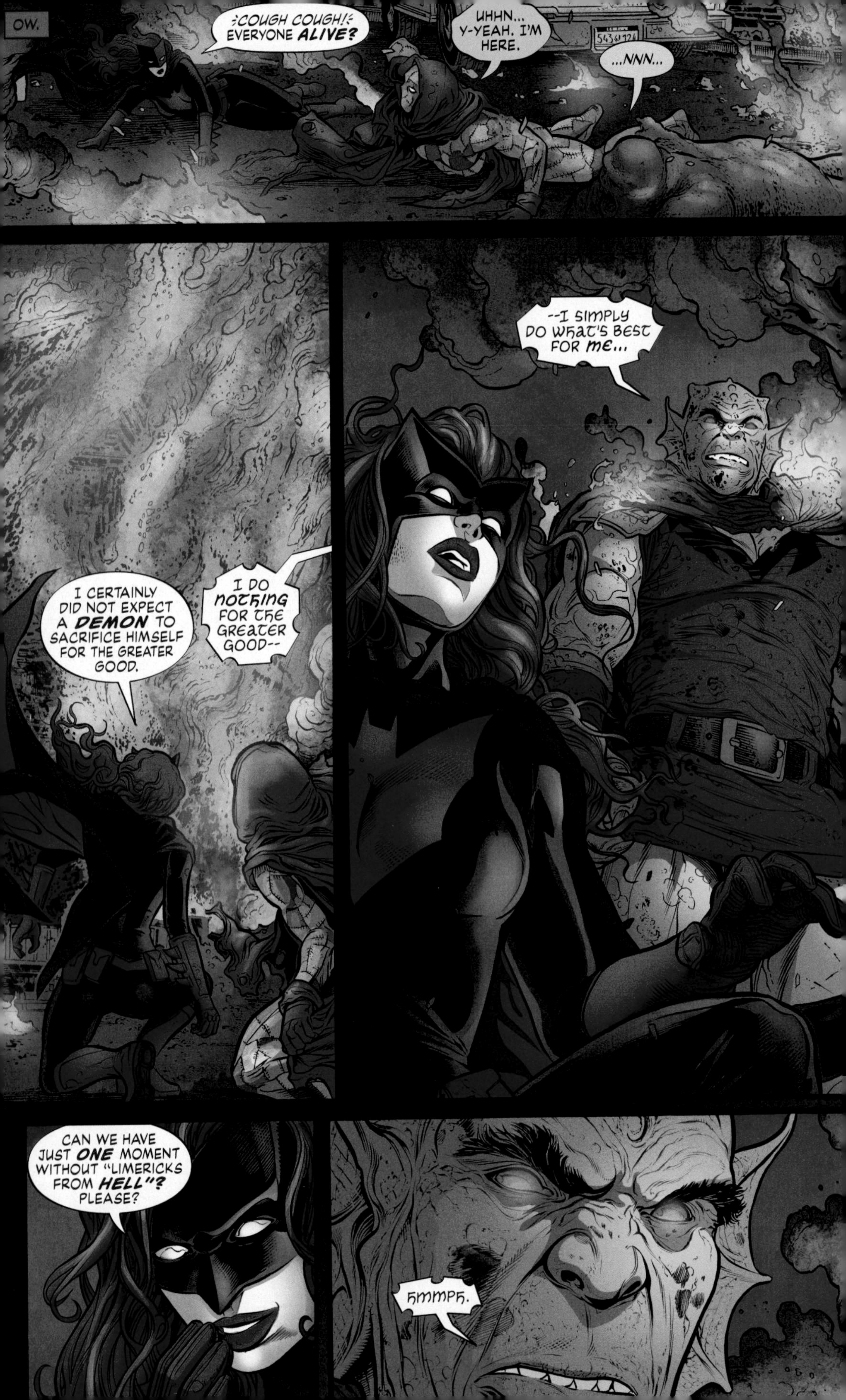
OW.
COUGH COUGH! EVERYONE ALIVE?
UHHN... Y-YEAH. I'M HERE.
...NNN...
I CERTAINLY DID NOT EXPECT A DEMON TO SACRIFICE HIMSELF FOR THE GREATER GOOD.
I DO NOTHING FOR THE GREATER GOOD--
--I SIMPLY DO WHAT'S BEST FOR ME...
CAN WE HAVE JUST ONE MOMENT WITHOUT "LIMERICKS FROM HELL"? PLEASE?
HMMPH.

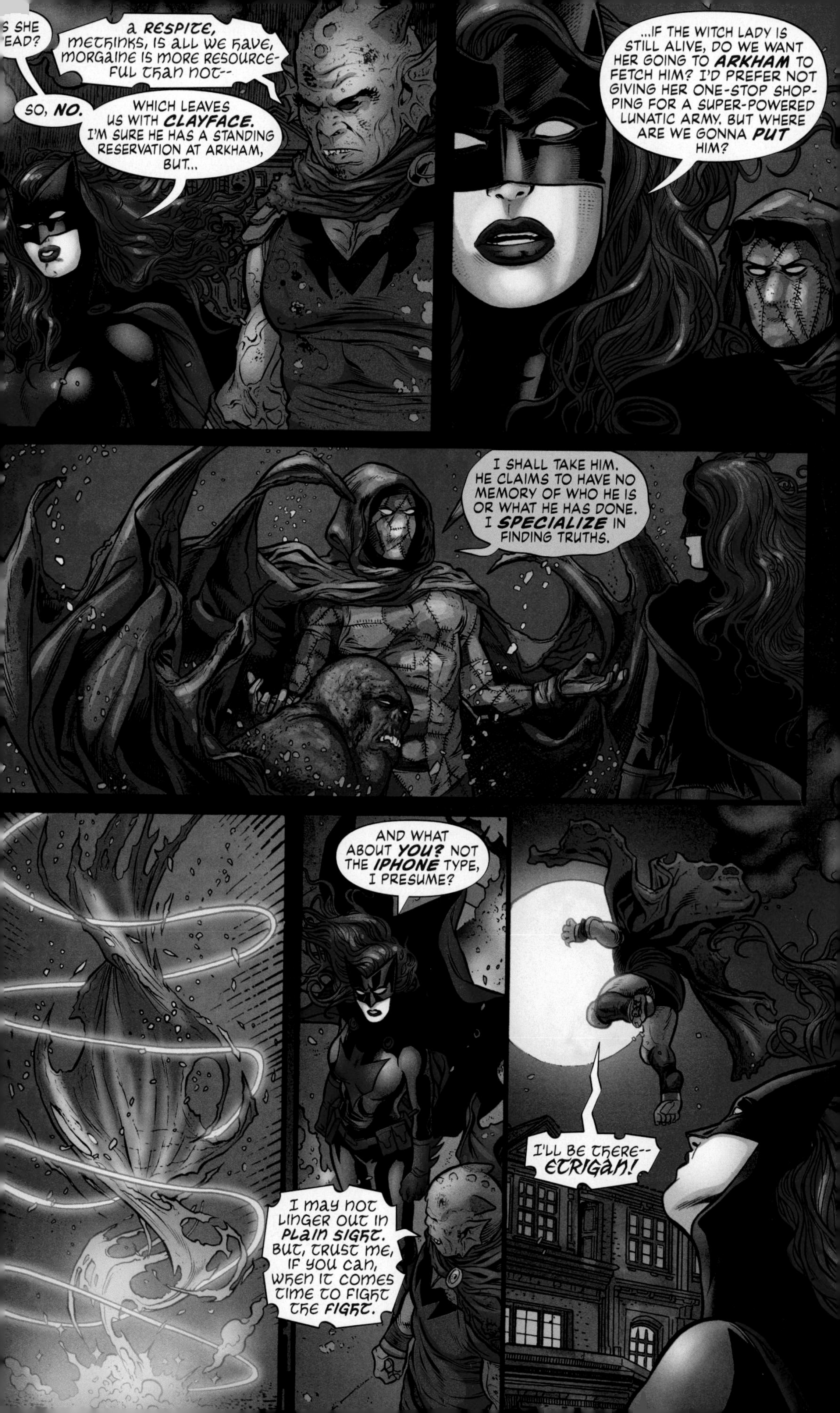
S SHE
EAD?
A RESPITE, METHINKS, IS ALL WE HAVE. MORGAINE IS MORE RESOURCE-FUL THAN NOT--
SO, NO.
WHICH LEAVES US WITH CLAYFACE. I'M SURE HE HAS A STANDING RESERVATION AT ARKHAM, BUT...
...IF THE WITCH LADY IS STILL ALIVE, DO WE WANT HER GOING TO ARKHAM TO FETCH HIM? I'D PREFER NOT GIVING HER ONE-STOP SHOP-PING FOR A SUPER-POWERED LUNATIC ARMY. BUT WHERE ARE WE GONNA PUT HIM?
I SHALL TAKE HIM. HE CLAIMS TO HAVE NO MEMORY OF WHO HE IS OR WHAT HE HAS DONE. I SPECIALIZE IN FINDING TRUTHS.
AND WHAT ABOUT YOU? NOT THE IPHONE TYPE, I PRESUME?
I MAY NOT LINGER OUT IN PLAIN SIGHT. BUT, TRUST ME, IF YOU CAN, WHEN IT COMES TIME TO FIGHT THE FIGHT.
I'LL BE THERE-- ETRIGAN!

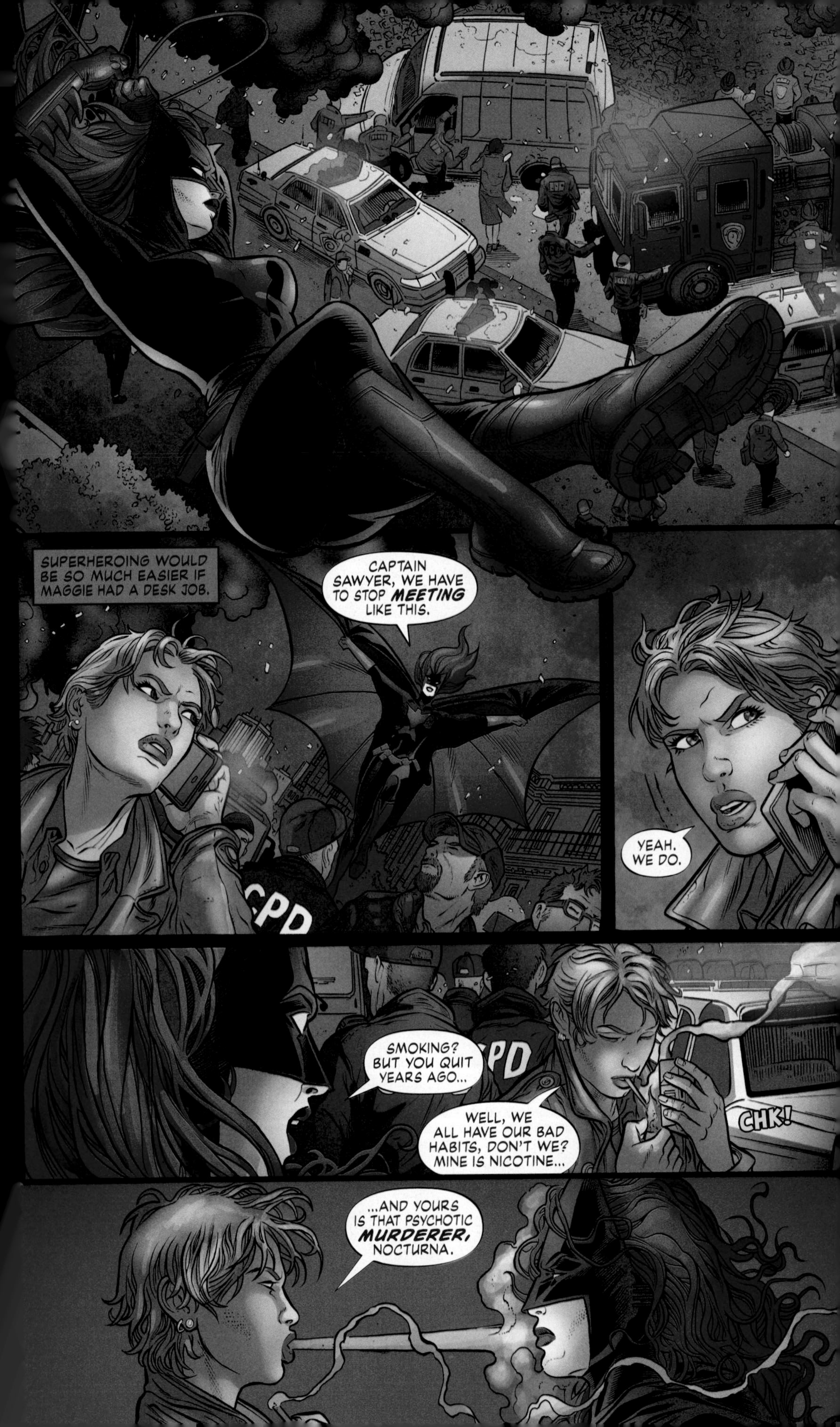
SUPERHEROING WOULD BE SO MUCH EASIER IF MAGGIE HAD A DESK JOB.
CAPTAIN SAWYER, WE HAVE TO STOP MEETING LIKE THIS.
GCPD
YEAH. WE DO.
SMOKING? BUT YOU QUIT YEARS AGO...
WELL, WE ALL HAVE OUR BAD HABITS, DON'T WE? MINE IS NICOTINE...
CHK!
...AND YOURS IS THAT PSYCHOTIC MURDERER, NOCTURNA.

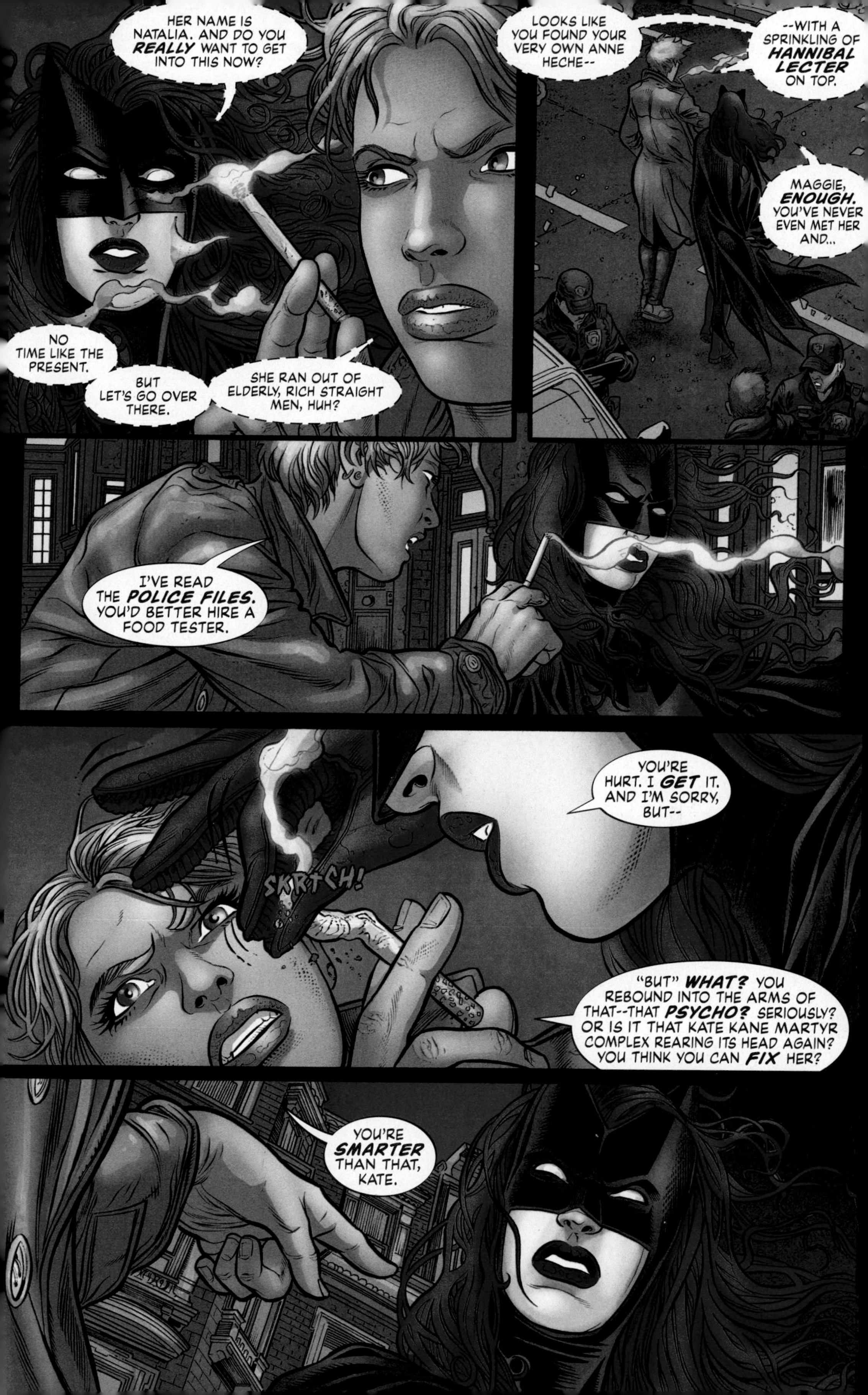
HER NAME IS NATALIA. AND DO YOU REALLY WANT TO GET INTO THIS NOW?
NO TIME LIKE THE PRESENT.
BUT LET'S GO OVER THERE.
SHE RAN OUT OF ELDERLY, RICH STRAIGHT MEN, HUH?
LOOKS LIKE YOU FOUND YOUR VERY OWN ANNE HECHE--
--WITH A SPRINKLING OF HANNIBAL LECTER ON TOP.
MAGGIE, ENOUGH. YOU'VE NEVER EVEN MET HER AND...
I'VE READ THE POLICE FILES. YOU'D BETTER HIRE A FOOD TESTER.
YOU'RE HURT. I GET IT. AND I'M SORRY, BUT--
SKRTCH!
"BUT" WHAT? YOU REBOUND INTO THE ARMS OF THAT--THAT PSYCHO? SERIOUSLY? OR IS IT THAT KATE KANE MARTYR COMPLEX REARING ITS HEAD AGAIN? YOU THINK YOU CAN FIX HER?
YOU'RE SMARTER THAN THAT, KATE.

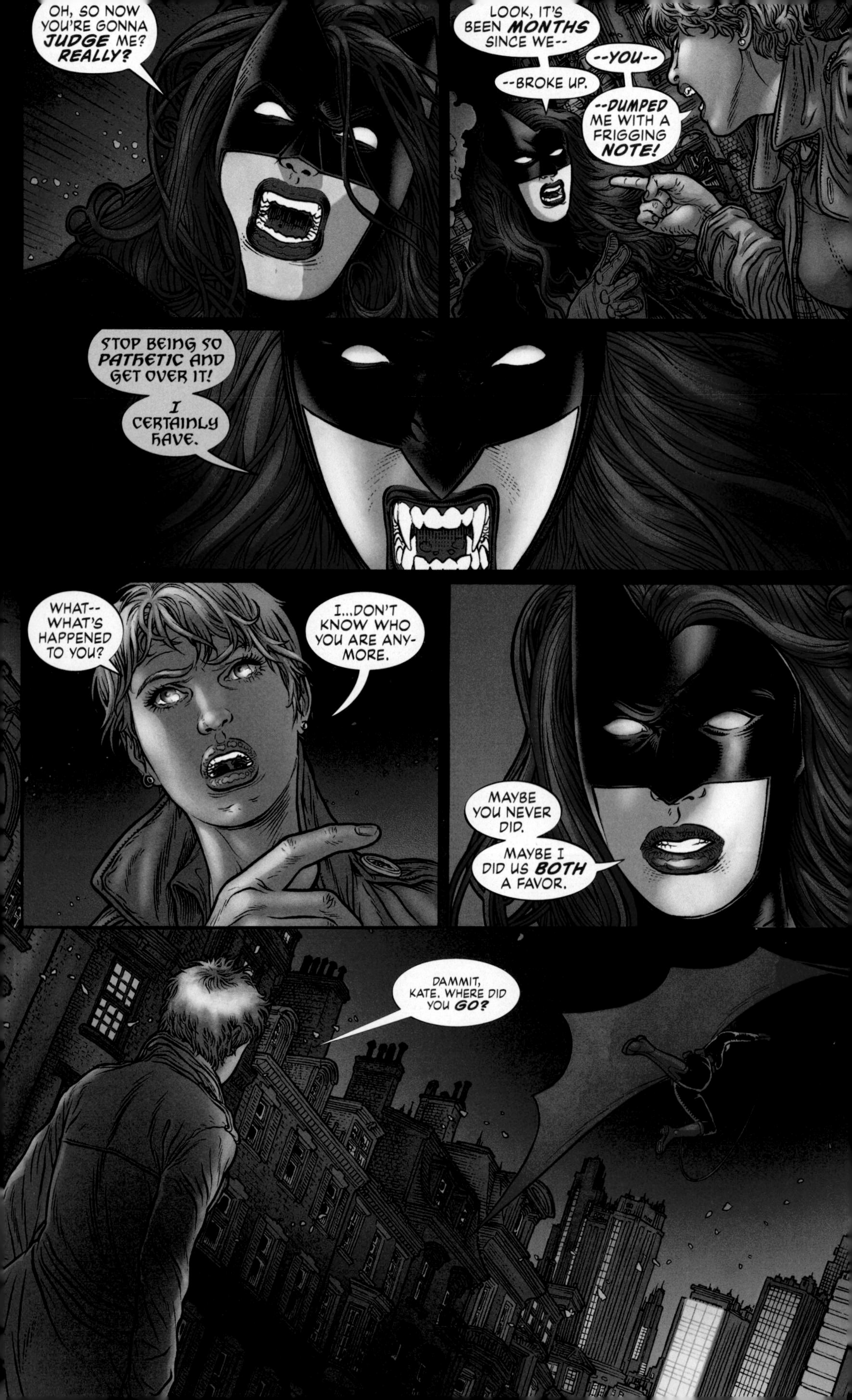

OH, SO NOW YOU'RE GONNA JUDGE ME? REALLY?
LOOK, IT'S BEEN MONTHS SINCE WE--
--BROKE UP.
--YOU--
--DUMPED ME WITH A FRIGGING NOTE!
STOP BEING SO PATHETIC AND GET OVER IT!
I CERTAINLY HAVE.
WHAT-- WHAT'S HAPPENED TO YOU?
I...DON'T KNOW WHO YOU ARE ANY-MORE.
MAYBE YOU NEVER DID.
MAYBE I DID US BOTH A FAVOR.
DAMMIT, KATE. WHERE DID YOU GO?

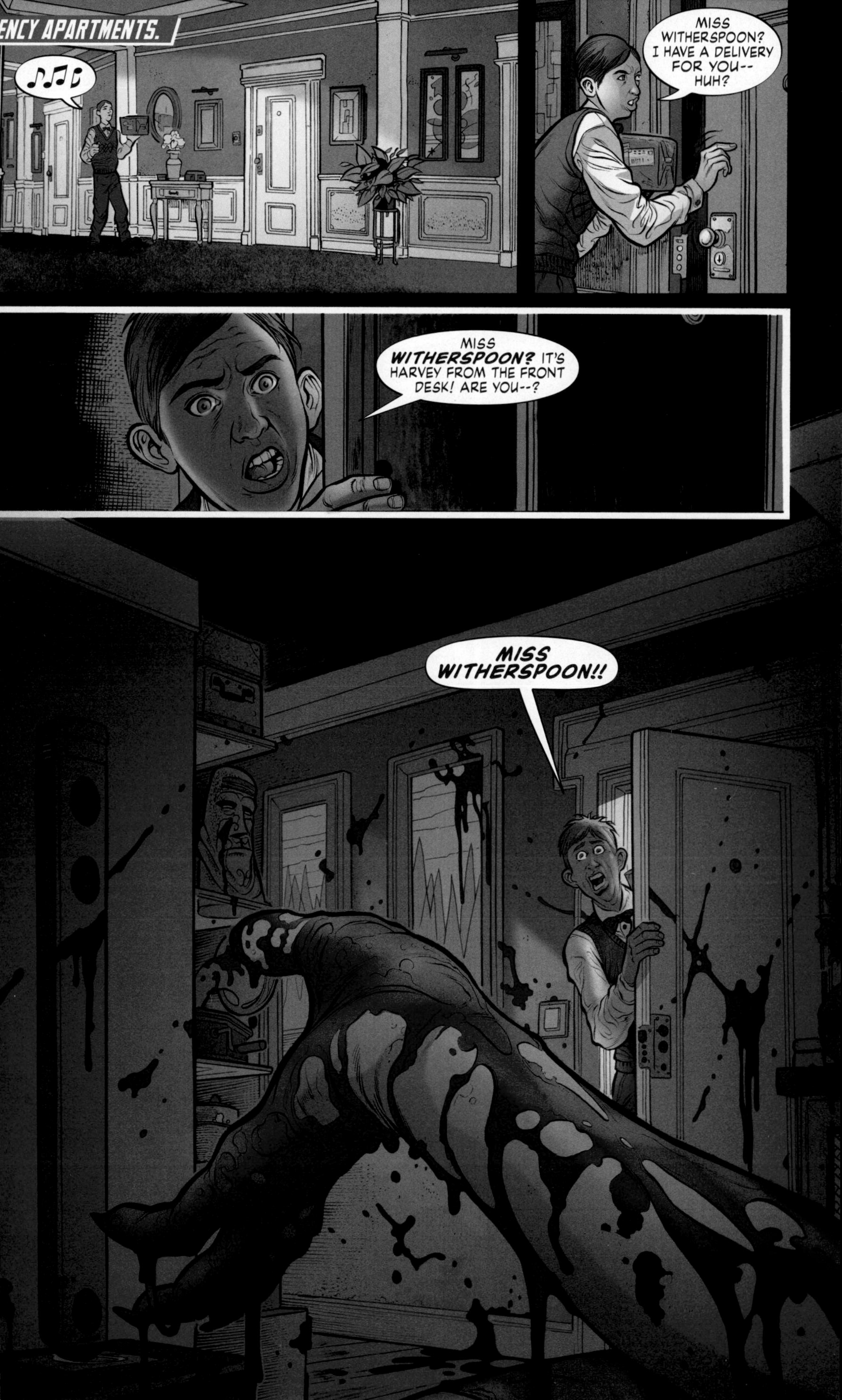

ENCY APARTMENTS.
♪♫♪
MISS WITHERSPOON? I HAVE A DELIVERY FOR YOU-- HUH?
MISS WITHERSPOON? IT'S HARVEY FROM THE FRONT DESK! ARE YOU--?
MISS WITHERSPOON!!

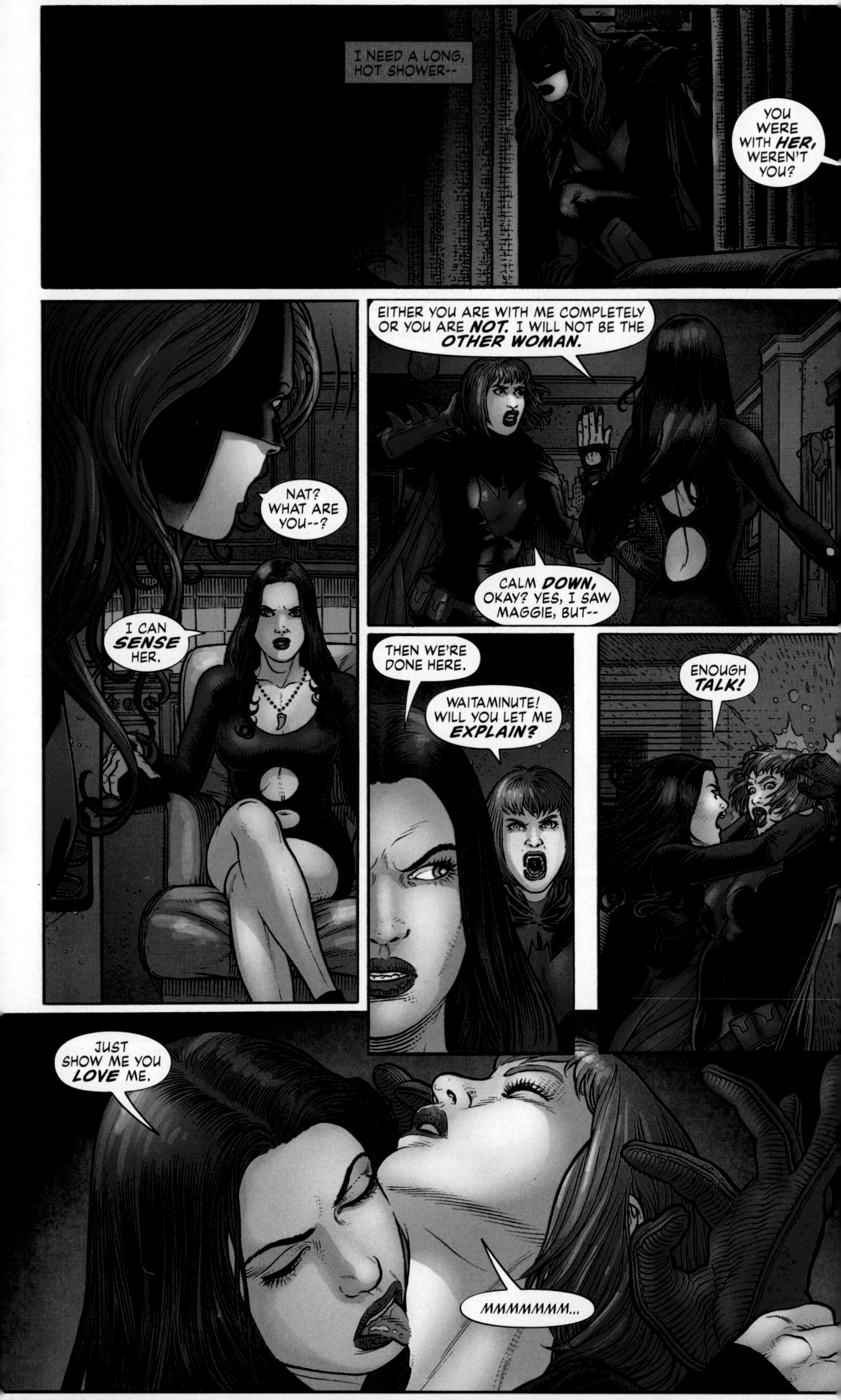
I NEED A LONG, HOT SHOWER--
YOU WERE WITH HER, WEREN'T YOU?
NAT? WHAT ARE YOU--?
I CAN SENSE HER.
EITHER YOU ARE WITH ME COMPLETELY OR YOU ARE NOT. I WILL NOT BE THE OTHER WOMAN.
CALM DOWN, OKAY? YES, I SAW MAGGIE, BUT--
THEN WE'RE DONE HERE.
WAITAMINUTE! WILL YOU LET ME EXPLAIN?
ENOUGH TALK!
JUST SHOW ME YOU LOVE ME.
MMMMMMM...

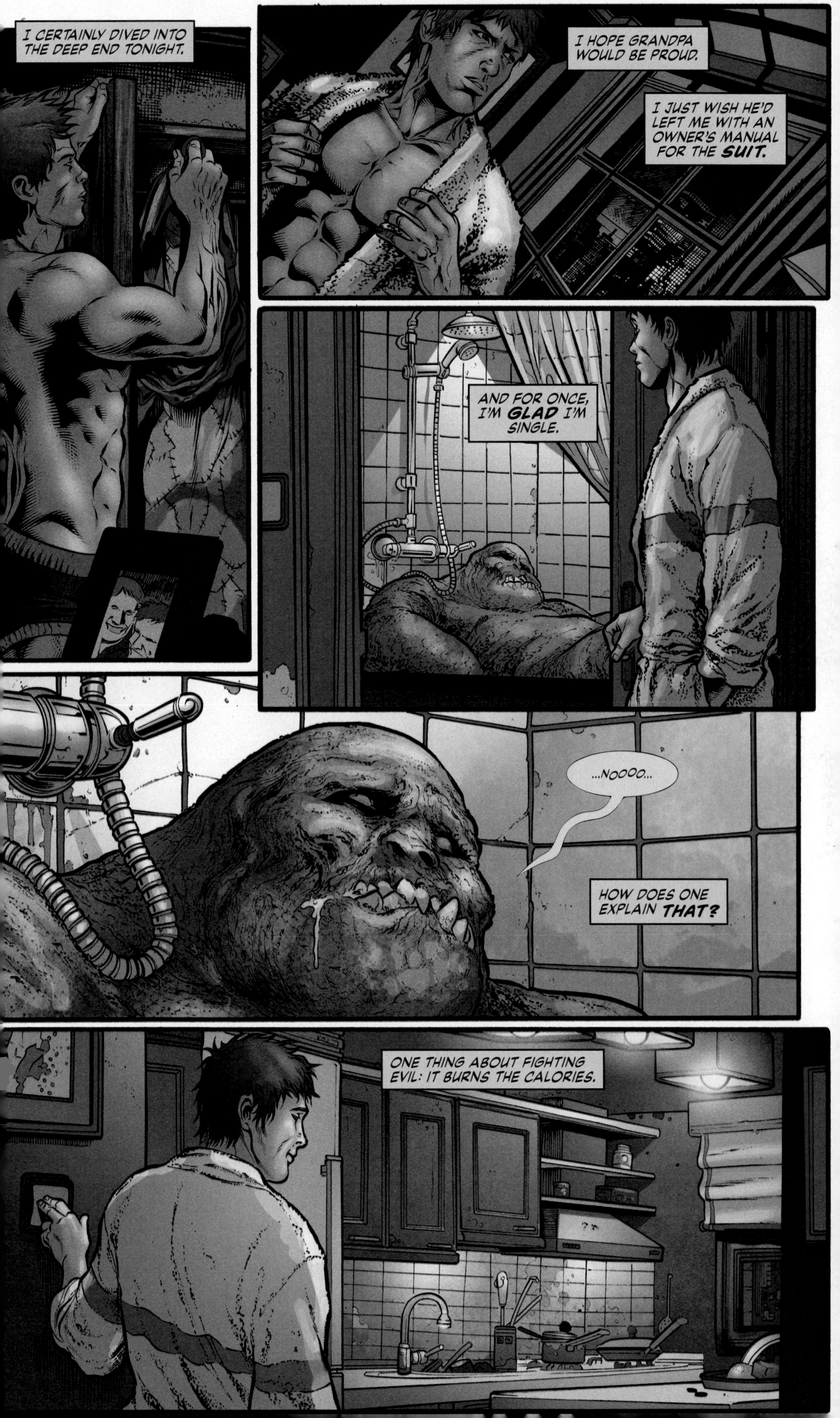
I CERTAINLY DIVED INTO THE DEEP END TONIGHT.
I HOPE GRANDPA WOULD BE PROUD.
I JUST WISH HE'D LEFT ME WITH AN OWNER'S MANUAL FOR THE SUIT.
AND FOR ONCE, I'M GLAD I'M SINGLE.
...NOOOO...
HOW DOES ONE EXPLAIN THAT?
ONE THING ABOUT FIGHTING EVIL: IT BURNS THE CALORIES.

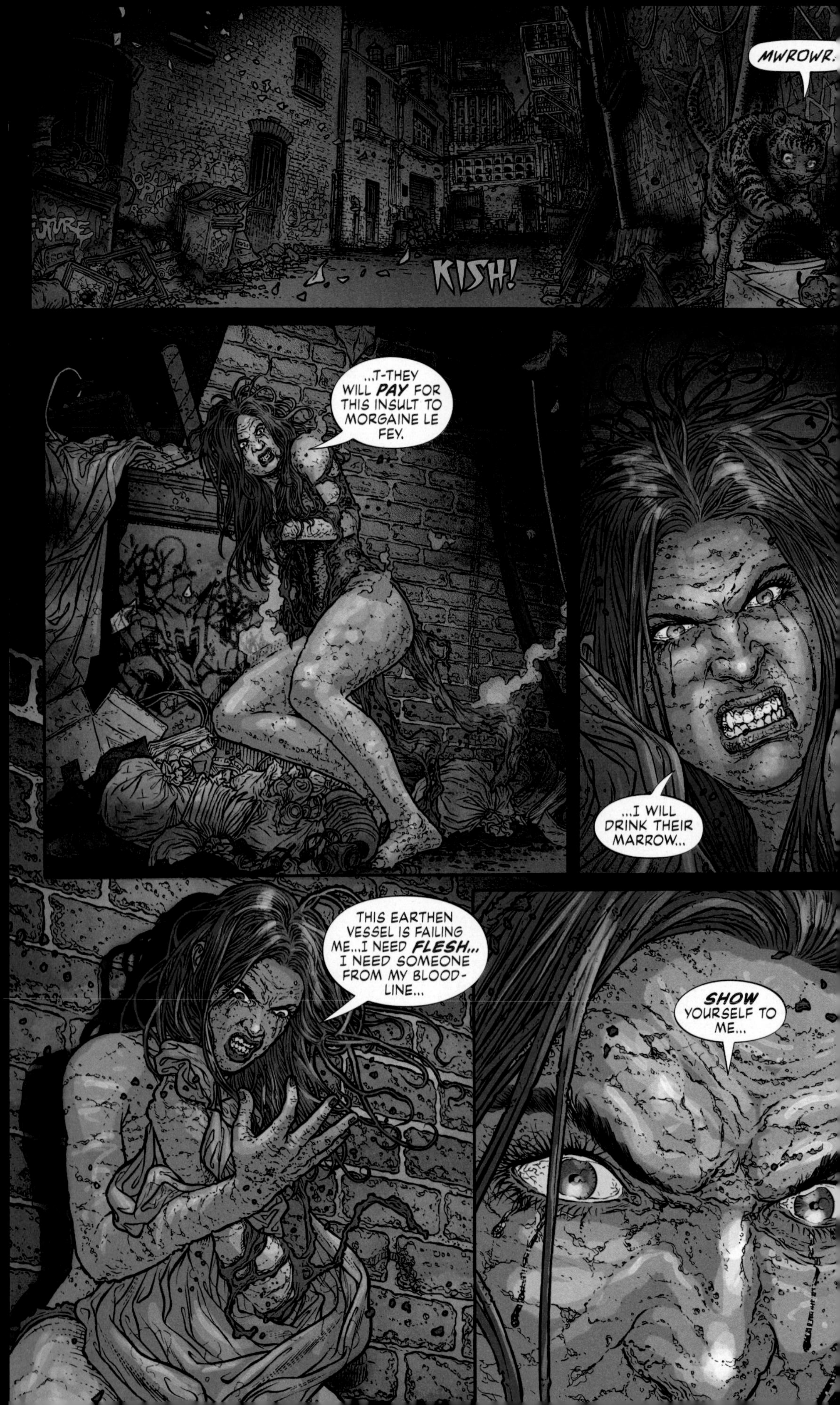
MWROWR.
KISH!
FUTURE
...T-THEY WILL PAY FOR THIS INSULT TO MORGAINE LE FEY.
...I WILL DRINK THEIR MARROW...
THIS EARTHEN VESSEL IS FAILING ME...I NEED FLESH... I NEED SOMEONE FROM MY BLOOD-LINE...
SHOW YOURSELF TO ME...

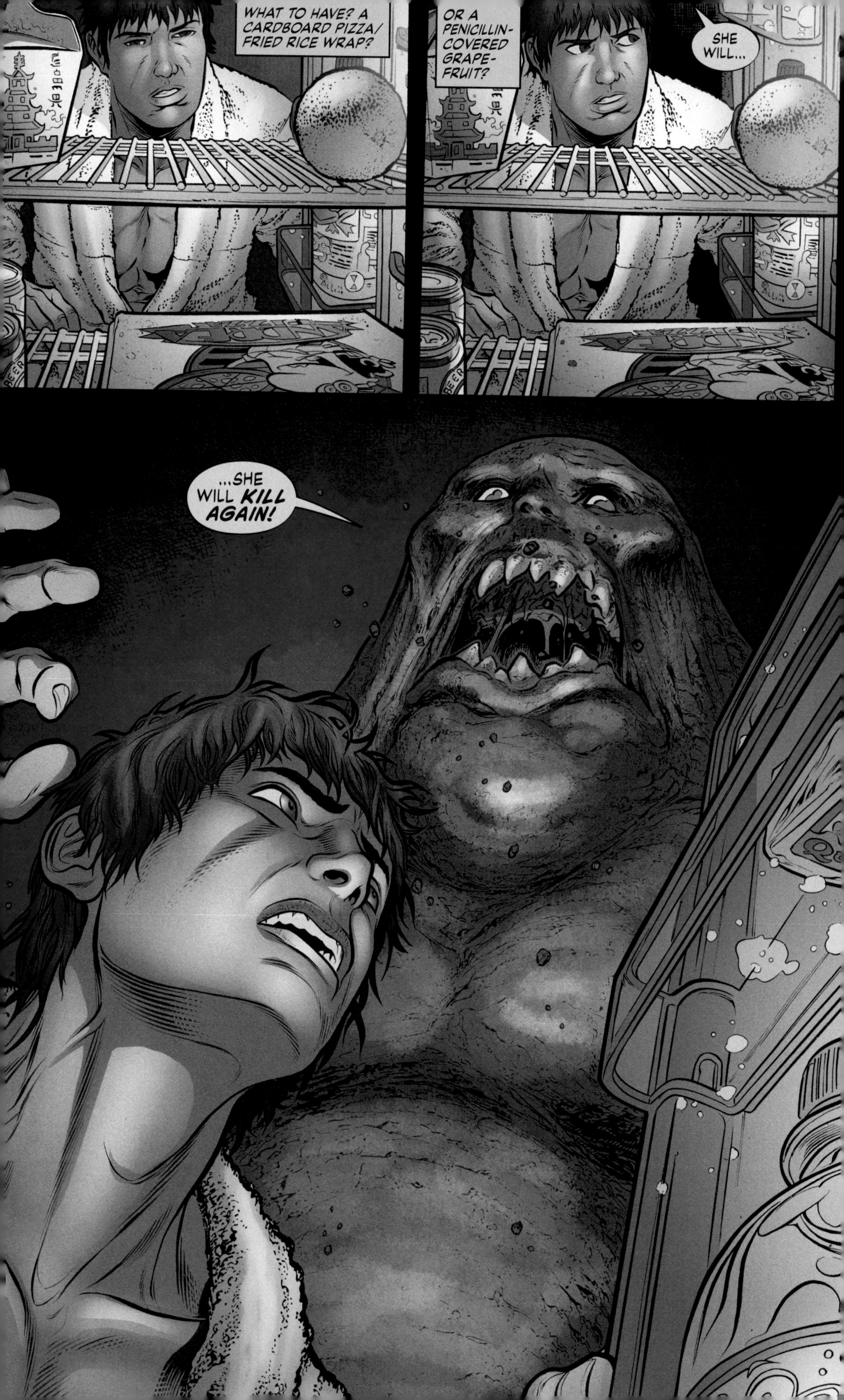
WHAT TO HAVE? A CARDBOARD PIZZA/ FRIED RICE WRAP?
OR A PENICILLIN-COVERED GRAPE-FRUIT?
SHE WILL...
...SHE WILL KILL AGAIN!

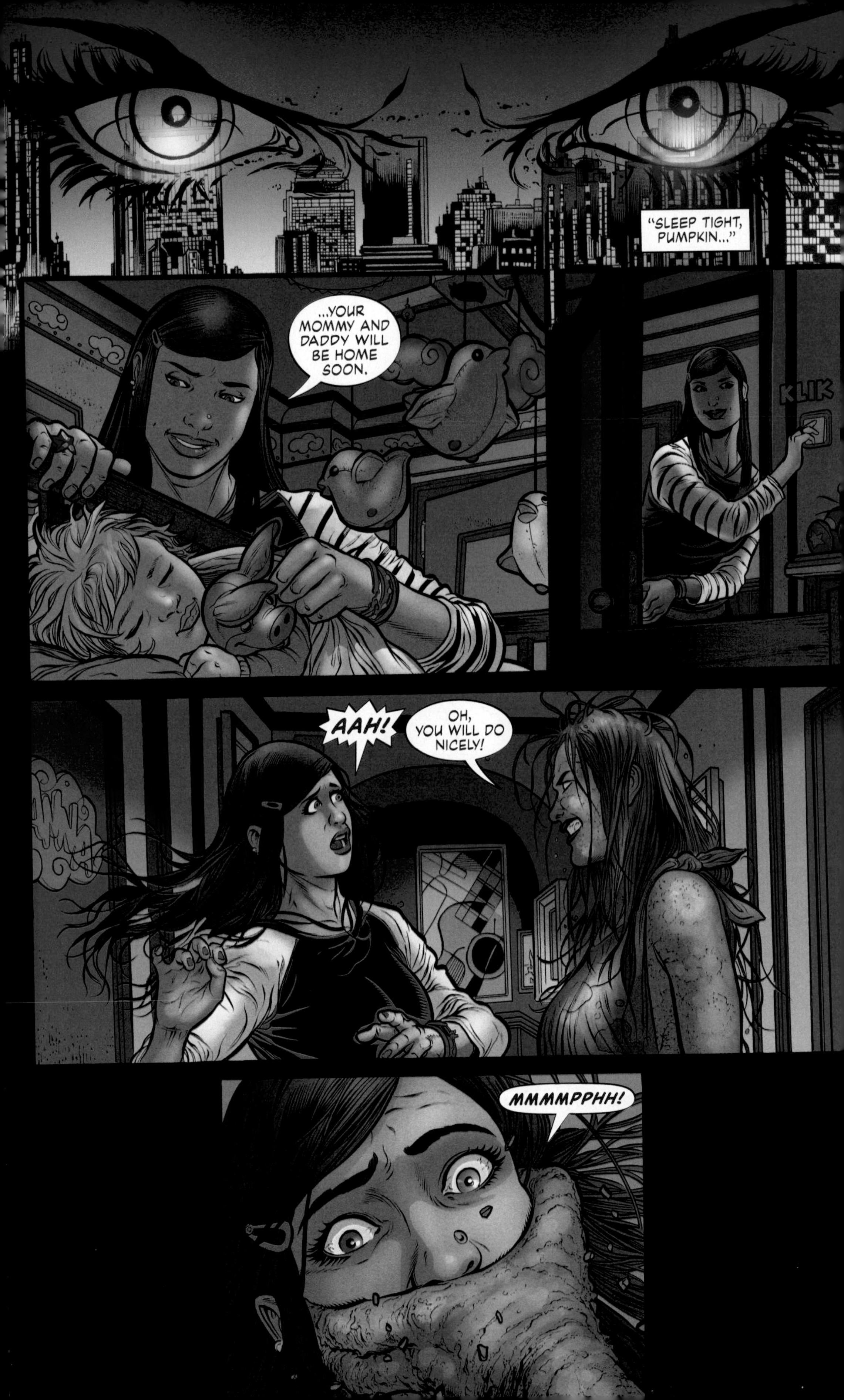
"SLEEP TIGHT, PUMPKIN..."
...YOUR MOMMY AND DADDY WILL BE HOME SOON.
KLIK
AAH!
OH, YOU WILL DO NICELY!
MMMMPPHH!

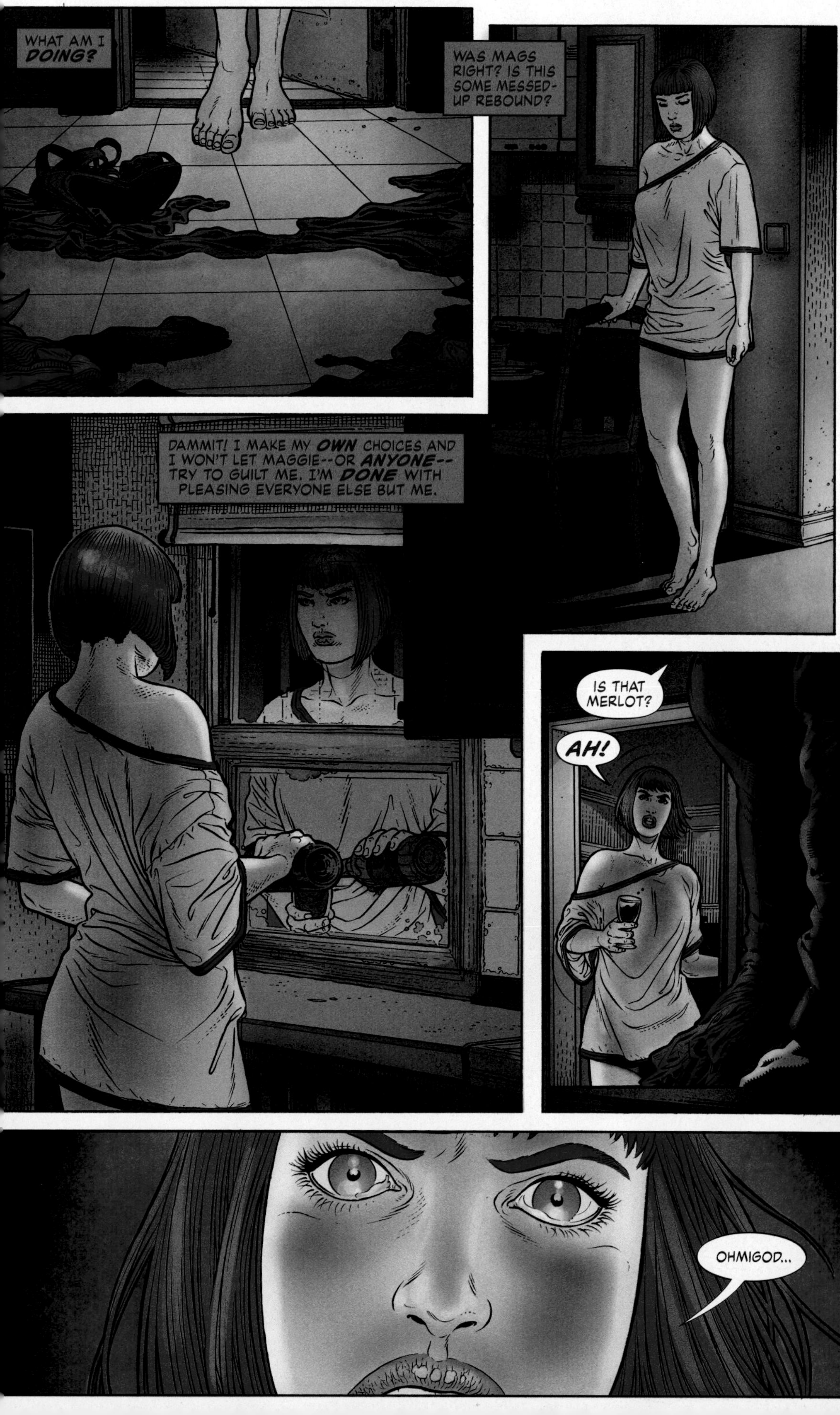
WHAT AM I DOING?
WAS MAGS RIGHT? IS THIS SOME MESSED-UP REBOUND?
DAMMIT! I MAKE MY OWN CHOICES AND I WON'T LET MAGGIE--OR ANYONE--TRY TO GUILT ME. I'M DONE WITH PLEASING EVERYONE ELSE BUT ME.
IS THAT MERLOT?
AH!
OHMIGOD...

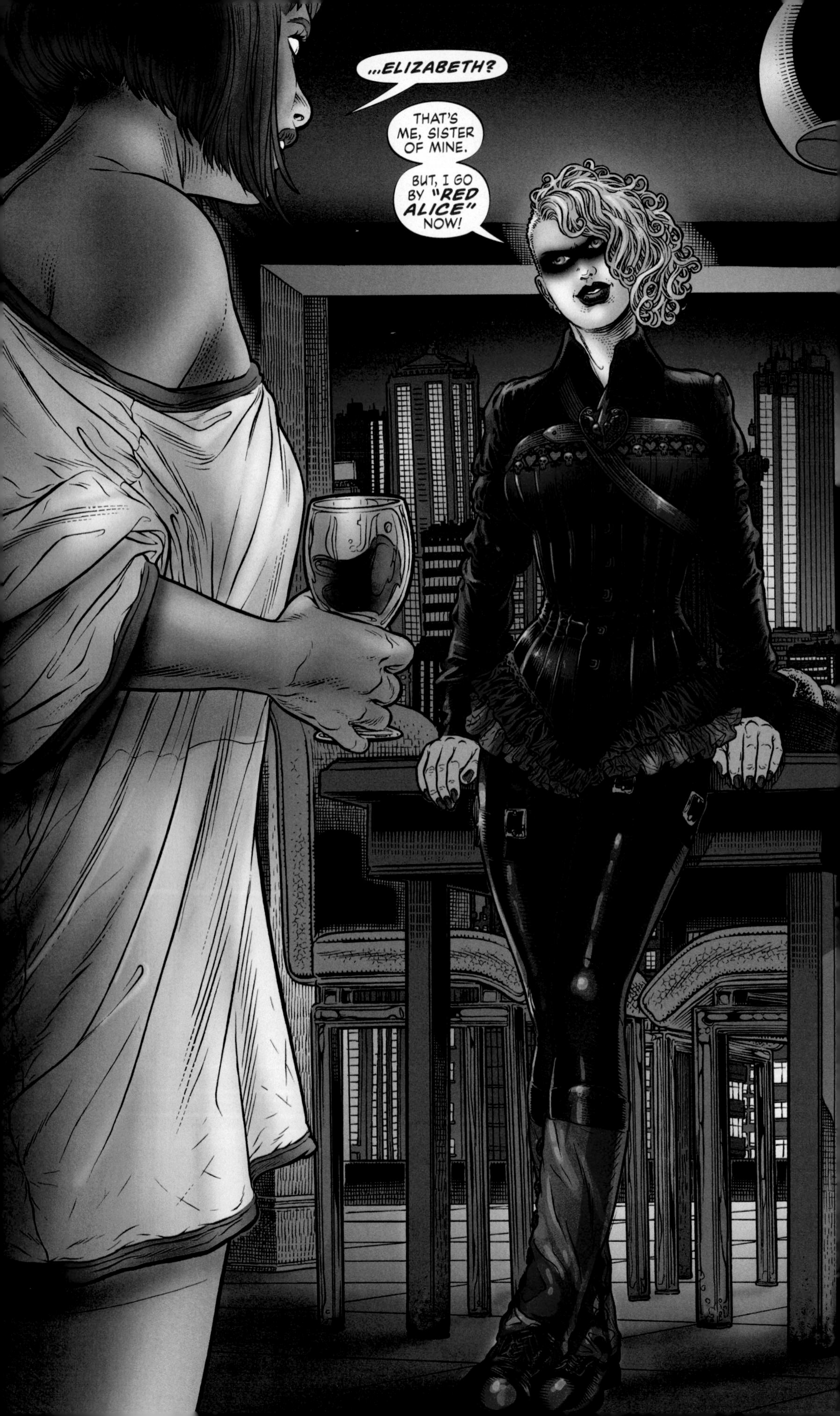

...ELIZABETH?
THAT'S ME, SISTER OF MINE.
BUT, I GO BY "RED ALICE" NOW!

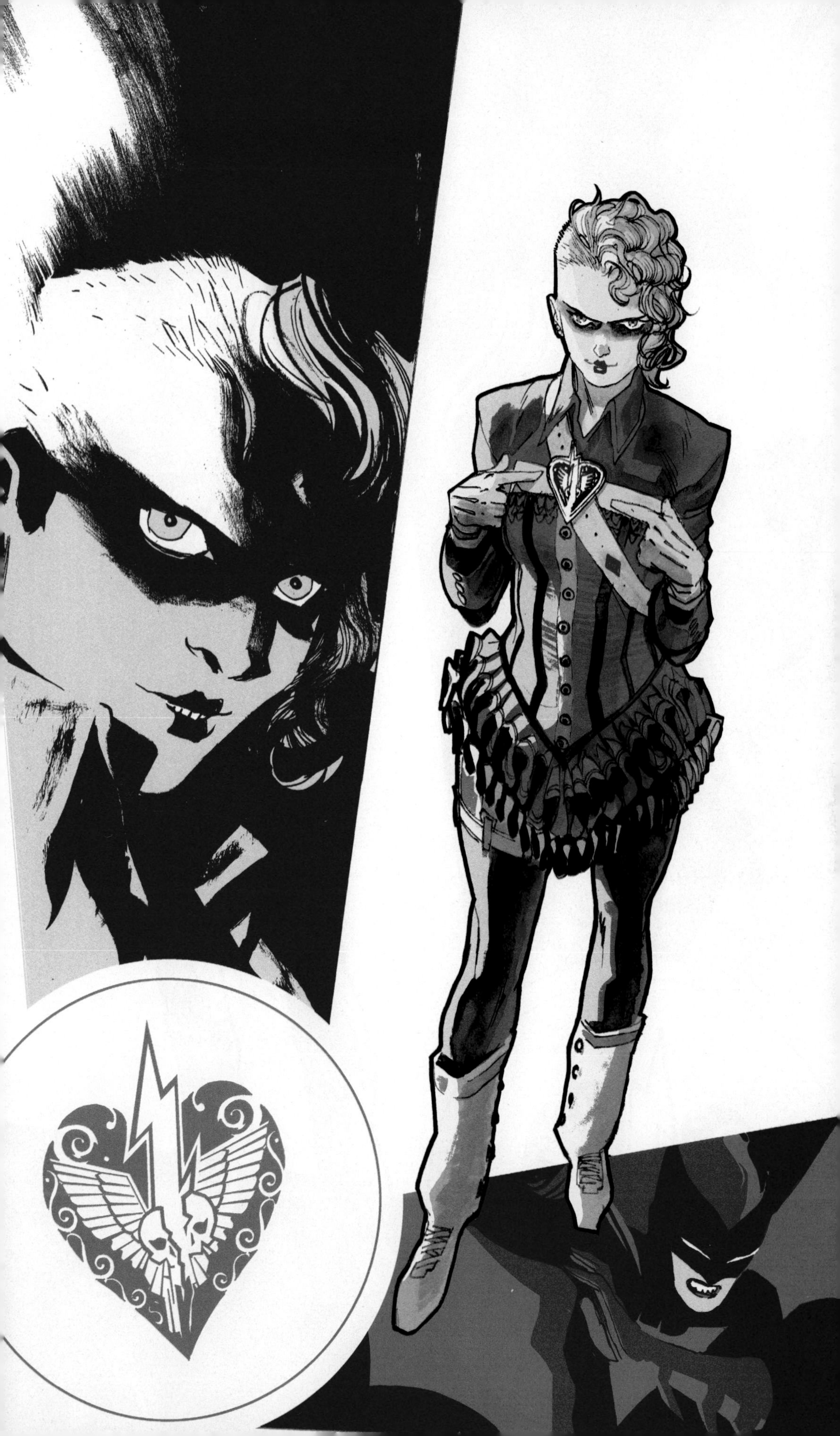

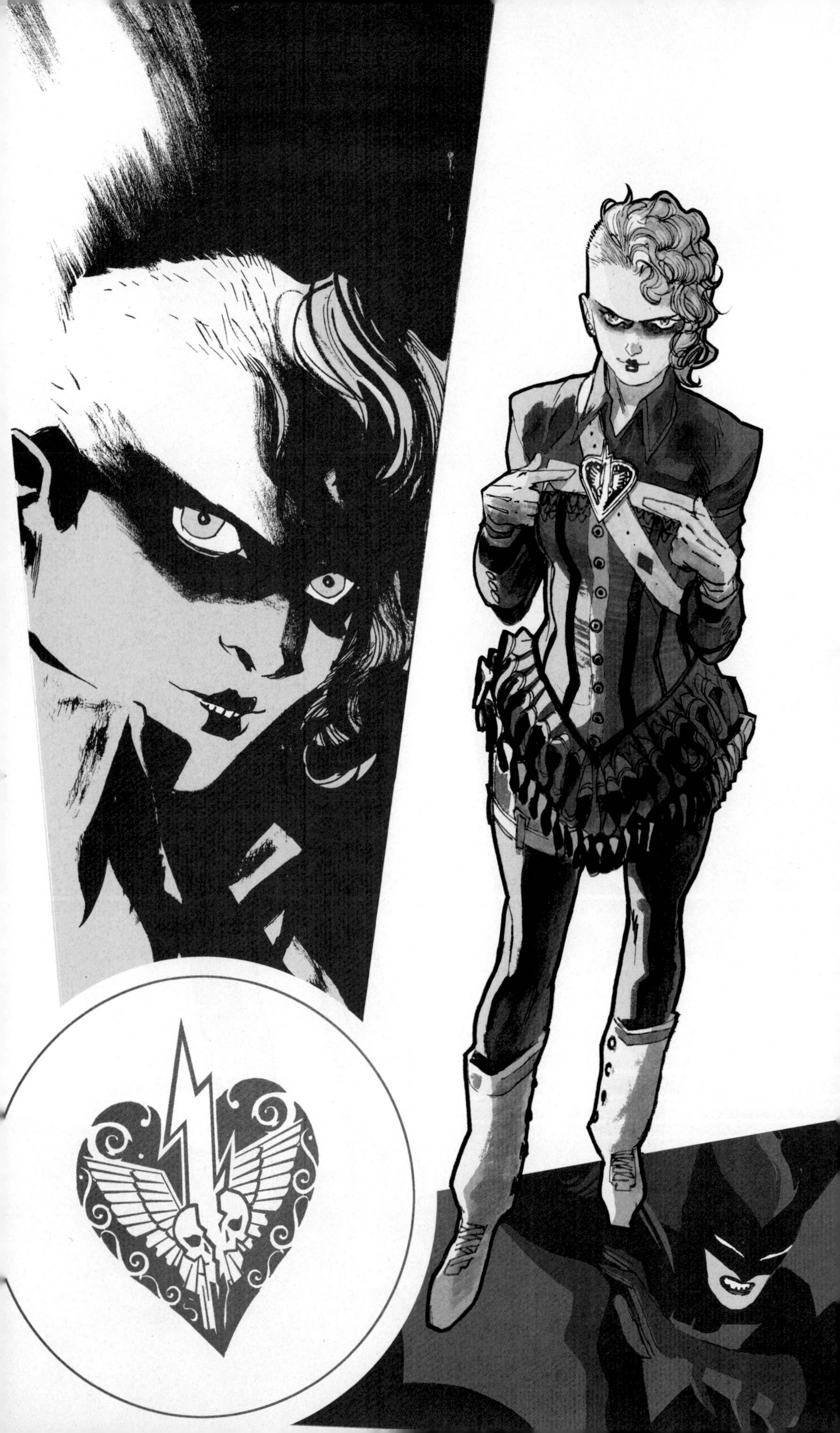

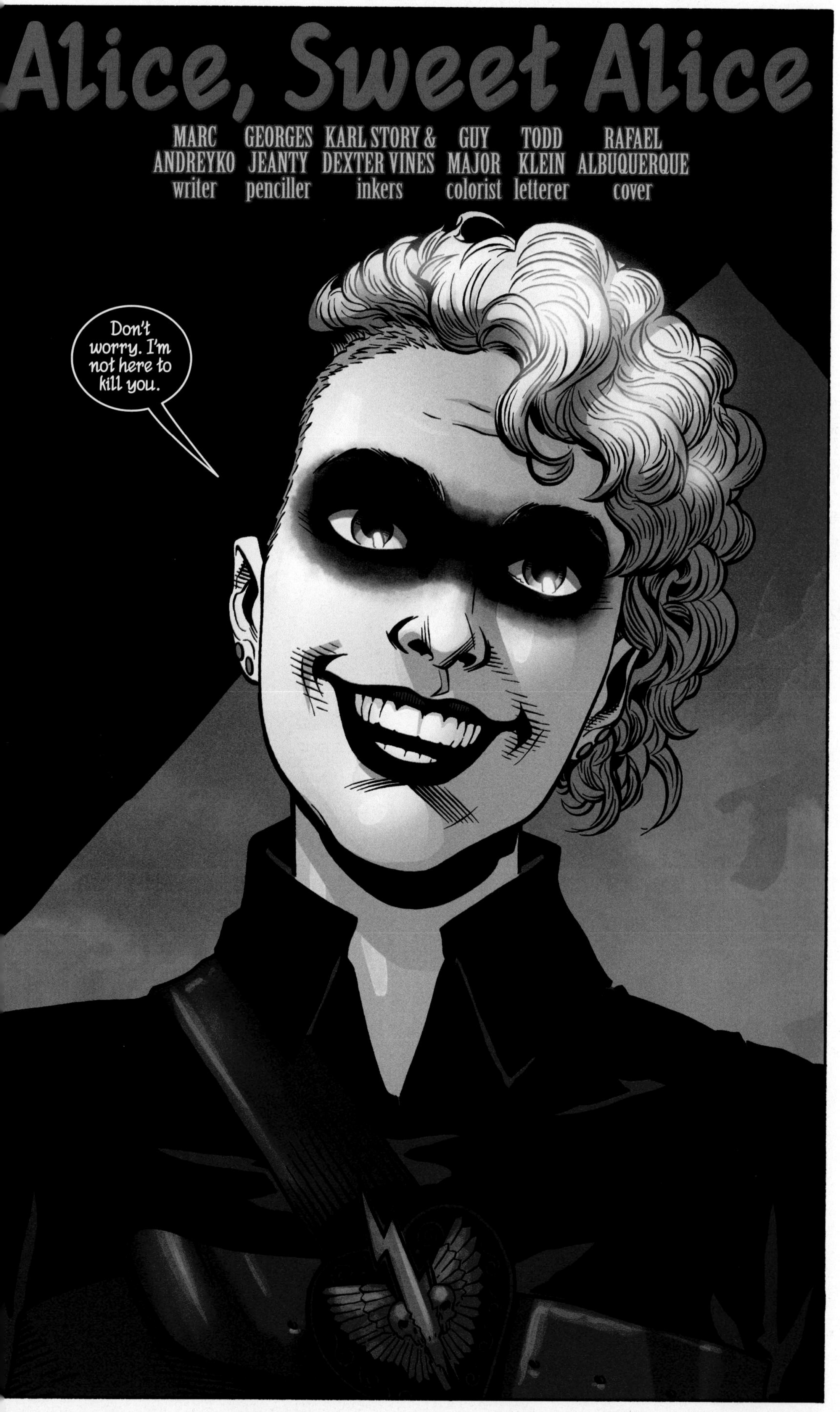
Alice, Sweet Alice
MARC ANDREYKO writer
GEORGES JEANTY penciller
KARL STORY & DEXTER VINES inkers
GUY MAJOR colorist
TODD KLEIN letterer
RAFAEL ALBUQUERQUE cover
Don't worry. I'm not here to kill you.

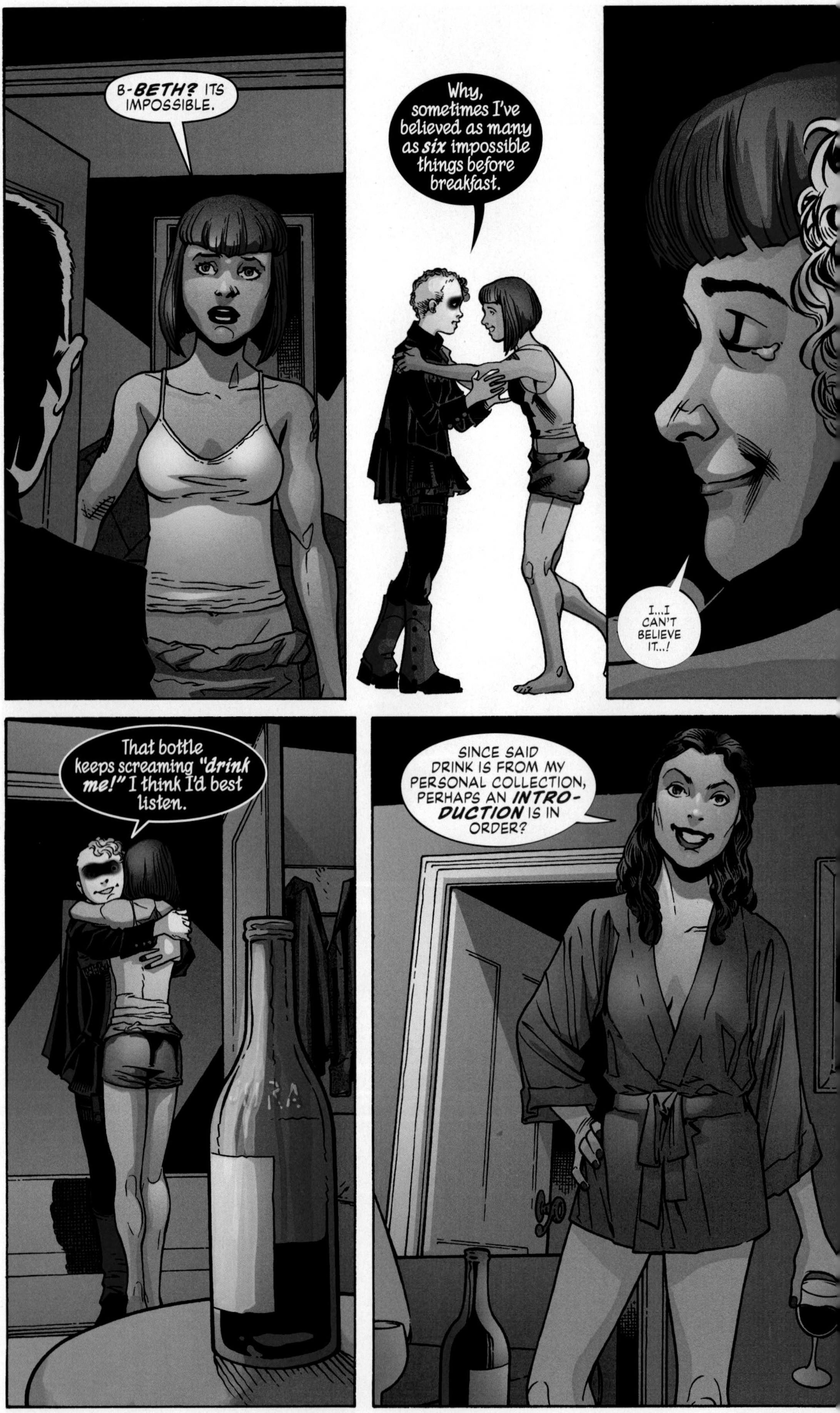
B-BETH? ITS IMPOSSIBLE.
Why, sometimes I've believed as many as six impossible things before breakfast.
I...I CAN'T BELIEVE IT...!
That bottle keeps screaming "drink me!" I think I'd best listen.
SINCE SAID DRINK IS FROM MY PERSONAL COLLECTION, PERHAPS AN INTRODUCTION IS IN ORDER?

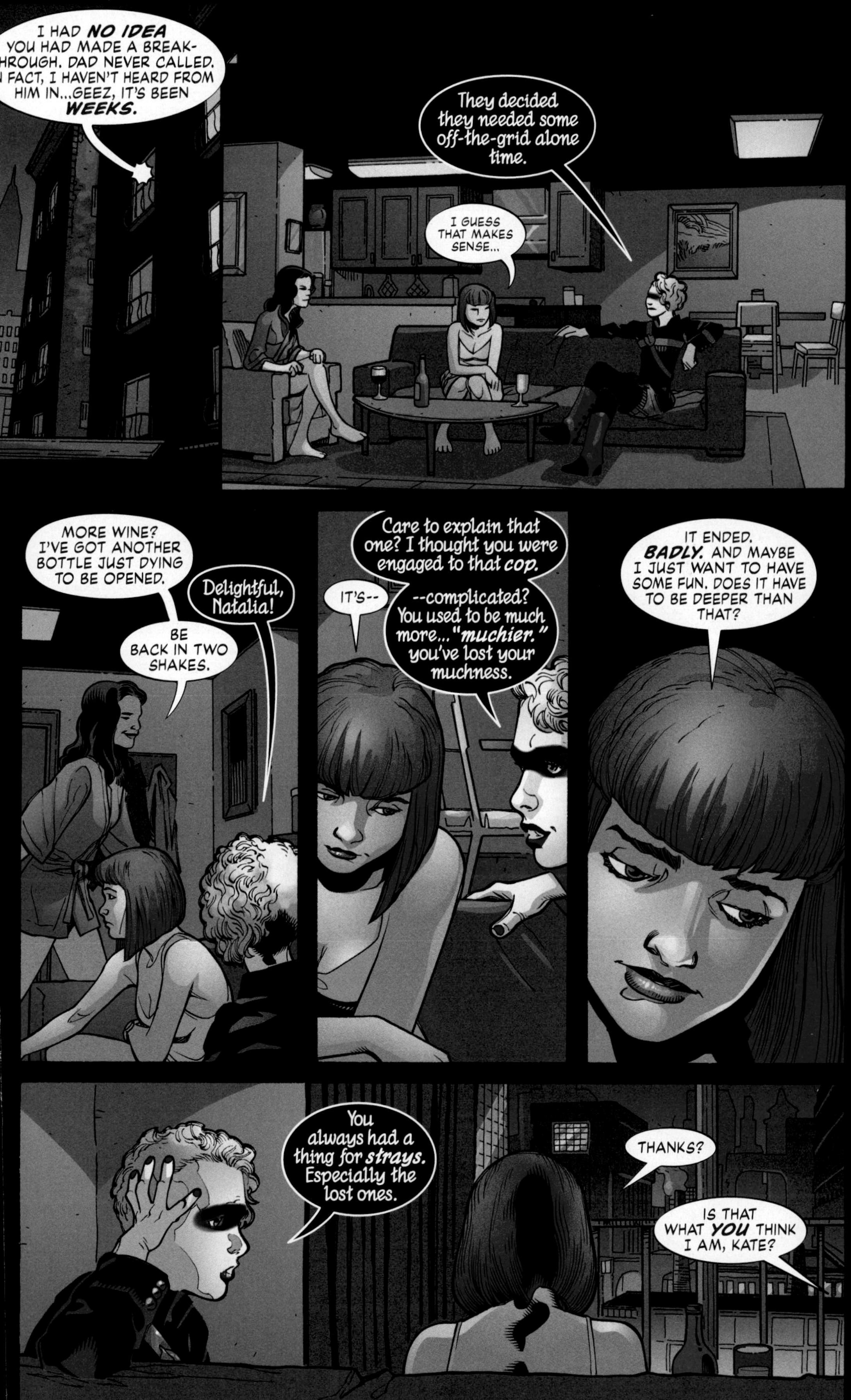

I HAD NO IDEA YOU HAD MADE A BREAK-THROUGH. DAD NEVER CALLED. IN FACT, I HAVEN'T HEARD FROM HIM IN...GEEZ, IT'S BEEN WEEKS.
They decided they needed some off-the-grid alone time.
I GUESS THAT MAKES SENSE...
MORE WINE? I'VE GOT ANOTHER BOTTLE JUST DYING TO BE OPENED.
Delightful, Natalia!
BE BACK IN TWO SHAKES.
Care to explain that one? I thought you were engaged to that cop.
IT'S--
--complicated? You used to be much more..."muchier." you've lost your muchness.
IT ENDED. BADLY. AND MAYBE I JUST WANT TO HAVE SOME FUN. DOES IT HAVE TO BE DEEPER THAN THAT?
You always had a thing for strays. Especially the lost ones.
THANKS?
IS THAT WHAT YOU THINK I AM, KATE?

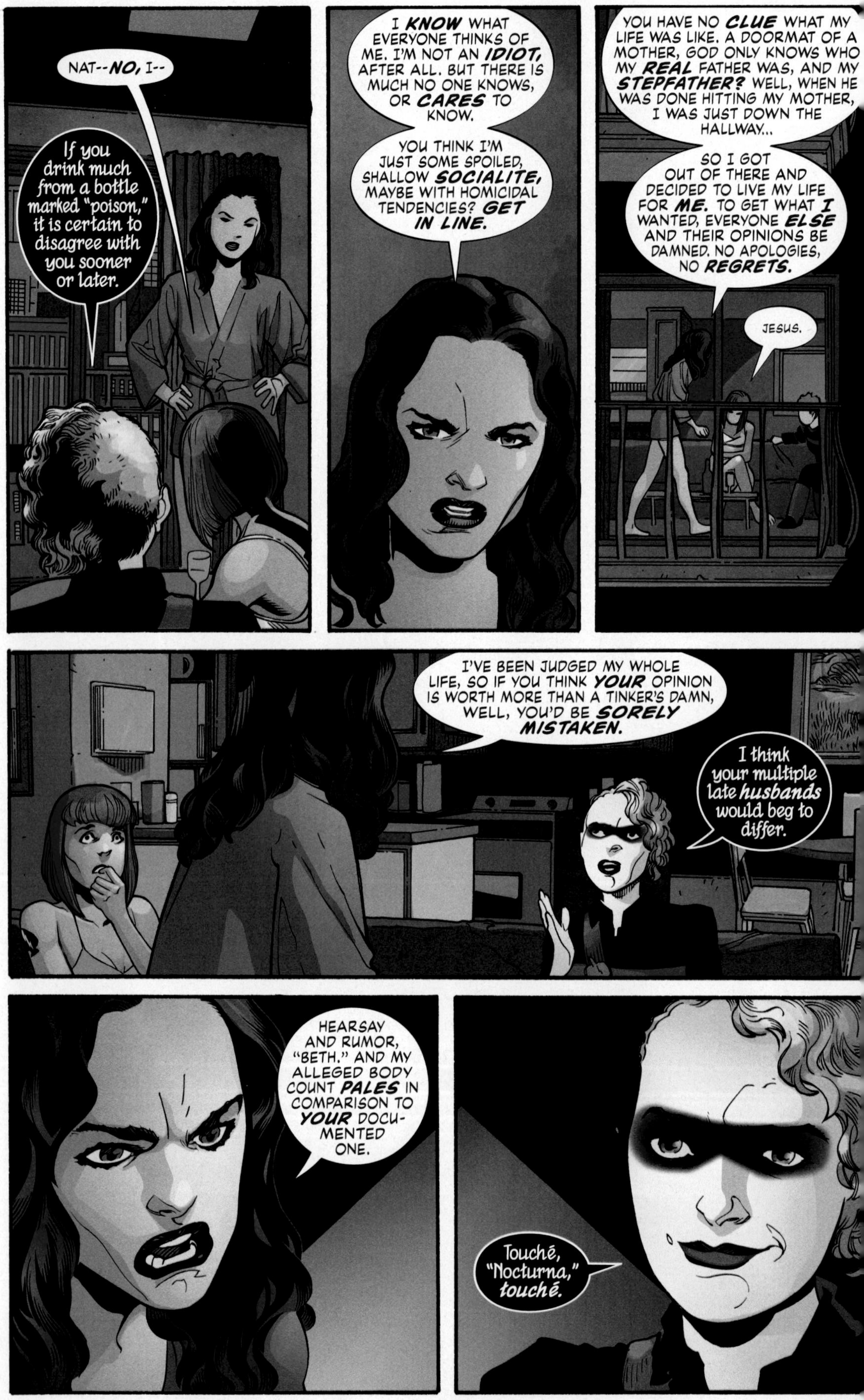
NAT--NO, I--
If you drink much from a bottle marked "poison," it is certain to disagree with you sooner or later.
I KNOW WHAT EVERYONE THINKS OF ME. I'M NOT AN IDIOT, AFTER ALL. BUT THERE IS MUCH NO ONE KNOWS, OR CARES TO KNOW.
YOU THINK I'M JUST SOME SPOILED, SHALLOW SOCIALITE, MAYBE WITH HOMICIDAL TENDENCIES? GET IN LINE.
YOU HAVE NO CLUE WHAT MY LIFE WAS LIKE. A DOORMAT OF A MOTHER, GOD ONLY KNOWS WHO MY REAL FATHER WAS, AND MY STEPFATHER? WELL, WHEN HE WAS DONE HITTING MY MOTHER, I WAS JUST DOWN THE HALLWAY...
SO I GOT OUT OF THERE AND DECIDED TO LIVE MY LIFE FOR ME. TO GET WHAT I WANTED, EVERYONE ELSE AND THEIR OPINIONS BE DAMNED. NO APOLOGIES, NO REGRETS.
JESUS.
I'VE BEEN JUDGED MY WHOLE LIFE, SO IF YOU THINK YOUR OPINION IS WORTH MORE THAN A TINKER'S DAMN, WELL, YOU'D BE SORELY MISTAKEN.
I think your multiple late husbands would beg to differ.
HEARSAY AND RUMOR, "BETH." AND MY ALLEGED BODY COUNT PALES IN COMPARISON TO YOUR DOCU-MENTED ONE.
Touché, "Nocturna," touché.

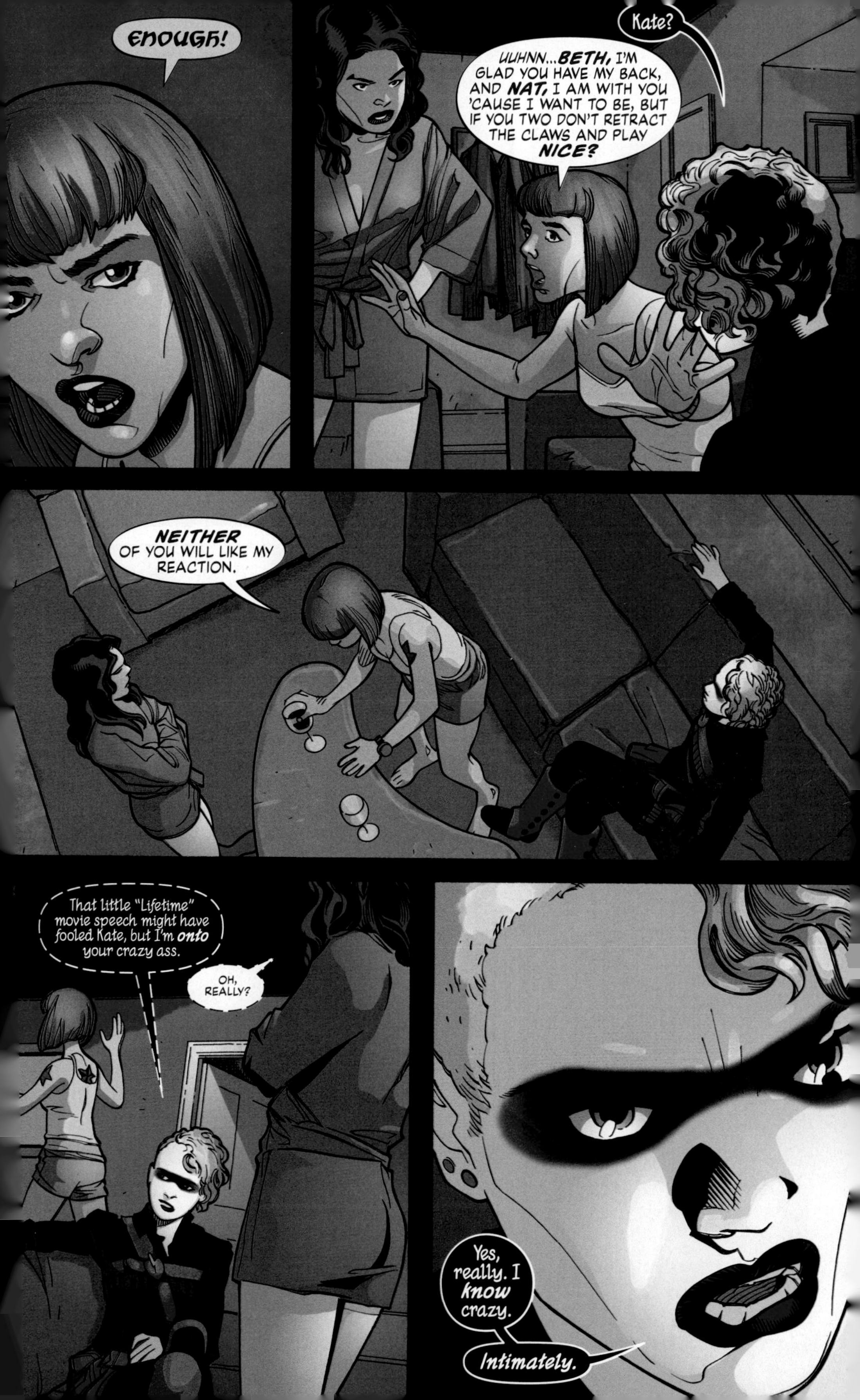
ENOUGH!
Kate?
UUHNN...BETH, I'M GLAD YOU HAVE MY BACK, AND NAT, I AM WITH YOU 'CAUSE I WANT TO BE, BUT IF YOU TWO DON'T RETRACT THE CLAWS AND PLAY NICE?
NEITHER OF YOU WILL LIKE MY REACTION.
That little "Lifetime" movie speech might have fooled Kate, but I'm onto your crazy ass.
OH, REALLY?
Yes, really. I know crazy.
Intimately.

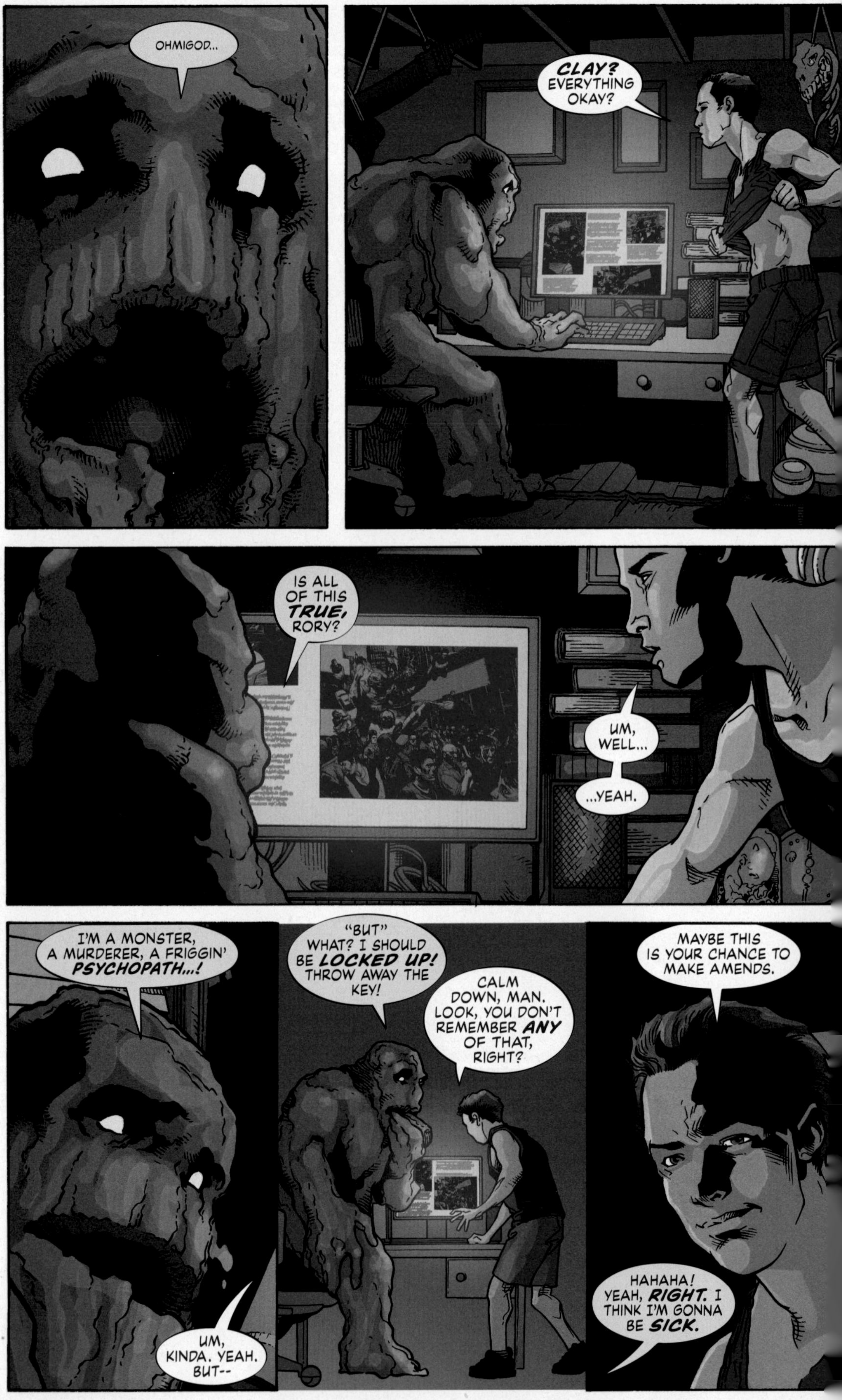
OHMIGOD...
CLAY? EVERYTHING OKAY?
IS ALL OF THIS TRUE, RORY?
UM, WELL...
...YEAH.
I'M A MONSTER, A MURDERER, A FRIGGIN' PSYCHOPATH...!
UM, KINDA. YEAH. BUT--
"BUT" WHAT? I SHOULD BE LOCKED UP! THROW AWAY THE KEY!
CALM DOWN, MAN. LOOK, YOU DON'T REMEMBER ANY OF THAT, RIGHT?
MAYBE THIS IS YOUR CHANCE TO MAKE AMENDS.
HAHAHA! YEAH, RIGHT. I THINK I'M GONNA BE SICK.

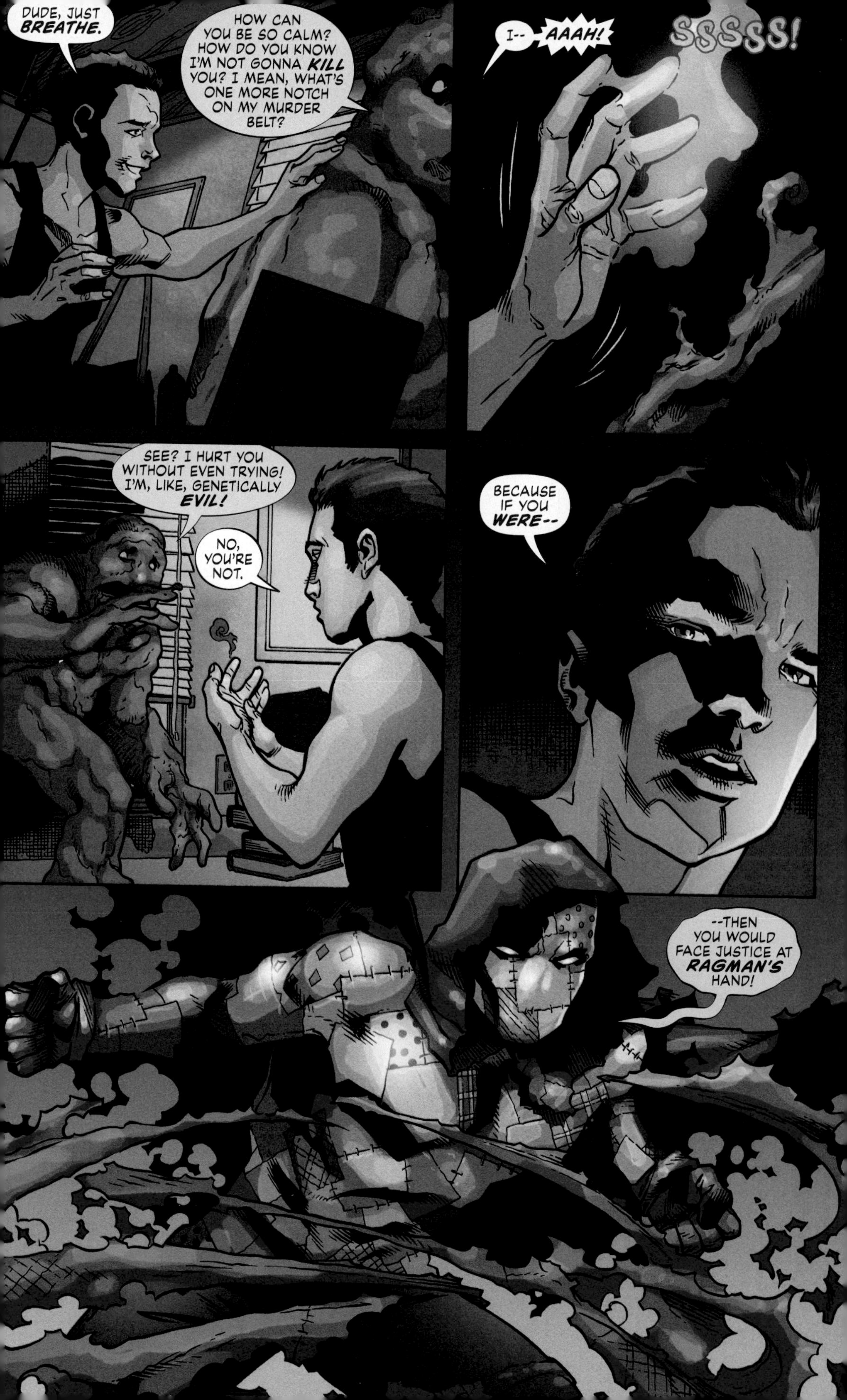
DUDE, JUST BREATHE.
HOW CAN YOU BE SO CALM? HOW DO YOU KNOW I'M NOT GONNA KILL YOU? I MEAN, WHAT'S ONE MORE NOTCH ON MY MURDER BELT?
I-- AAAH!
SSSSS!
SEE? I HURT YOU WITHOUT EVEN TRYING! I'M, LIKE, GENETICALLY EVIL!
NO, YOU'RE NOT.
BECAUSE IF YOU WERE--
--THEN YOU WOULD FACE JUSTICE AT RAGMAN'S HAND!

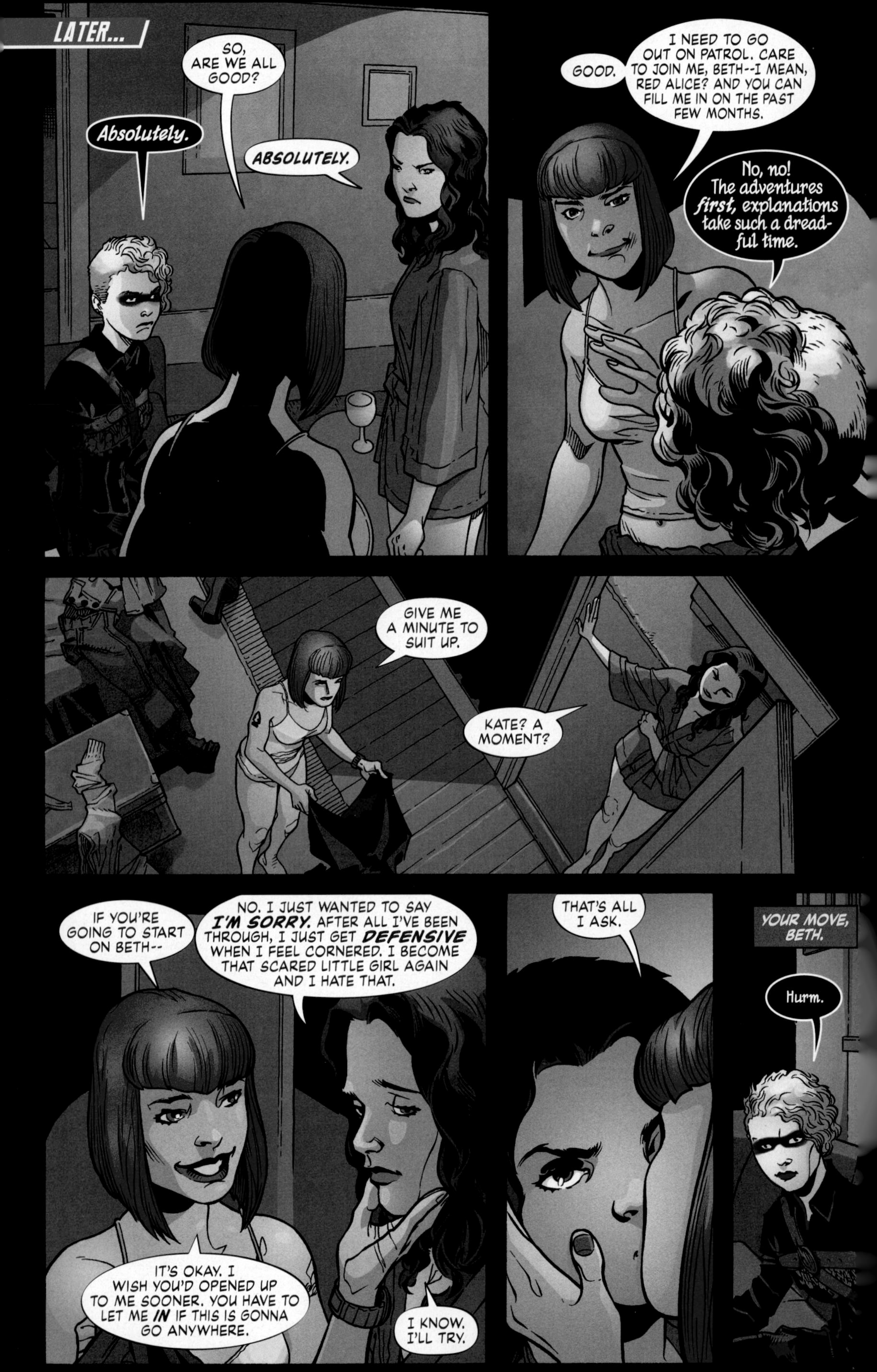
LATER...
SO, ARE WE ALL GOOD?
Absolutely.
ABSOLUTELY.
GOOD.
I NEED TO GO OUT ON PATROL. CARE TO JOIN ME, BETH--I MEAN, RED ALICE? AND YOU CAN FILL ME IN ON THE PAST FEW MONTHS.
No, no! The adventures *first*, explanations take such a dreadful time.
GIVE ME A MINUTE TO SUIT UP.
KATE? A MOMENT?
IF YOU'RE GOING TO START ON BETH--
NO. I JUST WANTED TO SAY ***I'M SORRY.*** AFTER ALL I'VE BEEN THROUGH, I JUST GET ***DEFENSIVE*** WHEN I FEEL CORNERED. I BECOME THAT SCARED LITTLE GIRL AGAIN AND I HATE THAT.
IT'S OKAY. I WISH YOU'D OPENED UP TO ME SOONER. YOU HAVE TO LET ME ***IN*** IF THIS IS GONNA GO ANYWHERE.
I KNOW. I'LL TRY.
THAT'S ALL I ASK.
YOUR MOVE, BETH.
Hurm.

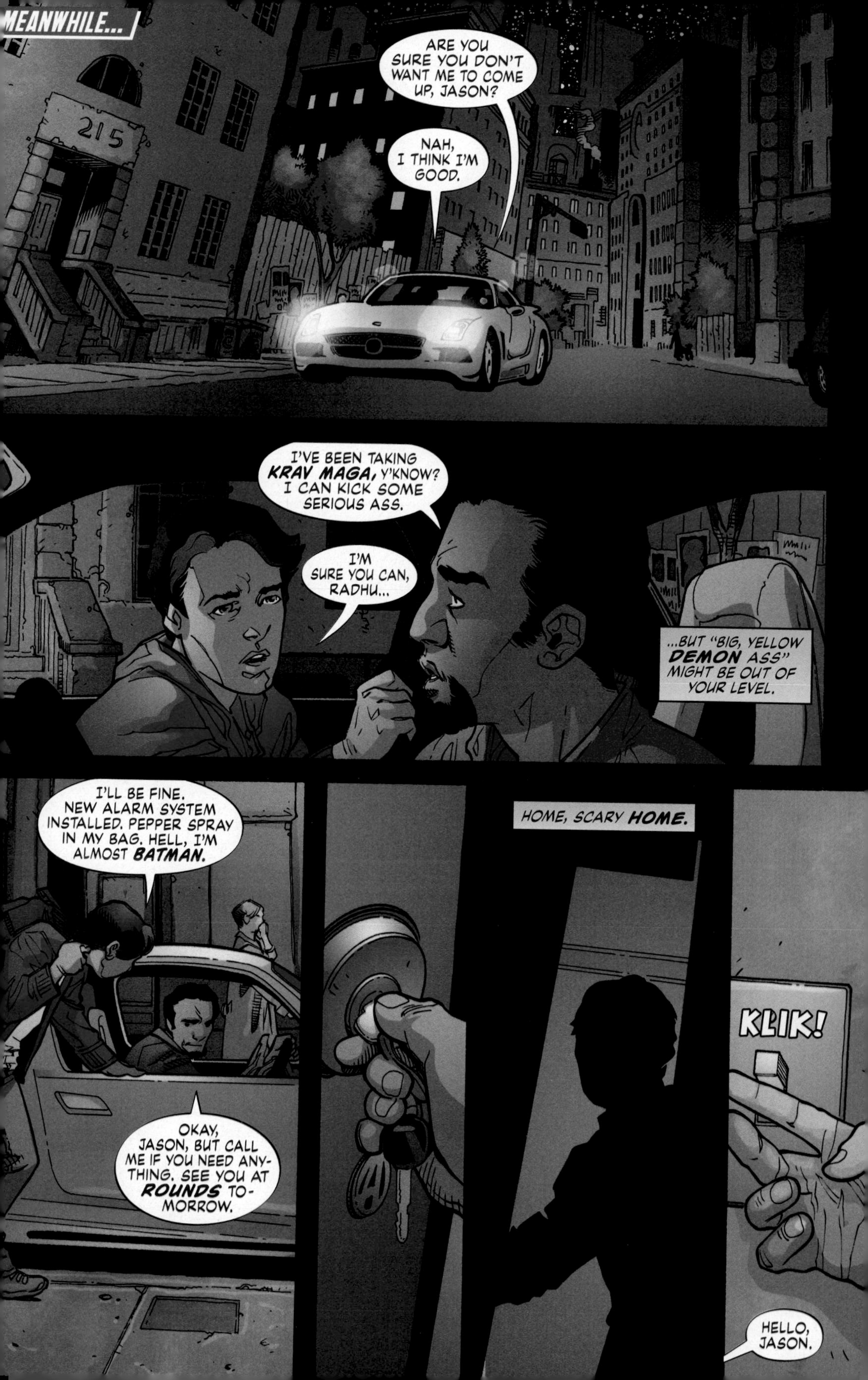
MEANWHILE...
ARE YOU SURE YOU DON'T WANT ME TO COME UP, JASON?
NAH, I THINK I'M GOOD.
215
I'VE BEEN TAKING KRAV MAGA, Y'KNOW? I CAN KICK SOME SERIOUS ASS.
I'M SURE YOU CAN, RADHU...
...BUT "BIG, YELLOW DEMON ASS" MIGHT BE OUT OF YOUR LEVEL.
I'LL BE FINE. NEW ALARM SYSTEM INSTALLED. PEPPER SPRAY IN MY BAG. HELL, I'M ALMOST BATMAN.
OKAY, JASON, BUT CALL ME IF YOU NEED ANY-THING. SEE YOU AT ROUNDS TO-MORROW.
HOME, SCARY HOME.
KLIK!
HELLO, JASON.

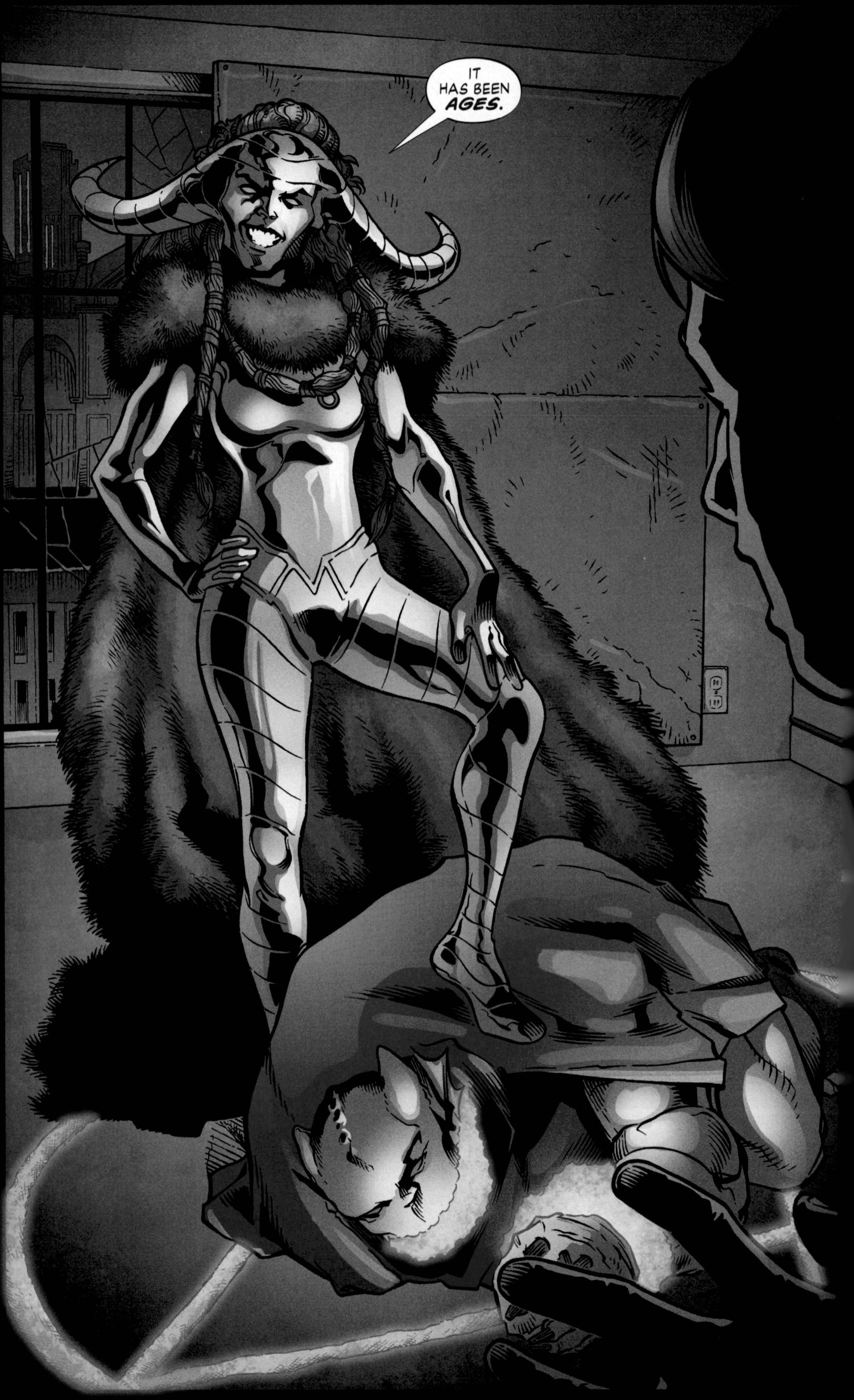
IT HAS BEEN *AGES.*

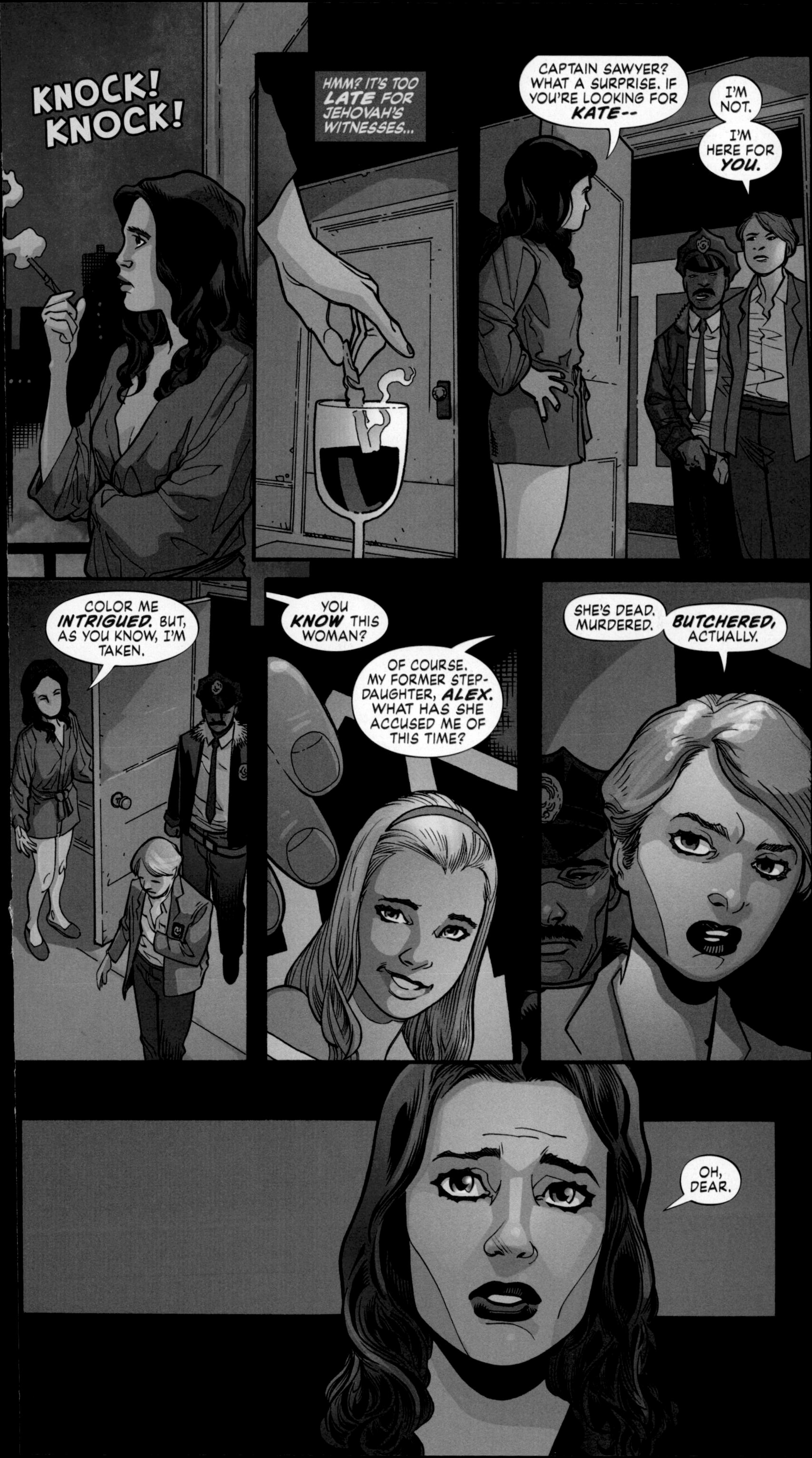
KNOCK! KNOCK!
HMM? IT'S TOO LATE FOR JEHOVAH'S WITNESSES...
CAPTAIN SAWYER? WHAT A SURPRISE. IF YOU'RE LOOKING FOR KATE--
I'M NOT.
I'M HERE FOR YOU.
COLOR ME INTRIGUED. BUT, AS YOU KNOW, I'M TAKEN.
YOU KNOW THIS WOMAN?
OF COURSE. MY FORMER STEP-DAUGHTER, ALEX. WHAT HAS SHE ACCUSED ME OF THIS TIME?
SHE'S DEAD. MURDERED.
BUTCHERED, ACTUALLY.
OH, DEAR.

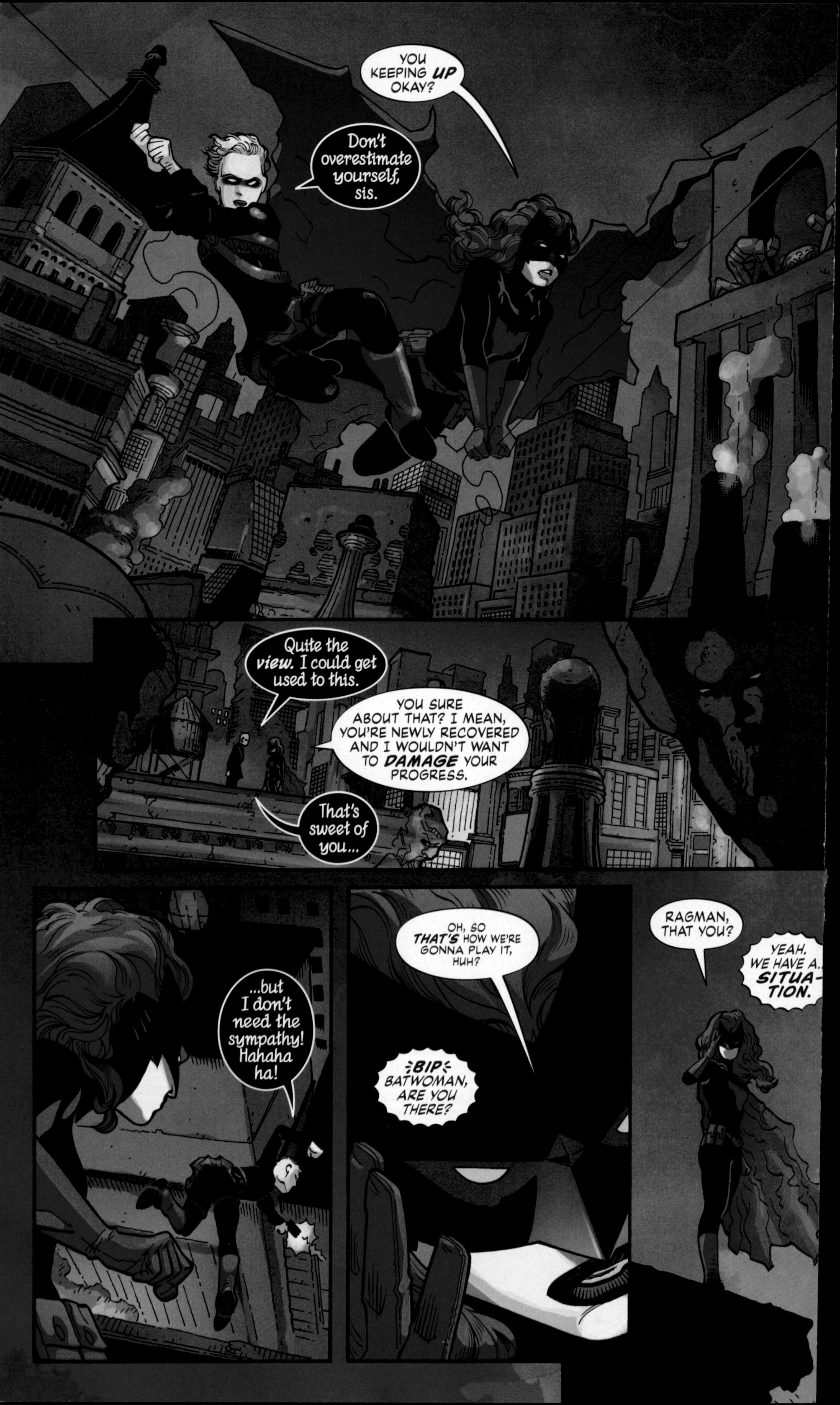
YOU KEEPING UP OKAY?
Don't overestimate yourself, sis.
Quite the view. I could get used to this.
YOU SURE ABOUT THAT? I MEAN, YOU'RE NEWLY RECOVERED AND I WOULDN'T WANT TO DAMAGE YOUR PROGRESS.
That's sweet of you...
...but I don't need the sympathy! Hahaha ha!
OH, SO THAT'S HOW WE'RE GONNA PLAY IT, HUH?
BIP
BATWOMAN, ARE YOU THERE?
RAGMAN, THAT YOU?
YEAH. WE HAVE A... SITUATION.

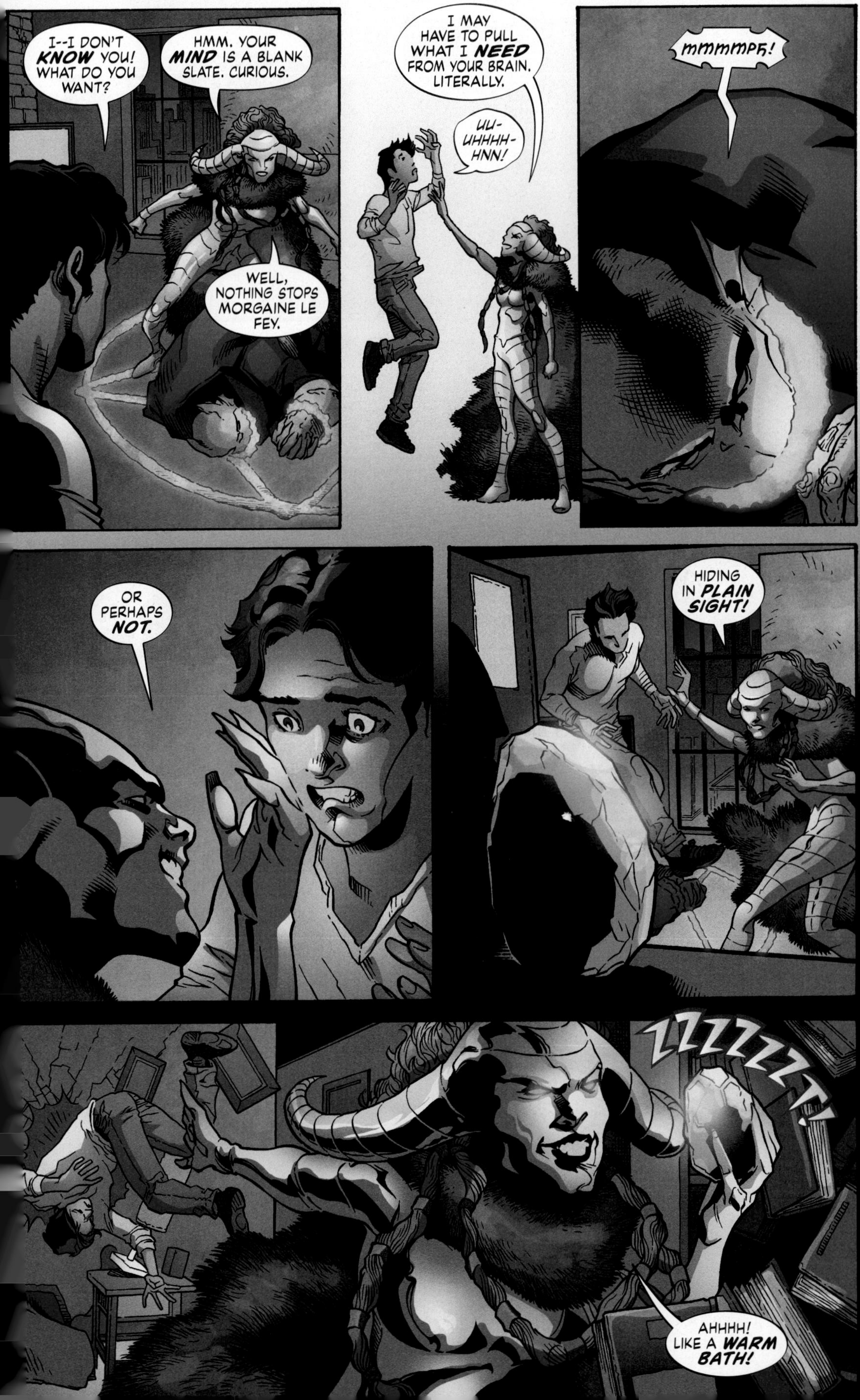
I--I DON'T KNOW YOU! WHAT DO YOU WANT?
HMM. YOUR MIND IS A BLANK SLATE. CURIOUS.
WELL, NOTHING STOPS MORGAINE LE FEY.
I MAY HAVE TO PULL WHAT I NEED FROM YOUR BRAIN. LITERALLY.
UU-UHHHH-HNN!
MMMMPH!
OR PERHAPS NOT.
HIDING IN PLAIN SIGHT!
ZZZZZZT!
AHHHH! LIKE A WARM BATH!

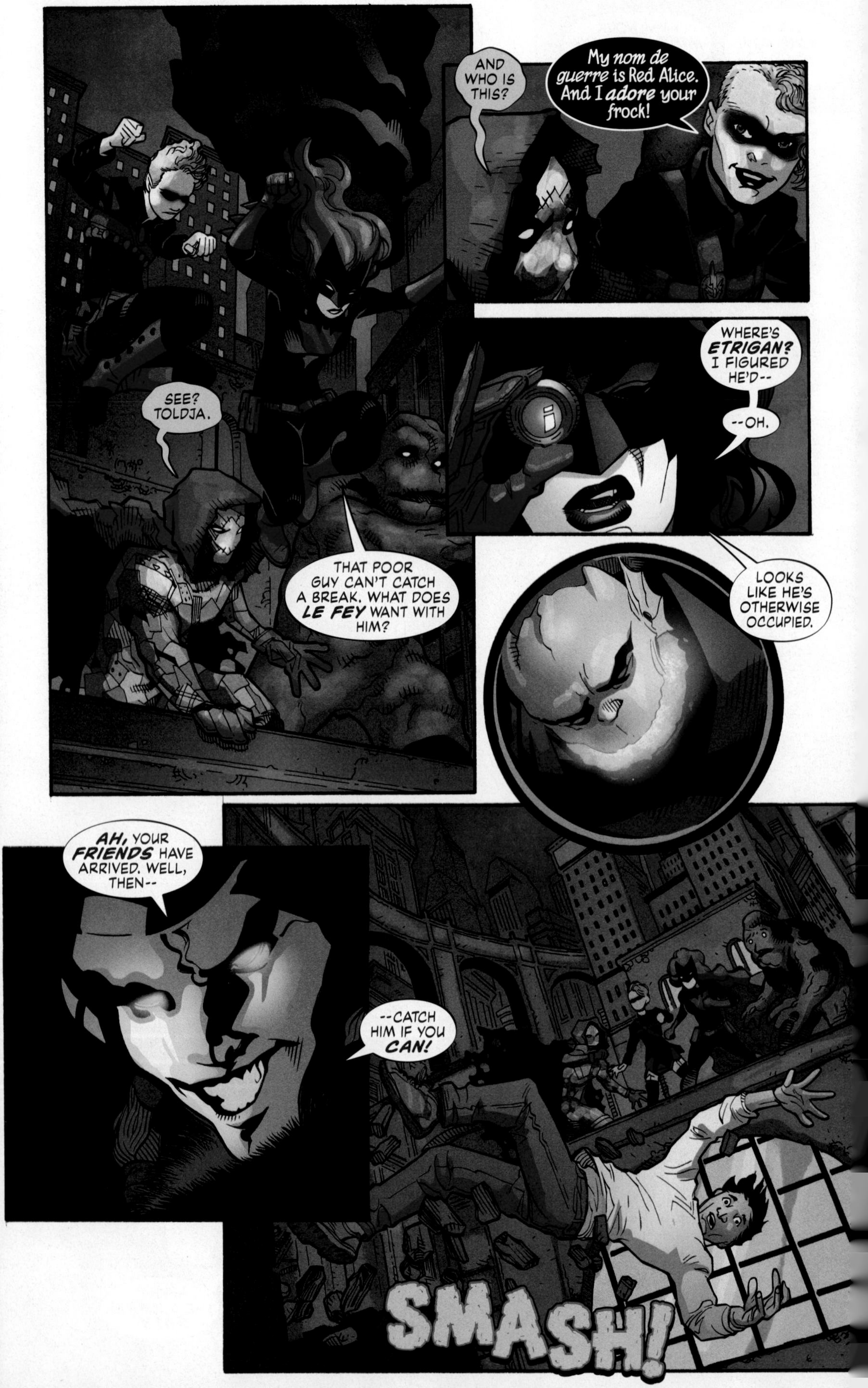
AND WHO IS THIS?
My nom de guerre is Red Alice. And I adore your frock!
SEE? TOLDJA.
THAT POOR GUY CAN'T CATCH A BREAK. WHAT DOES LE FEY WANT WITH HIM?
WHERE'S ETRIGAN? I FIGURED HE'D--
--OH.
LOOKS LIKE HE'S OTHERWISE OCCUPIED.
AH, YOUR FRIENDS HAVE ARRIVED. WELL, THEN--
--CATCH HIM IF YOU CAN!
SMASH!

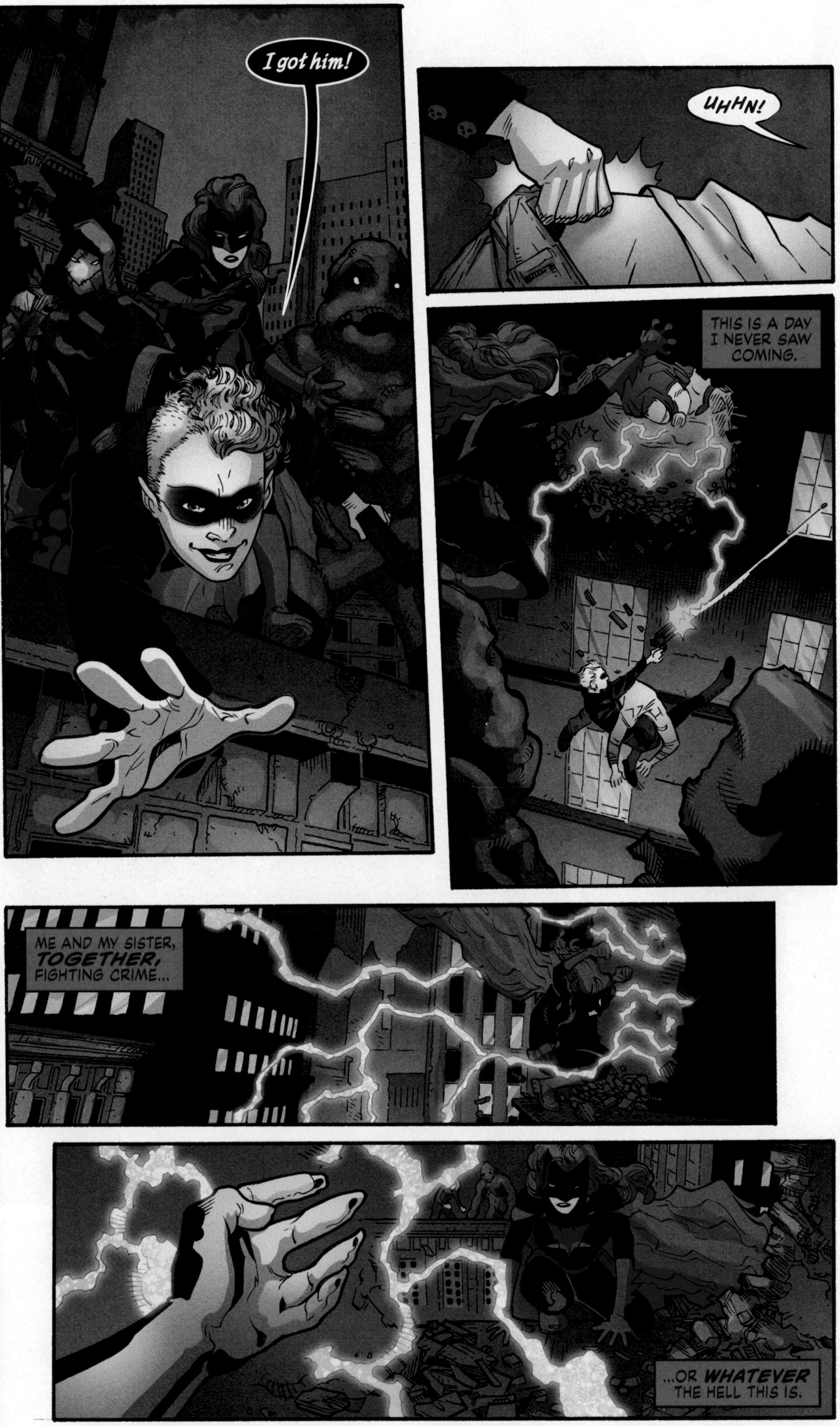
I got him!
UHHN!
THIS IS A DAY I NEVER SAW COMING.
ME AND MY SISTER, *TOGETHER,* FIGHTING CRIME...
...OR *WHATEVER* THE HELL THIS IS.

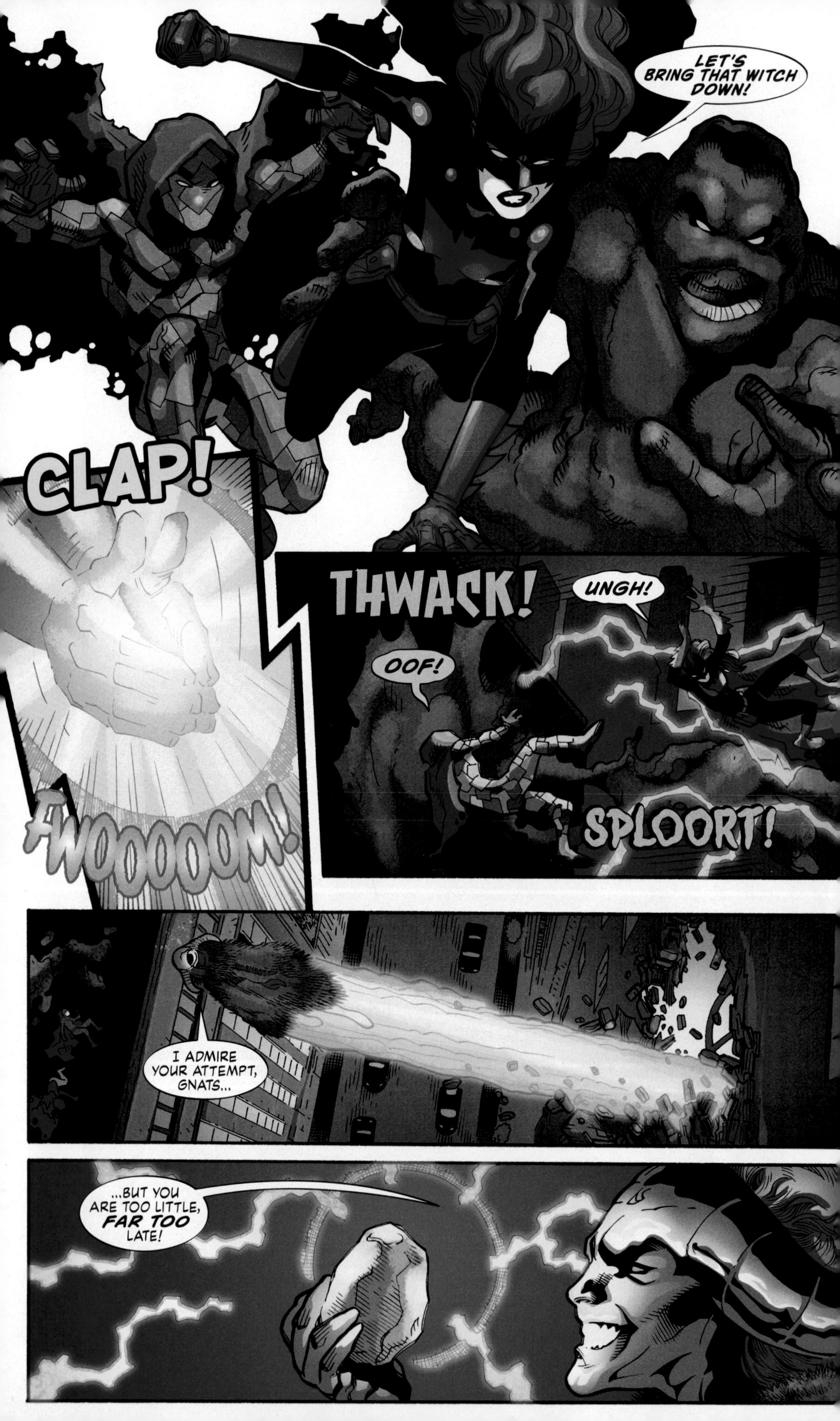
LET'S BRING THAT WITCH DOWN!
CLAP!
FWOOOOOM!
THWACK!
UNGH!
OOF!
SPLOORT!
I ADMIRE YOUR ATTEMPT, GNATS...
...BUT YOU ARE TOO LITTLE, FAR TOO LATE!

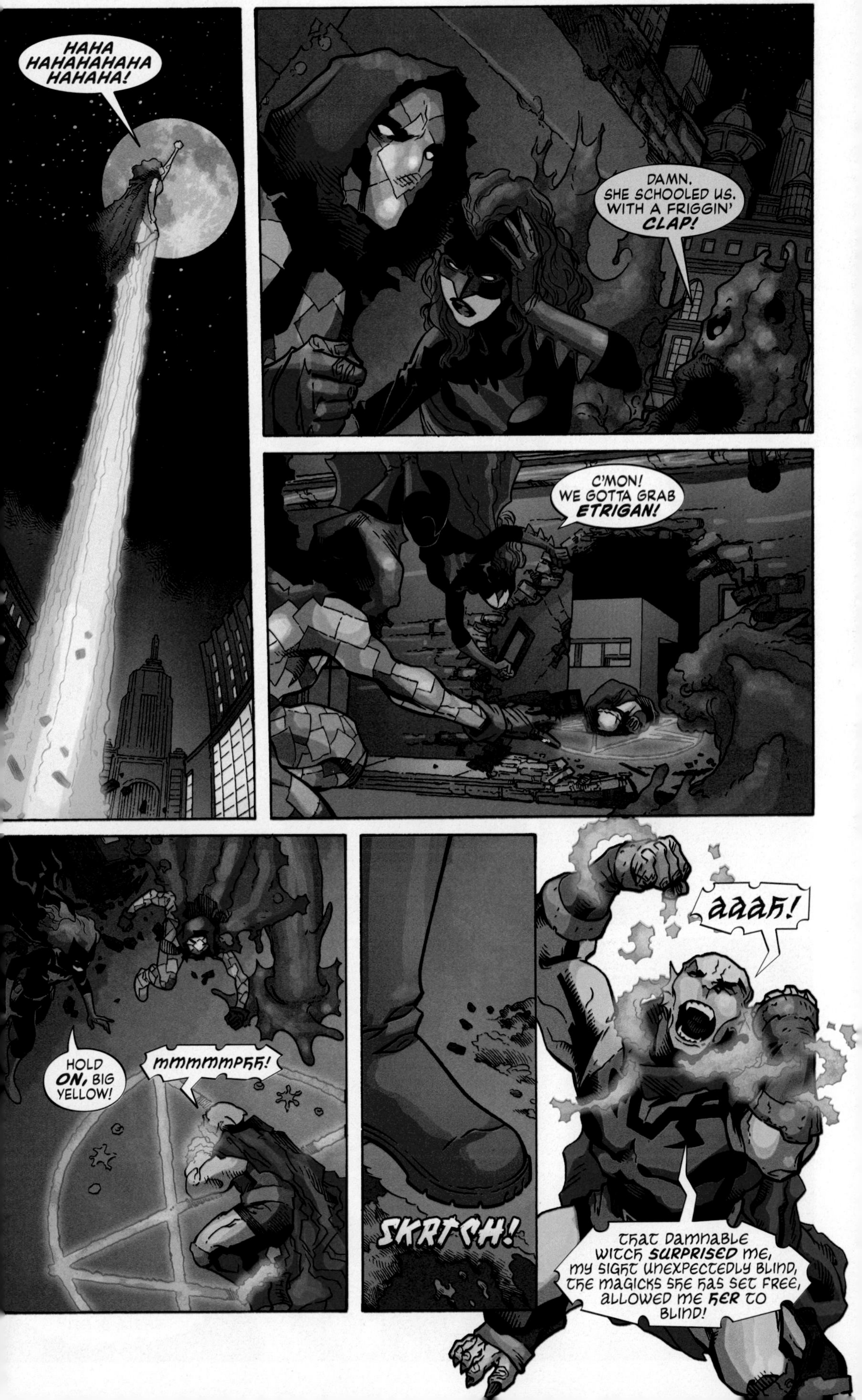
HAHA HAHAHAHAHA HAHAHA!
DAMN. SHE SCHOOLED US. WITH A FRIGGIN' CLAP!
C'MON! WE GOTTA GRAB ETRIGAN!
HOLD ON, BIG YELLOW!
MMMMMPHH!
SKRTCH!
AAAH!
THAT DAMNABLE WITCH SURPRISED ME, MY SIGHT UNEXPECTEDLY BLIND, THE MAGICKS SHE HAS SET FREE, ALLOWED ME HER TO BLIND!

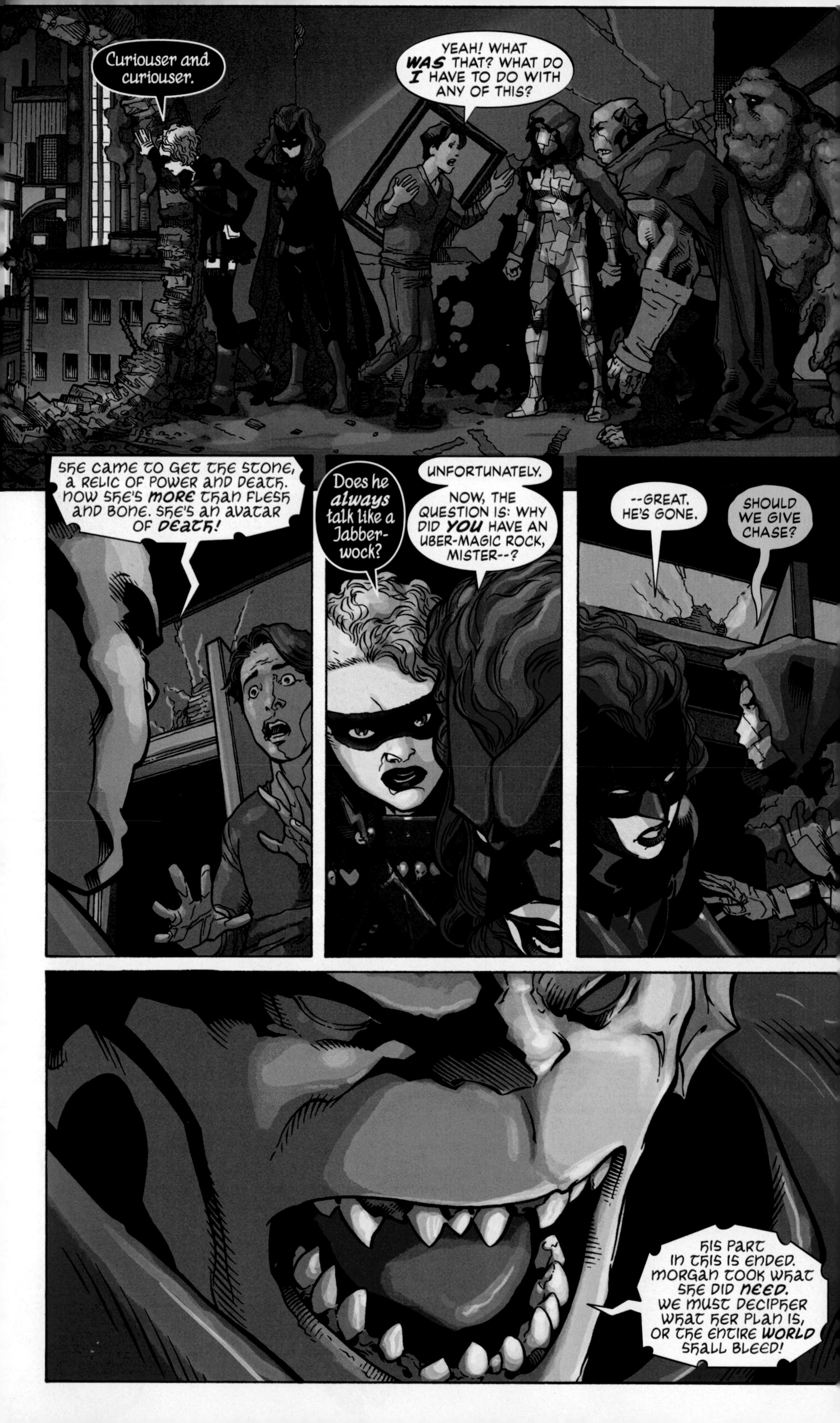
Curiouser and curiouser.
YEAH! WHAT WAS THAT? WHAT DO I HAVE TO DO WITH ANY OF THIS?
SHE CAME TO GET THE STONE, A RELIC OF POWER AND DEATH. NOW SHE'S MORE THAN FLESH AND BONE. SHE'S AN AVATAR OF DEATH!
Does he always talk like a Jabber-wock?
UNFORTUNATELY.
NOW, THE QUESTION IS: WHY DID YOU HAVE AN UBER-MAGIC ROCK, MISTER--?
--GREAT. HE'S GONE.
SHOULD WE GIVE CHASE?
HIS PART IN THIS IS ENDED. MORGAN TOOK WHAT SHE DID NEED. WE MUST DECIPHER WHAT HER PLAN IS, OR THE ENTIRE WORLD SHALL BLEED!

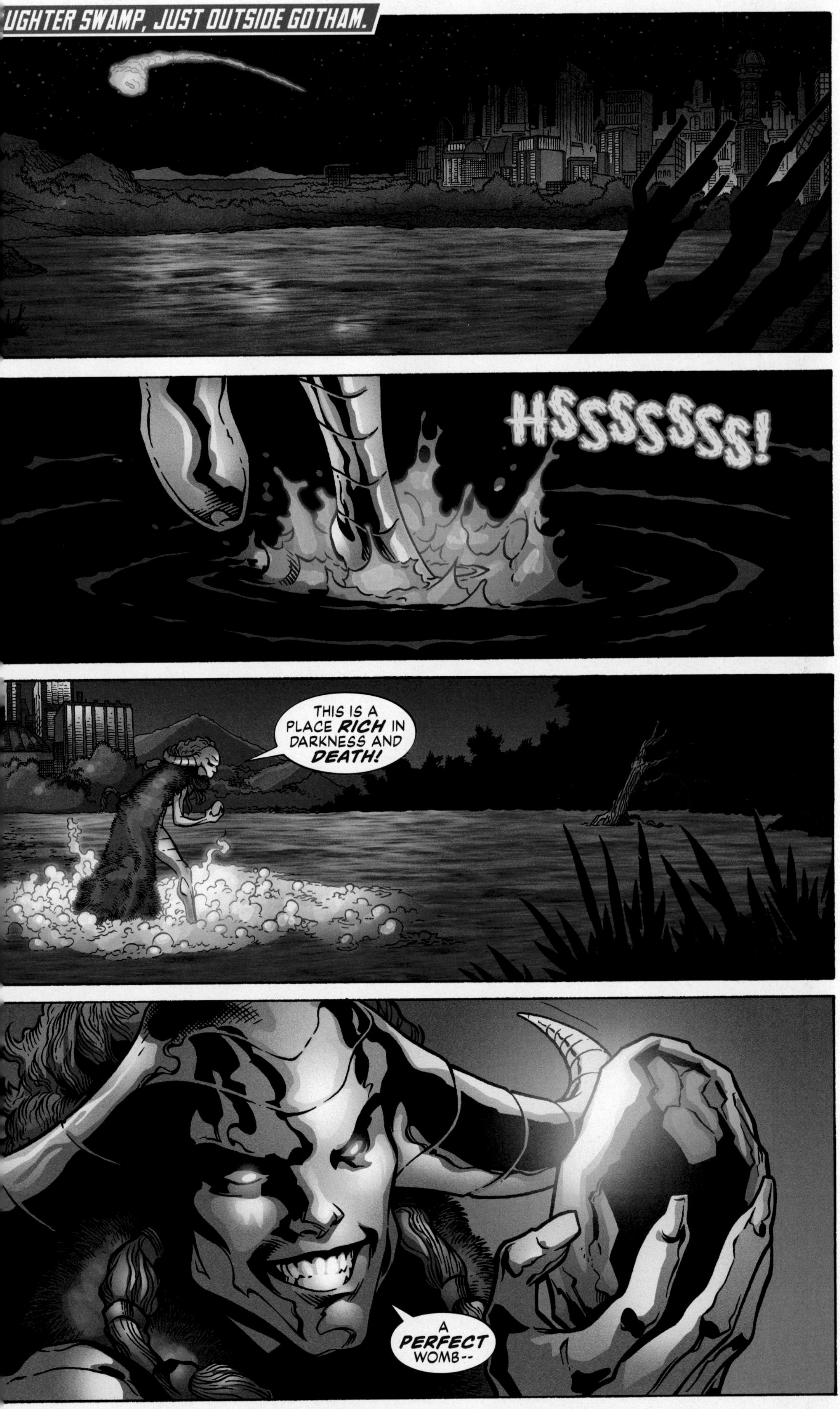
UGHTER SWAMP, JUST OUTSIDE GOTHAM.
HSSSSSSS!
THIS IS A PLACE RICH IN DARKNESS AND DEATH!
A PERFECT WOMB--

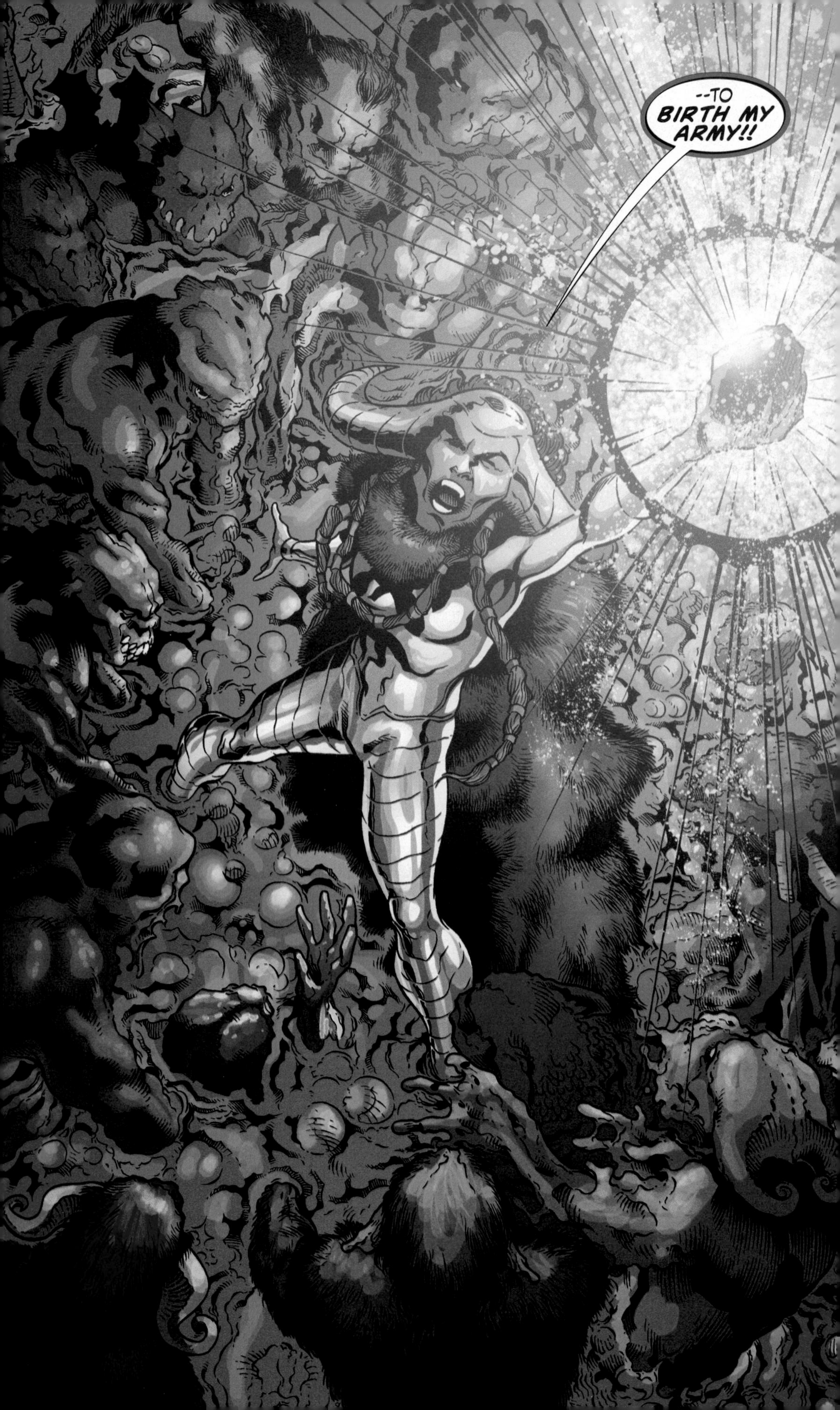
--TO BIRTH MY ARMY!!

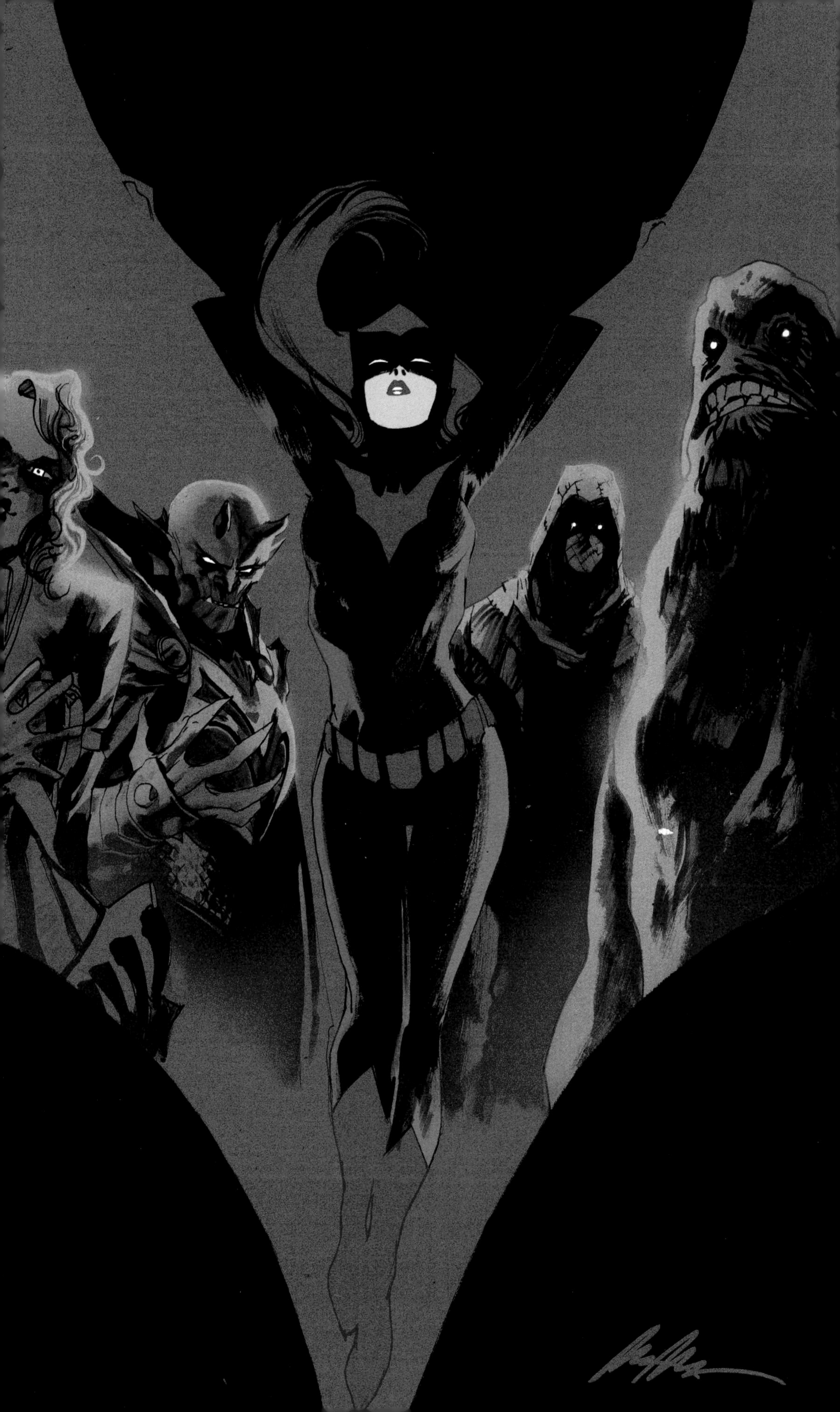

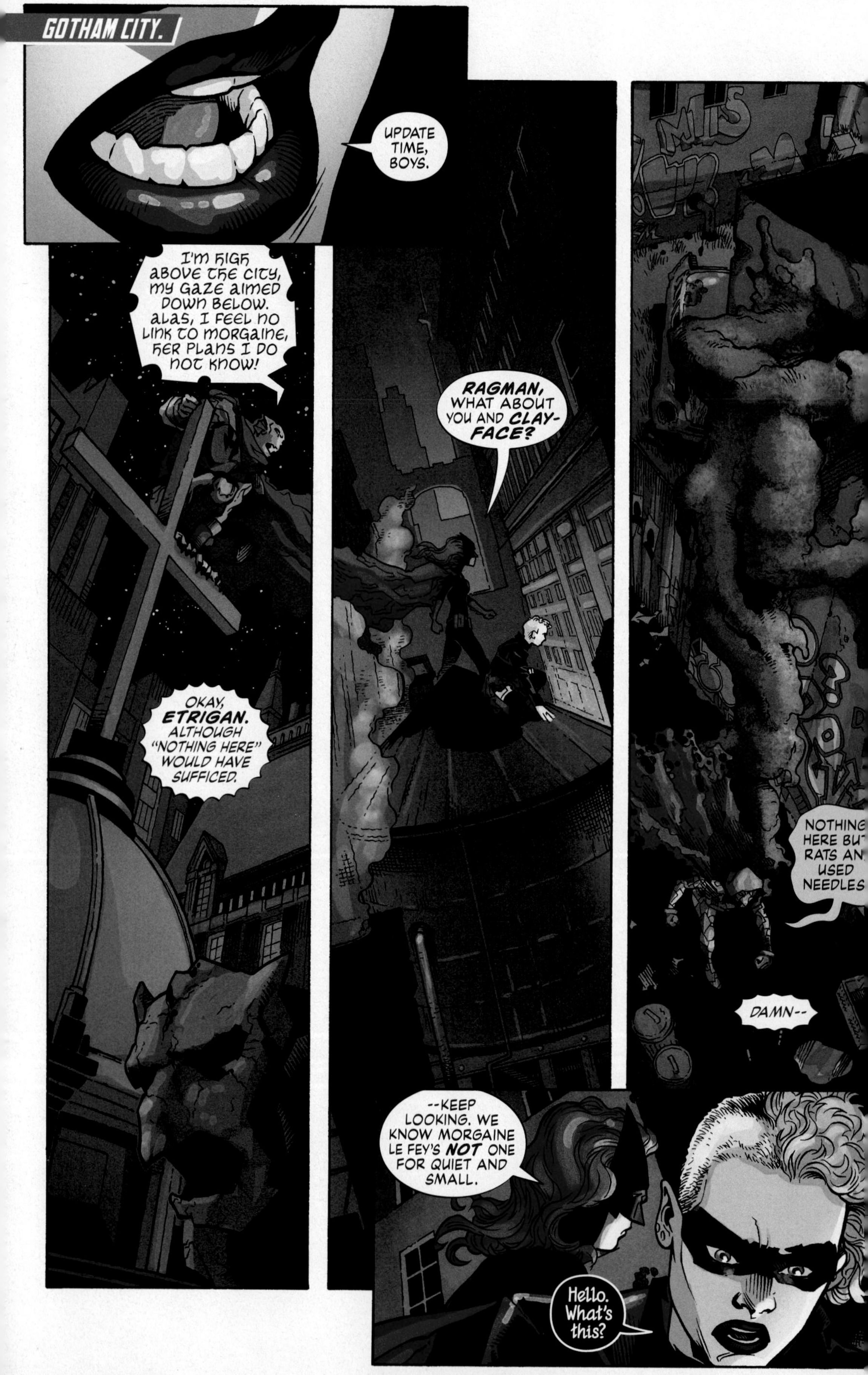
GOTHAM CITY.
UPDATE TIME, BOYS.
I'M HIGH ABOVE THE CITY, MY GAZE AIMED DOWN BELOW. ALAS, I FEEL NO LINK TO MORGAINE, HER PLANS I DO NOT KNOW!
OKAY, ETRIGAN. ALTHOUGH "NOTHING HERE" WOULD HAVE SUFFICED.
RAGMAN, WHAT ABOUT YOU AND CLAY-FACE?
NOTHING HERE BU RATS AN USED NEEDLES
DAMN--
--KEEP LOOKING. WE KNOW MORGAINE LE FEY'S NOT ONE FOR QUIET AND SMALL.
Hello. What's this?

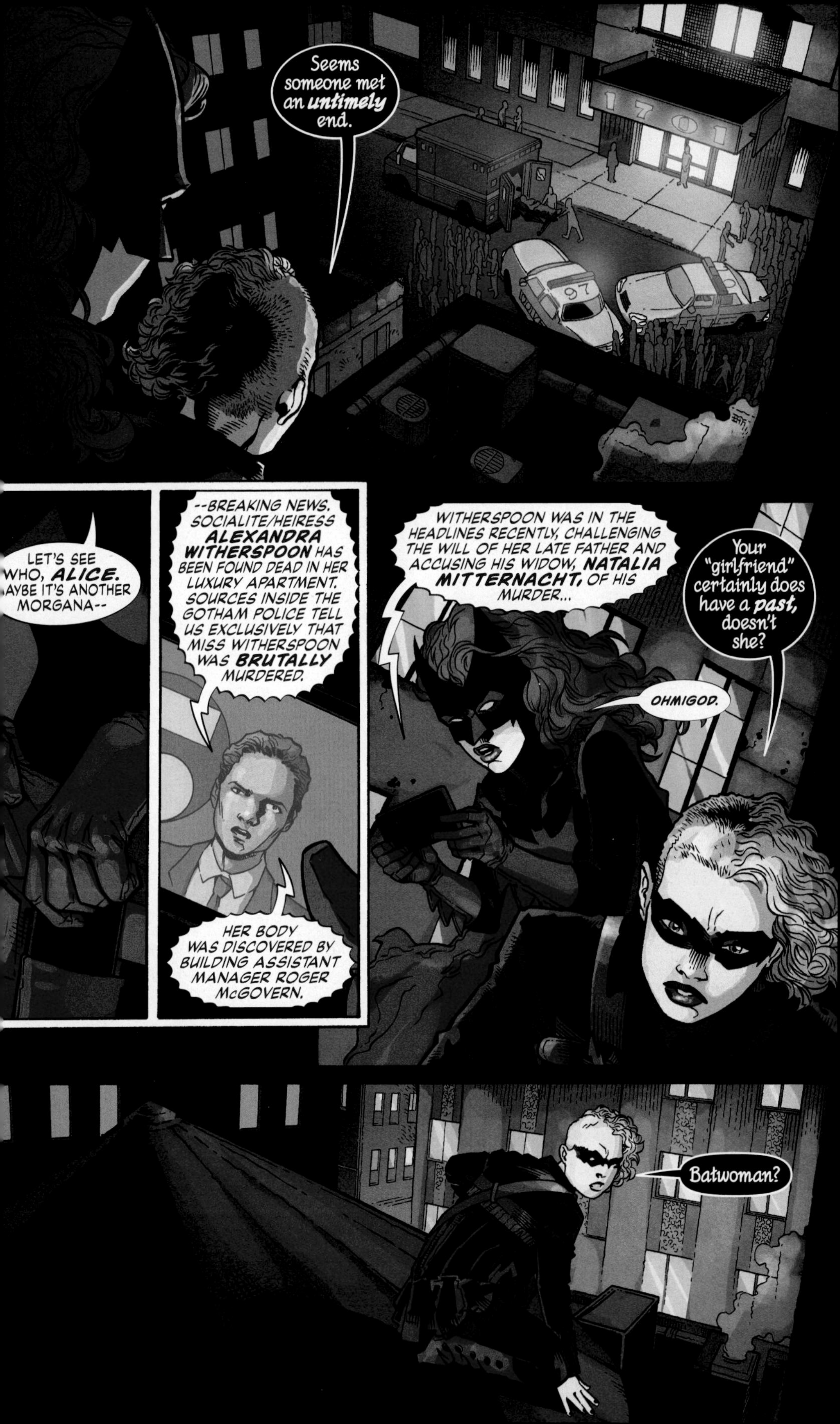
Seems someone met an *untimely* end.
LET'S SEE WHO, **ALICE.** AYBE IT'S ANOTHER MORGANA--
--BREAKING NEWS. SOCIALITE/HEIRESS **ALEXANDRA WITHERSPOON** HAS BEEN FOUND DEAD IN HER LUXURY APARTMENT. SOURCES INSIDE THE GOTHAM POLICE TELL US EXCLUSIVELY THAT MISS WITHERSPOON WAS **BRUTALLY** MURDERED.
HER BODY WAS DISCOVERED BY BUILDING ASSISTANT MANAGER ROGER McGOVERN.
WITHERSPOON WAS IN THE HEADLINES RECENTLY, CHALLENGING THE WILL OF HER LATE FATHER AND ACCUSING HIS WIDOW, **NATALIA MITTERNACHT,** OF HIS MURDER...
Your "girlfriend" certainly does have a *past,* doesn't she?
OHMIGOD.
Batwoman?

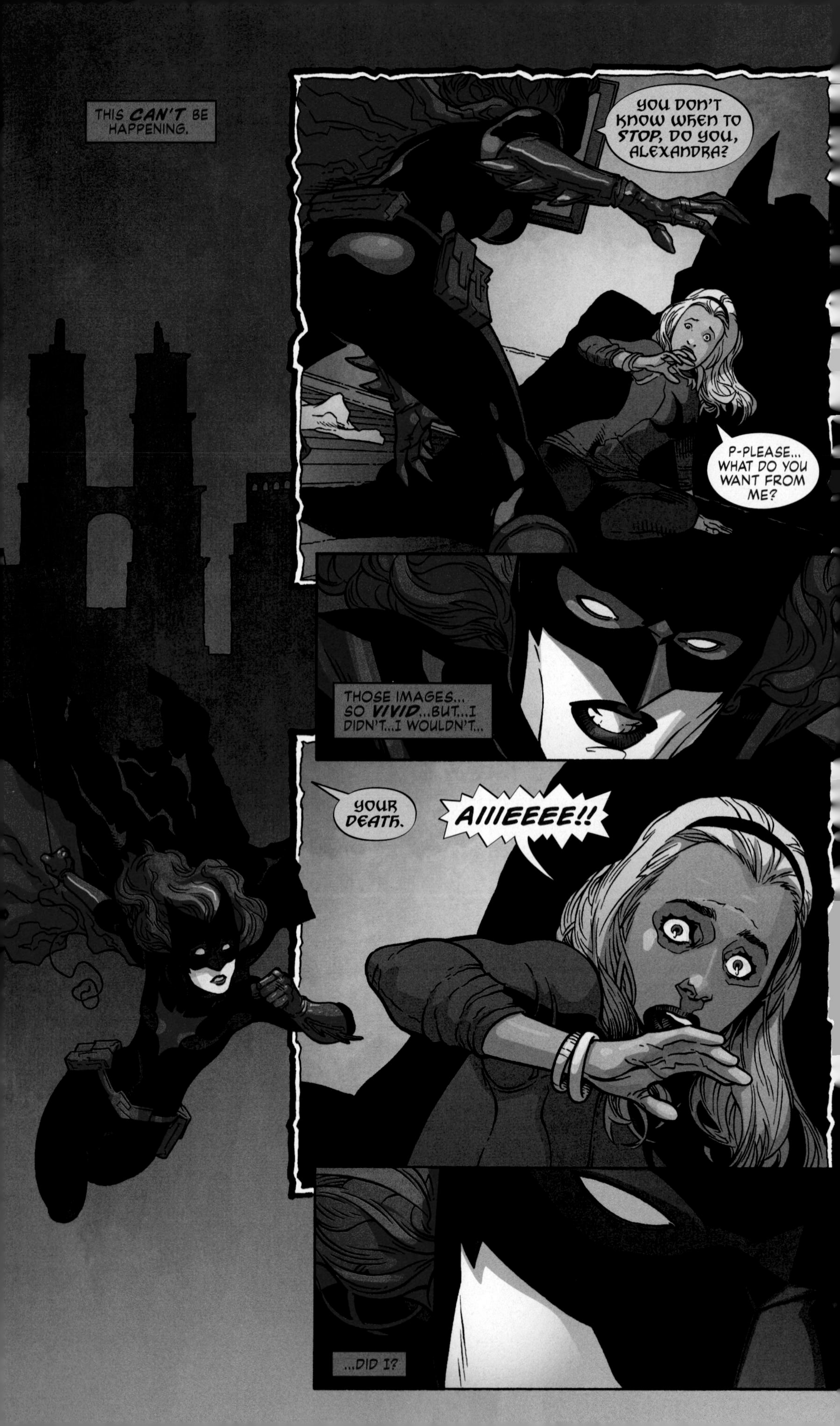
THIS CAN'T BE HAPPENING.
YOU DON'T KNOW WHEN TO STOP, DO YOU, ALEXANDRA?
P-PLEASE... WHAT DO YOU WANT FROM ME?
THOSE IMAGES... SO VIVID...BUT...I DIDN'T...I WOULDN'T...
YOUR DEATH.
AIIIEEEE!!
...DID I?

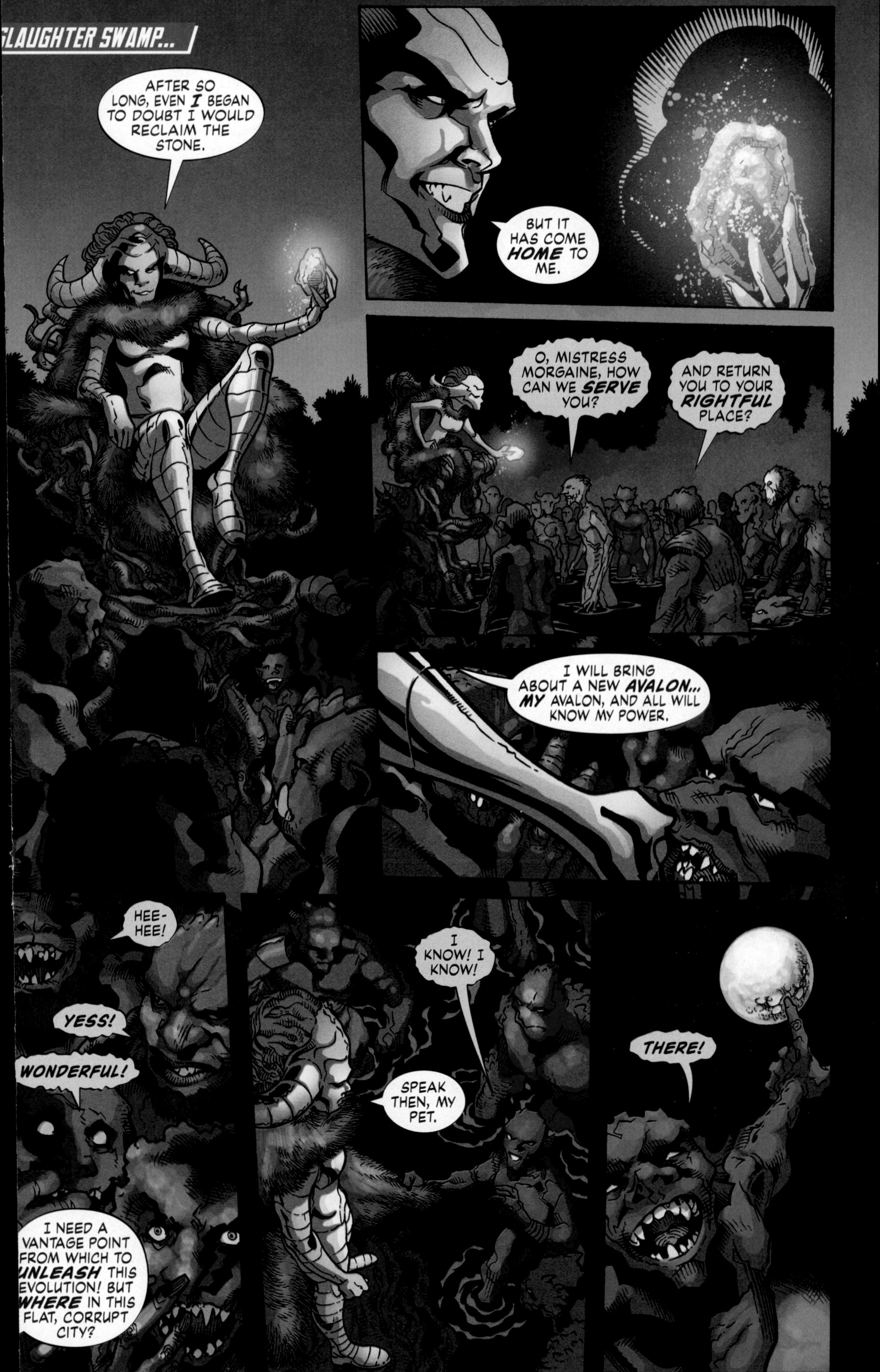
SLAUGHTER SWAMP...
AFTER SO LONG, EVEN I BEGAN TO DOUBT I WOULD RECLAIM THE STONE.
BUT IT HAS COME HOME TO ME.
O, MISTRESS MORGAINE, HOW CAN WE SERVE YOU?
AND RETURN YOU TO YOUR RIGHTFUL PLACE?
I WILL BRING ABOUT A NEW AVALON... MY AVALON, AND ALL WILL KNOW MY POWER.
HEE-HEE!
YESS!
WONDERFUL!
I NEED A VANTAGE POINT FROM WHICH TO UNLEASH THIS EVOLUTION! BUT WHERE IN THIS FLAT, CORRUPT CITY?
I KNOW! I KNOW!
SPEAK THEN, MY PET.
THERE!

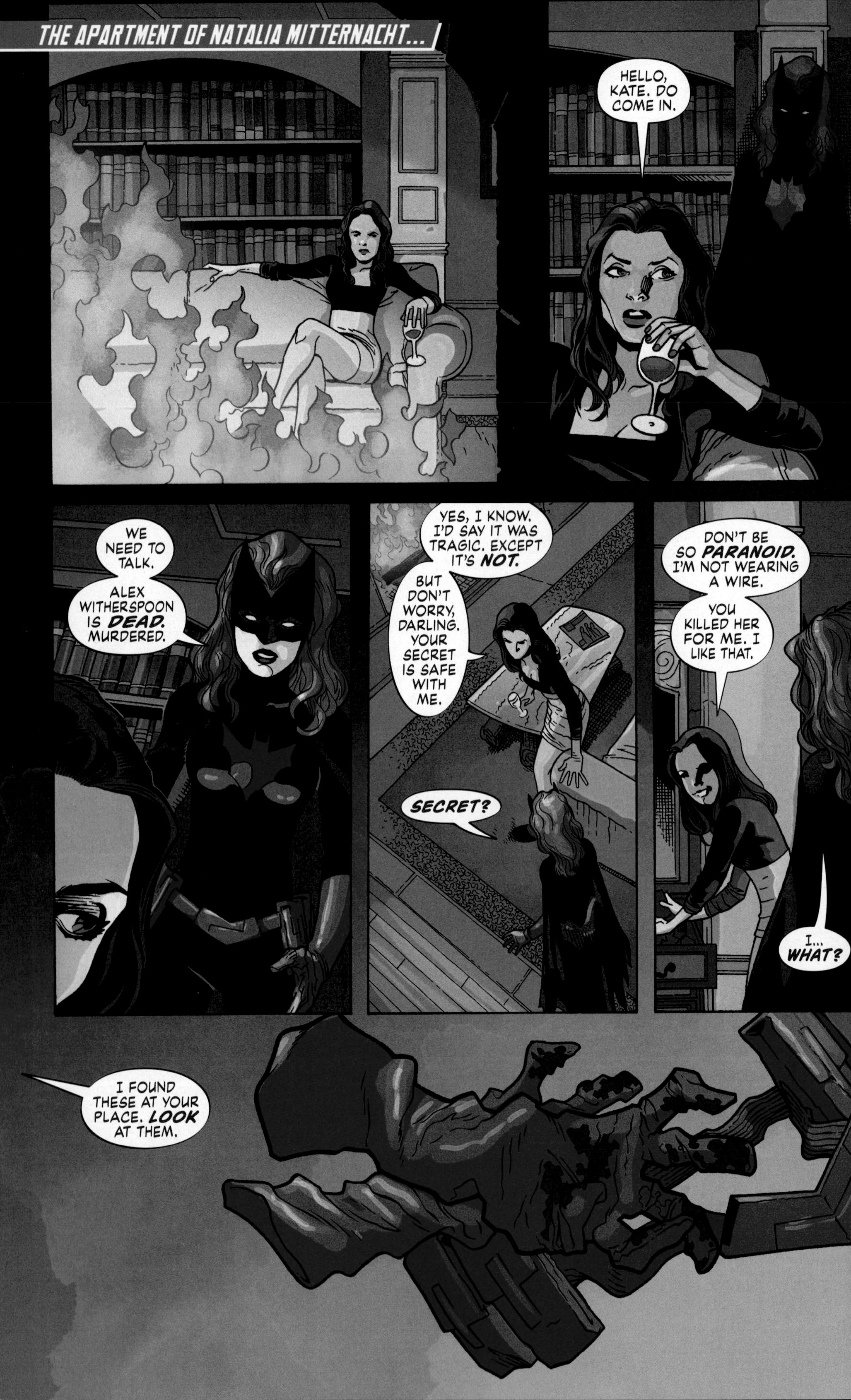
THE APARTMENT OF NATALIA MITTERNACHT...
HELLO, KATE. DO COME IN.
WE NEED TO TALK.
ALEX WITHERSPOON IS DEAD. MURDERED.
YES, I KNOW. I'D SAY IT WAS TRAGIC. EXCEPT IT'S NOT.
BUT DON'T WORRY, DARLING. YOUR SECRET IS SAFE WITH ME.
SECRET?
DON'T BE SO PARANOID. I'M NOT WEARING A WIRE.
YOU KILLED HER FOR ME. I LIKE THAT.
I... WHAT?
I FOUND THESE AT YOUR PLACE. LOOK AT THEM.

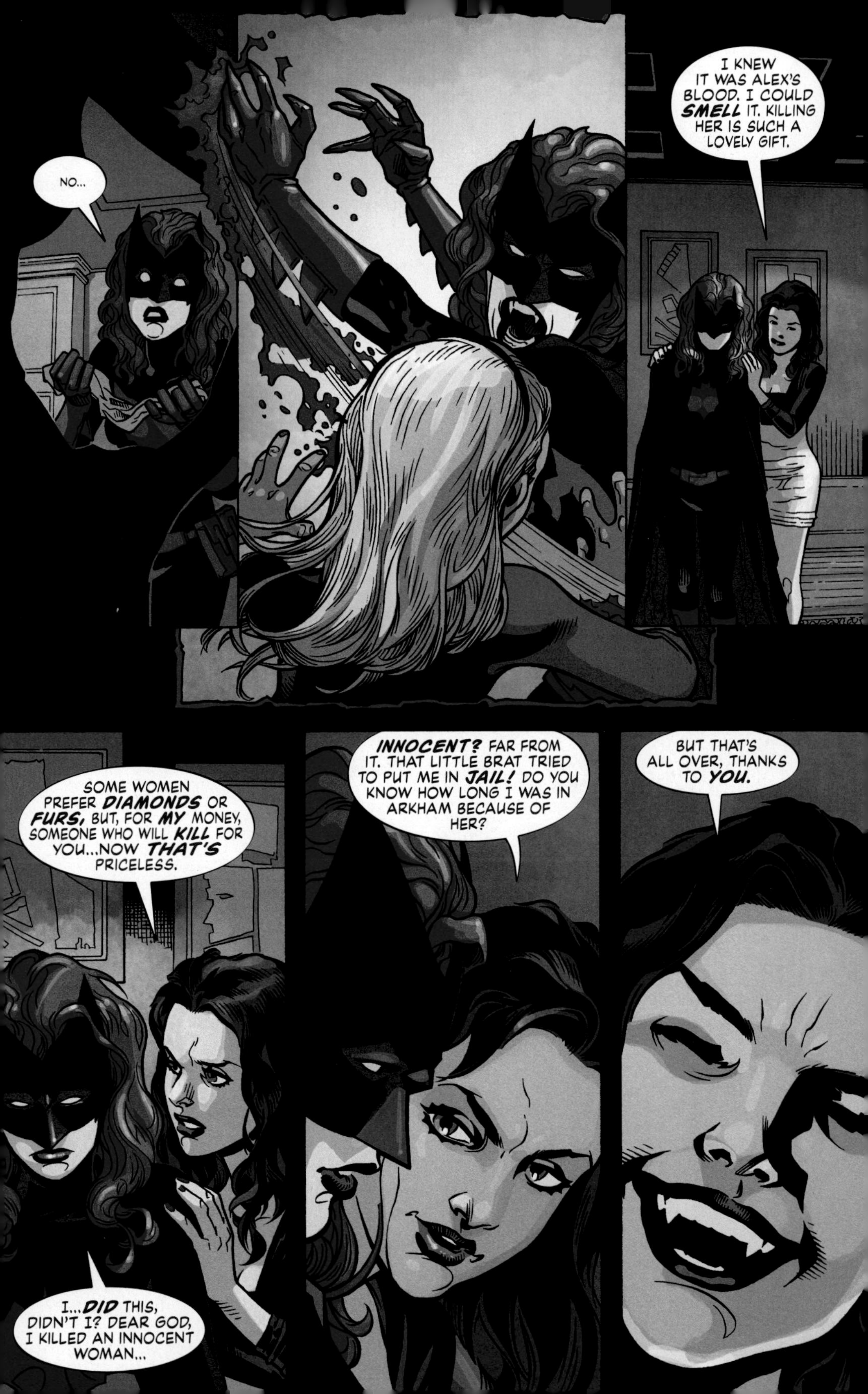
NO...
I KNEW IT WAS ALEX'S BLOOD. I COULD SMELL IT. KILLING HER IS SUCH A LOVELY GIFT.
SOME WOMEN PREFER DIAMONDS OR FURS, BUT, FOR MY MONEY, SOMEONE WHO WILL KILL FOR YOU...NOW THAT'S PRICELESS.
I...DID THIS, DIDN'T I? DEAR GOD, I KILLED AN INNOCENT WOMAN...
INNOCENT? FAR FROM IT. THAT LITTLE BRAT TRIED TO PUT ME IN JAIL! DO YOU KNOW HOW LONG I WAS IN ARKHAM BECAUSE OF HER?
BUT THAT'S ALL OVER, THANKS TO YOU.

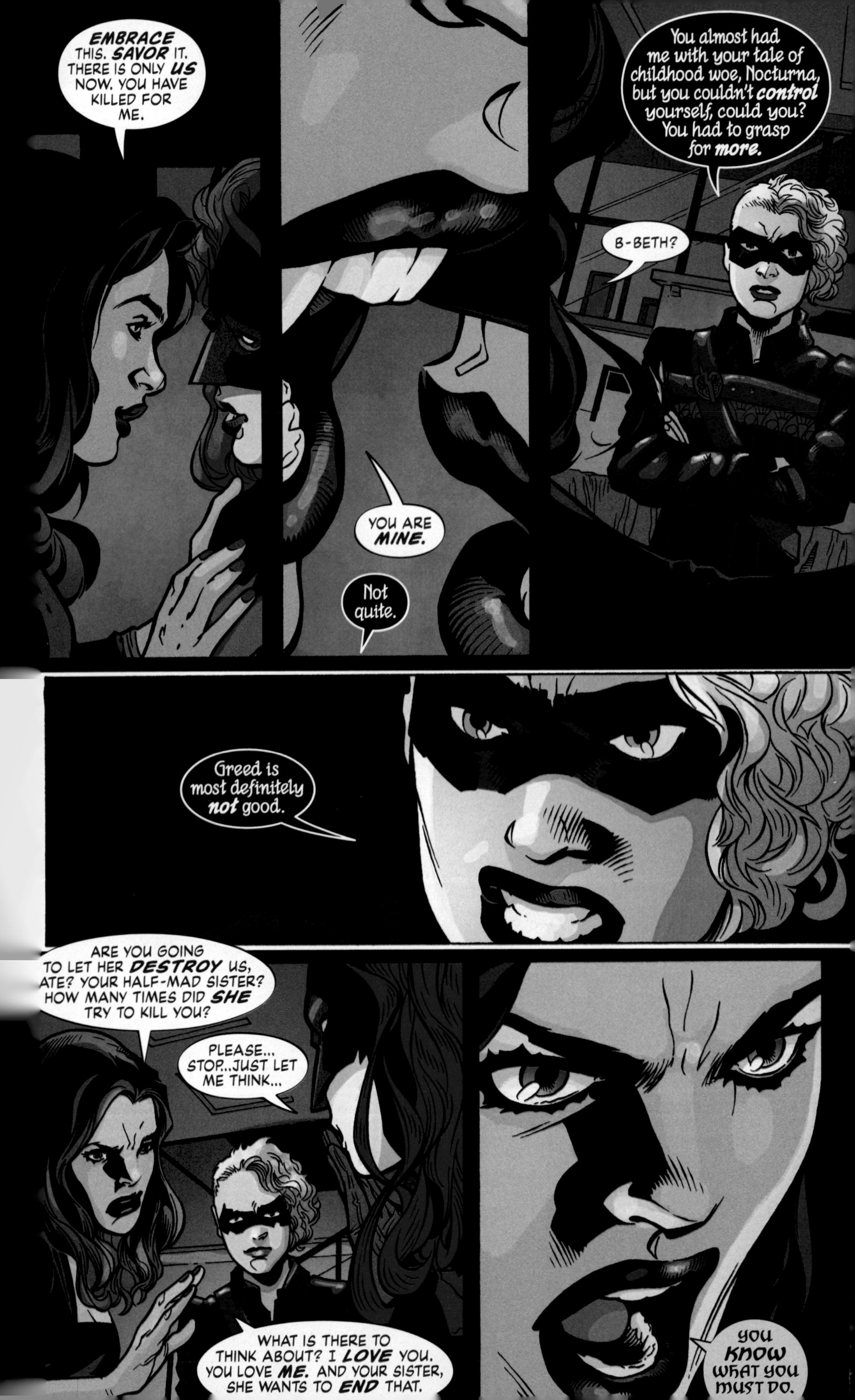
EMBRACE THIS. SAVOR IT. THERE IS ONLY US NOW. YOU HAVE KILLED FOR ME.
YOU ARE MINE.
Not quite.
You almost had me with your tale of childhood woe, Nocturna, but you couldn't control yourself, could you? You had to grasp for more.
B-BETH?
Greed is most definitely not good.
ARE YOU GOING TO LET HER DESTROY US, ATE? YOUR HALF-MAD SISTER? HOW MANY TIMES DID SHE TRY TO KILL YOU?
PLEASE... STOP...JUST LET ME THINK...
WHAT IS THERE TO THINK ABOUT? I LOVE YOU. YOU LOVE ME. AND YOUR SISTER, SHE WANTS TO END THAT.
YOU KNOW WHAT YOU MUST DO.

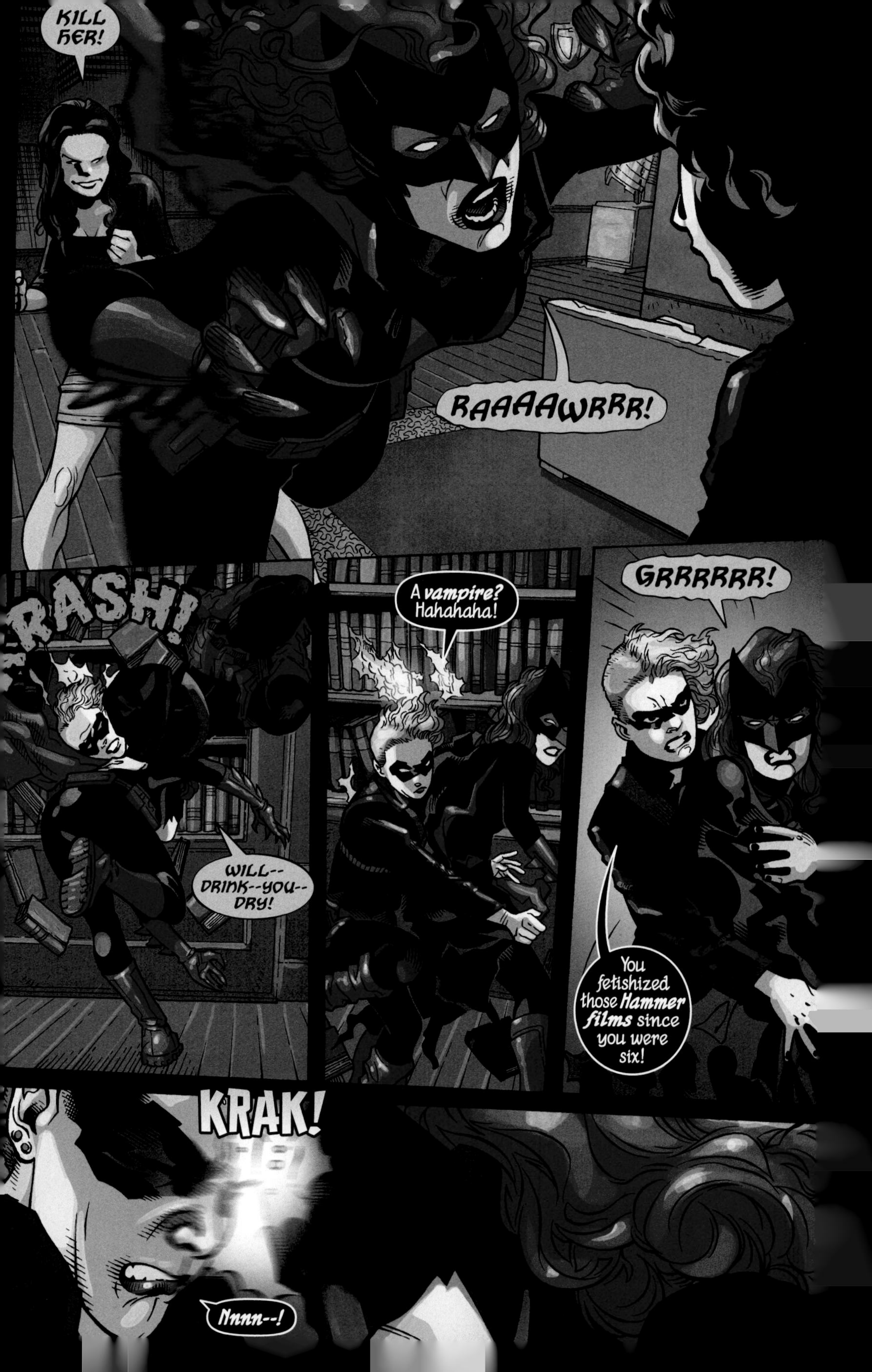
KILL HER!
RAAAAWRRR!
RASH!
WILL-- DRINK--YOU-- DRY!
A vampire? Hahahaha!
GRRRRRR!
You fetishized those Hammer films since you were six!
KRAK!
Nnnn--!

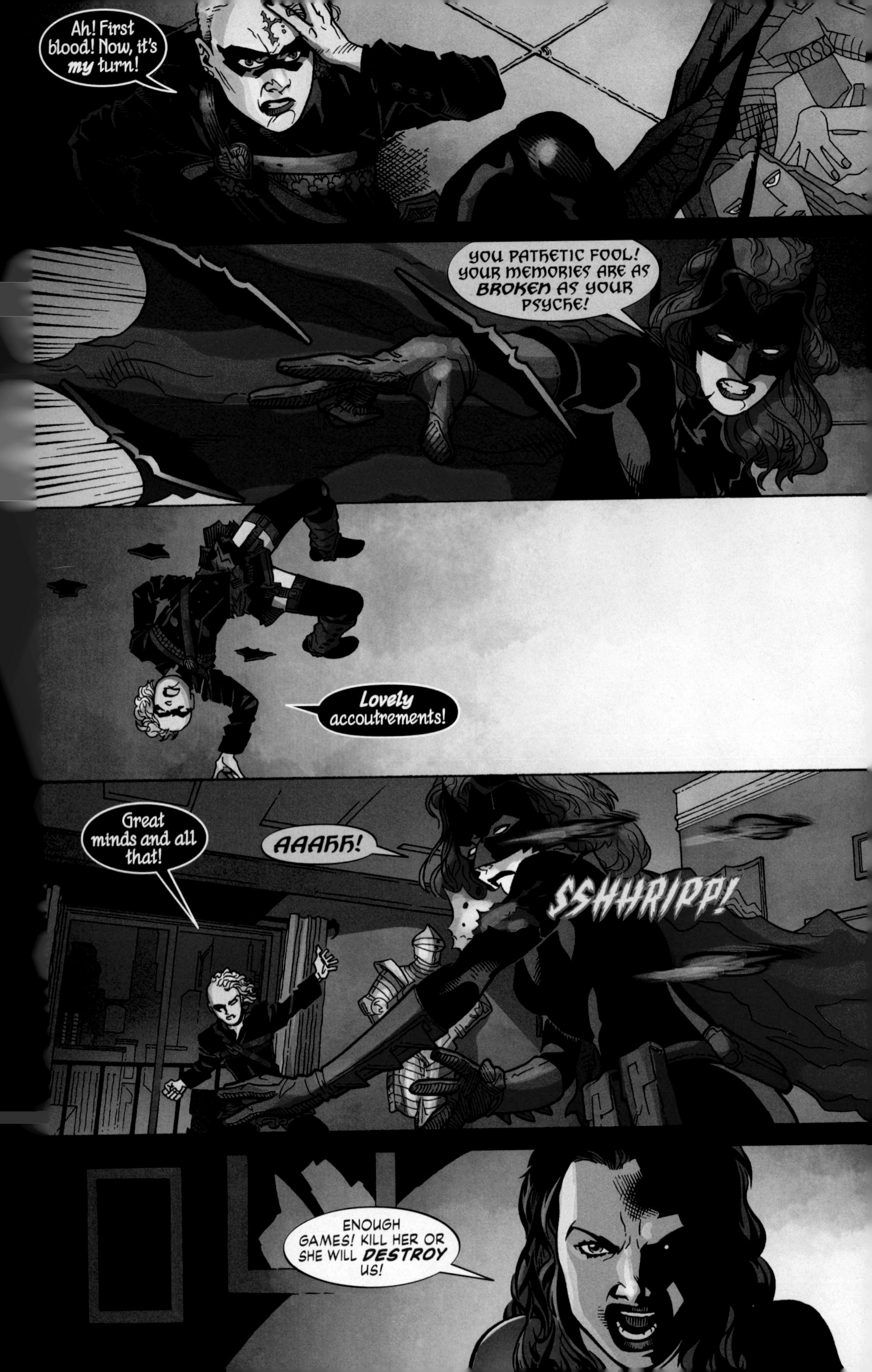

Ah! First blood! Now, it's *my* turn!
YOU PATHETIC FOOL! YOUR MEMORIES ARE AS **BROKEN** AS YOUR PSYCHE!
Lovely accoutrements!
Great minds and all that!
AAAHH!
SSHHRIPP!
ENOUGH GAMES! KILL HER OR SHE WILL ***DESTROY*** US!

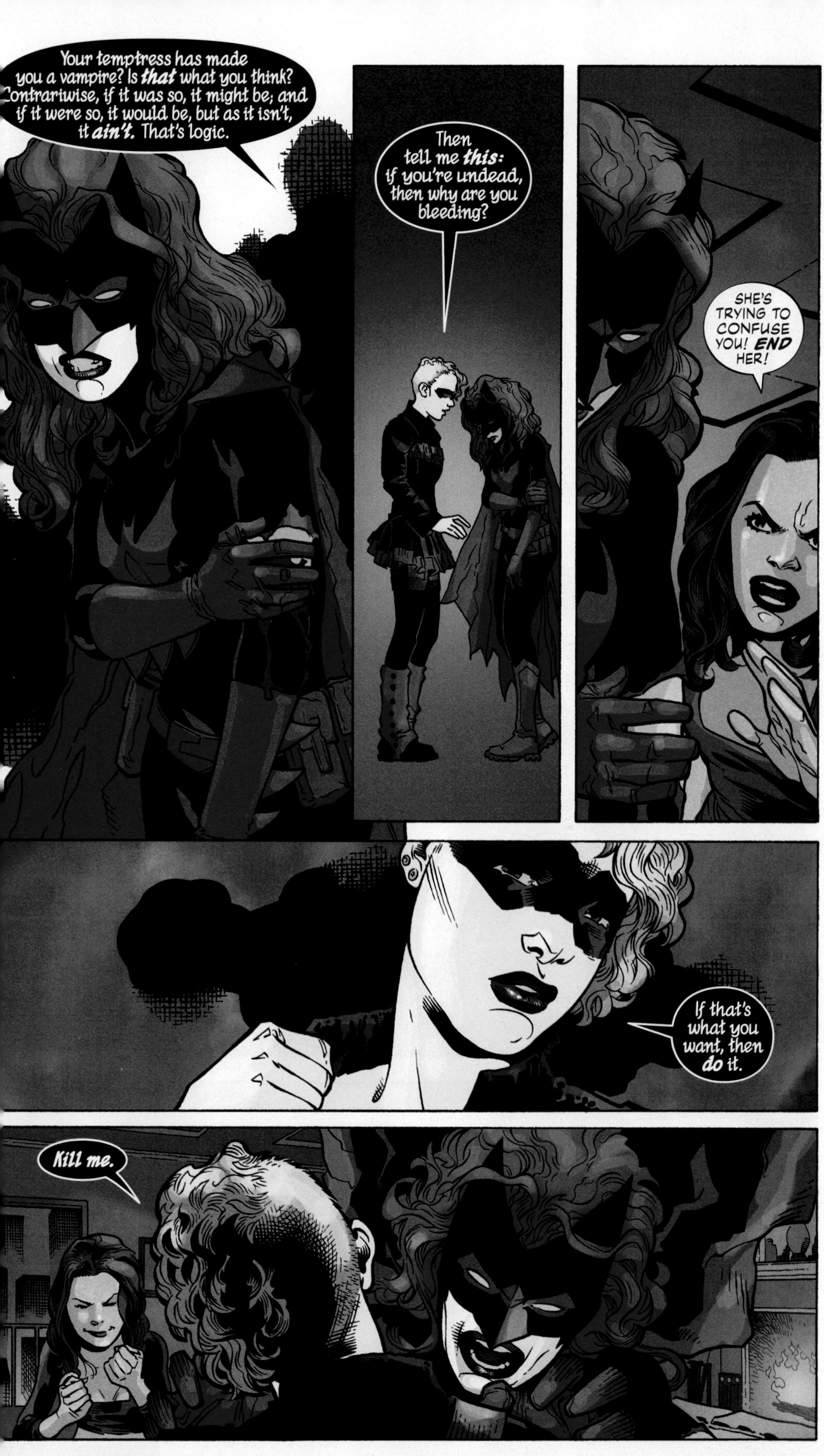
Your temptress has made you a vampire? Is that what you think? Contrariwise, if it was so, it might be; and if it were so, it would be, but as it isn't, it ain't. That's logic.
Then tell me this: if you're undead, then why are you bleeding?
SHE'S TRYING TO CONFUSE YOU! END HER!
If that's what you want, then do it.
Kill me.

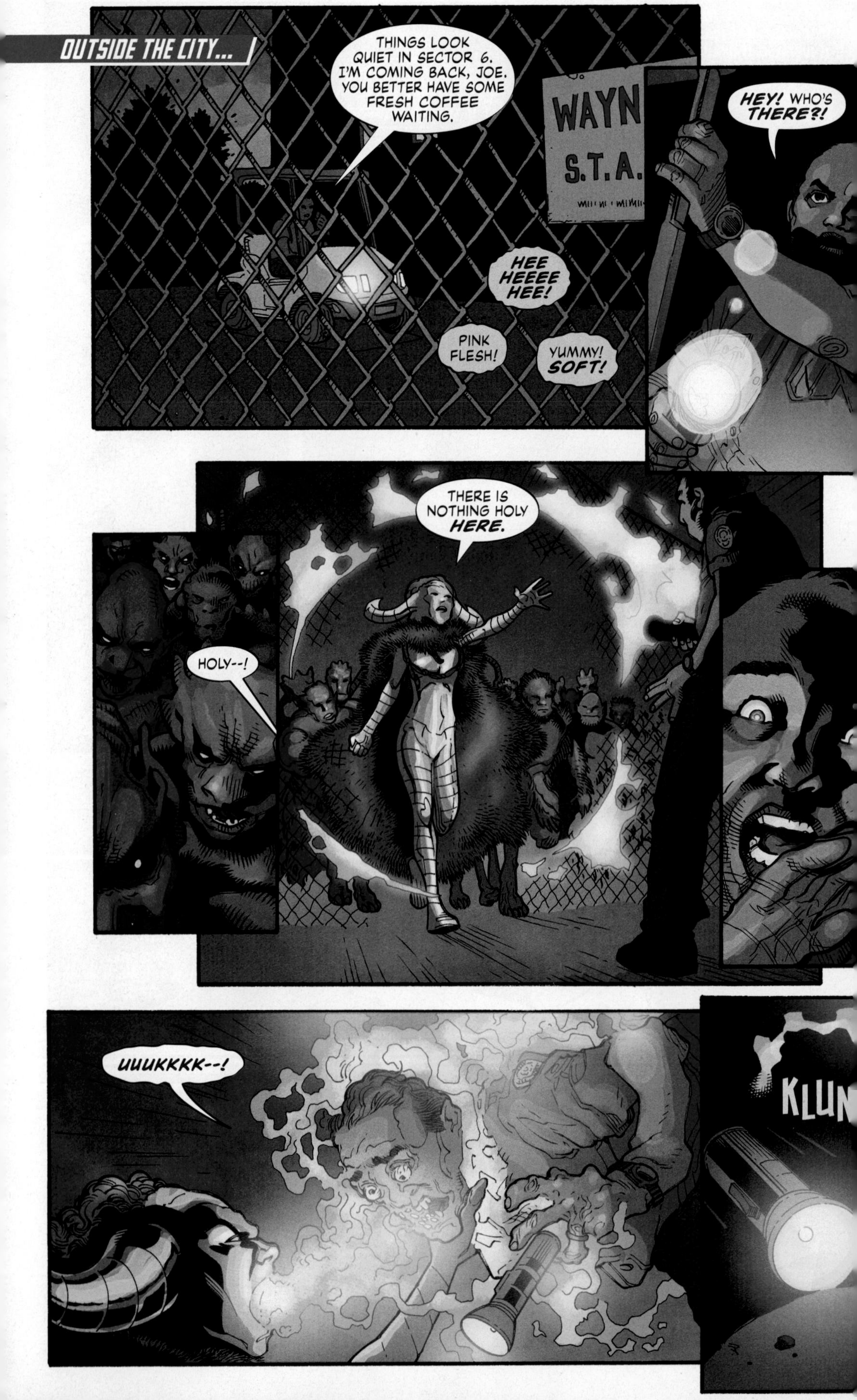
OUTSIDE THE CITY...
THINGS LOOK QUIET IN SECTOR 6. I'M COMING BACK, JOE. YOU BETTER HAVE SOME FRESH COFFEE WAITING.
WAYN
S.T.A.
HEY! WHO'S THERE?!
HEE HEEEE HEE!
PINK FLESH!
YUMMY! SOFT!
THERE IS NOTHING HOLY HERE.
HOLY--!
UUUKKKK--!
KLUN

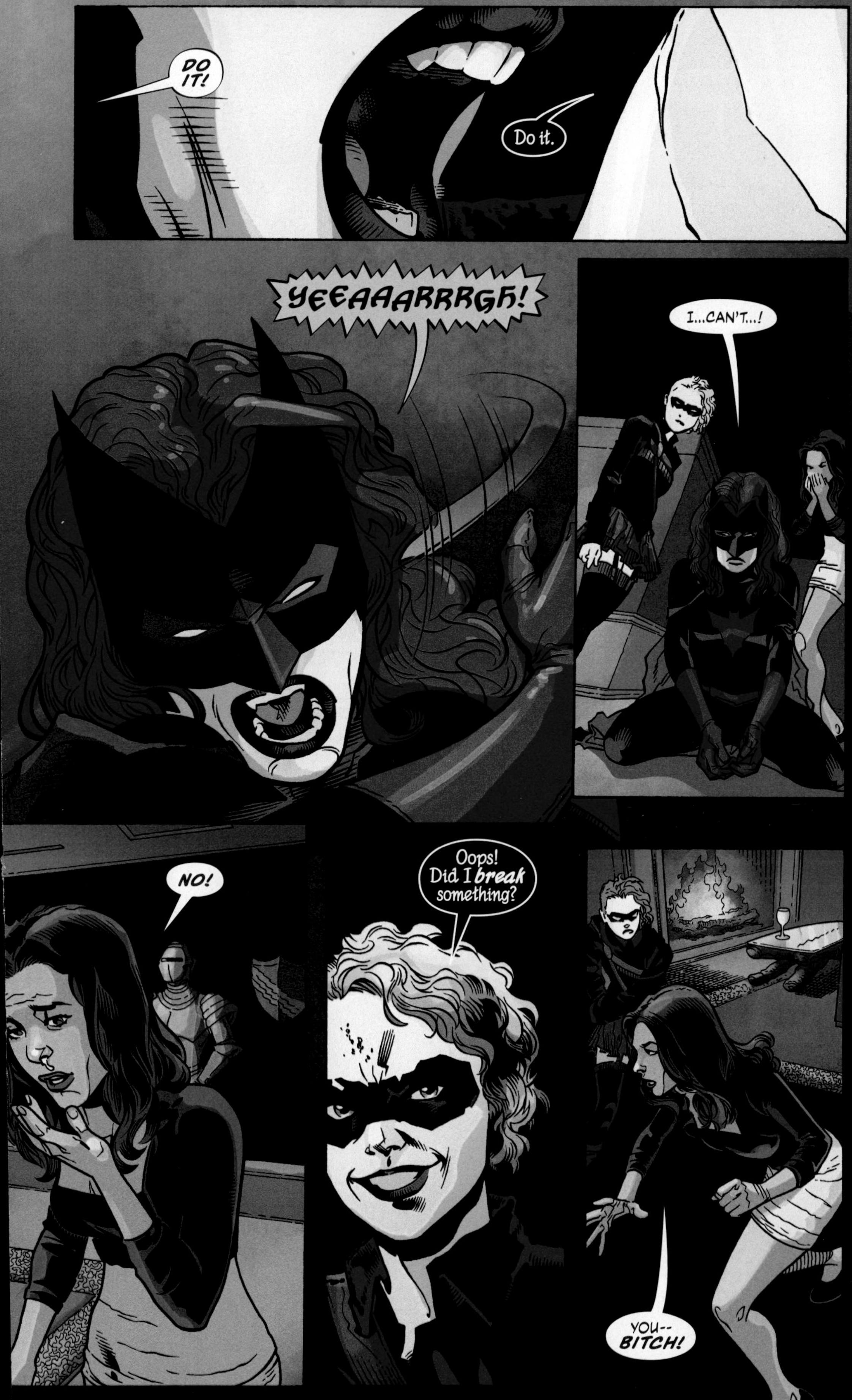
DO IT!
Do it.
YEEAAARRRGH!
I...CAN'T...!
NO!
Oops! Did I break something?
YOU-- BITCH!

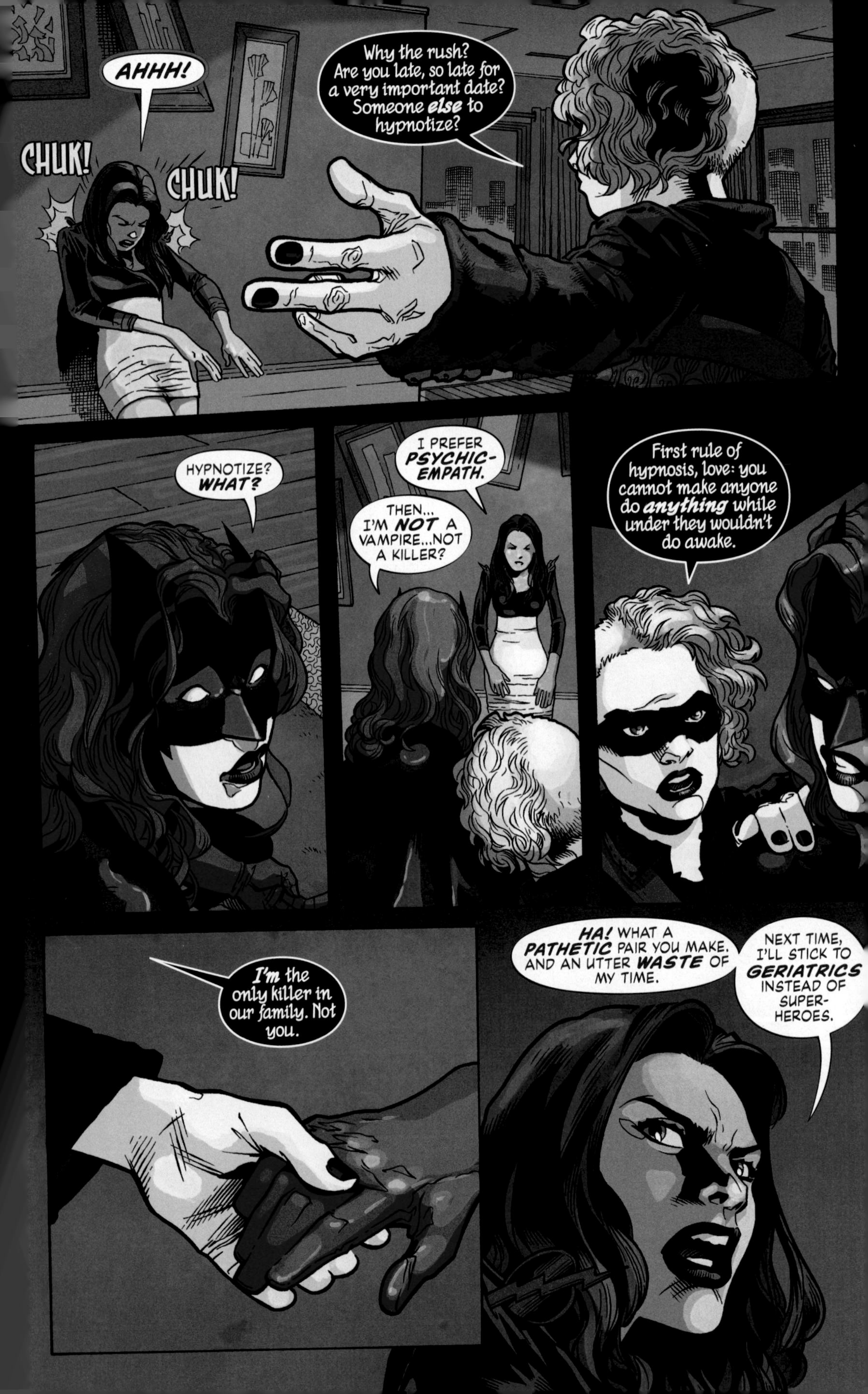

AHHH!
CHUK!
CHUK!
Why the rush? Are you late, so late for a very important date? Someone else to hypnotize?
HYPNOTIZE? WHAT?
I PREFER PSYCHIC-EMPATH.
THEN... I'M NOT A VAMPIRE...NOT A KILLER?
First rule of hypnosis, love: you cannot make anyone do anything while under they wouldn't do awake.
I'm the only killer in our family. Not you.
HA! WHAT A PATHETIC PAIR YOU MAKE. AND AN UTTER WASTE OF MY TIME.
NEXT TIME, I'LL STICK TO GERIATRICS INSTEAD OF SUPER-HEROES.

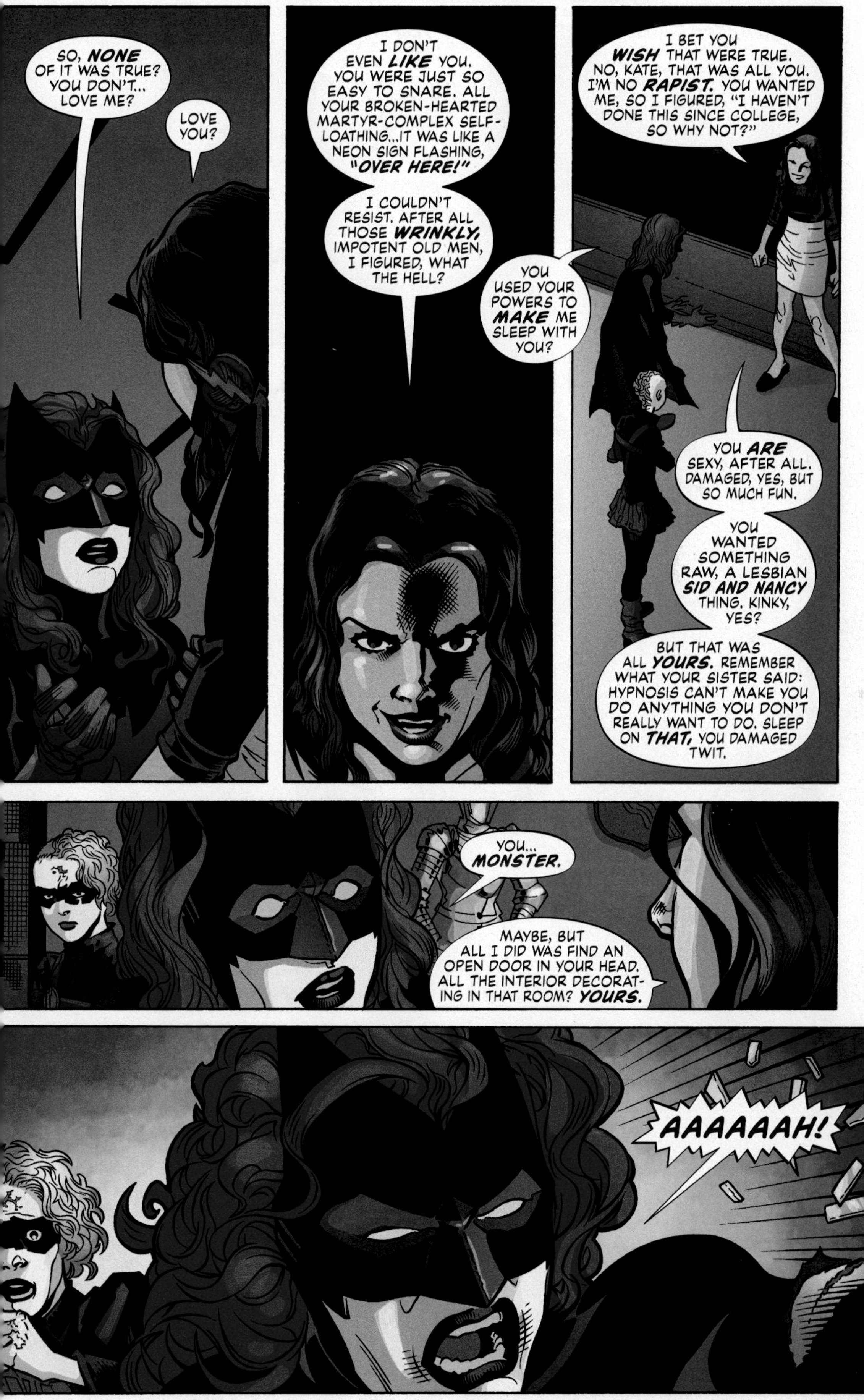

SO, NONE OF IT WAS TRUE? YOU DON'T... LOVE ME?
LOVE YOU?
I DON'T EVEN LIKE YOU. YOU WERE JUST SO EASY TO SNARE. ALL YOUR BROKEN-HEARTED MARTYR-COMPLEX SELF-LOATHING...IT WAS LIKE A NEON SIGN FLASHING, "OVER HERE!"
I COULDN'T RESIST. AFTER ALL THOSE WRINKLY, IMPOTENT OLD MEN, I FIGURED, WHAT THE HELL?
YOU USED YOUR POWERS TO MAKE ME SLEEP WITH YOU?
I BET YOU WISH THAT WERE TRUE. NO, KATE, THAT WAS ALL YOU. I'M NO RAPIST. YOU WANTED ME, SO I FIGURED, "I HAVEN'T DONE THIS SINCE COLLEGE, SO WHY NOT?"
YOU ARE SEXY, AFTER ALL. DAMAGED, YES, BUT SO MUCH FUN.
YOU WANTED SOMETHING RAW, A LESBIAN SID AND NANCY THING. KINKY, YES?
BUT THAT WAS ALL YOURS. REMEMBER WHAT YOUR SISTER SAID: HYPNOSIS CAN'T MAKE YOU DO ANYTHING YOU DON'T REALLY WANT TO DO. SLEEP ON THAT, YOU DAMAGED TWIT.
YOU... MONSTER.
MAYBE, BUT ALL I DID WAS FIND AN OPEN DOOR IN YOUR HEAD. ALL THE INTERIOR DECORATING IN THAT ROOM? YOURS.
AAAAAAH!

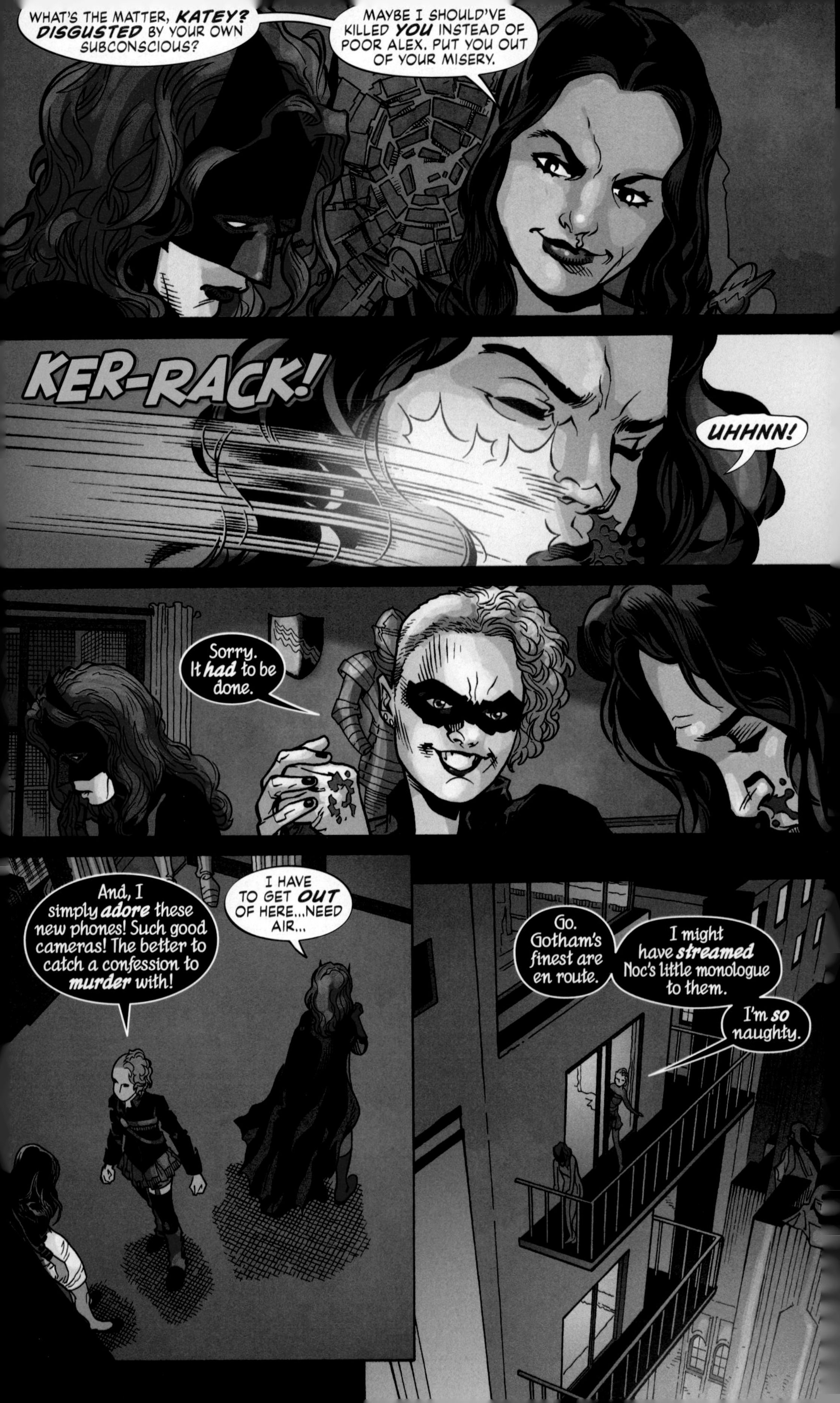
WHAT'S THE MATTER, KATEY? DISGUSTED BY YOUR OWN SUBCONSCIOUS?
MAYBE I SHOULD'VE KILLED YOU INSTEAD OF POOR ALEX. PUT YOU OUT OF YOUR MISERY.
KER-RACK!
UHHNN!
Sorry. It had to be done.
And, I simply adore these new phones! Such good cameras! The better to catch a confession to murder with!
I HAVE TO GET OUT OF HERE...NEED AIR...
Go. Gotham's finest are en route.
I might have streamed Noc's little monologue to them.
I'm so naughty.

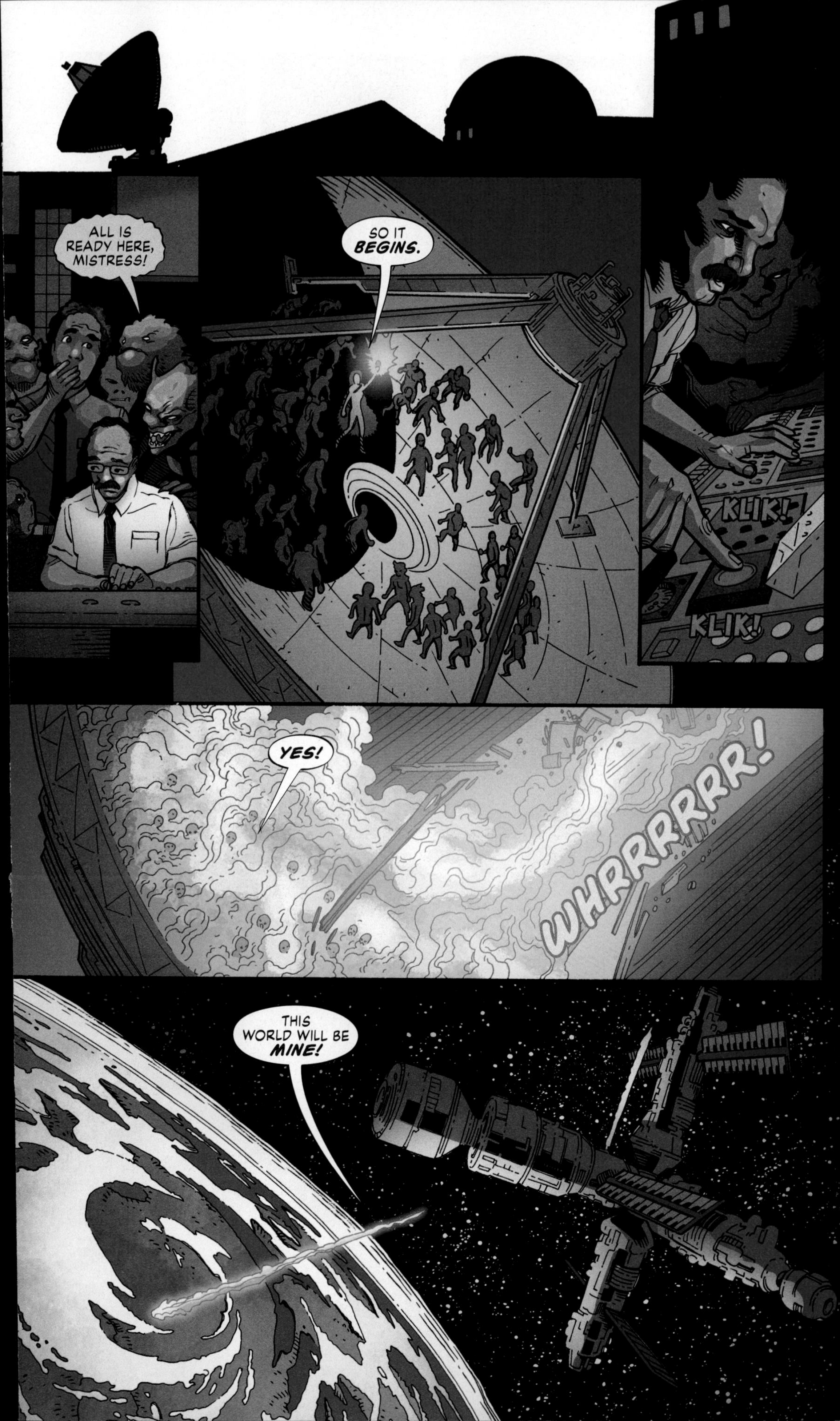
ALL IS READY HERE, MISTRESS!
SO IT BEGINS.
KLIK!
KLIK!
YES!
WHRRRRRR!
THIS WORLD WILL BE MINE!

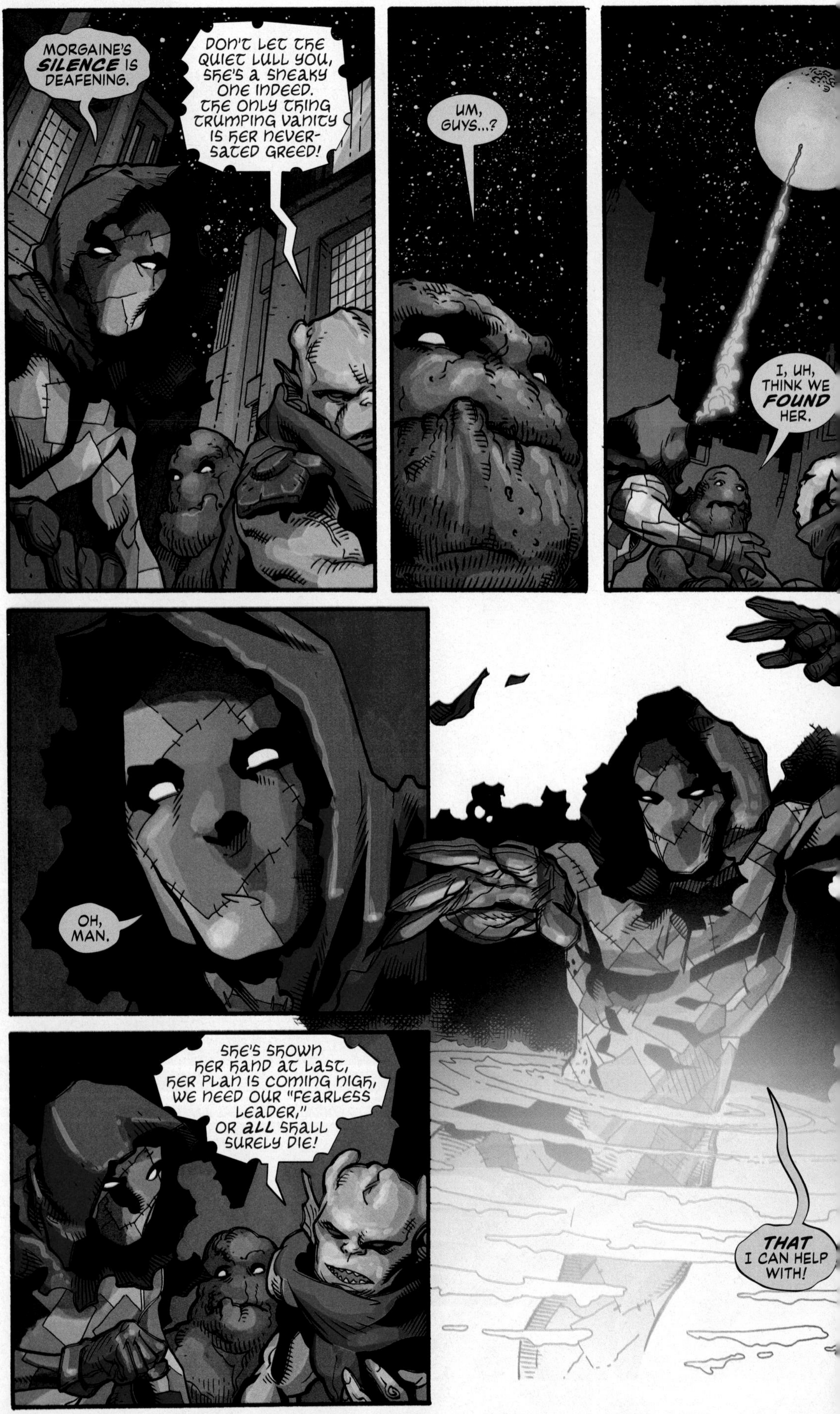
MORGAINE'S SILENCE IS DEAFENING.
DON'T LET THE QUIET LULL YOU, SHE'S A SNEAKY ONE INDEED. THE ONLY THING TRUMPING VANITY IS HER NEVER-SATED GREED!
UM, GUYS...?
I, UH, THINK WE FOUND HER.
OH, MAN.
SHE'S SHOWN HER HAND AT LAST, HER PLAN IS COMING HIGH, WE NEED OUR "FEARLESS LEADER," OR ALL SHALL SURELY DIE!
THAT I CAN HELP WITH!

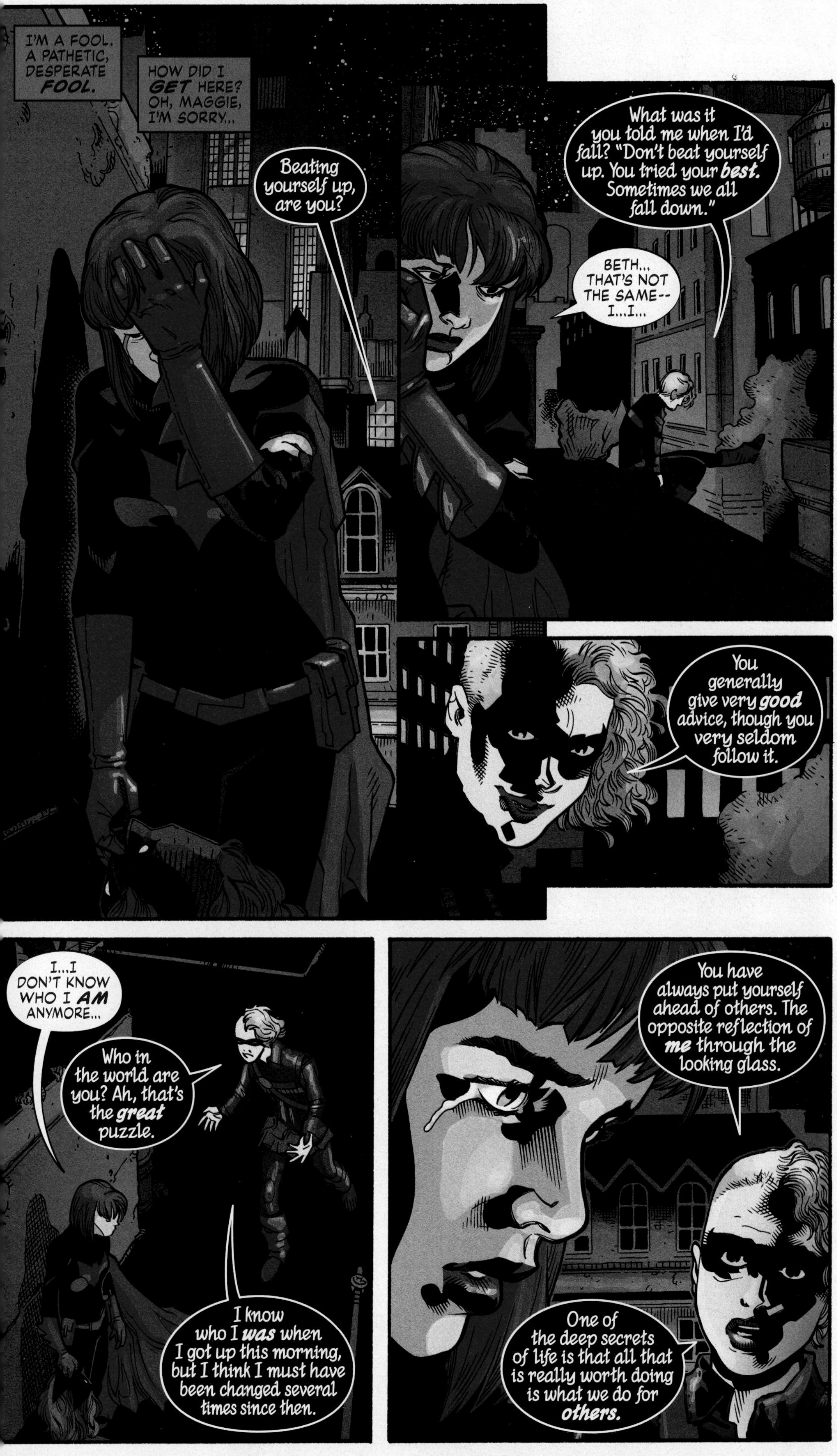
I'M A FOOL. A PATHETIC, DESPERATE FOOL.
HOW DID I GET HERE? OH, MAGGIE, I'M SORRY...
Beating yourself up, are you?
What was it you told me when I'd fall? "Don't beat yourself up. You tried your best. Sometimes we all fall down."
BETH... THAT'S NOT THE SAME-- I...I...
You generally give very good advice, though you very seldom follow it.
I...I DON'T KNOW WHO I AM ANYMORE...
Who in the world are you? Ah, that's the great puzzle.
I know who I was when I got up this morning, but I think I must have been changed several times since then.
You have always put yourself ahead of others. The opposite reflection of me through the looking glass.
One of the deep secrets of life is that all that is really worth doing is what we do for others.

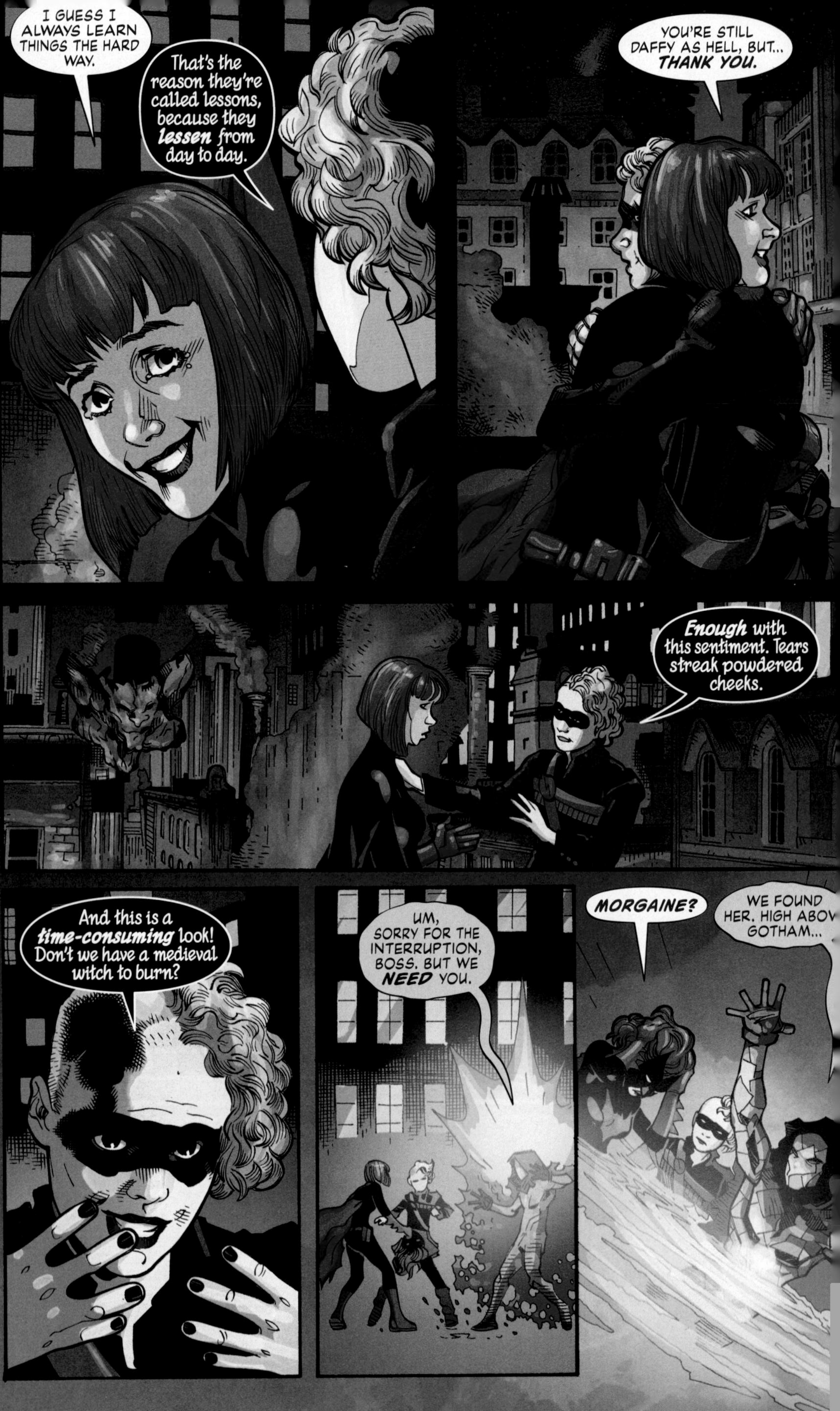
I GUESS I ALWAYS LEARN THINGS THE HARD WAY.
That's the reason they're called lessons, because they **lessen** from day to day.
YOU'RE STILL DAFFY AS HELL, BUT... ***THANK YOU.***
Enough with this sentiment. Tears streak powdered cheeks.
And this is a ***time-consuming*** look! Don't we have a medieval witch to burn?
UM, SORRY FOR THE INTERRUPTION, BOSS. BUT WE ***NEED*** YOU.
MORGAINE?
WE FOUND HER. HIGH ABOV GOTHAM...

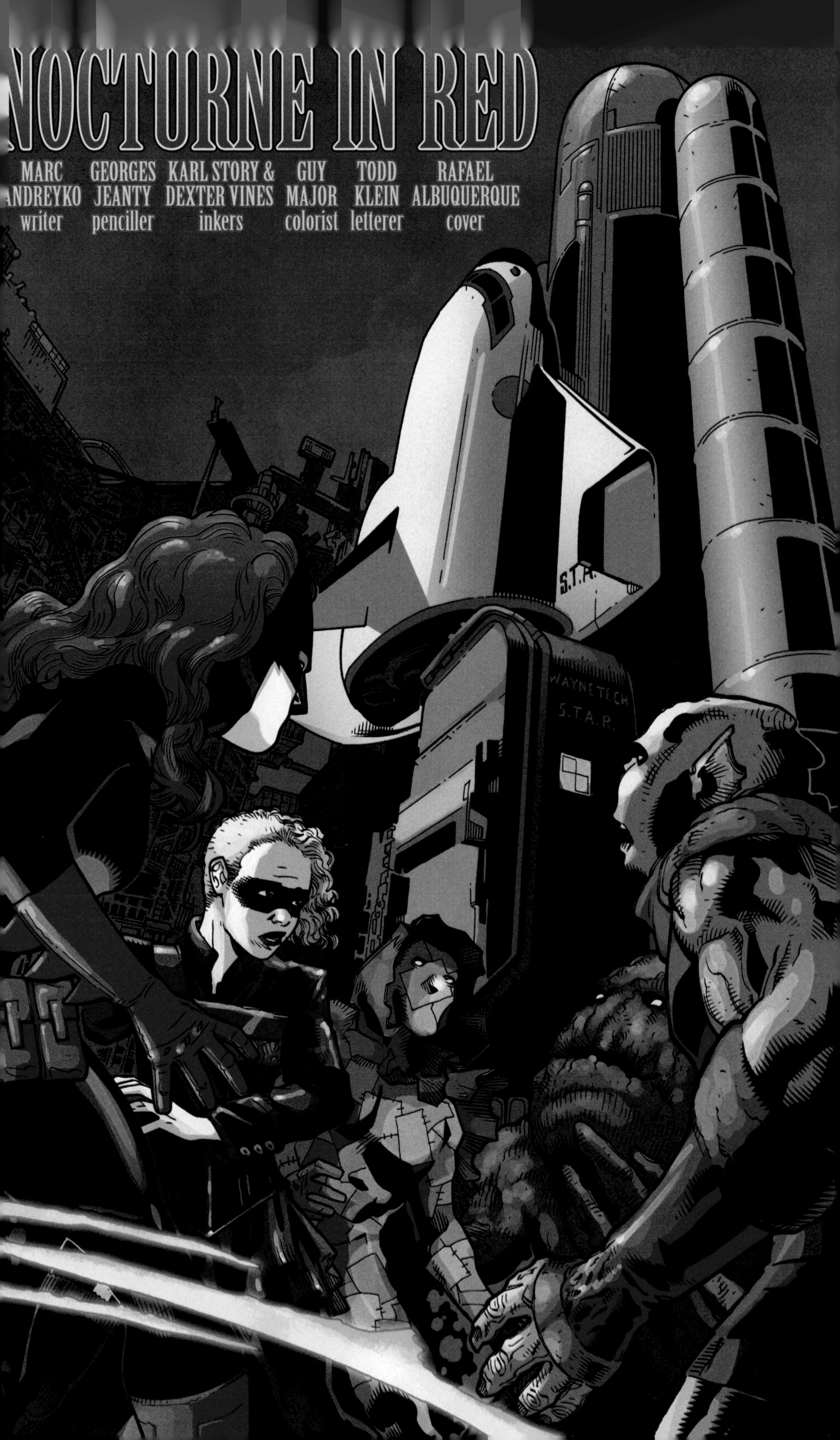
NOCTURNE IN RED
MARC ANDREYKO writer
GEORGES JEANTY penciller
KARL STORY & DEXTER VINES inkers
GUY MAJOR colorist
TODD KLEIN letterer
RAFAEL ALBUQUERQUE cover
S.T.A.
WAYNETECH
S.T.A.R.

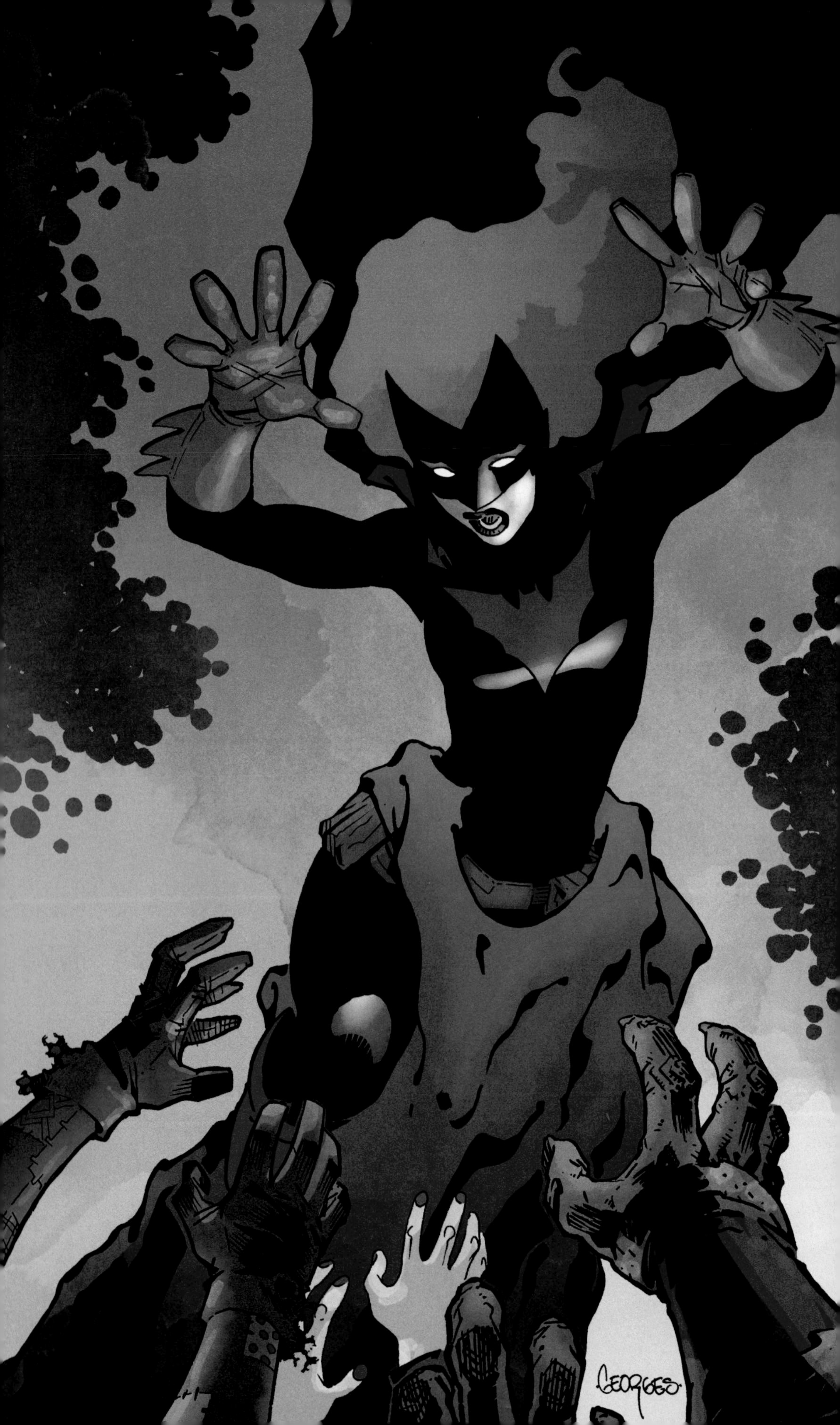
GEORGES

SO THIS IS HOW IT **ENDS,** HUH?

FALLING TO EARTH, WRAPPED IN CLAY-FACE. TRUE STORY.

AFTER ALL I'VE BEEN THROUGH, ALL THE DEMONS I'VE BATTLED, LITERAL AND **NOT,** YOU'D THINK I DESERVE A BREAK.

I GUESS KARMA IS A **MYTH.**

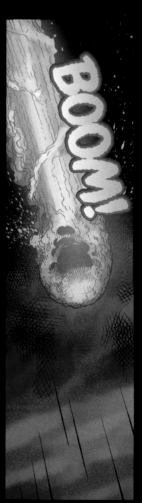

BOOM!

FWEEEEEEEEE

SPLASH!

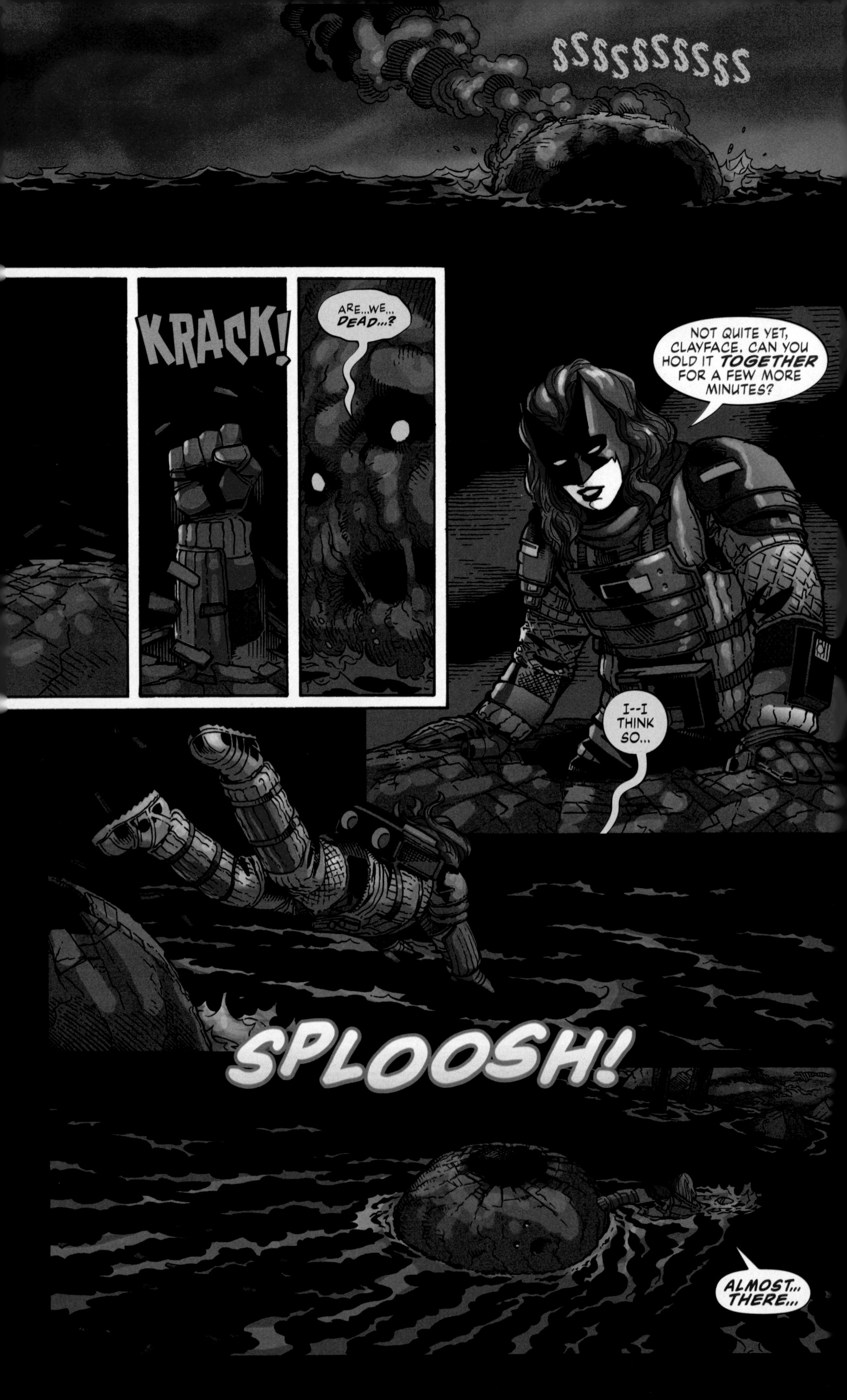
SSSSSSSSSS
KRACK!
ARE...WE... DEAD...?
NOT QUITE YET, CLAYFACE. CAN YOU HOLD IT TOGETHER FOR A FEW MORE MINUTES?
I--I THINK SO...
SPLOOSH!
ALMOST... THERE...

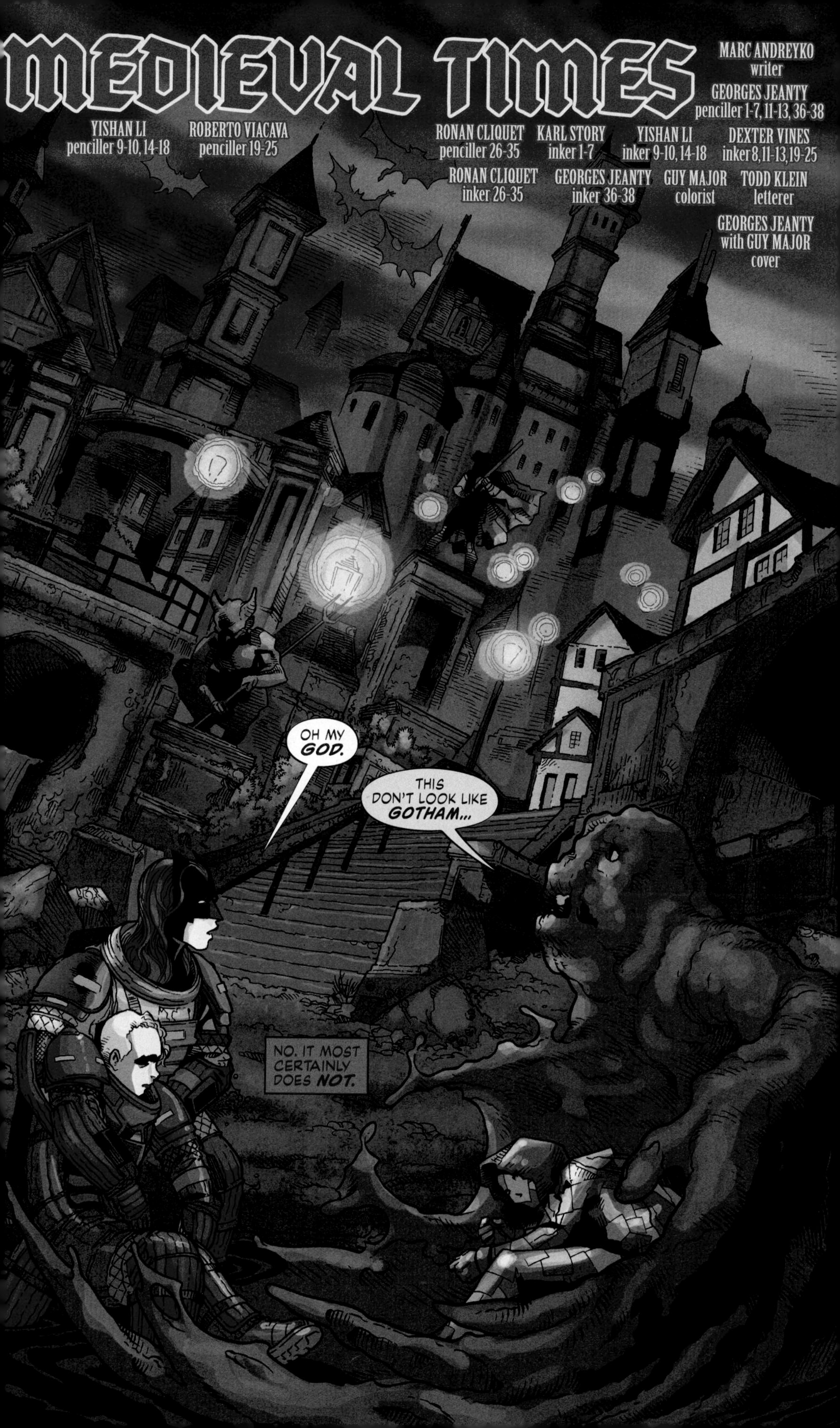
MEDIEVAL TIMES
MARC ANDREYKO writer
GEORGES JEANTY penciller 1-7, 11-13, 36-38
YISHAN LI penciller 9-10, 14-18
ROBERTO VIACAVA penciller 19-25
RONAN CLIQUET penciller 26-35
KARL STORY inker 1-7
YISHAN LI inker 9-10, 14-18
DEXTER VINES inker 8, 11-13, 19-25
RONAN CLIQUET inker 26-35
GEORGES JEANTY inker 36-38
GUY MAJOR colorist
TODD KLEIN letterer
GEORGES JEANTY with GUY MAJOR cover
OH MY GOD.
THIS DON'T LOOK LIKE GOTHAM...
NO. IT MOST CERTAINLY DOES NOT.

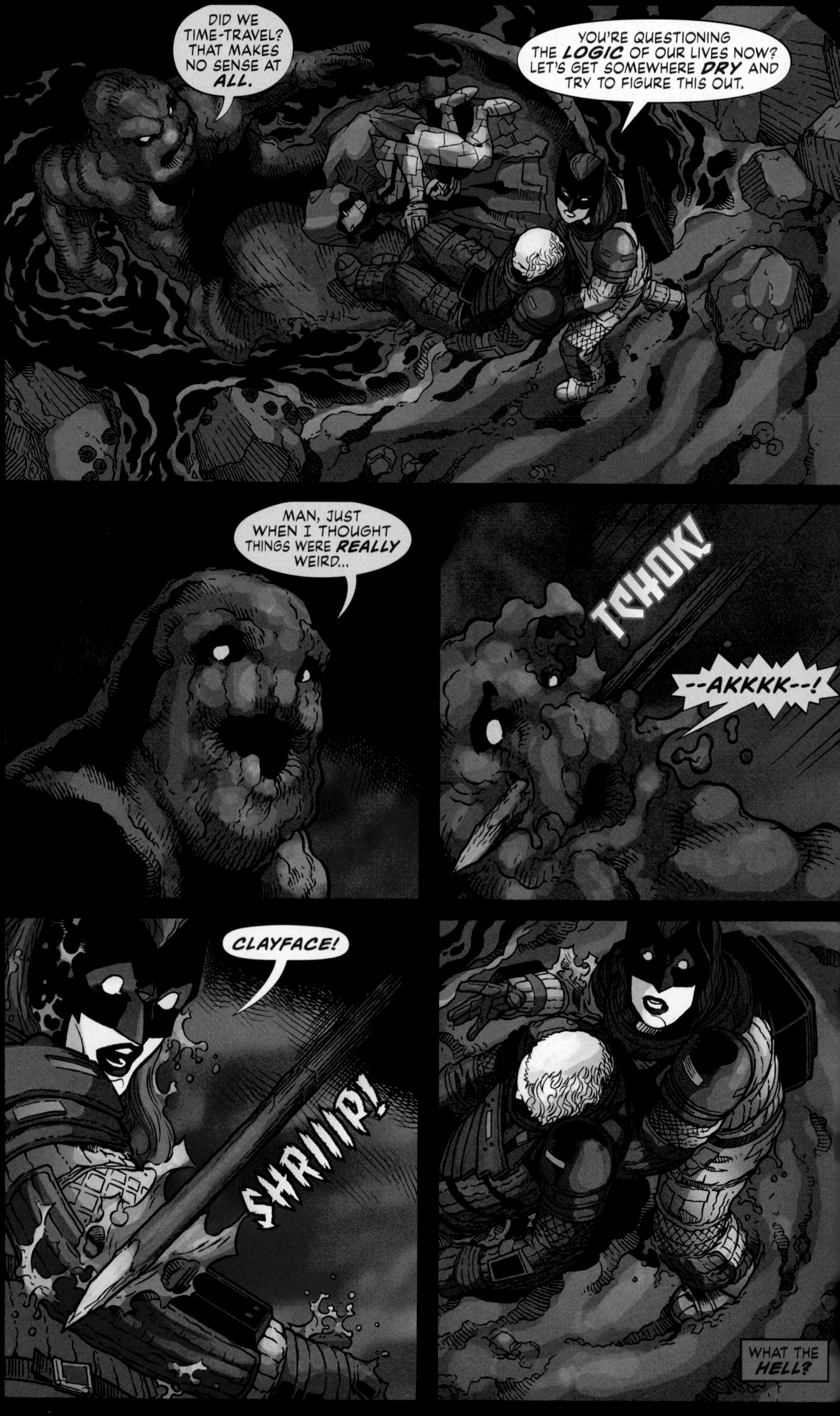
DID WE TIME-TRAVEL? THAT MAKES NO SENSE AT ALL.
YOU'RE QUESTIONING THE LOGIC OF OUR LIVES NOW? LET'S GET SOMEWHERE DRY AND TRY TO FIGURE THIS OUT.
MAN, JUST WHEN I THOUGHT THINGS WERE REALLY WEIRD...
TCHOK!
--AKKKK--!
CLAYFACE!
SHRIIP!
WHAT THE HELL?

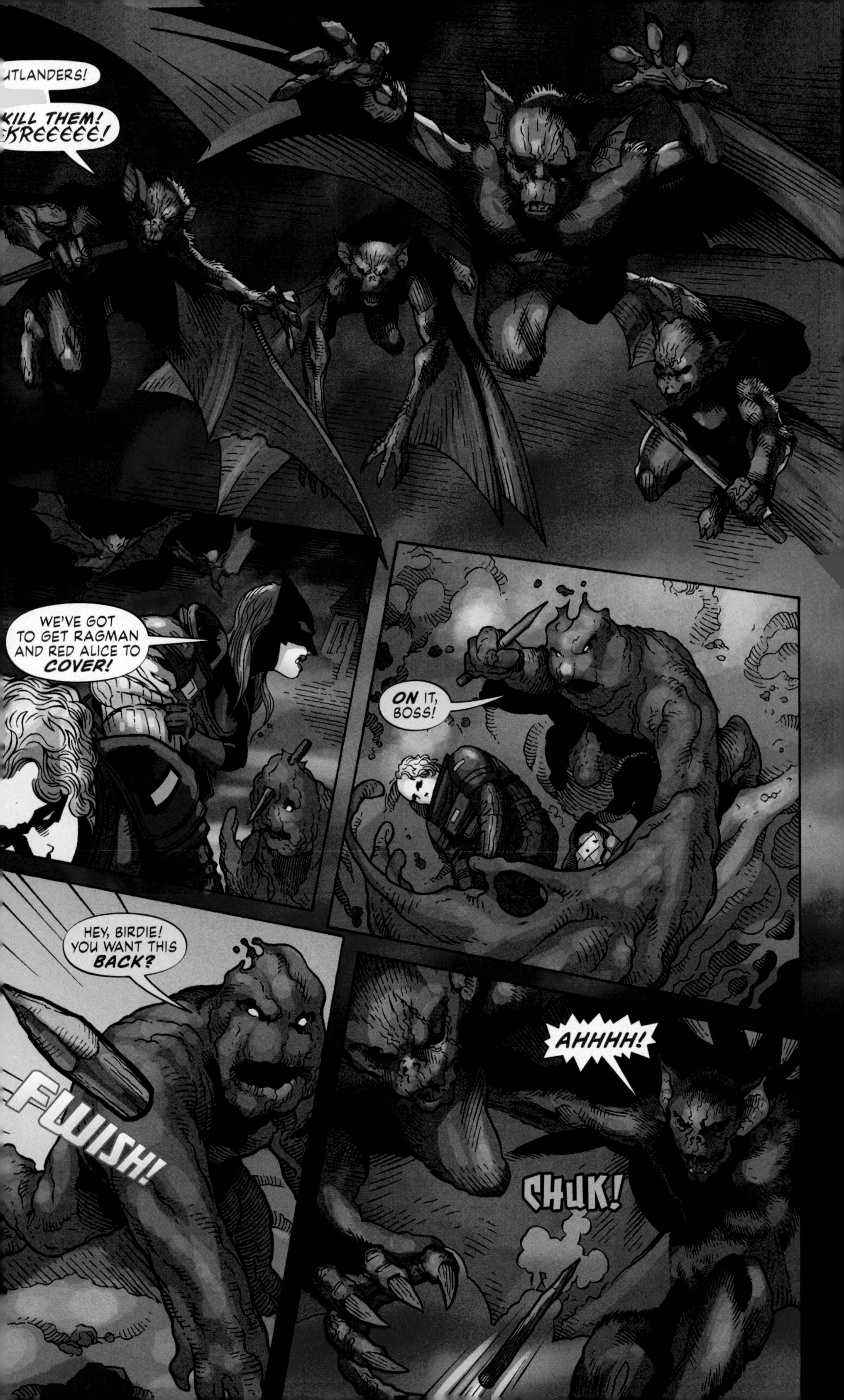

...TLANDERS!
KILL THEM! SKREEEEEE!
WE'VE GOT TO GET RAGMAN AND RED ALICE TO COVER!
ON IT, BOSS!
HEY, BIRDIE! YOU WANT THIS BACK?
FWISH!
AHHHH!
CHUK!

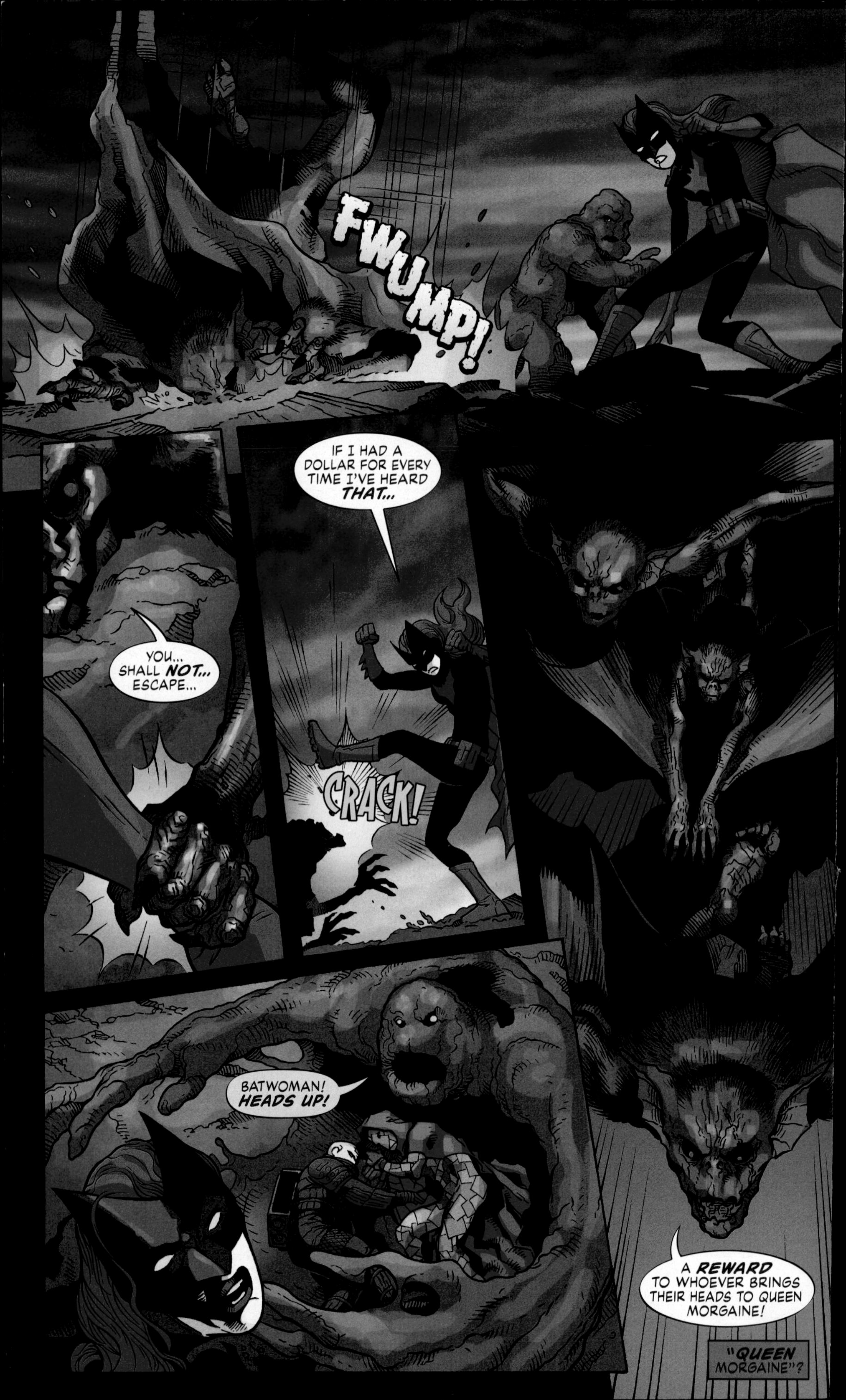
FWUMP!
YOU... SHALL NOT... ESCAPE...
IF I HAD A DOLLAR FOR EVERY TIME I'VE HEARD THAT...
CRACK!
BATWOMAN! HEADS UP!
A REWARD TO WHOEVER BRINGS THEIR HEADS TO QUEEN MORGAINE!
"QUEEN MORGAINE"?

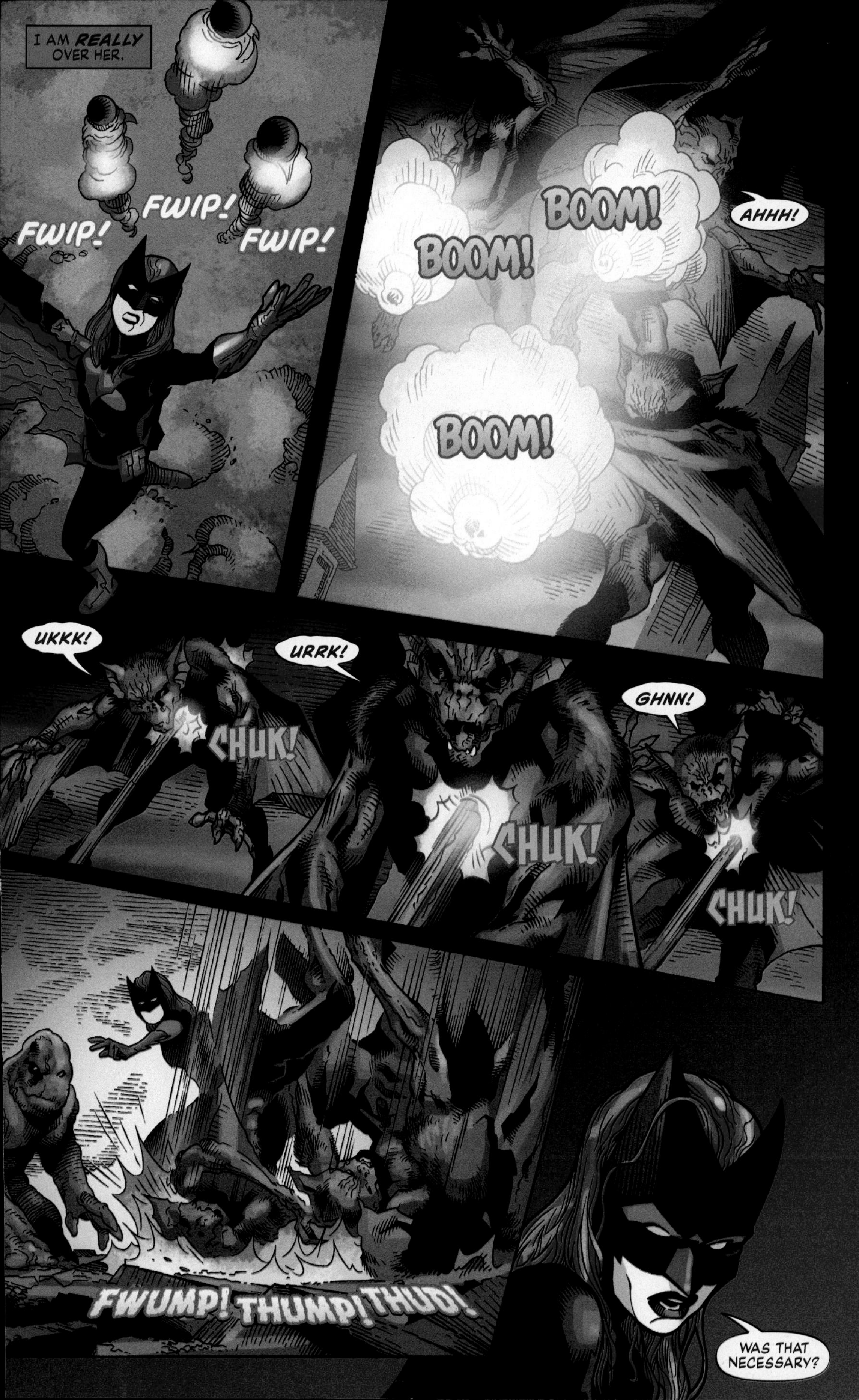
I AM REALLY OVER HER.
FWIP!
FWIP!
FWIP!
BOOM!
BOOM!
AHHH!
BOOM!
UKKK!
URRK!
GHNN!
CHUK!
CHUK!
CHUK!
FWUMP! THUMP! THUD!
WAS THAT NECESSARY?

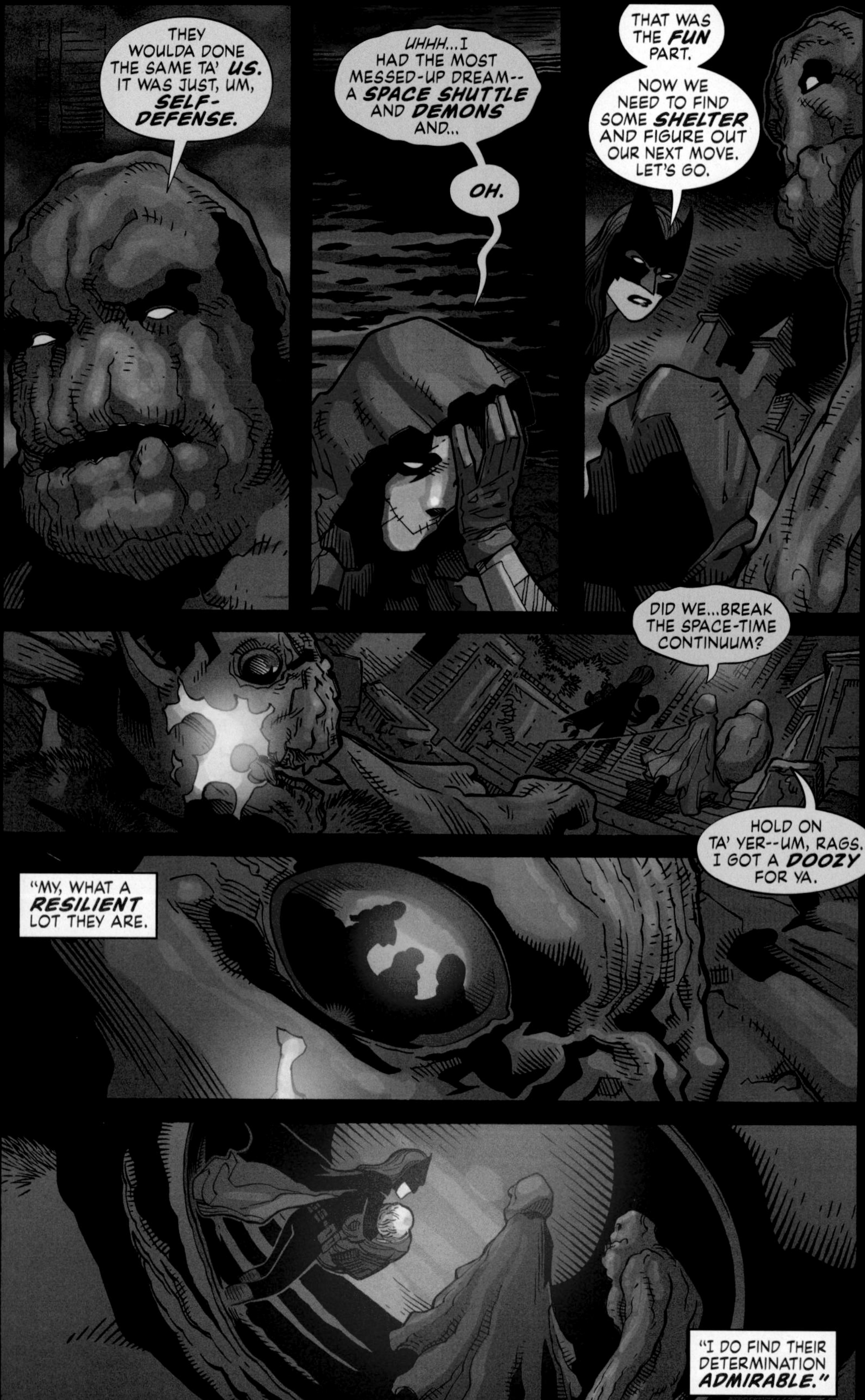
THEY WOULDA DONE THE SAME TA' US. IT WAS JUST, UM, SELF-DEFENSE.
UHHH...I HAD THE MOST MESSED-UP DREAM-- A SPACE SHUTTLE AND DEMONS AND...
OH.
THAT WAS THE FUN PART.
NOW WE NEED TO FIND SOME SHELTER AND FIGURE OUT OUR NEXT MOVE. LET'S GO.
DID WE...BREAK THE SPACE-TIME CONTINUUM?
HOLD ON TA' YER--UM, RAGS. I GOT A DOOZY FOR YA.
"MY, WHAT A RESILIENT LOT THEY ARE.
"I DO FIND THEIR DETERMINATION ADMIRABLE."

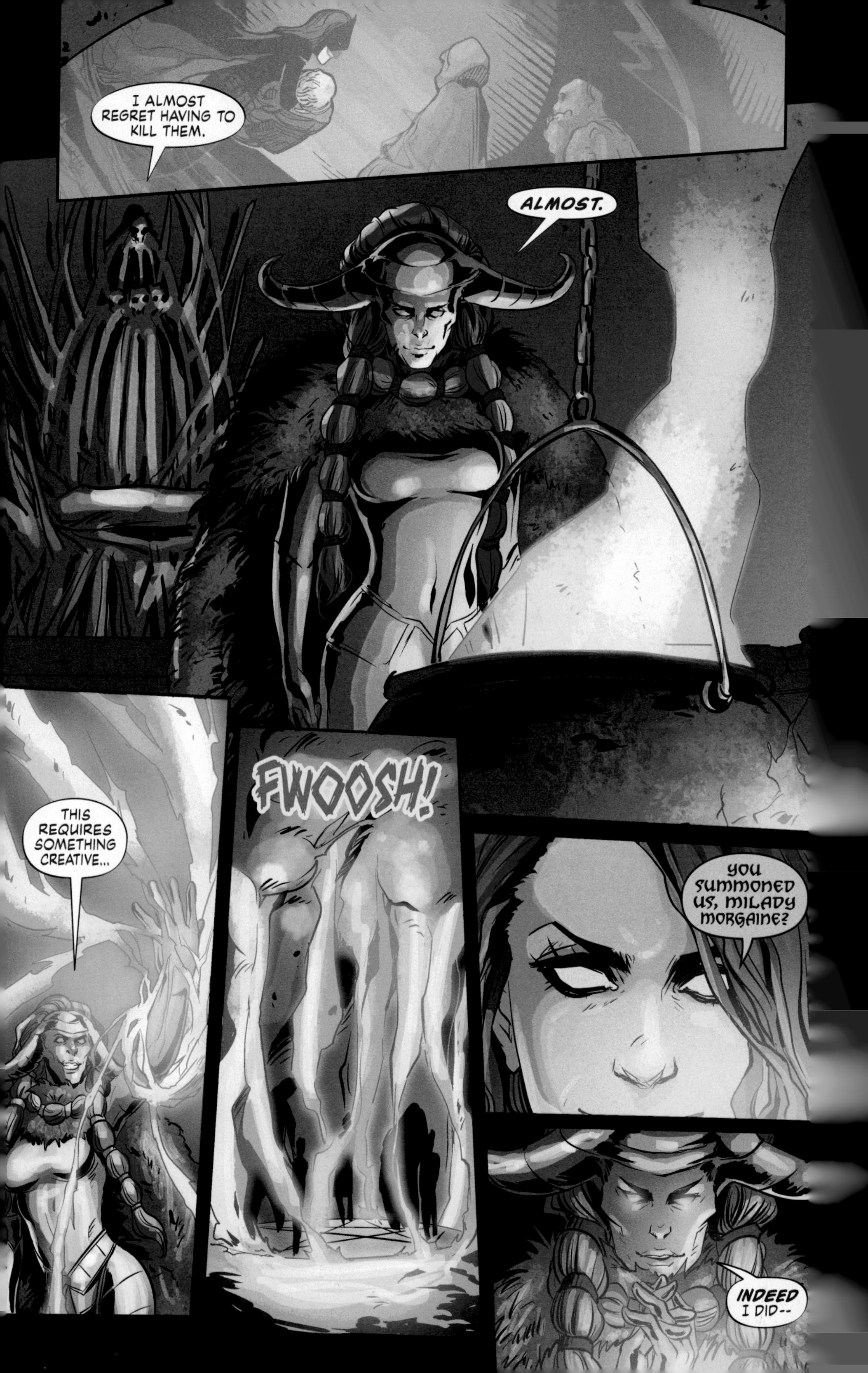
I ALMOST REGRET HAVING TO KILL THEM.
ALMOST.
THIS REQUIRES SOMETHING CREATIVE...
FWOOSH!
YOU SUMMONED US, MILADY MORGAINE?
INDEED I DID--

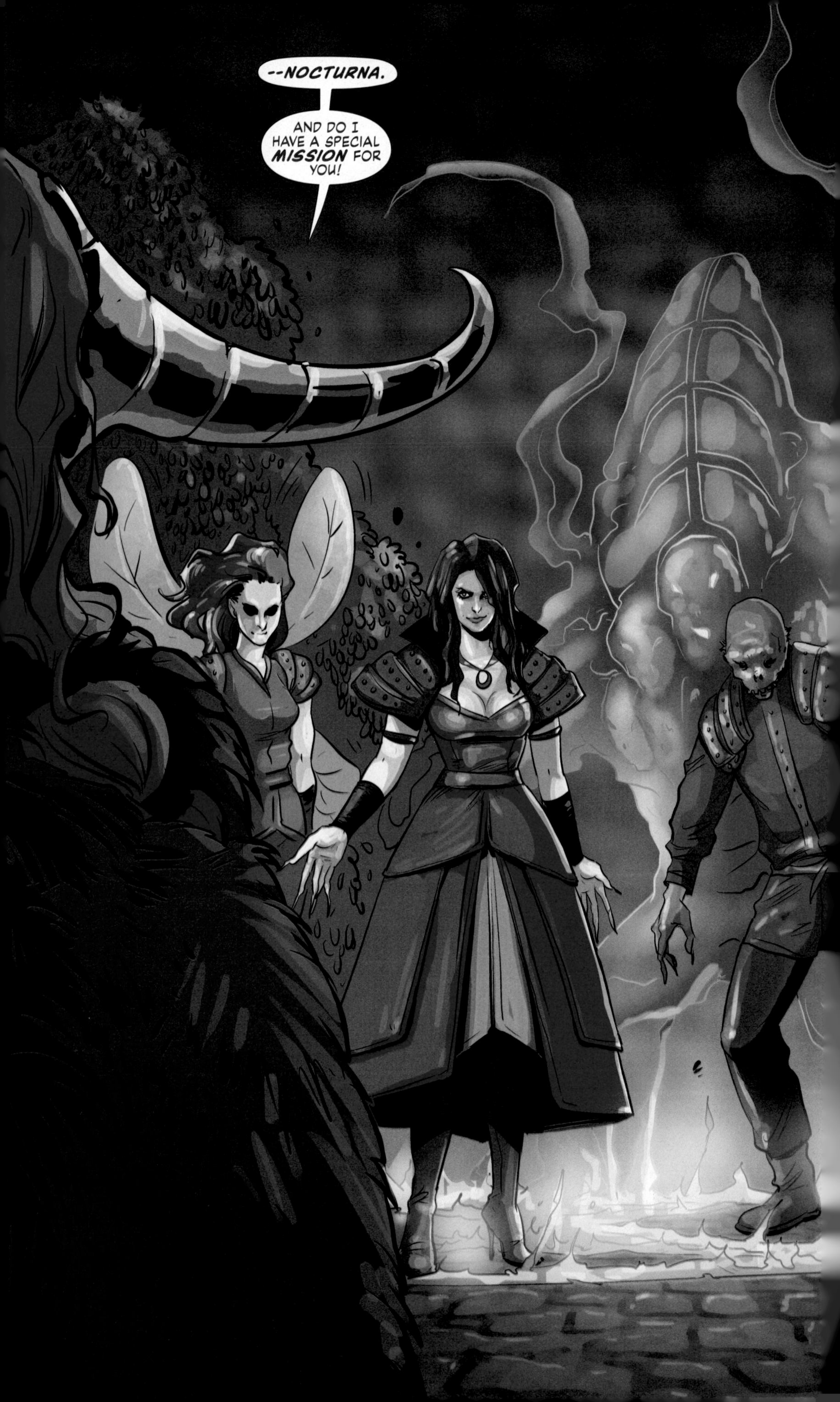
--NOCTURNA.
AND DO I HAVE A SPECIAL MISSION FOR YOU!

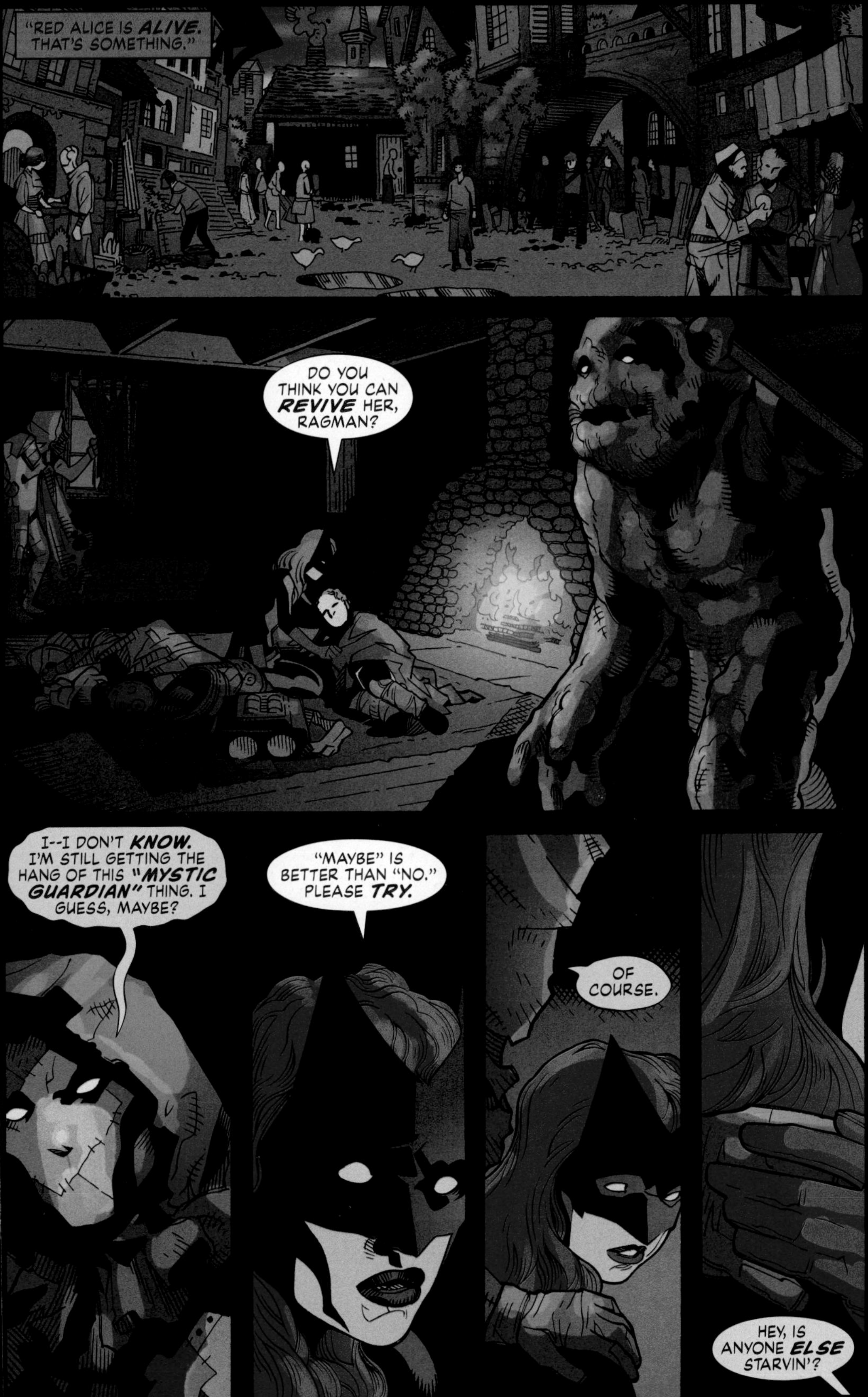
"RED ALICE IS ALIVE. THAT'S SOMETHING."
DO YOU THINK YOU CAN REVIVE HER, RAGMAN?
I--I DON'T KNOW. I'M STILL GETTING THE HANG OF THIS "MYSTIC GUARDIAN" THING. I GUESS, MAYBE?
"MAYBE" IS BETTER THAN "NO." PLEASE TRY.
OF COURSE.
HEY, IS ANYONE ELSE STARVIN'?

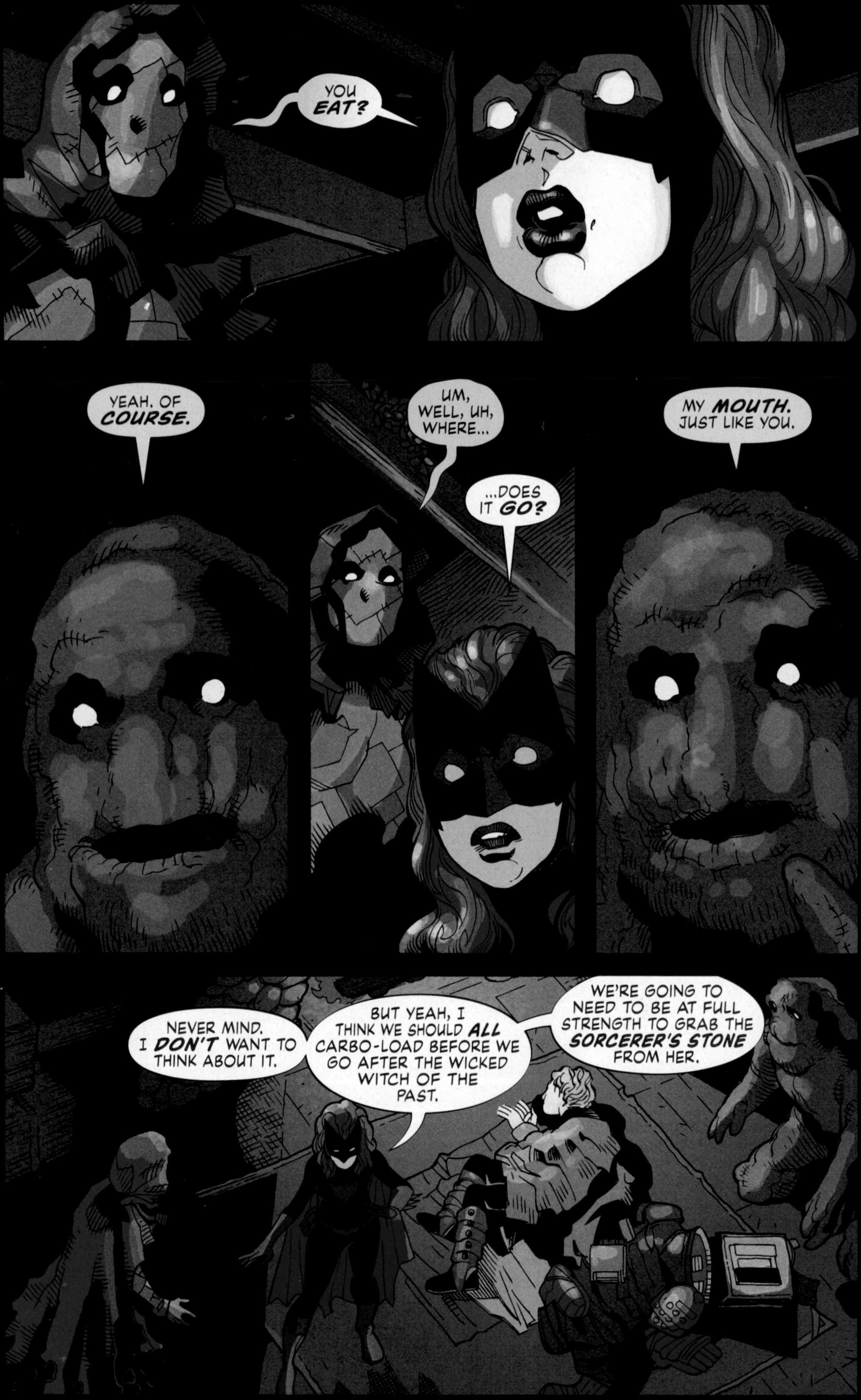
YOU EAT?
YEAH. OF COURSE.
UM, WELL, UH, WHERE...
...DOES IT GO?
MY MOUTH. JUST LIKE YOU.
NEVER MIND. I DON'T WANT TO THINK ABOUT IT.
BUT YEAH, I THINK WE SHOULD ALL CARBO-LOAD BEFORE WE GO AFTER THE WICKED WITCH OF THE PAST.
WE'RE GOING TO NEED TO BE AT FULL STRENGTH TO GRAB THE SORCERER'S STONE FROM HER.

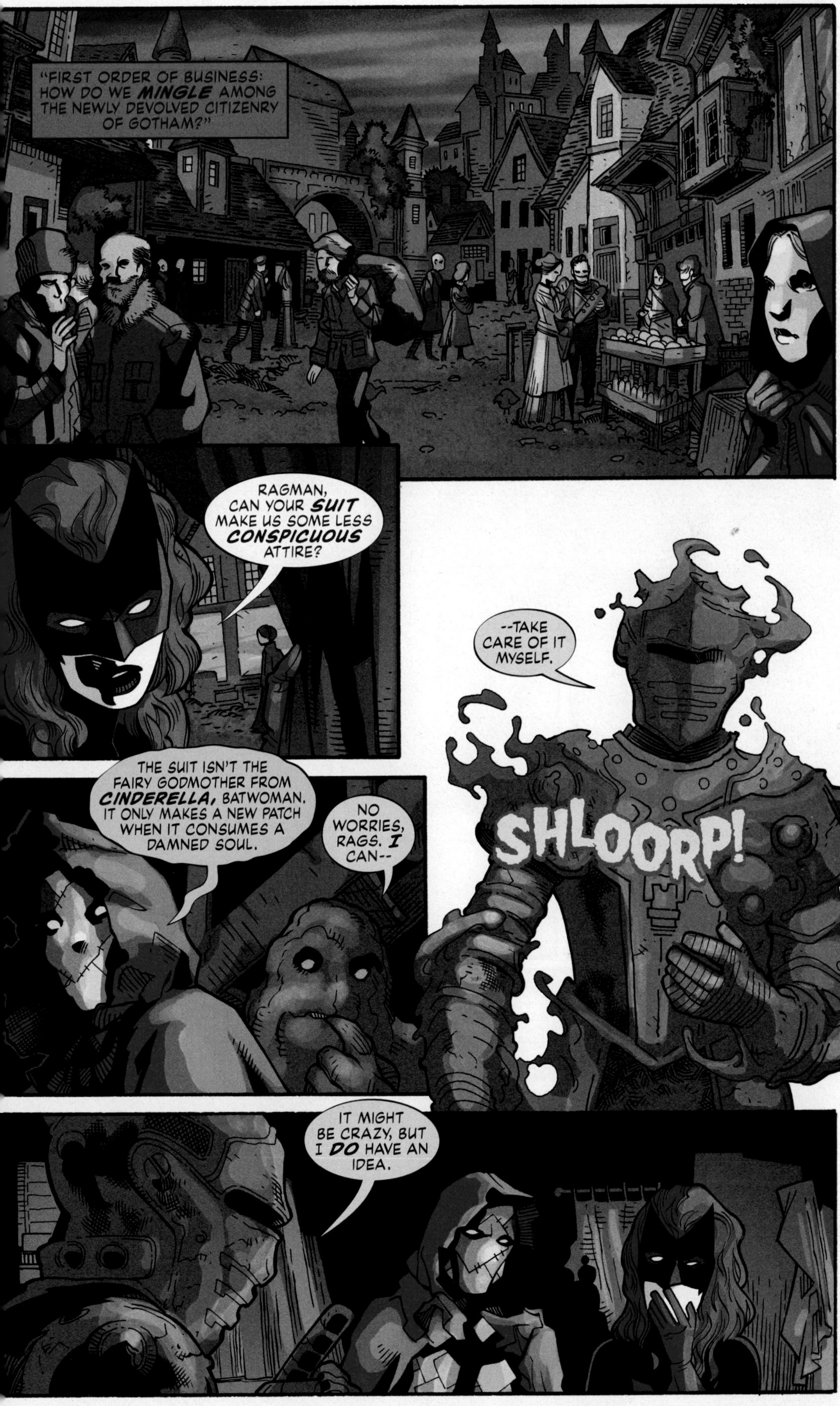
"FIRST ORDER OF BUSINESS: HOW DO WE MINGLE AMONG THE NEWLY DEVOLVED CITIZENRY OF GOTHAM?"
RAGMAN, CAN YOUR SUIT MAKE US SOME LESS CONSPICUOUS ATTIRE?
THE SUIT ISN'T THE FAIRY GODMOTHER FROM CINDERELLA, BATWOMAN. IT ONLY MAKES A NEW PATCH WHEN IT CONSUMES A DAMNED SOUL.
NO WORRIES, RAGS. I CAN--
--TAKE CARE OF IT MYSELF.
SHLOORP!
IT MIGHT BE CRAZY, BUT I DO HAVE AN IDEA.

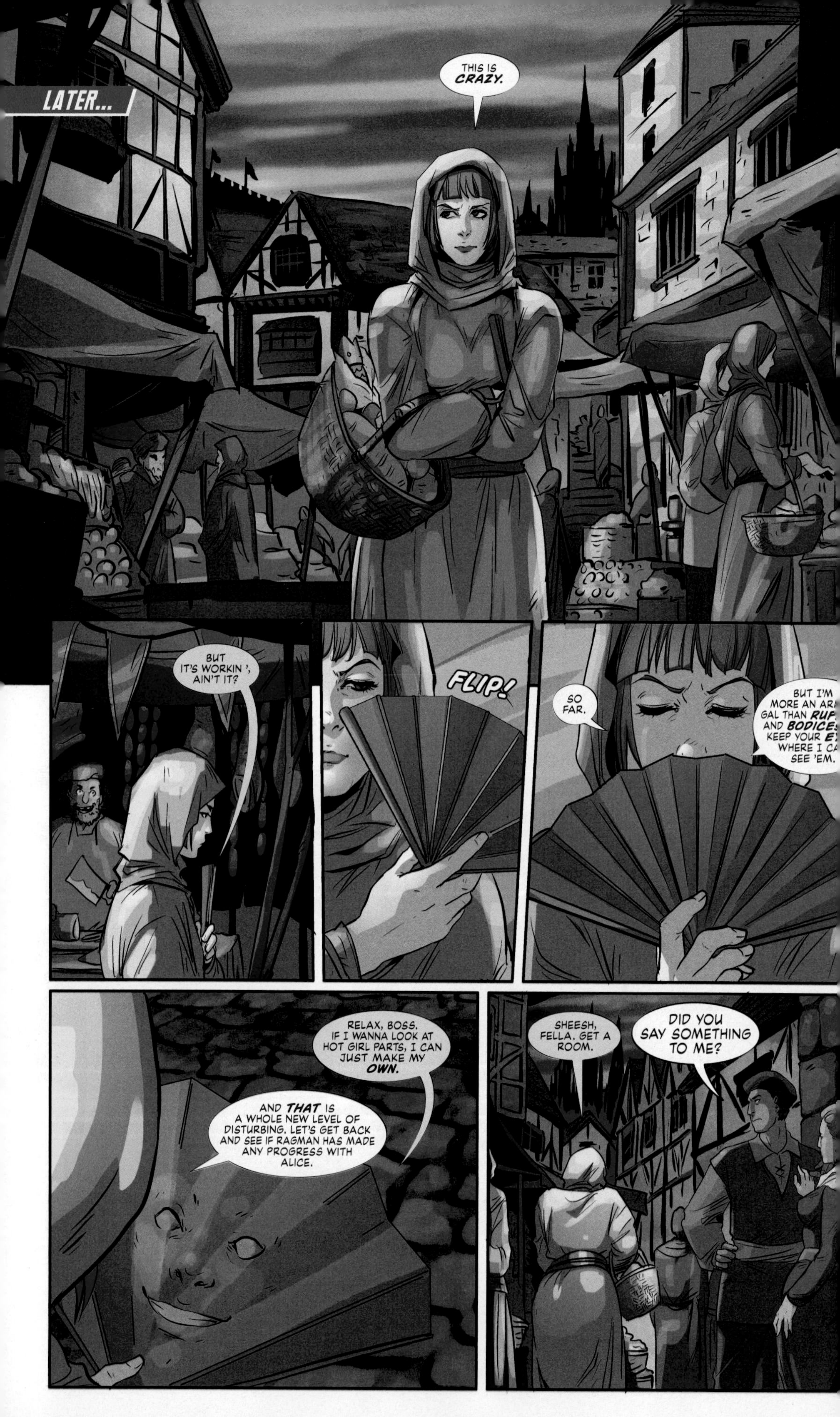
LATER...
THIS IS CRAZY.
BUT IT'S WORKIN', AIN'T IT?
FLIP!
SO FAR.
BUT I'M MORE AN ARA GAL THAN RUF AND BODICES KEEP YOUR EY WHERE I CA SEE 'EM.
RELAX, BOSS. IF I WANNA LOOK AT HOT GIRL PARTS, I CAN JUST MAKE MY OWN.
AND THAT IS A WHOLE NEW LEVEL OF DISTURBING. LET'S GET BACK AND SEE IF RAGMAN HAS MADE ANY PROGRESS WITH ALICE.
SHEESH, FELLA. GET A ROOM.
DID YOU SAY SOMETHING TO ME?

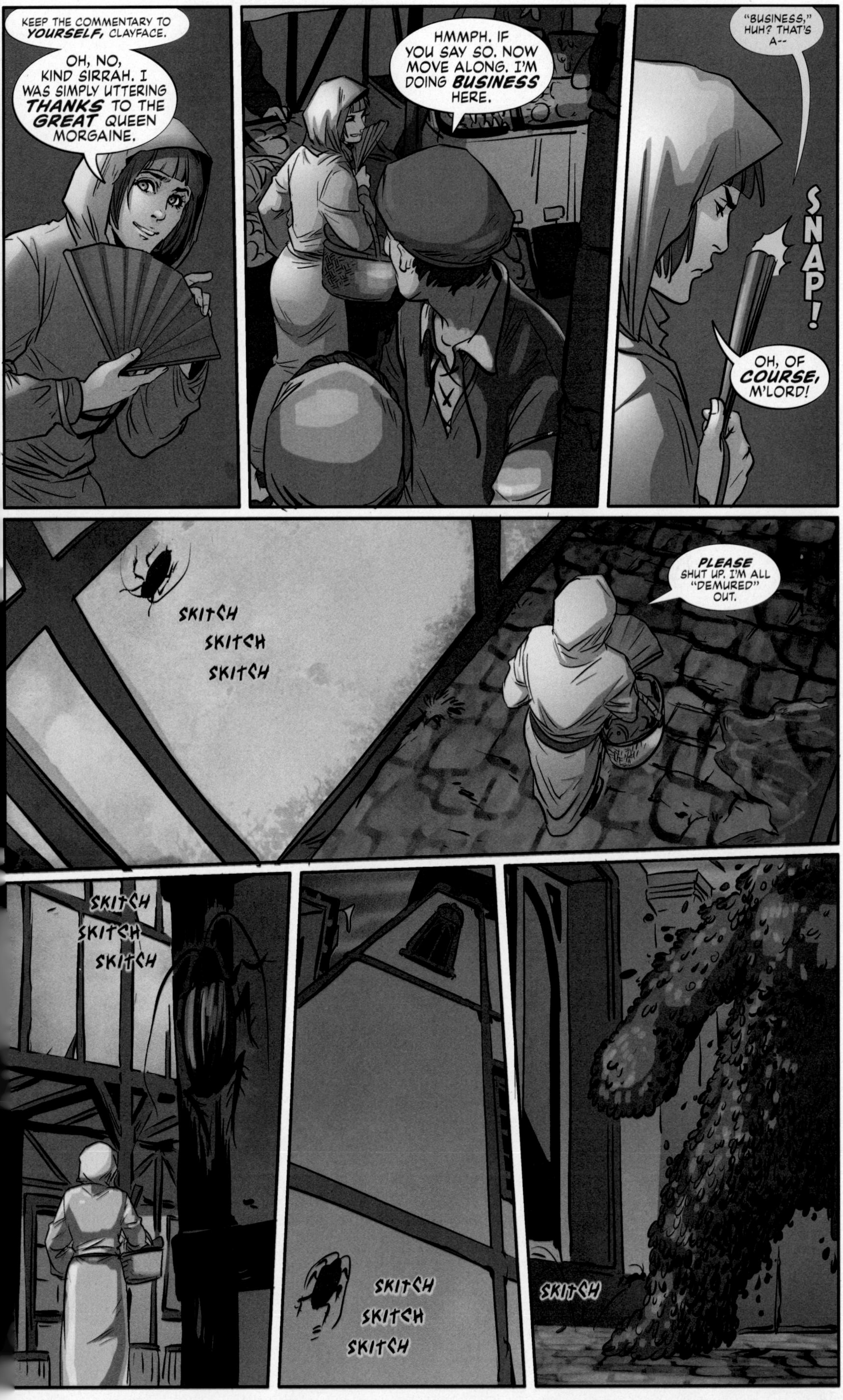
KEEP THE COMMENTARY TO YOURSELF, CLAYFACE.
OH, NO, KIND SIRRAH. I WAS SIMPLY UTTERING THANKS TO THE GREAT QUEEN MORGAINE.
HMMPH. IF YOU SAY SO. NOW MOVE ALONG. I'M DOING BUSINESS HERE.
"BUSINESS," HUH? THAT'S A--
SNAP!
OH, OF COURSE, M'LORD!
SKITCH SKITCH SKITCH
PLEASE SHUT UP. I'M ALL "DEMURED" OUT.
SKITCH SKITCH SKITCH
SKITCH SKITCH SKITCH
SKITCH

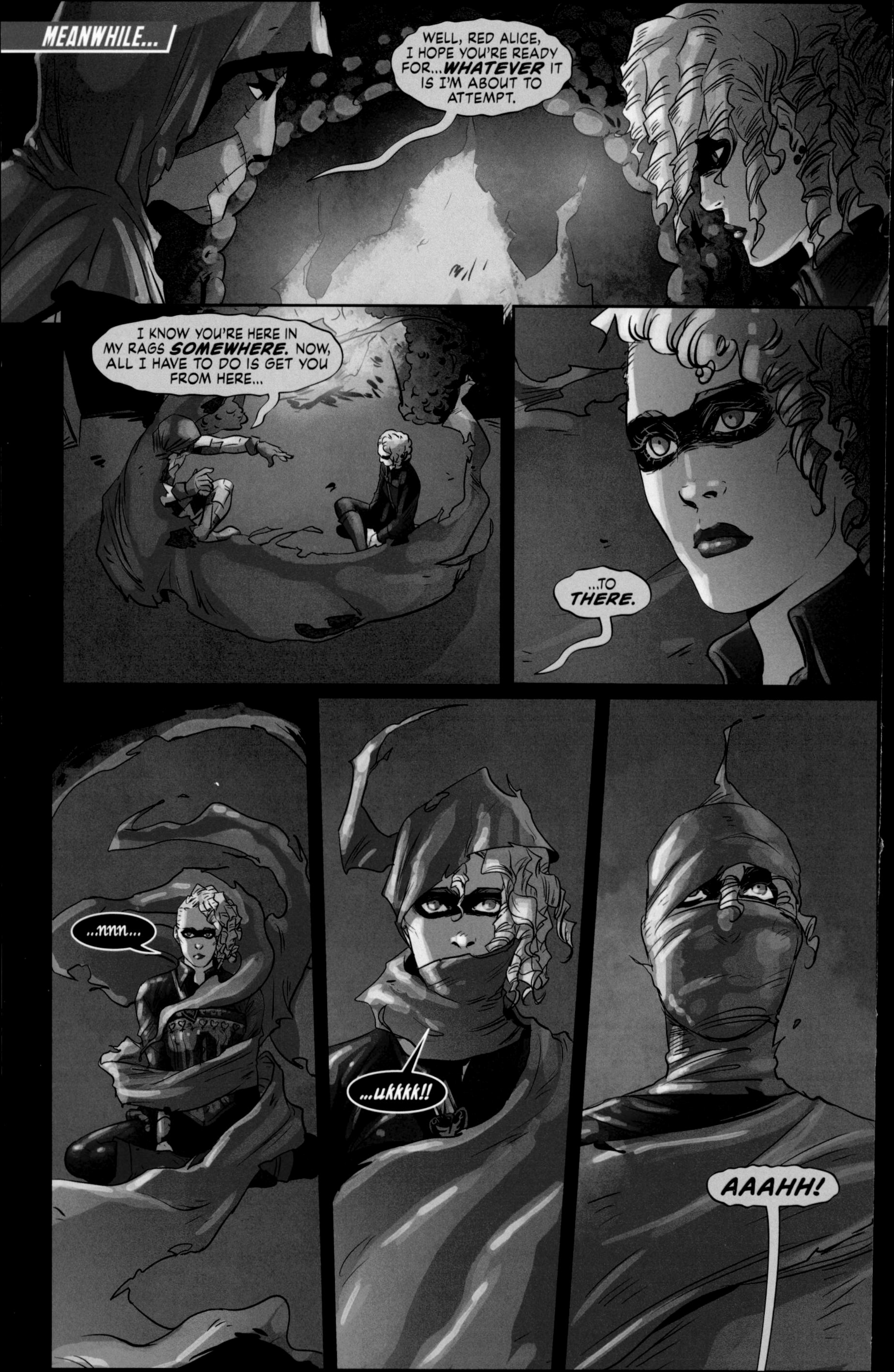
MEANWHILE...
WELL, RED ALICE, I HOPE YOU'RE READY FOR... WHATEVER IT IS I'M ABOUT TO ATTEMPT.
I KNOW YOU'RE HERE IN MY RAGS SOMEWHERE. NOW, ALL I HAVE TO DO IS GET YOU FROM HERE...
...TO THERE.
...nnn...
...ukkkk!!
AAAHH!

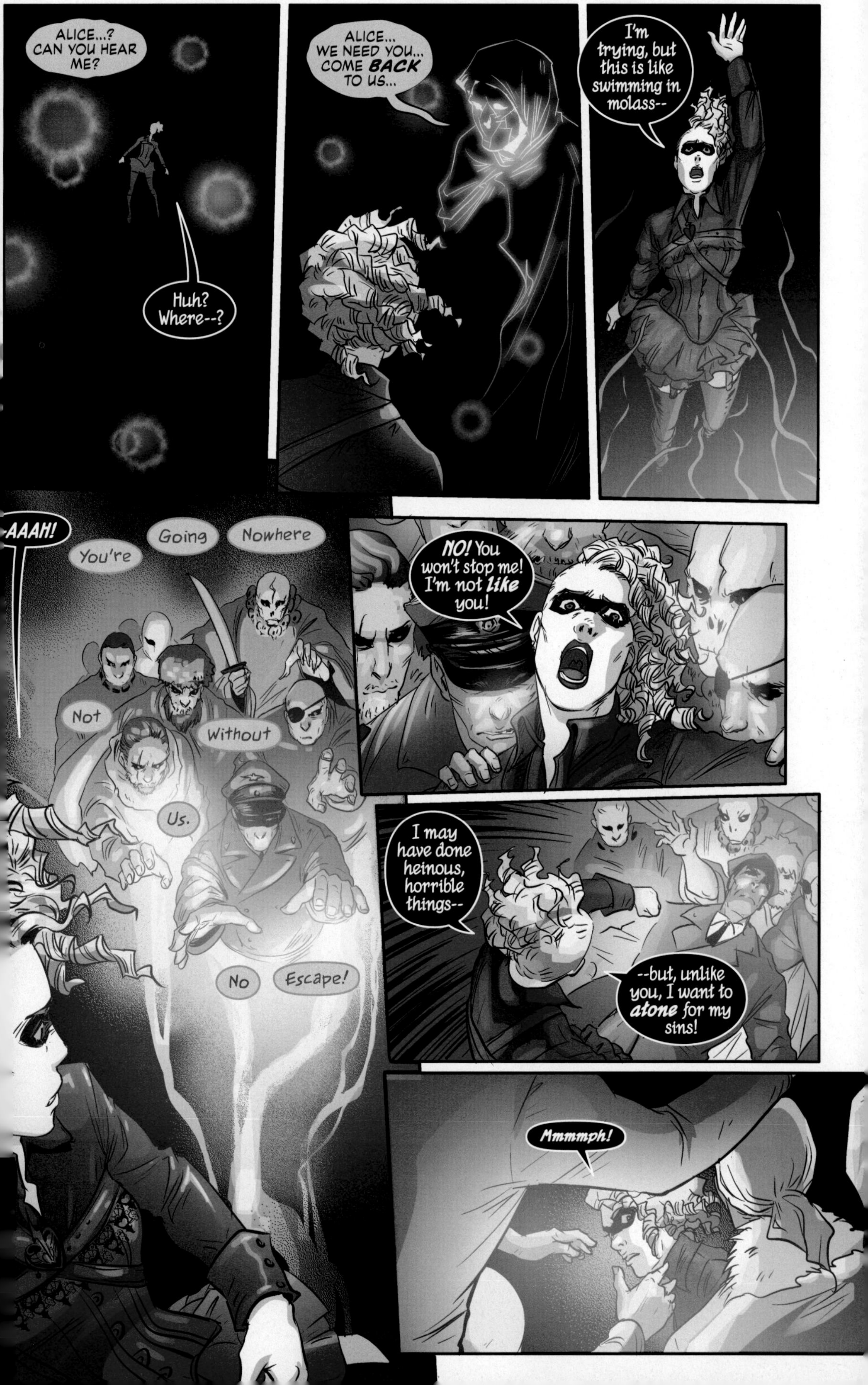
ALICE...? CAN YOU HEAR ME?
Huh? Where--?
ALICE... WE NEED YOU... COME BACK TO US...
I'm trying, but this is like swimming in molass--
-AAAH!
You're
Going
Nowhere
Not
Without
Us.
No
Escape!
NO! You won't stop me! I'm not like you!
I may have done heinous, horrible things--
--but, unlike you, I want to atone for my sins!
Mmmmph!

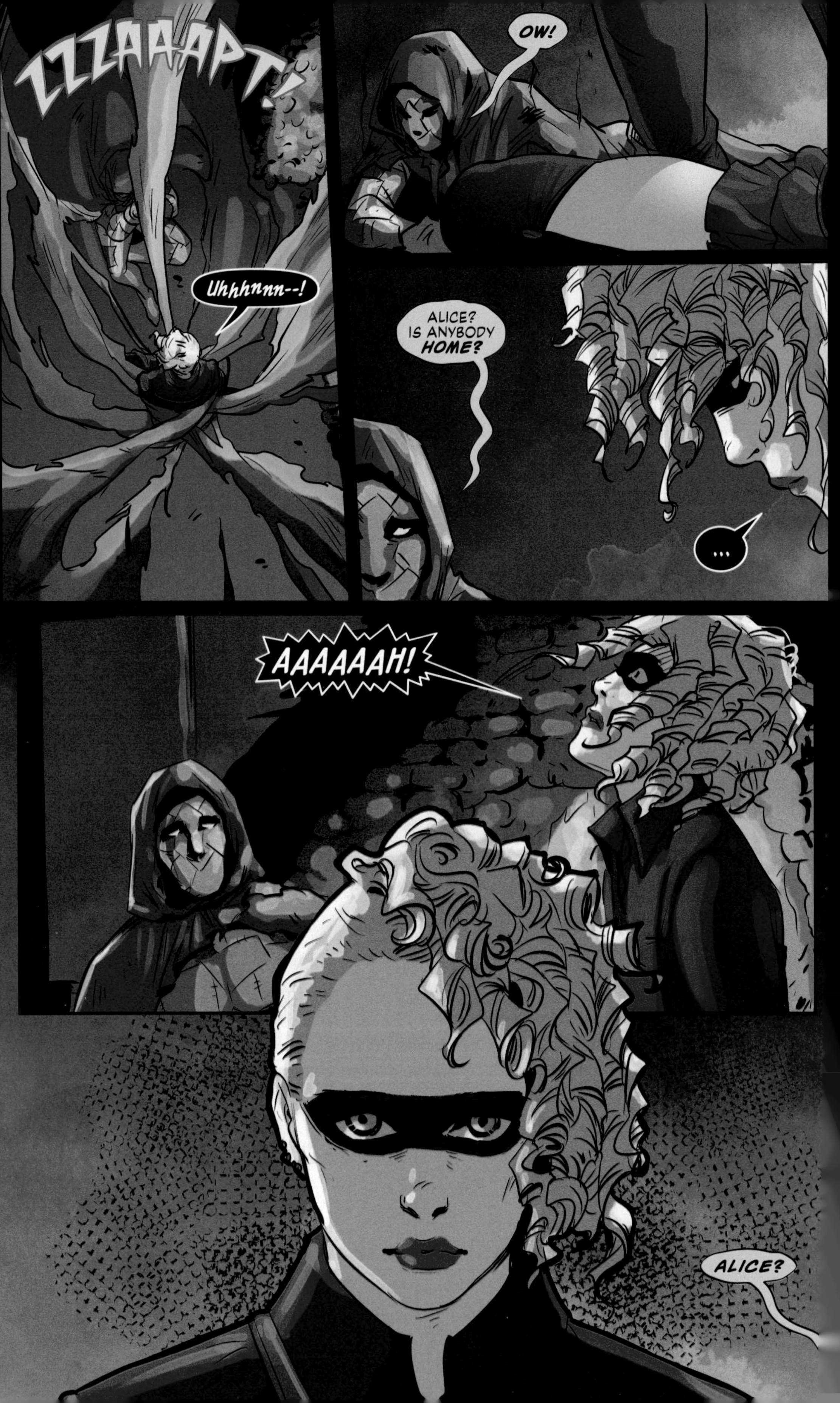
ZZZAAAAPT!
OW!
Uhhhnnn--!
ALICE? IS ANYBODY HOME?
...
AAAAAAH!
ALICE?

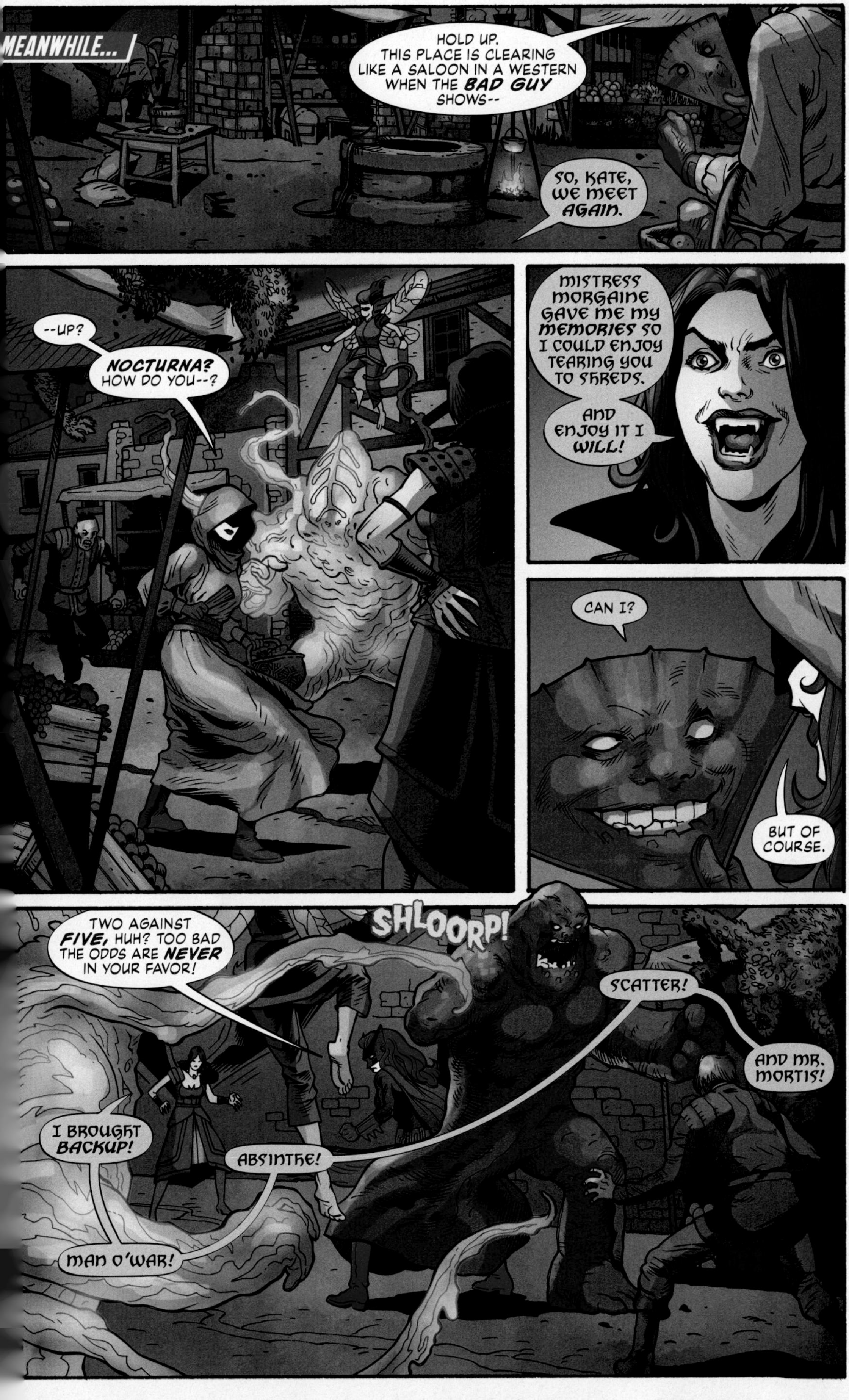
MEANWHILE...
HOLD UP. THIS PLACE IS CLEARING LIKE A SALOON IN A WESTERN WHEN THE BAD GUY SHOWS--
SO, KATE, WE MEET AGAIN.
--UP?
NOCTURNA? HOW DO YOU--?
MISTRESS MORGAINE GAVE ME MY MEMORIES SO I COULD ENJOY TEARING YOU TO SHREDS.
AND ENJOY IT I WILL!
CAN I?
BUT OF COURSE.
TWO AGAINST FIVE, HUH? TOO BAD THE ODDS ARE NEVER IN YOUR FAVOR!
SHLOORP!
I BROUGHT BACKUP!
MAN O'WAR!
ABSINTHE!
SCATTER!
AND MR. MORTIS!

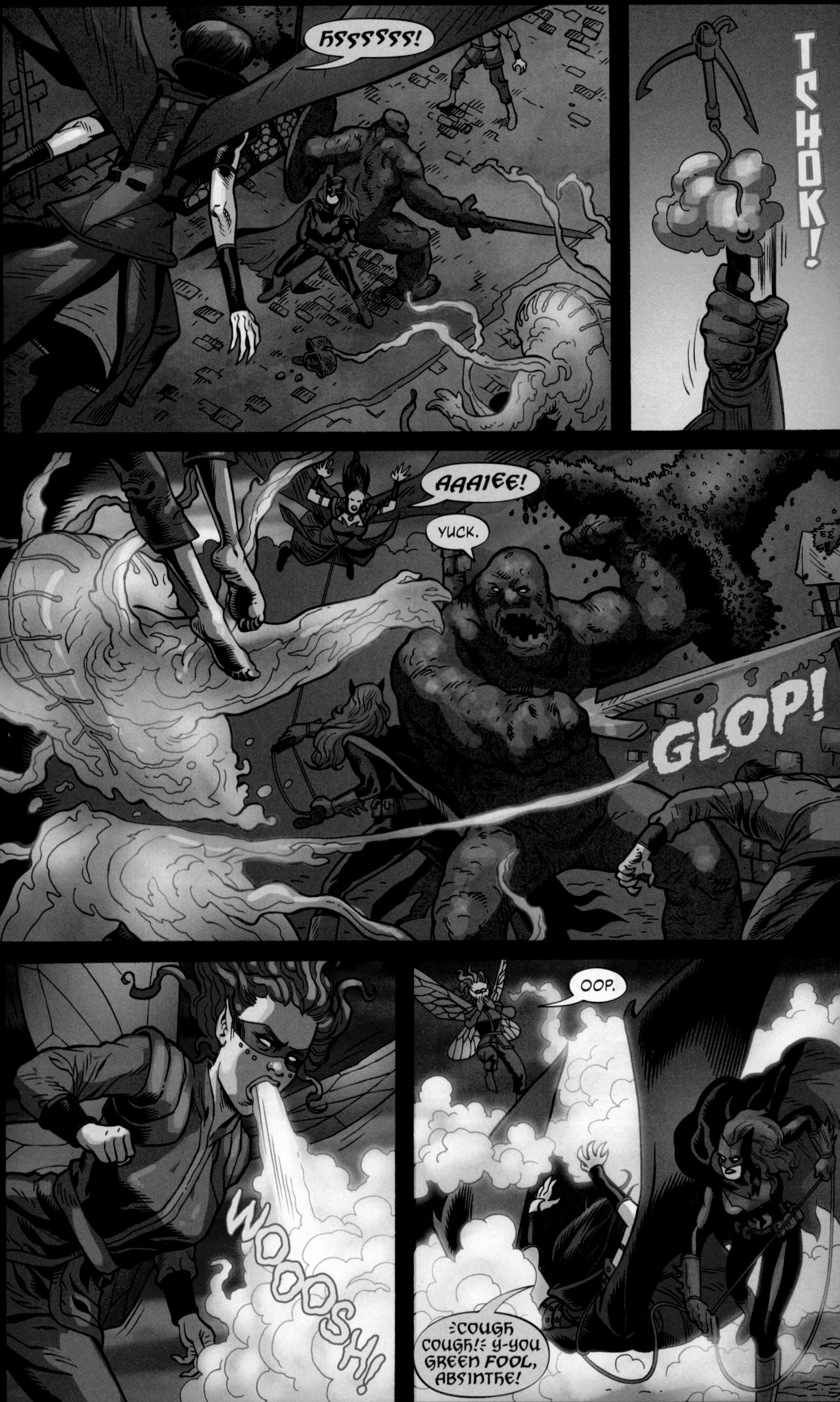
HSSSSSS!
TCHOK!
AAAIEE!
YUCK.
GLOP!
WOOOSH!
OOP.
COUGH COUGH! Y-YOU GREEN FOOL, ABSINTHE!

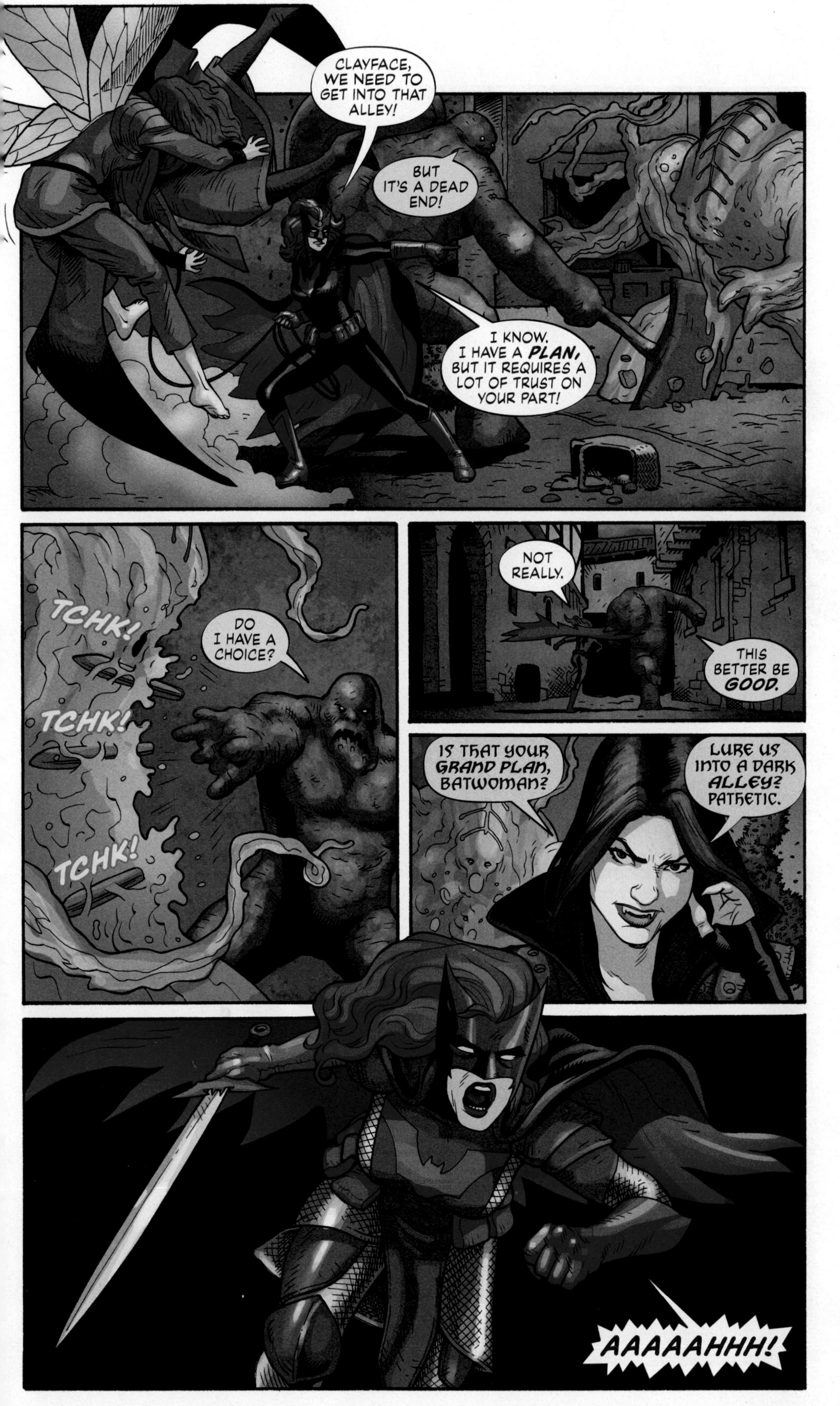
CLAYFACE, WE NEED TO GET INTO THAT ALLEY!
BUT IT'S A DEAD END!
I KNOW. I HAVE A PLAN, BUT IT REQUIRES A LOT OF TRUST ON YOUR PART!
TCHK!
TCHK!
TCHK!
DO I HAVE A CHOICE?
NOT REALLY.
THIS BETTER BE GOOD.
IS THAT YOUR GRAND PLAN, BATWOMAN?
LURE US INTO A DARK ALLEY? PATHETIC.
AAAAAHHH!

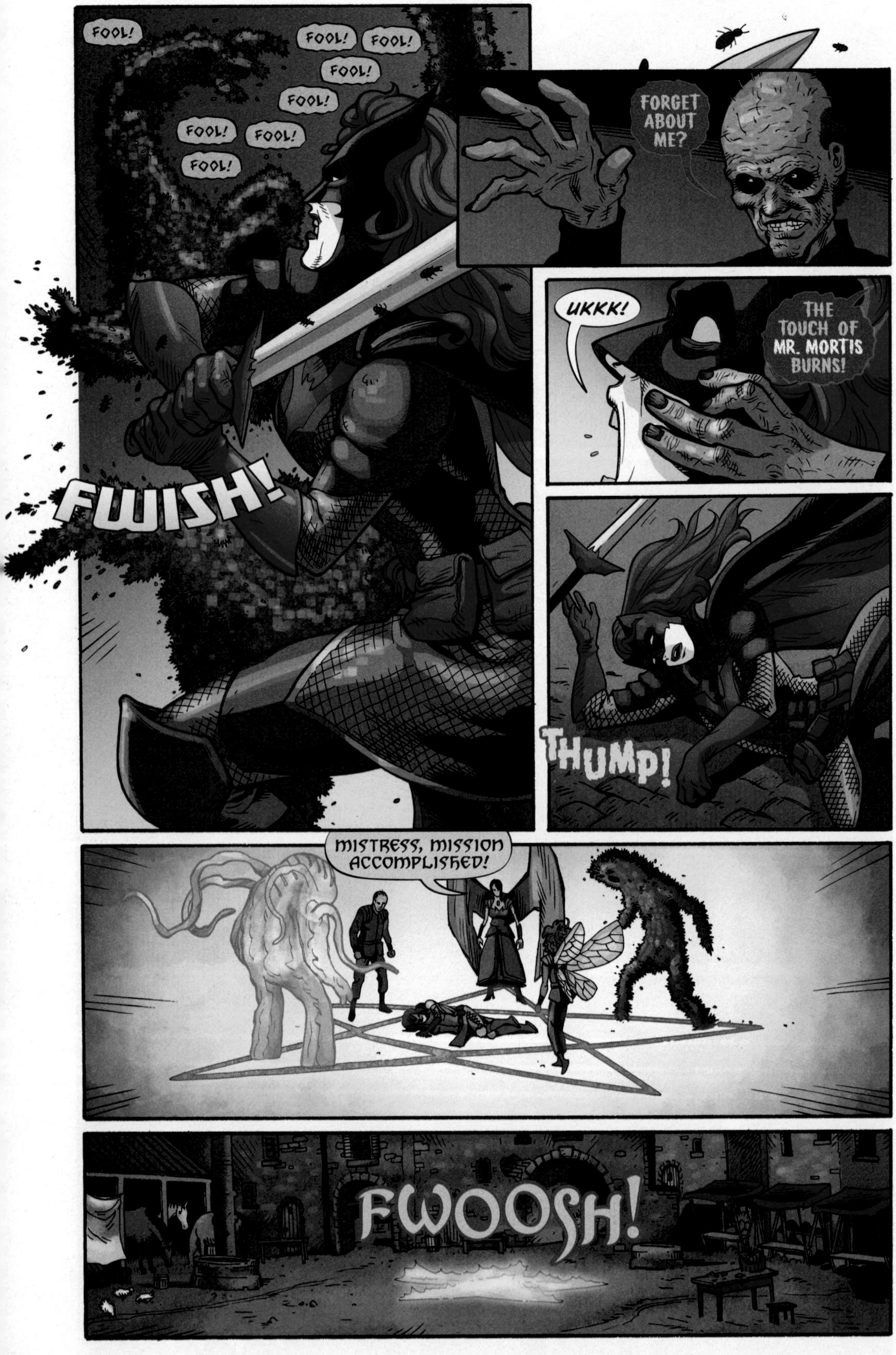
FOOL!
FOOL!
FOOL!
FOOL!
FOOL!
FOOL!
FOOL!
FOOL!
FWISH!
FORGET ABOUT ME?
UKKK!
THE TOUCH OF MR. MORTIS BURNS!
THUMP!
MISTRESS, MISSION ACCOMPLISHED!
FWOOSH!

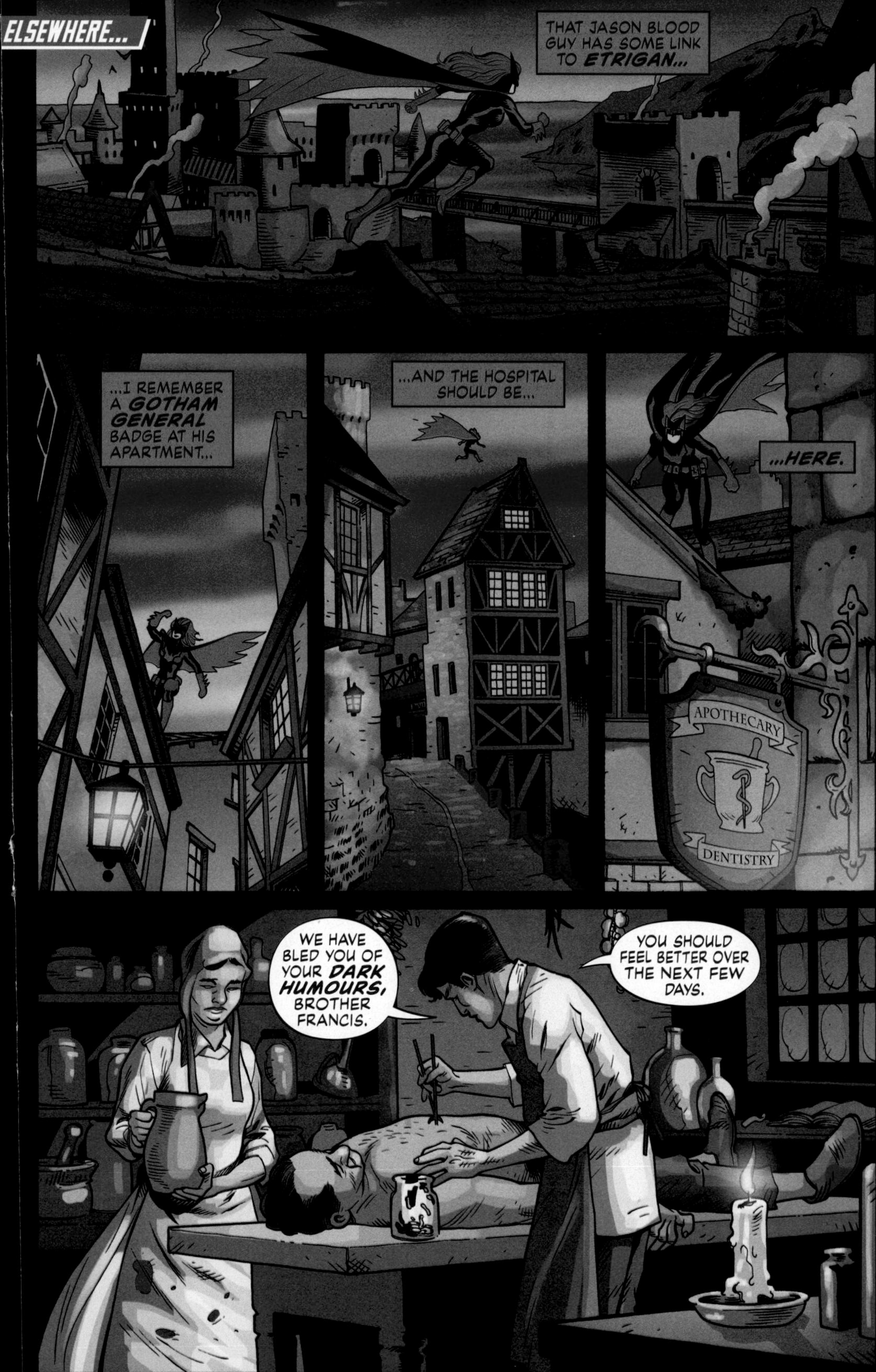
ELSEWHERE...
THAT JASON BLOOD GUY HAS SOME LINK TO ETRIGAN...
...I REMEMBER A GOTHAM GENERAL BADGE AT HIS APARTMENT...
...AND THE HOSPITAL SHOULD BE...
...HERE.
APOTHECARY
DENTISTRY
WE HAVE BLED YOU OF YOUR DARK HUMOURS, BROTHER FRANCIS.
YOU SHOULD FEEL BETTER OVER THE NEXT FEW DAYS.

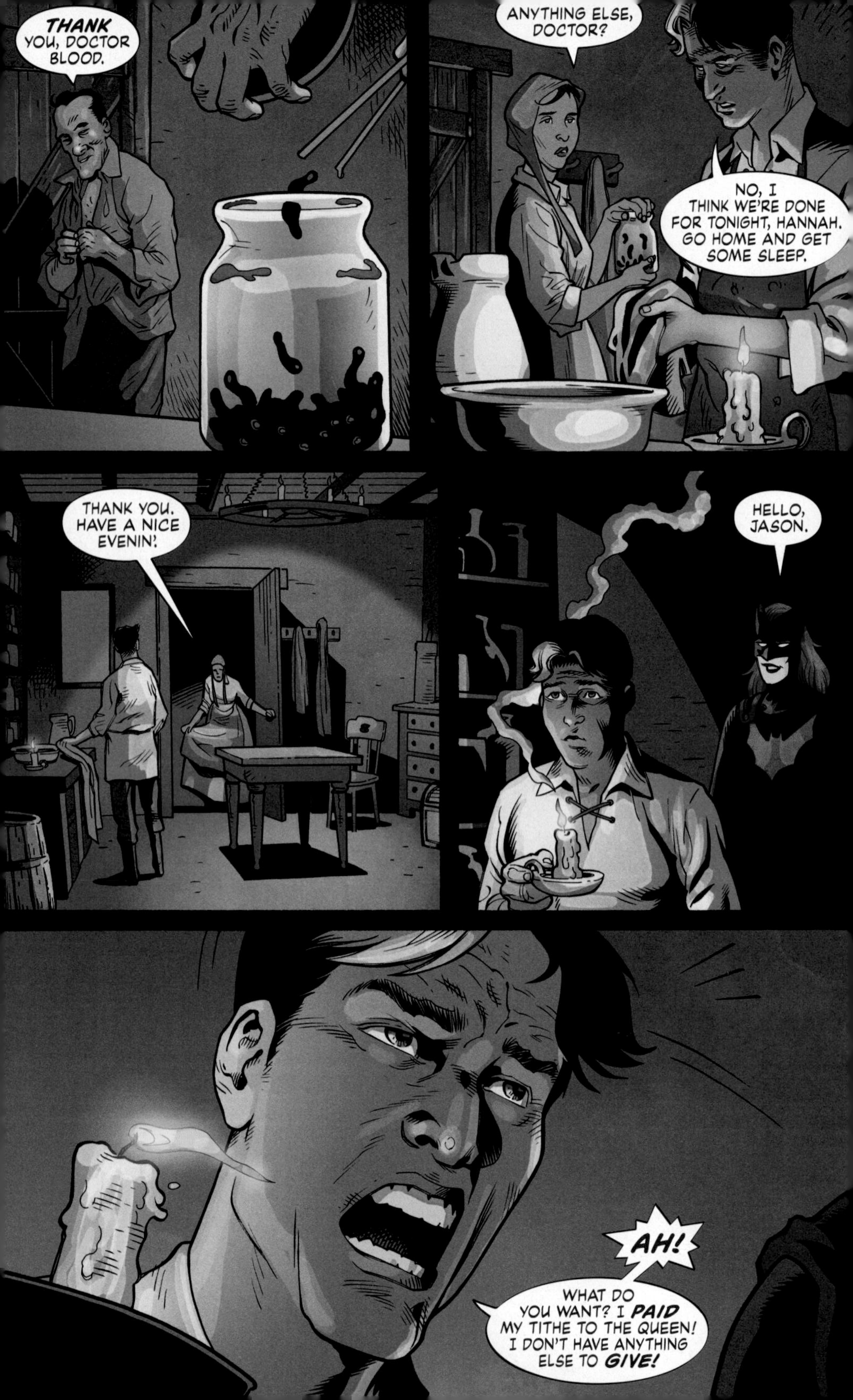
THANK YOU, DOCTOR BLOOD.
ANYTHING ELSE, DOCTOR?
NO, I THINK WE'RE DONE FOR TONIGHT, HANNAH. GO HOME AND GET SOME SLEEP.
THANK YOU. HAVE A NICE EVENIN'.
HELLO, JASON.
AH!
WHAT DO YOU WANT? I PAID MY TITHE TO THE QUEEN! I DON'T HAVE ANYTHING ELSE TO GIVE!

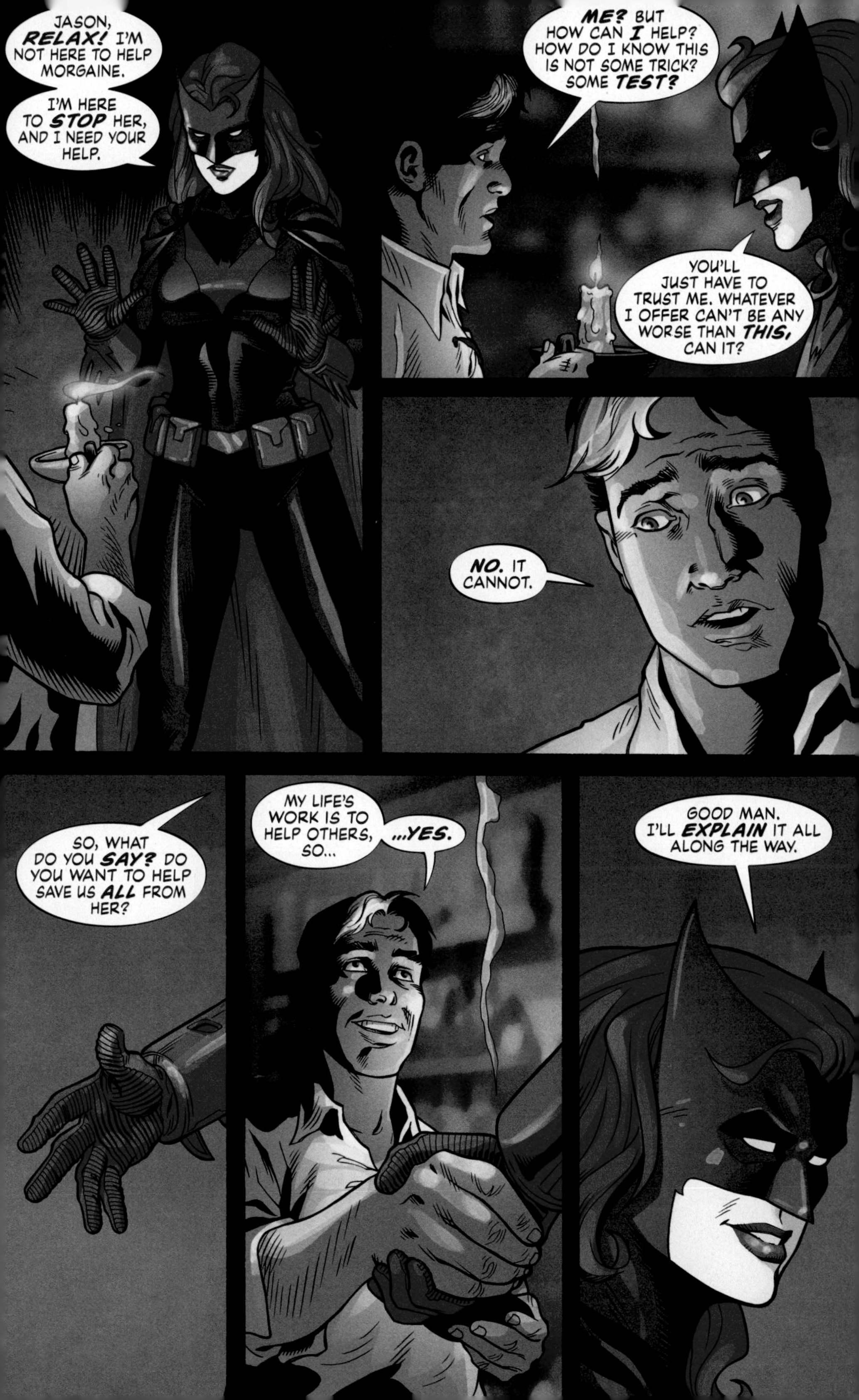
JASON, RELAX! I'M NOT HERE TO HELP MORGAINE.
I'M HERE TO STOP HER, AND I NEED YOUR HELP.
ME? BUT HOW CAN I HELP? HOW DO I KNOW THIS IS NOT SOME TRICK? SOME TEST?
YOU'LL JUST HAVE TO TRUST ME. WHATEVER I OFFER CAN'T BE ANY WORSE THAN THIS, CAN IT?
NO. IT CANNOT.
SO, WHAT DO YOU SAY? DO YOU WANT TO HELP SAVE US ALL FROM HER?
MY LIFE'S WORK IS TO HELP OTHERS, SO...
...YES.
GOOD MAN. I'LL EXPLAIN IT ALL ALONG THE WAY.

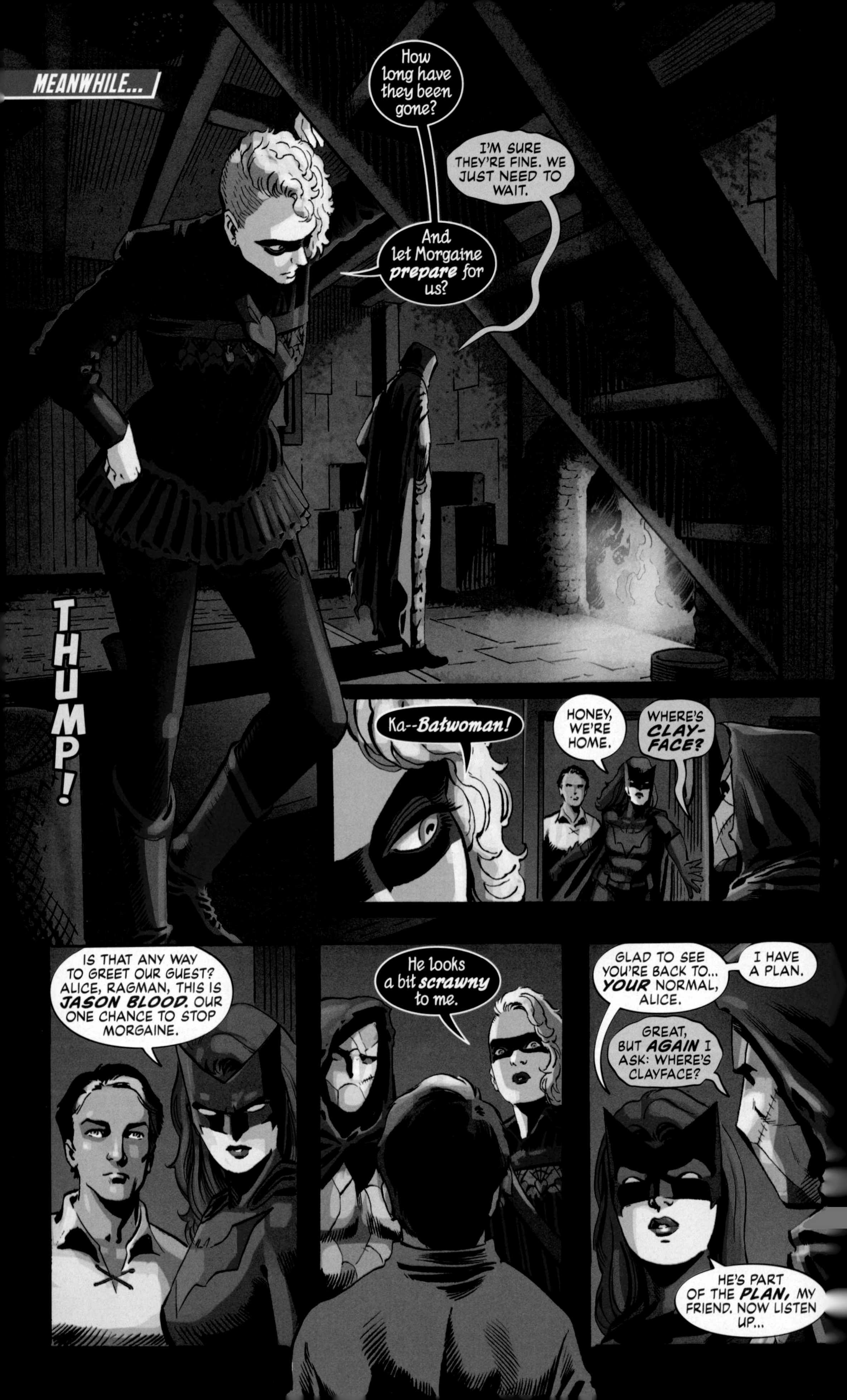
MEANWHILE...
How long have they been gone?
I'M SURE THEY'RE FINE. WE JUST NEED TO WAIT.
And let Morgaine prepare for us?
THUMP!
Ka--Batwoman!
HONEY, WE'RE HOME.
WHERE'S CLAYFACE?
IS THAT ANY WAY TO GREET OUR GUEST? ALICE, RAGMAN, THIS IS JASON BLOOD. OUR ONE CHANCE TO STOP MORGAINE.
He looks a bit scrawny to me.
GLAD TO SEE YOU'RE BACK TO... YOUR NORMAL, ALICE.
I HAVE A PLAN.
GREAT, BUT AGAIN I ASK: WHERE'S CLAYFACE?
HE'S PART OF THE PLAN, MY FRIEND. NOW LISTEN UP...

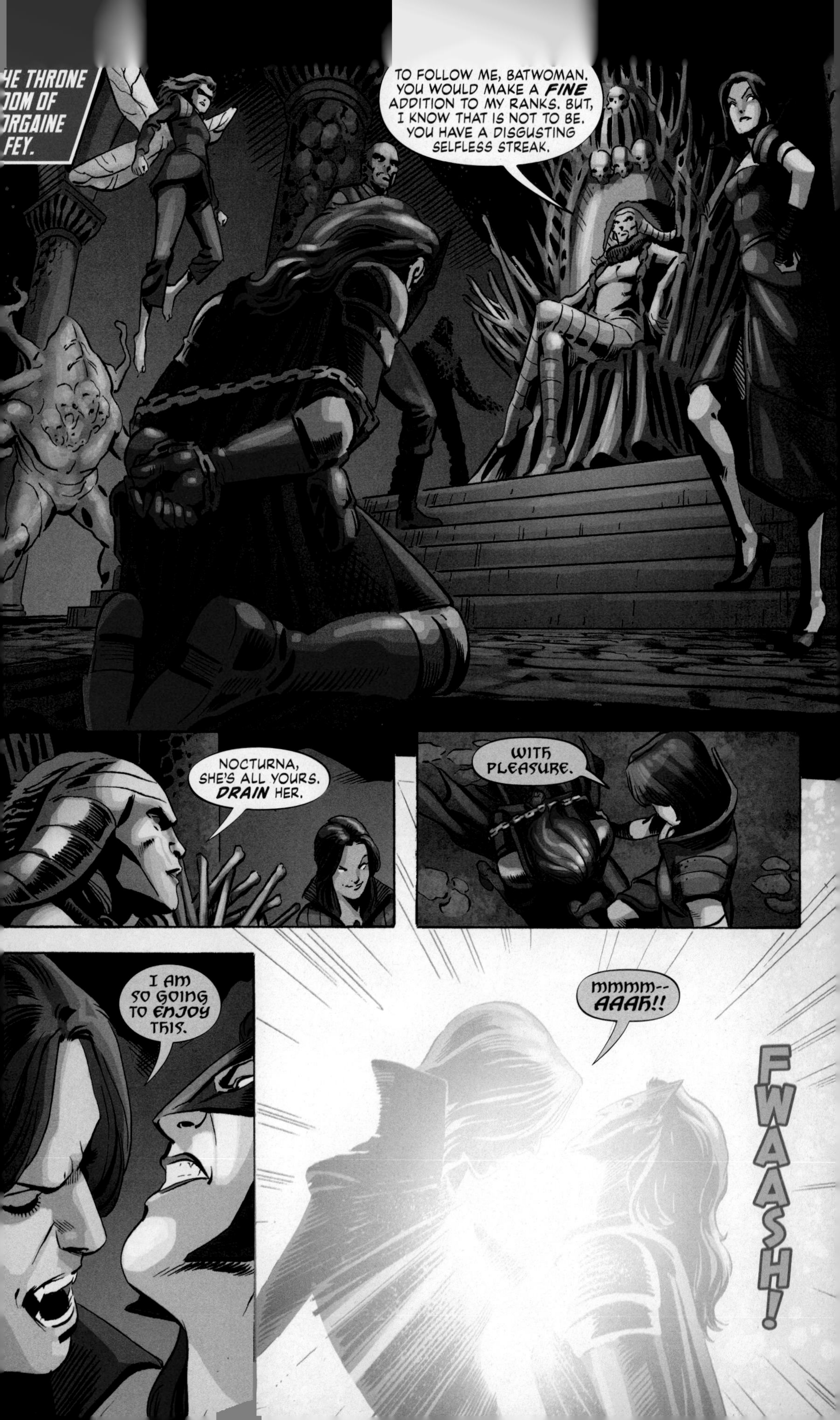
HE THRONE
OOM OF
ORGAINE
FEY.
TO FOLLOW ME, BATWOMAN. YOU WOULD MAKE A FINE ADDITION TO MY RANKS. BUT, I KNOW THAT IS NOT TO BE. YOU HAVE A DISGUSTING SELFLESS STREAK.
NOCTURNA, SHE'S ALL YOURS. DRAIN HER.
WITH PLEASURE.
I AM SO GOING TO ENJOY THIS.
MMMM-- AAAH!!
FWAASH!

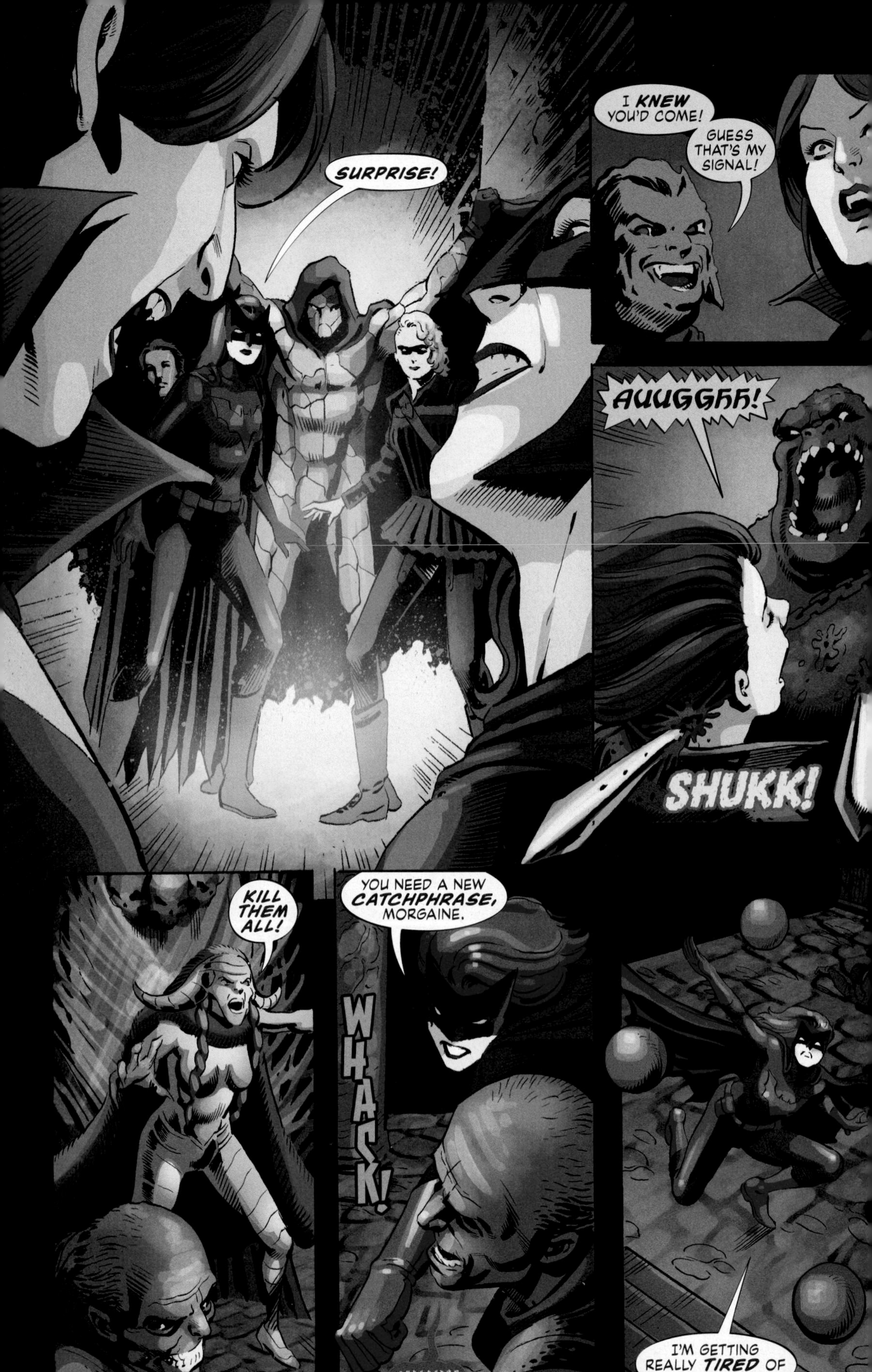
SURPRISE!
I KNEW YOU'D COME!
GUESS THAT'S MY SIGNAL!
AUUGGHH!
SHUKK!
KILL THEM ALL!
YOU NEED A NEW CATCHPHRASE, MORGAINE.
WHASK!
UHHN!
I'M GETTING REALLY TIRED OF THAT ONE!

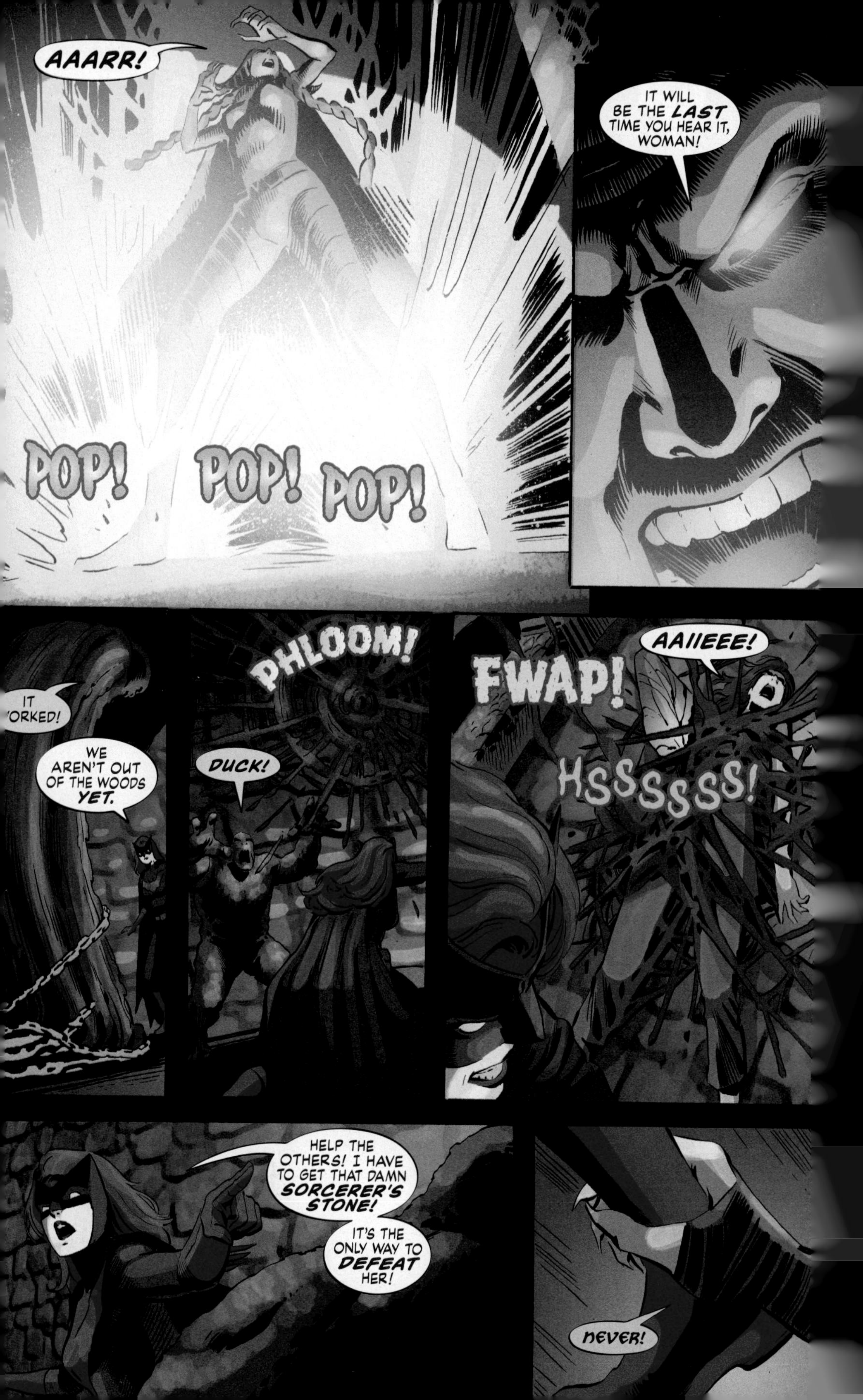
AAARR!
POP! POP! POP!
IT WILL BE THE LAST TIME YOU HEAR IT, WOMAN!
IT 'ORKED!
WE AREN'T OUT OF THE WOODS YET.
PHLOOM!
DUCK!
FWAP!
AAIIEEE!
HSSSSSS!
HELP THE OTHERS! I HAVE TO GET THAT DAMN SORCERER'S STONE!
IT'S THE ONLY WAY TO DEFEAT HER!
NEVER!

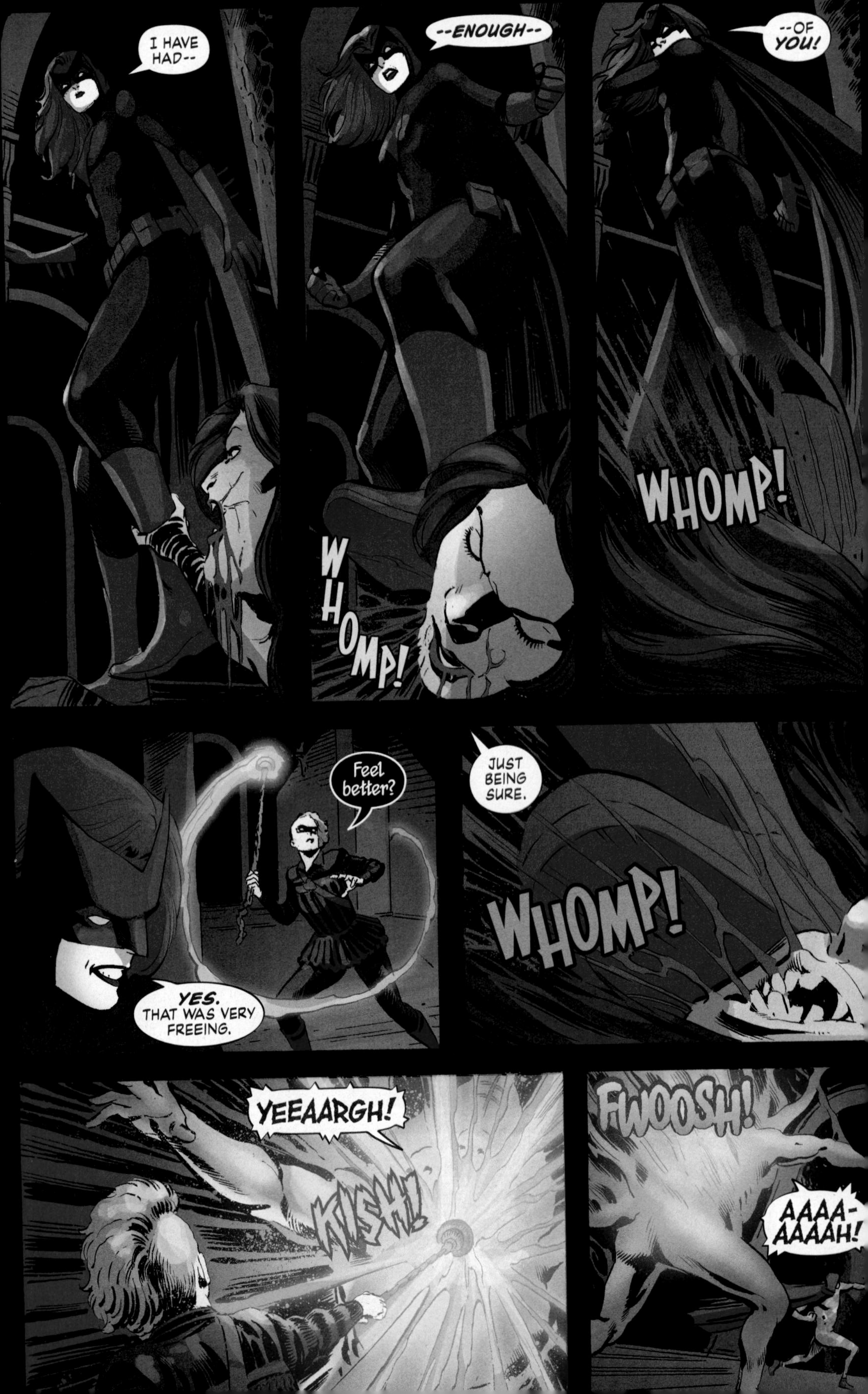
I HAVE HAD--
--ENOUGH--
--OF YOU!
WHOMP!
WHOMP!
Feel better?
YES. THAT WAS VERY FREEING.
JUST BEING SURE.
WHOMP!
YEEAARGH!
KISH!
FWOOSH!
AAAA-AAAAH!

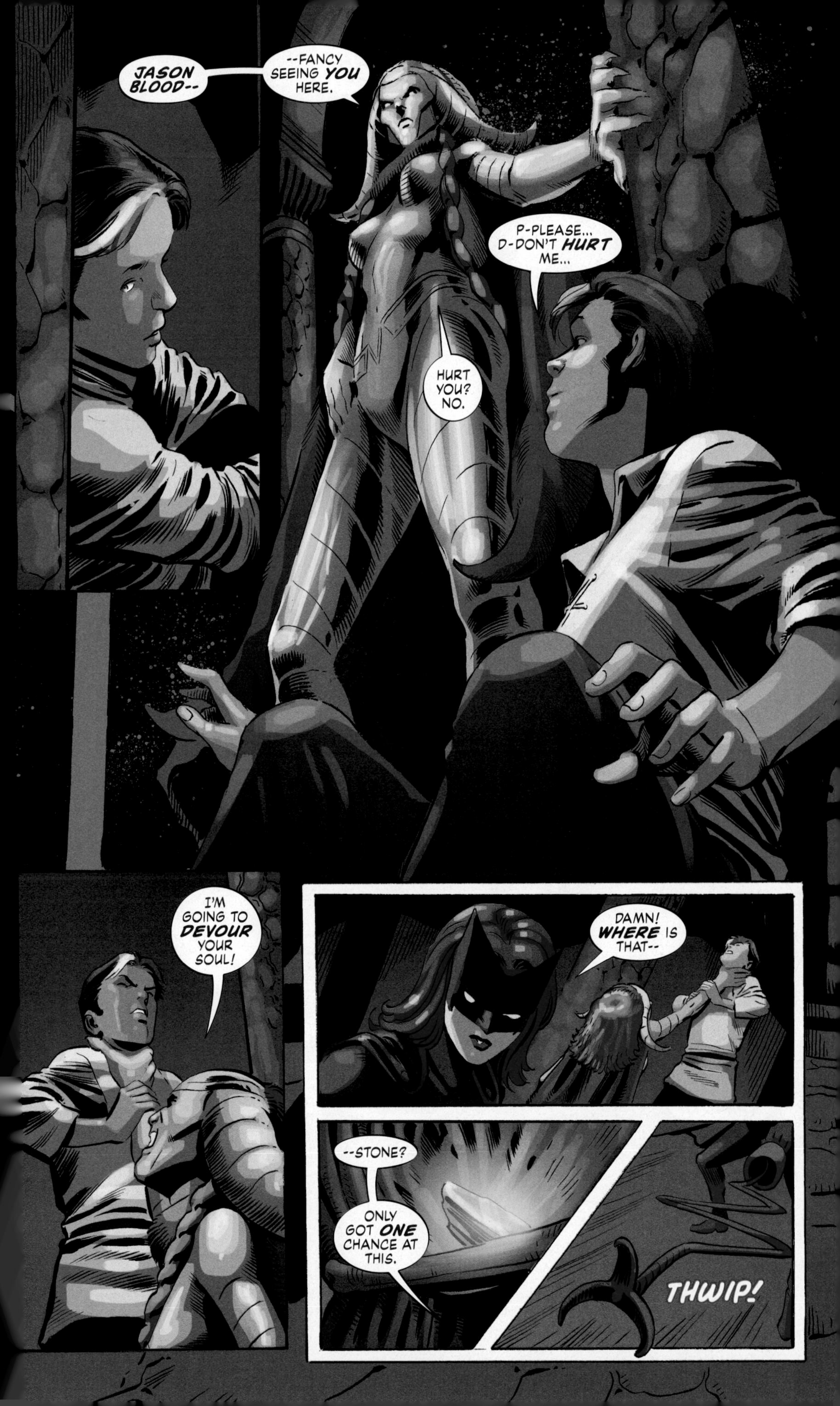

JASON BLOOD--
--FANCY SEEING YOU HERE.
P-PLEASE... D-DON'T HURT ME...
HURT YOU? NO.
I'M GOING TO DEVOUR YOUR SOUL!
DAMN! WHERE IS THAT--
--STONE?
ONLY GOT ONE CHANCE AT THIS.
THWIP!

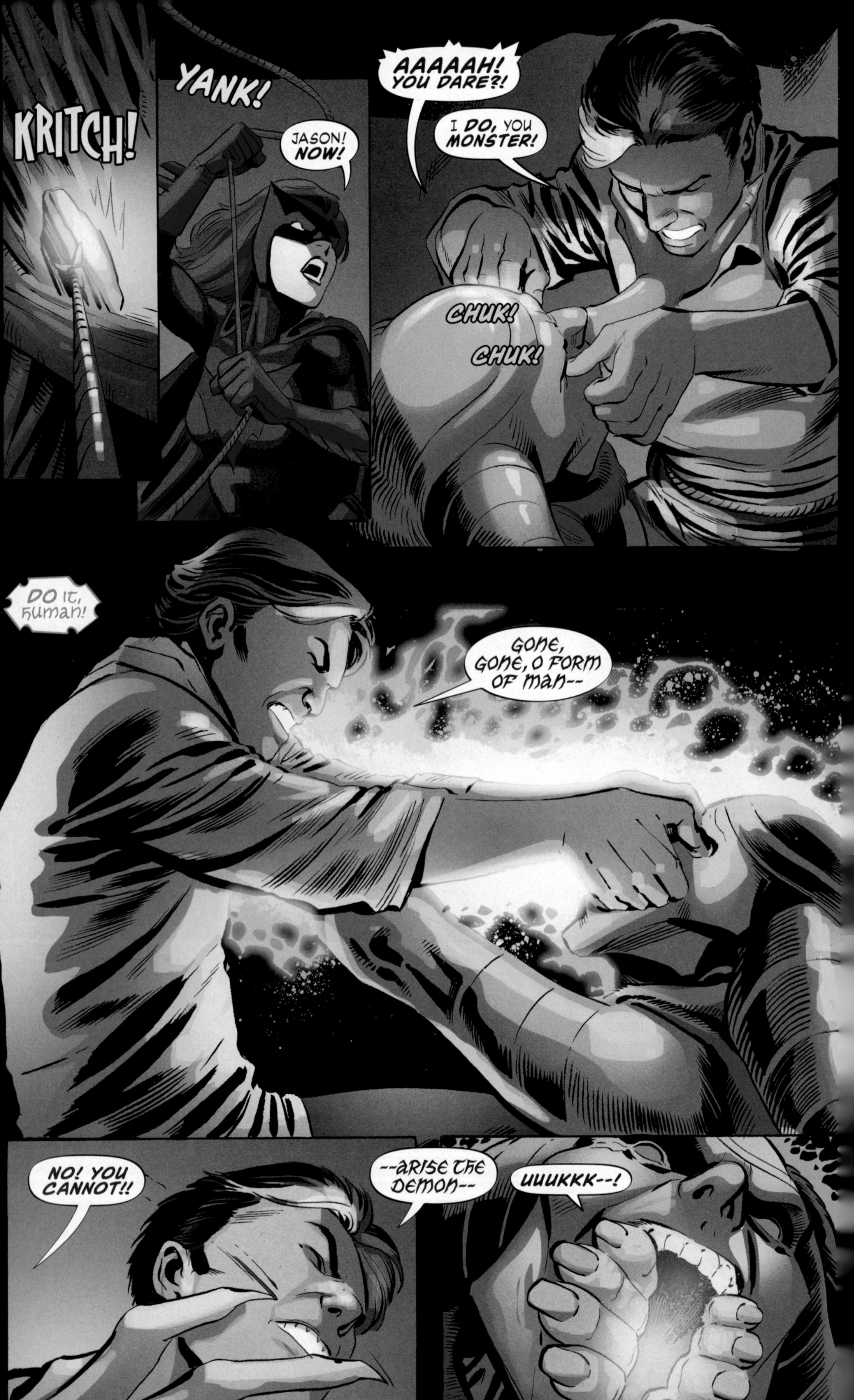

KRITCH!
YANK!
JASON! NOW!
AAAAAH! YOU DARE?!
I DO, YOU MONSTER!
CHUK!
CHUK!
DO IT, HUMAN!
GONE, GONE, O FORM OF MAN--
NO! YOU CANNOT!!
--ARISE THE DEMON--
UUUKKK--!

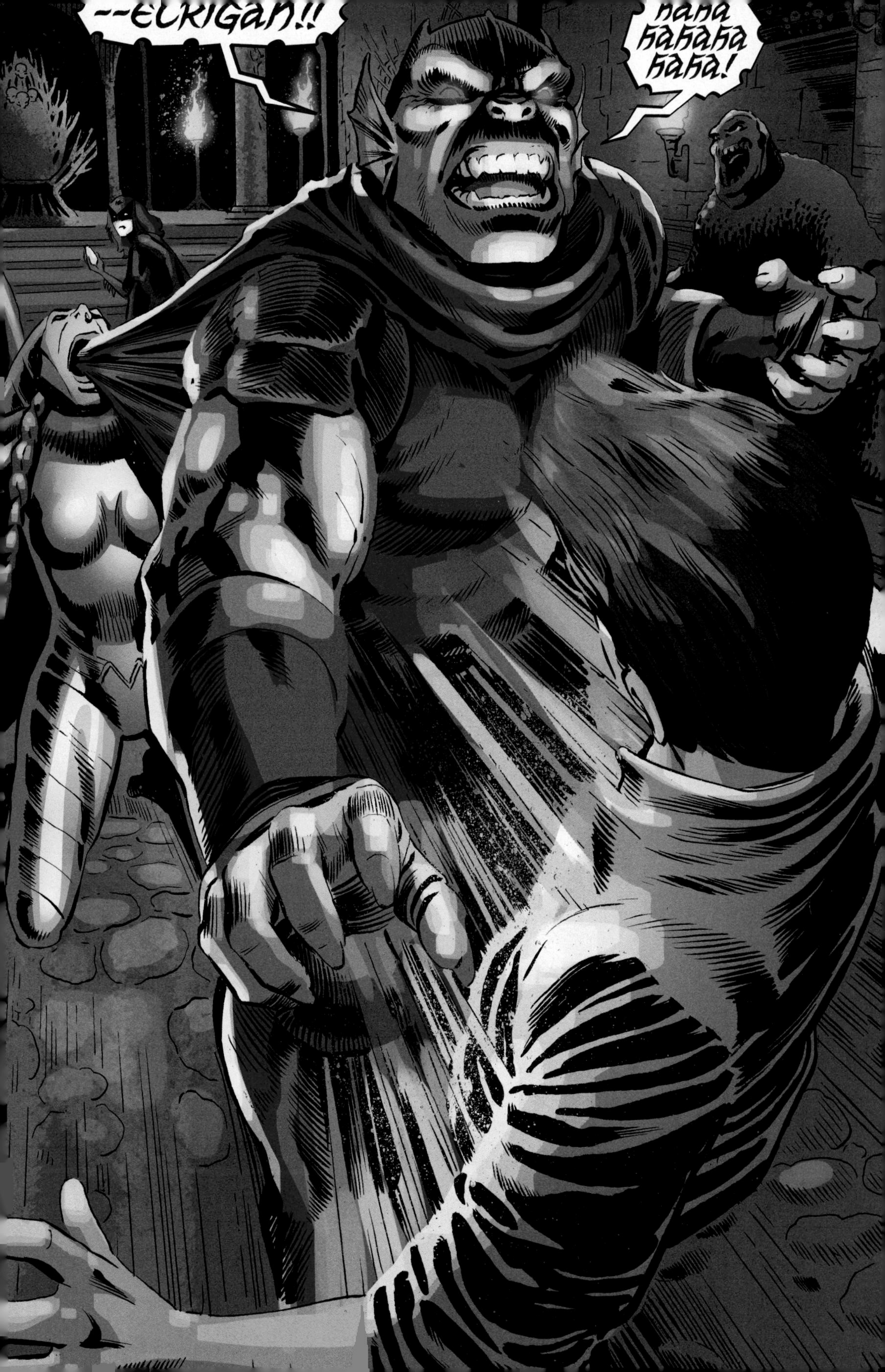
--ETRIGAN!!
HAHA HAHAHA HAHA!

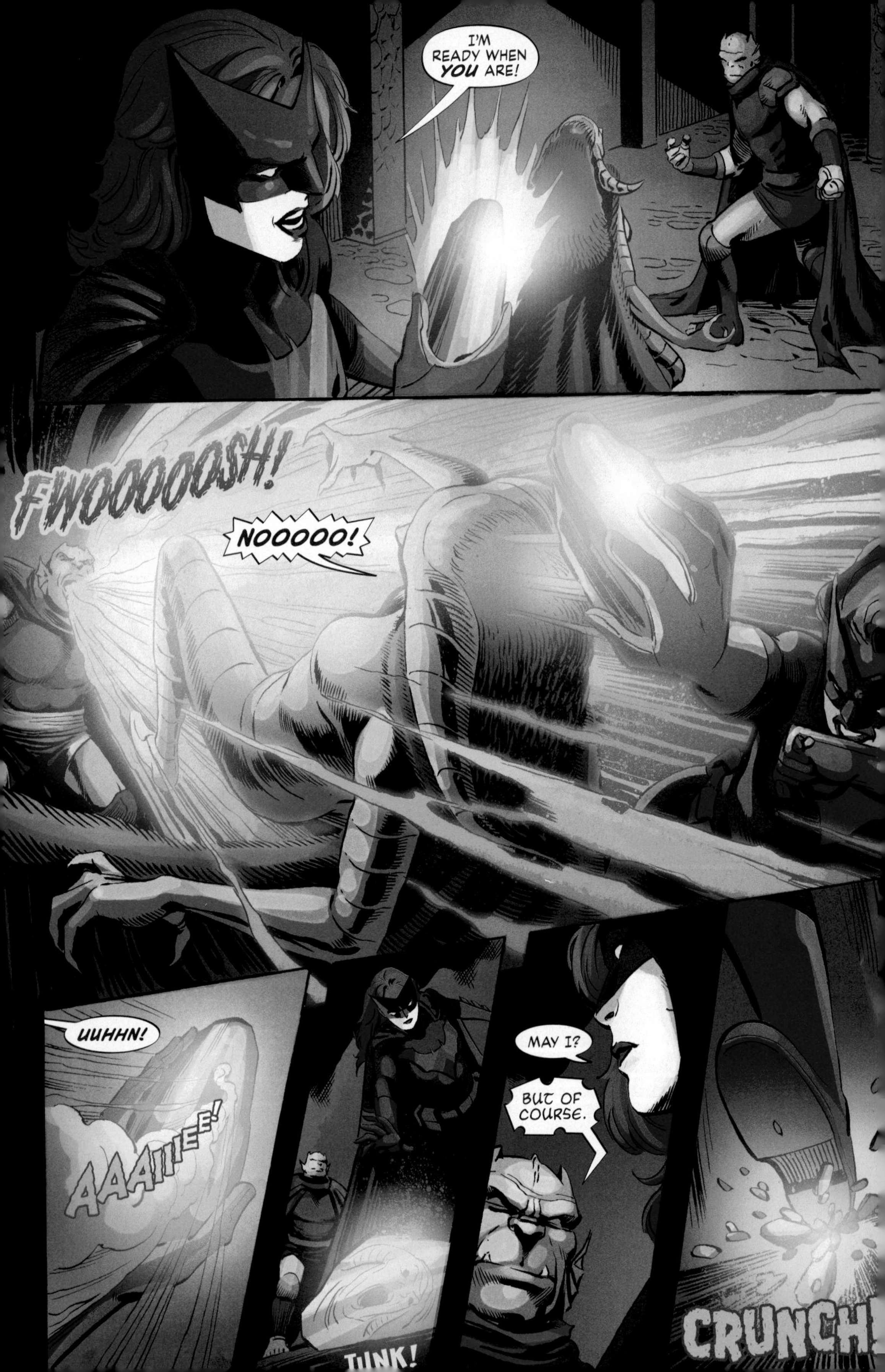
I'M READY WHEN YOU ARE!
FWOOOOOSH!
NOOOOO!
UUHHN!
AAAIIIEEE!
MAY I?
BUT OF COURSE.
TINK!
CRUNCH!

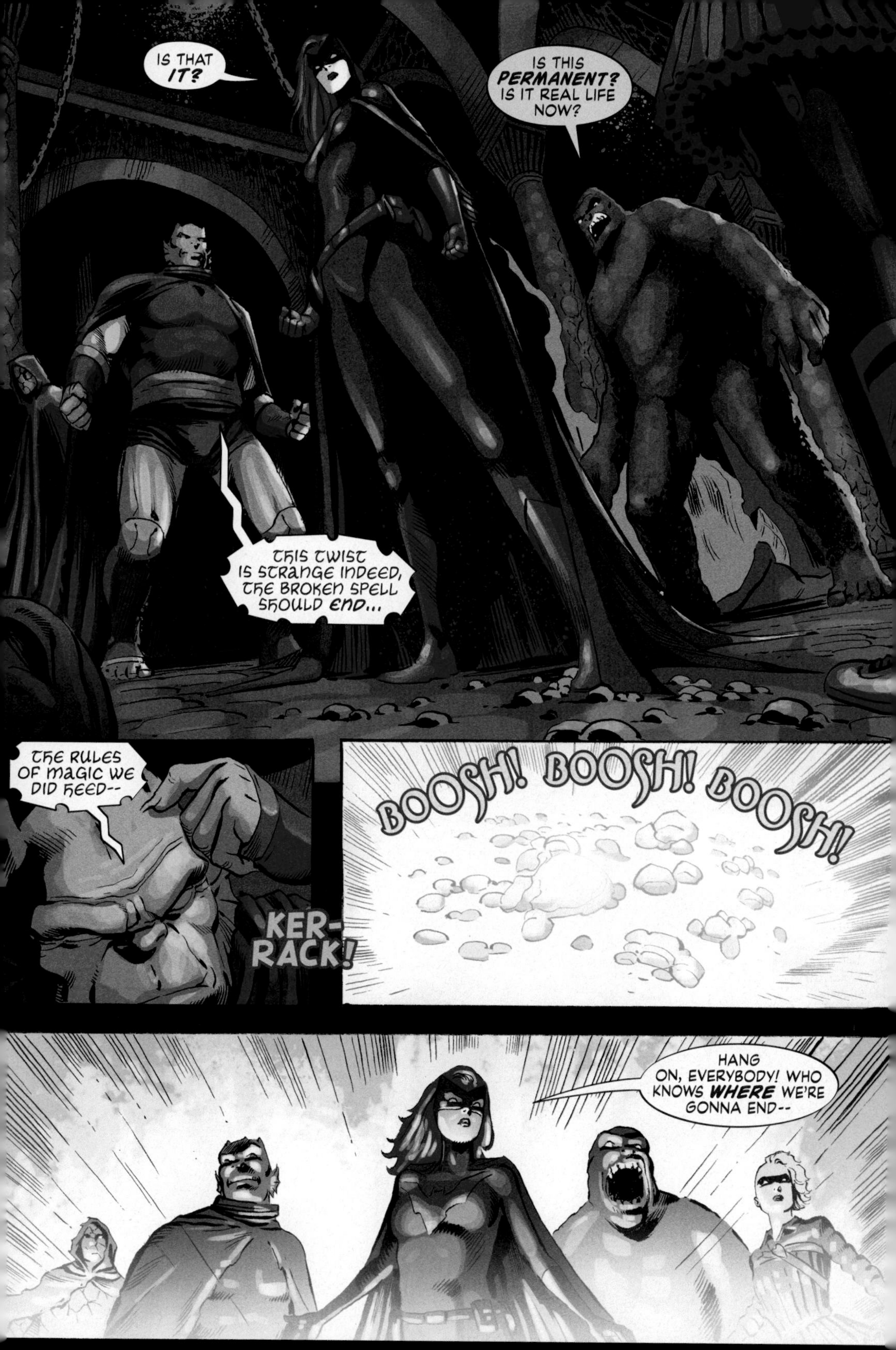
IS THAT IT?
IS THIS PERMANENT? IS IT REAL LIFE NOW?
THIS TWIST IS STRANGE INDEED, THE BROKEN SPELL SHOULD END...
THE RULES OF MAGIC WE DID HEED--
KER-RACK!
BOOSH! BOOSH! BOOSH!
HANG ON, EVERYBODY! WHO KNOWS WHERE WE'RE GONNA END--

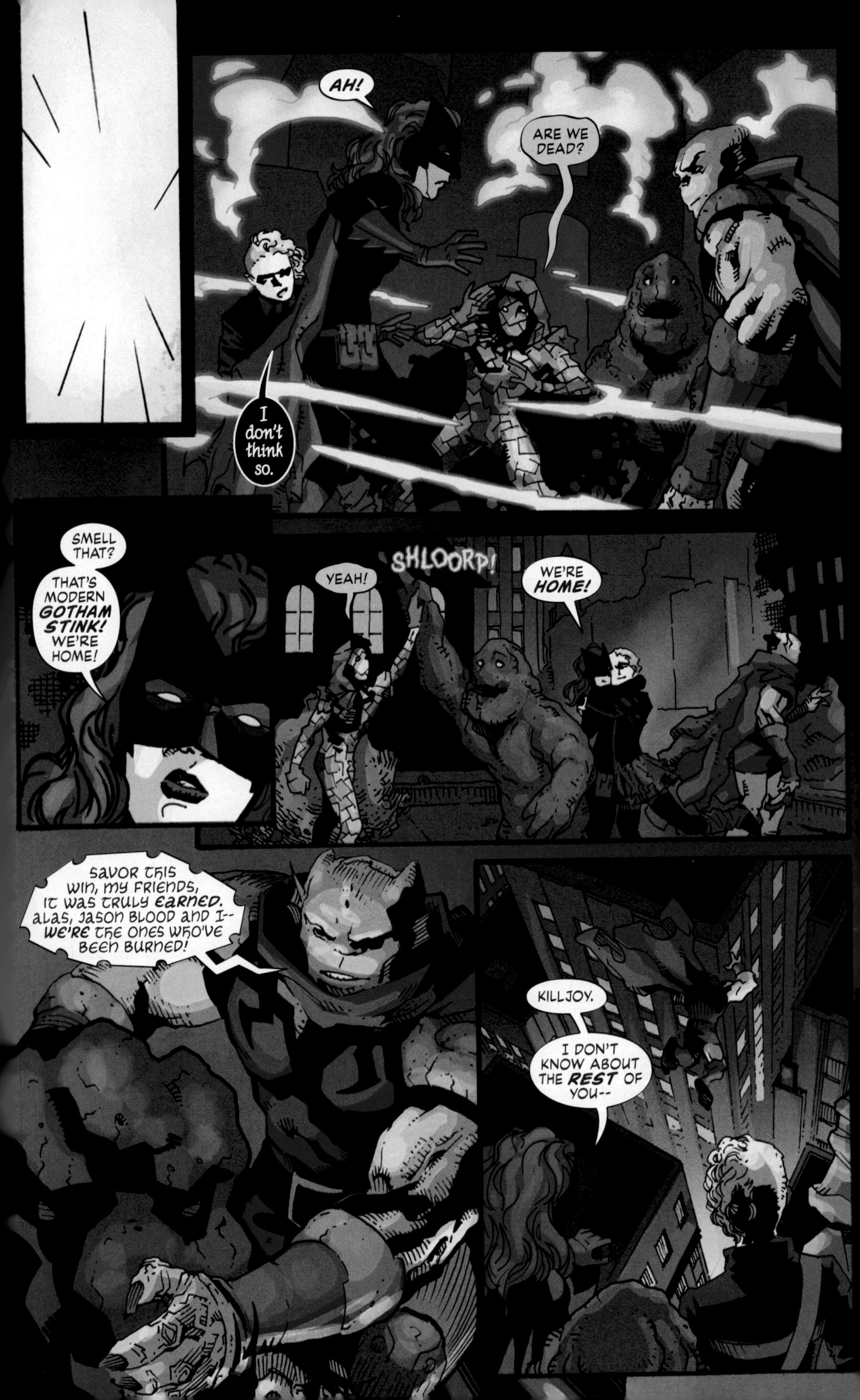

AH!
ARE WE DEAD?
I don't think so.
SMELL THAT?
THAT'S MODERN GOTHAM STINK! WE'RE HOME!
SHLOORP!
YEAH!
WE'RE HOME!
SAVOR THIS WIN, MY FRIENDS, IT WAS TRULY EARNED. ALAS, JASON BLOOD AND I-- WE'RE THE ONES WHO'VE BEEN BURNED!
KILLJOY.
I DON'T KNOW ABOUT THE REST OF YOU--

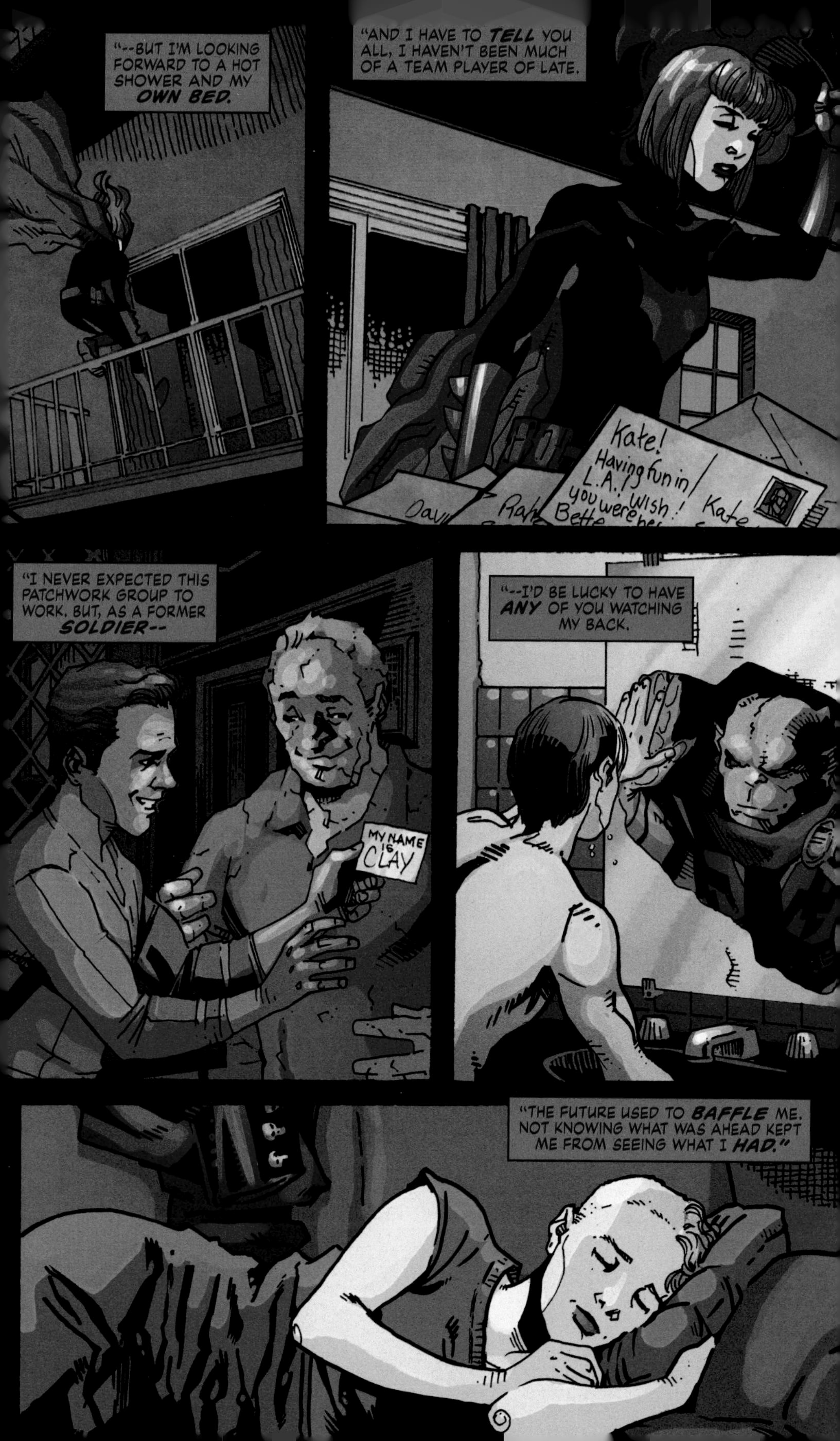
"--BUT I'M LOOKING FORWARD TO A HOT SHOWER AND MY OWN BED.
"AND I HAVE TO TELL YOU ALL, I HAVEN'T BEEN MUCH OF A TEAM PLAYER OF LATE.
Kate! Having fun in L.A.! Wish you were he
Kate
"I NEVER EXPECTED THIS PATCHWORK GROUP TO WORK. BUT, AS A FORMER SOLDIER--
MY NAME IS CLAY
"--I'D BE LUCKY TO HAVE ANY OF YOU WATCHING MY BACK.
"THE FUTURE USED TO BAFFLE ME. NOT KNOWING WHAT WAS AHEAD KEPT ME FROM SEEING WHAT I HAD."

"BUT THAT'S *OVER* NOW.

KNOCK KNOCK!

"I ACCEPT THE *UNCERTAINTY* OF LIFE...

"...THE FRAGILITY..."

KATE?

HI, MAGGIE. WE NEED TO TALK.

"AND YOU KNOW WHAT?"

...

COME IN.

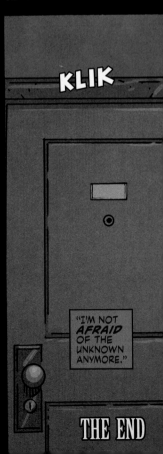

KLIK

"I'M NOT *AFRAID* OF THE UNKNOWN ANYMORE."

THE END

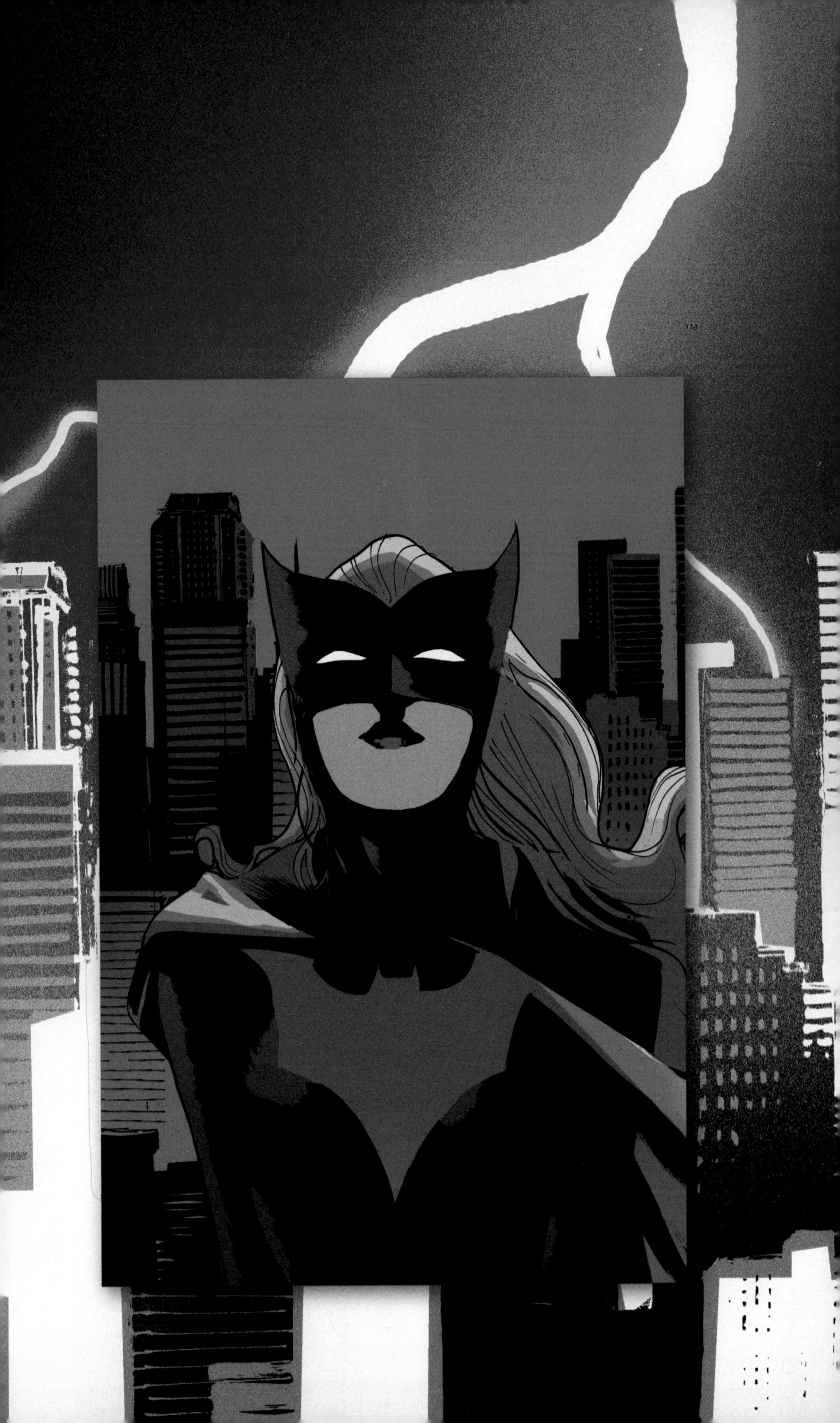
TM

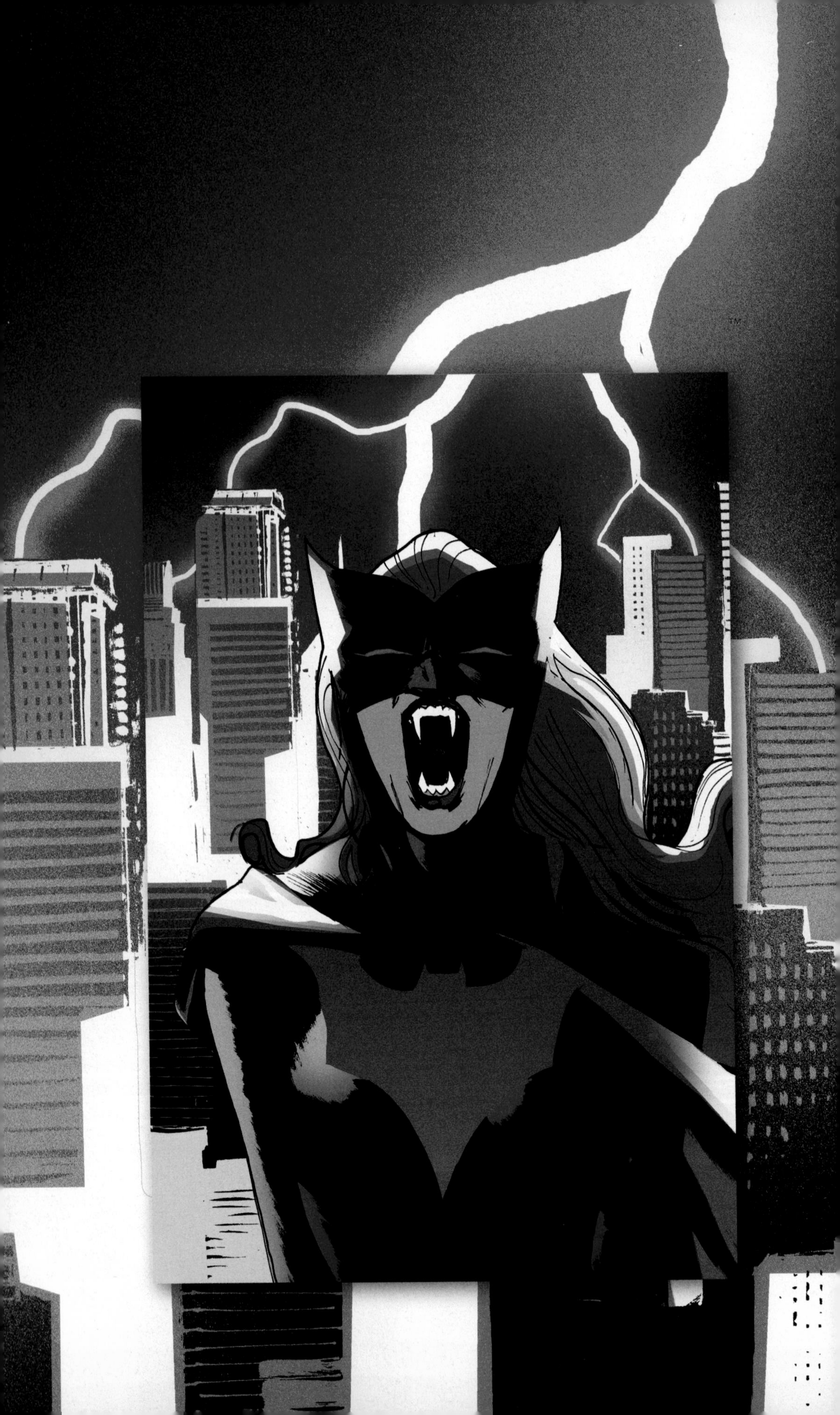

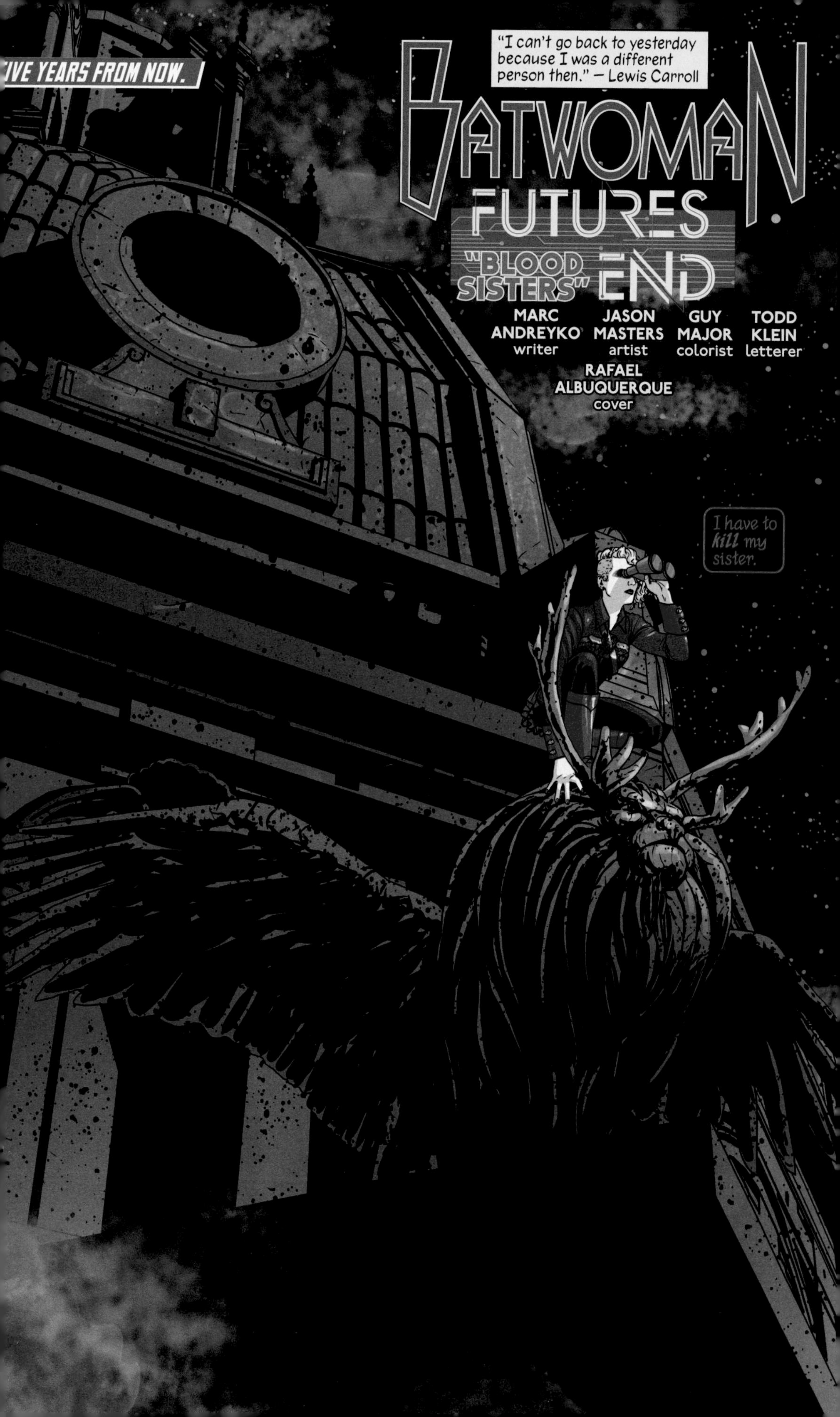

IVE YEARS FROM NOW.
"I can't go back to yesterday because I was a different person then." — Lewis Carroll
BATWOMAN
FUTURES END
"BLOOD SISTERS"
MARC ANDREYKO writer
JASON MASTERS artist
GUY MAJOR colorist
TODD KLEIN letterer
RAFAEL ALBUQUERQUE cover
I have to kill my sister.

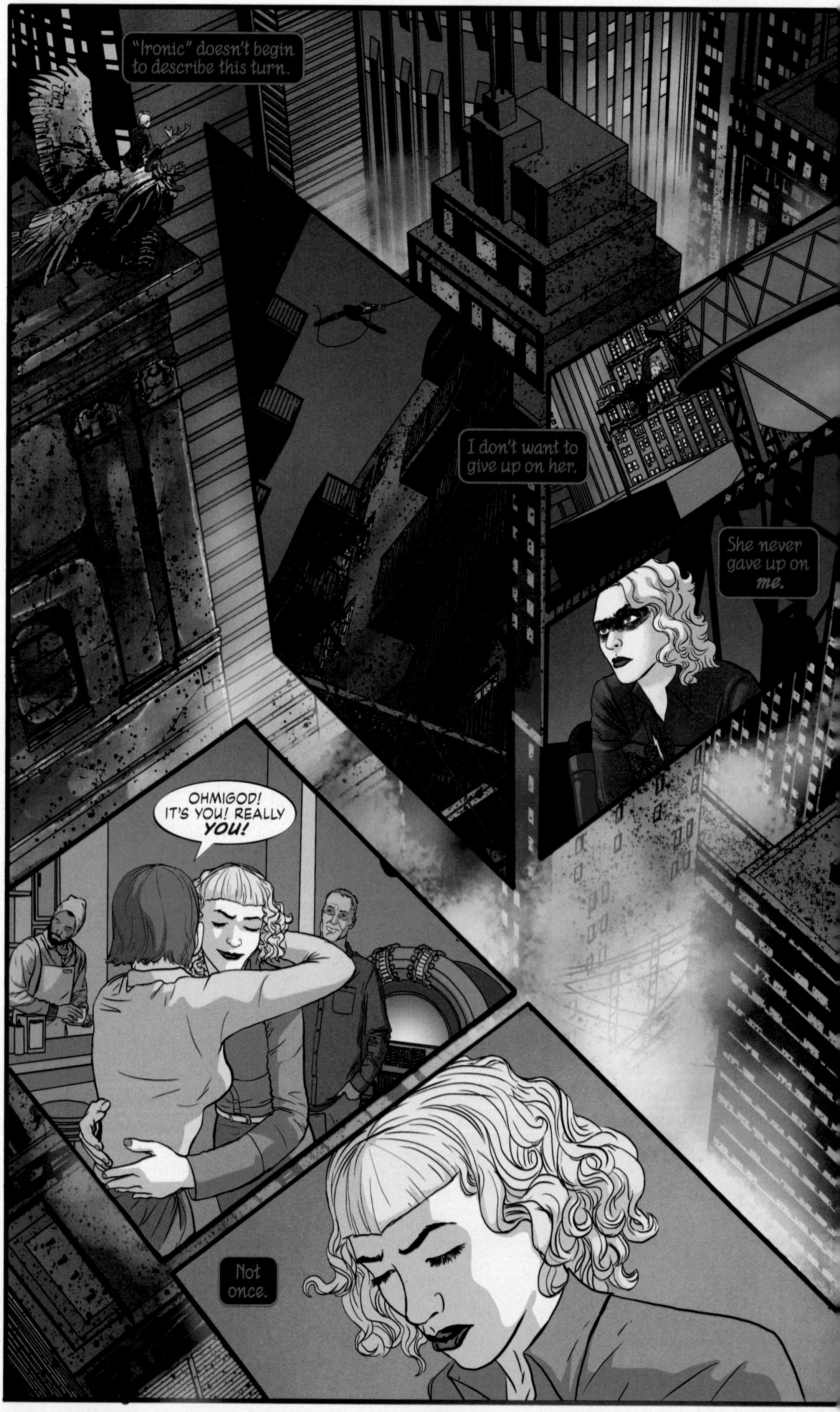
"Ironic" doesn't begin to describe this turn.
I don't want to give up on her.
She never gave up on *me.*
OHMIGOD! IT'S YOU! REALLY *YOU!*
Not once.

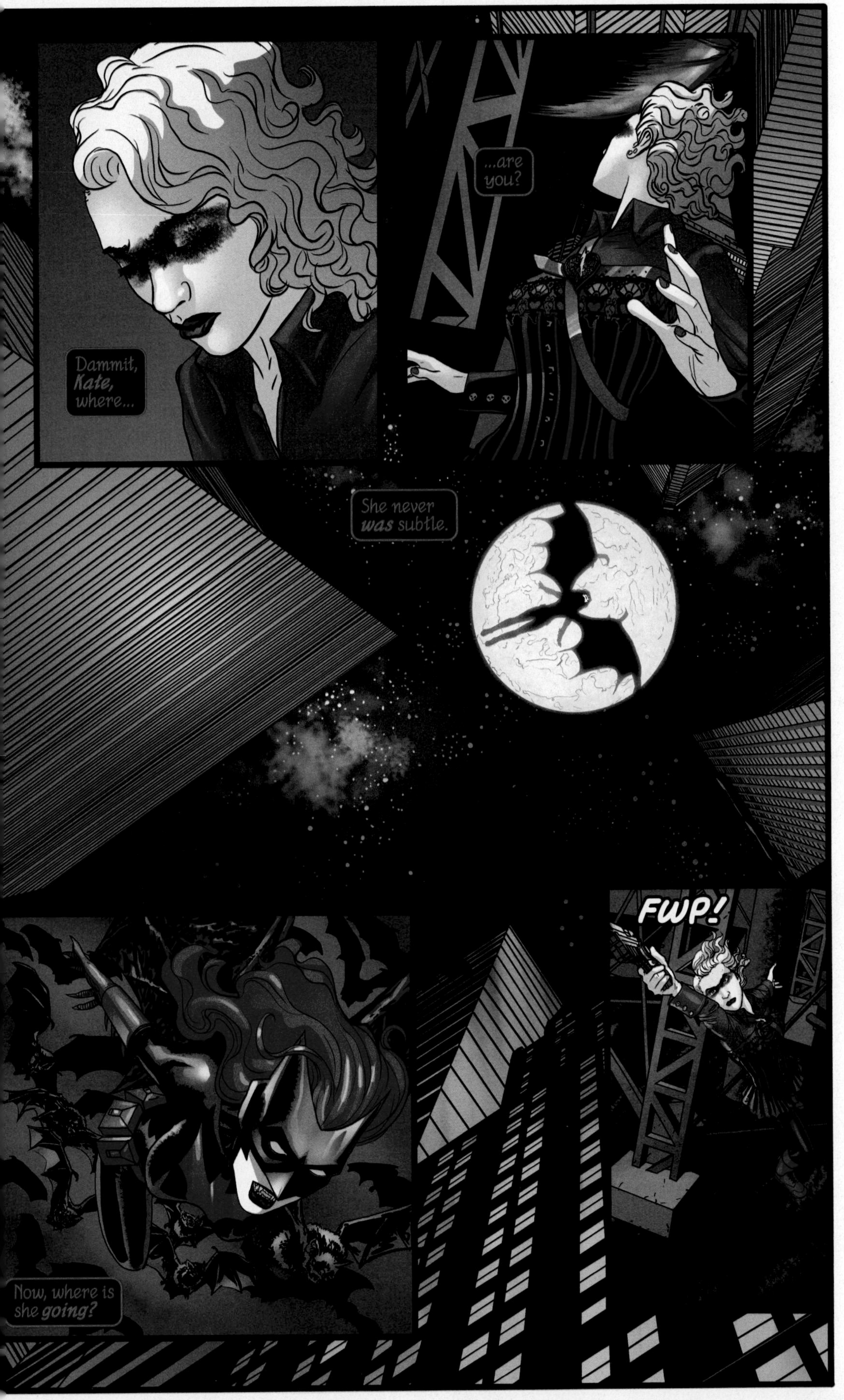
Dammit, Kate, where...
...are you?
She never was subtle.
Now, where is she going?
FWP!

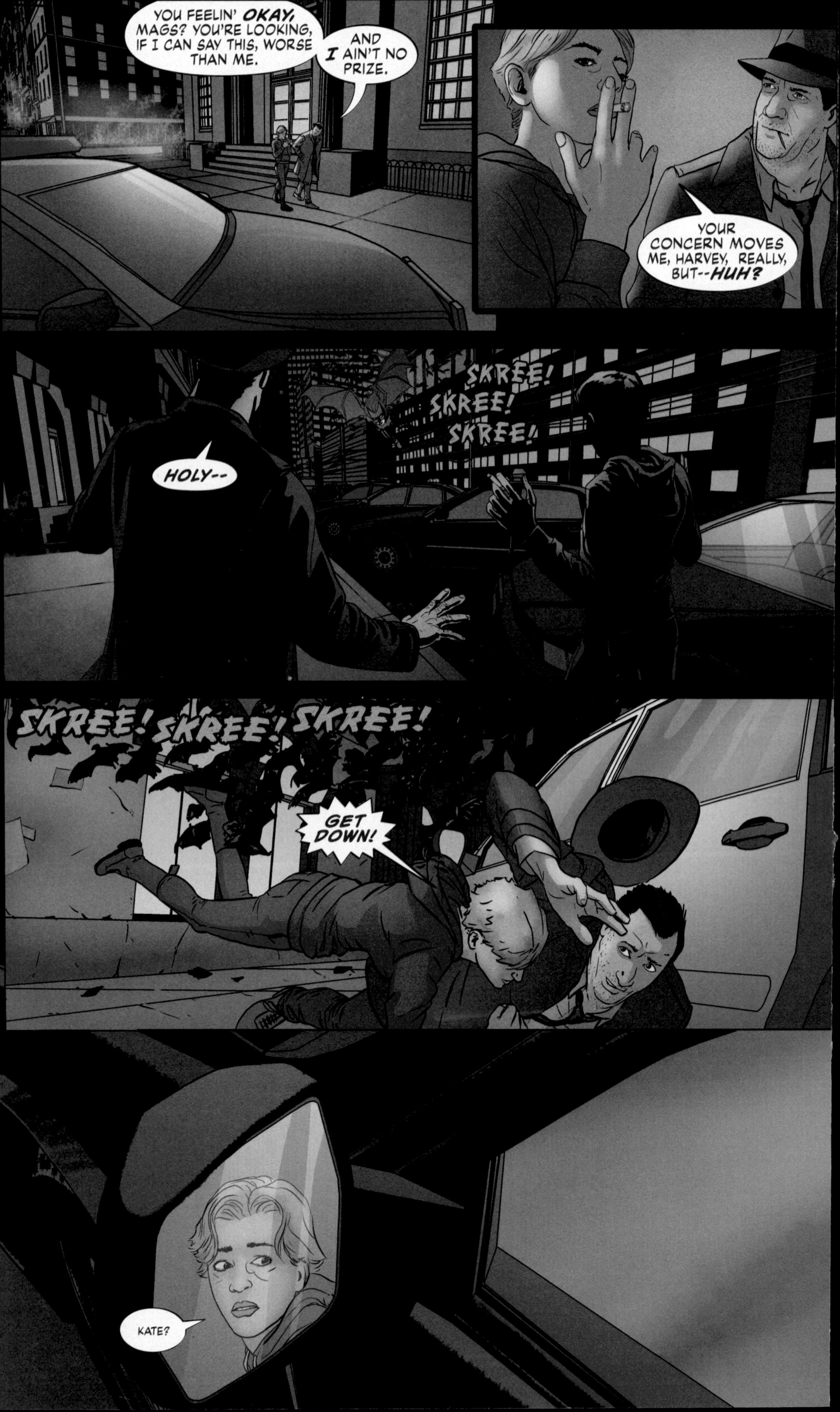
YOU FEELIN' OKAY, MAGS? YOU'RE LOOKING, IF I CAN SAY THIS, WORSE THAN ME.
AND I AIN'T NO PRIZE.
YOUR CONCERN MOVES ME, HARVEY, REALLY, BUT--HUH?
SKREE! SKREE! SKREE!
HOLY--
SKREE! SKREE! SKREE!
GET DOWN!
KATE?

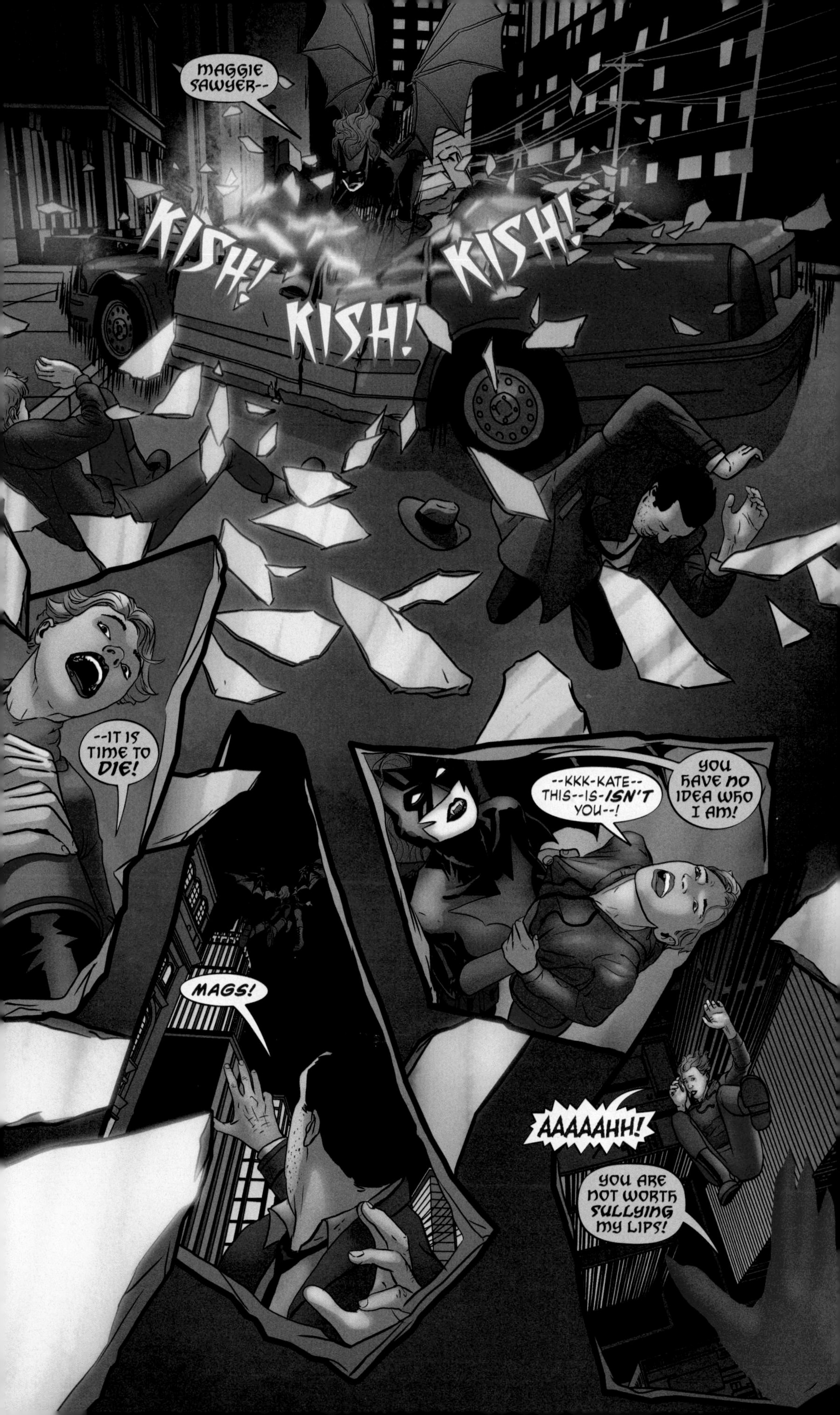
MAGGIE SAWYER--
KISH!
KISH!
KISH!
--IT IS TIME TO DIE!
--KKK-KATE-- THIS--IS-ISN'T YOU--!
YOU HAVE NO IDEA WHO I AM!
MAGS!
AAAAAHH!
YOU ARE NOT WORTH SULLYING MY LIPS!

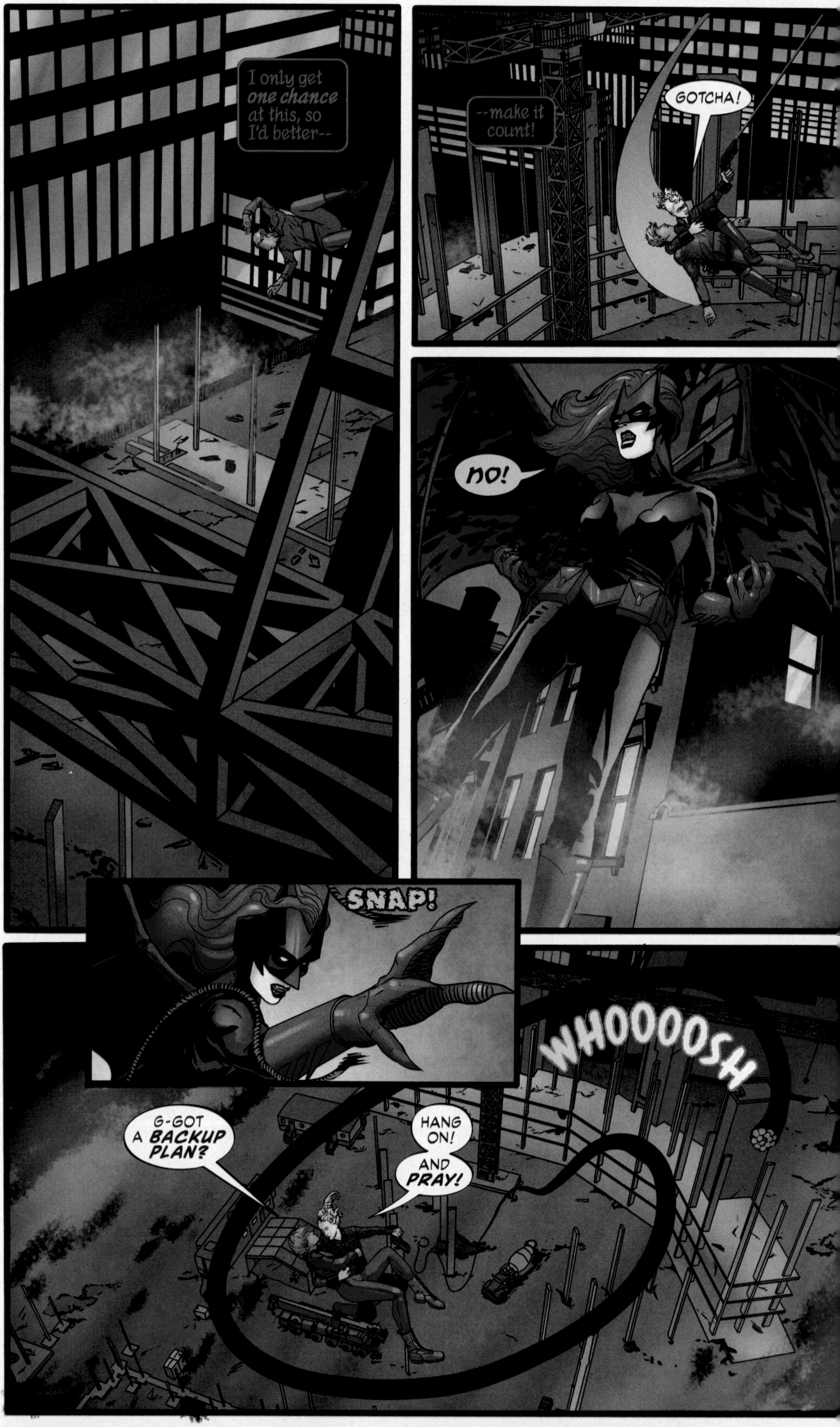
I only get one chance at this, so I'd better--
--make it count!
GOTCHA!
no!
SNAP!
WHOOOOSH
G-GOT A BACKUP PLAN?
HANG ON! AND PRAY!

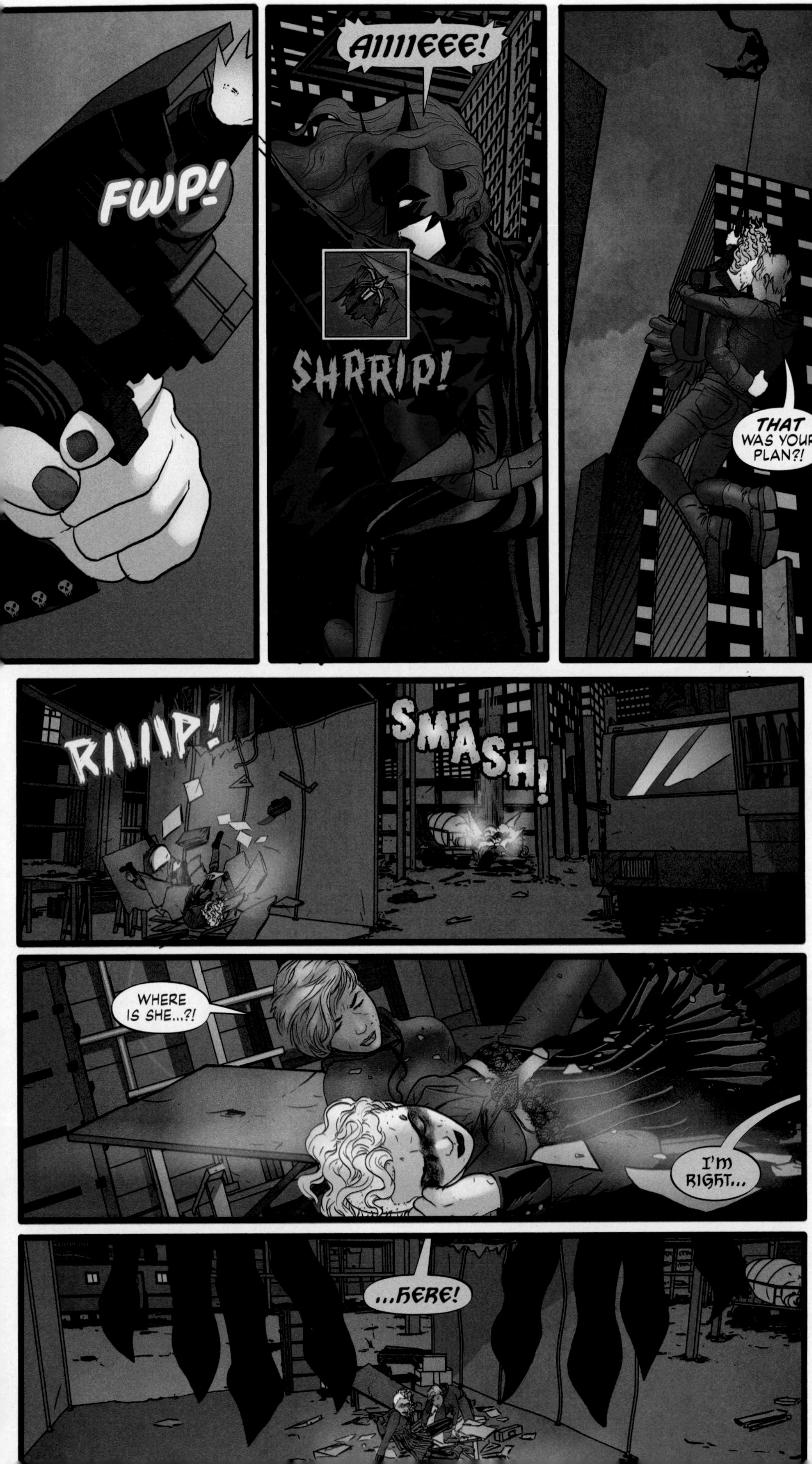
FWP!
AIIIIEEE!
SHRRIP!
THAT WAS YOUR PLAN?!
RIIIIP!
SMASH!
WHERE IS SHE...?!
I'M RIGHT...
...HERE!

REMEMBER *RORY,* KATE?

SHUK!

--MMMPPh--!

BATWOMAN, *STOP!* YOU MUST *FIGHT* THIS! DON'T GIVE IN!

YOU THINK YOU'RE MY *FRIEND?* YOU ARE NOTHING TO ME...

--KKK--

CHOK!

...LESS THAN NOTHING!

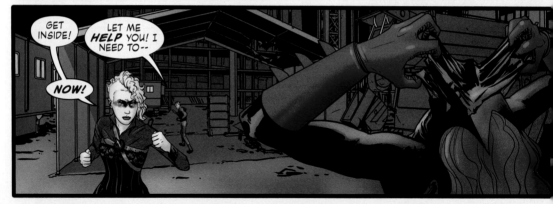

GET INSIDE!

LET ME *HELP* YOU! I NEED TO--

NOW!

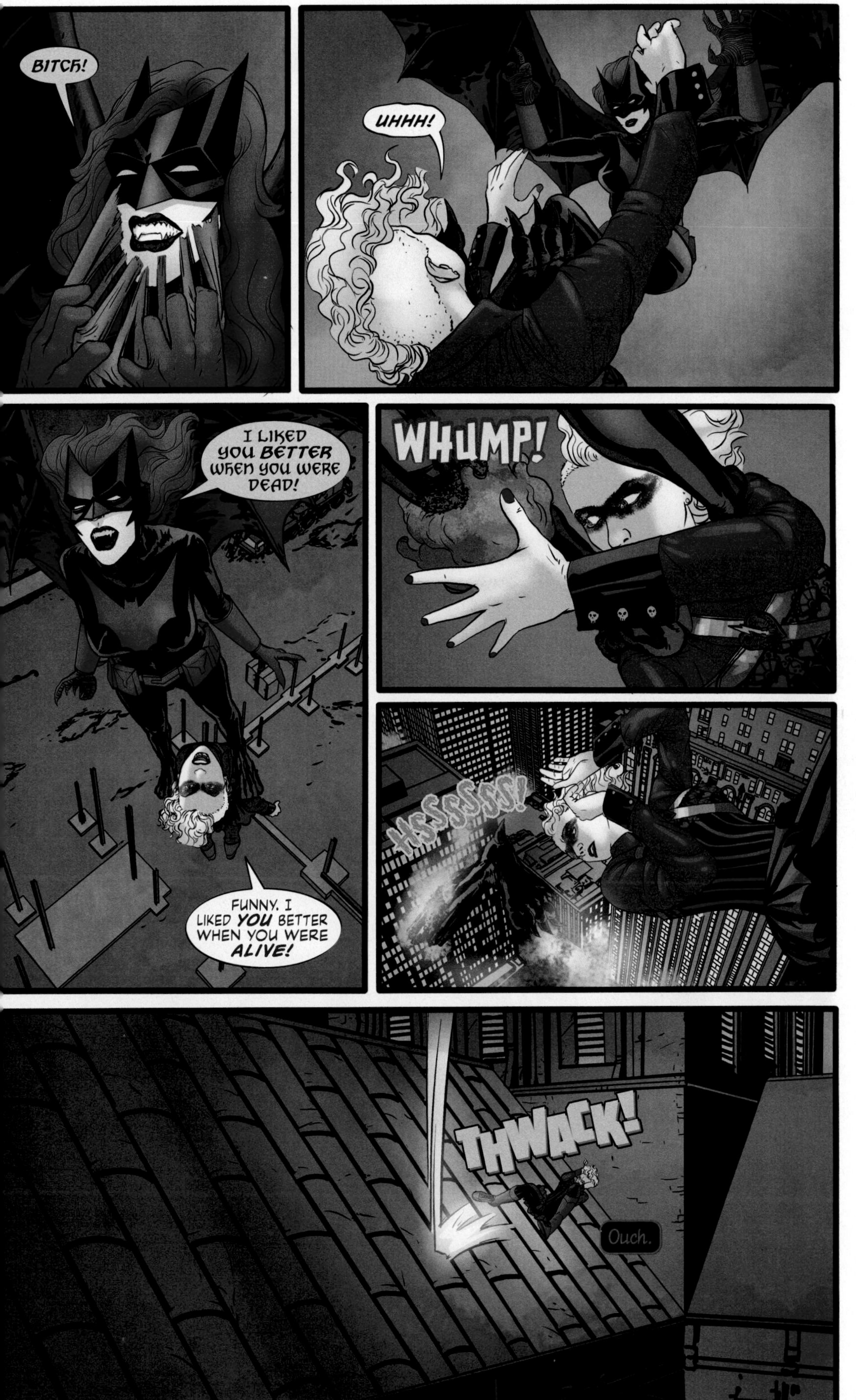
BITCH!
UHHH!
I LIKED YOU BETTER WHEN YOU WERE DEAD!
FUNNY. I LIKED YOU BETTER WHEN YOU WERE ALIVE!
WHUMP!
HSSSSSS!
THWACK!
Ouch.

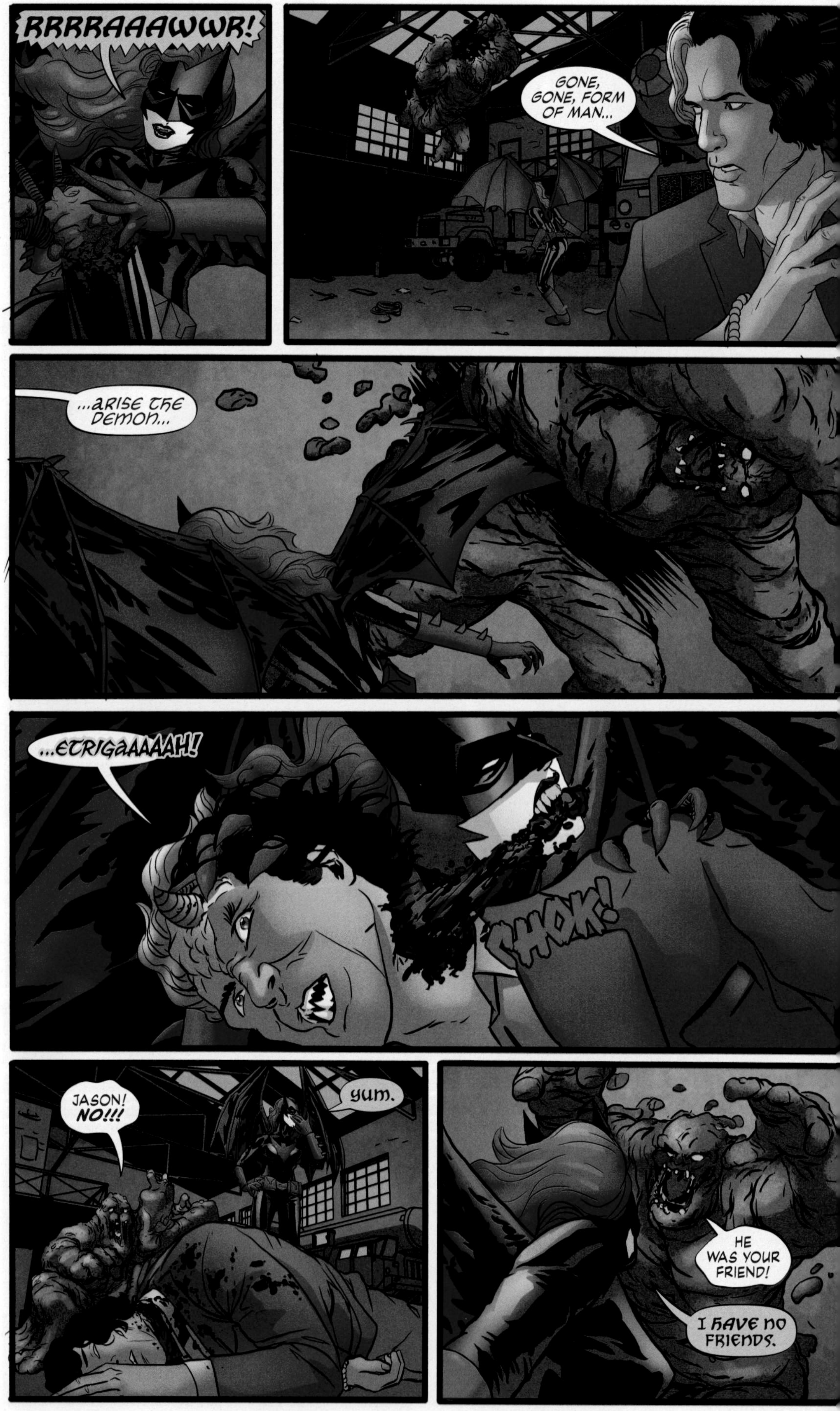
RRRRAAAWWR!
GONE, GONE, FORM OF MAN...
...ARISE THE DEMON...
...ETRIGAAAAAH!
CHOK!
JASON! NO!!!
YUM.
HE WAS YOUR FRIEND!
I HAVE NO FRIENDS.

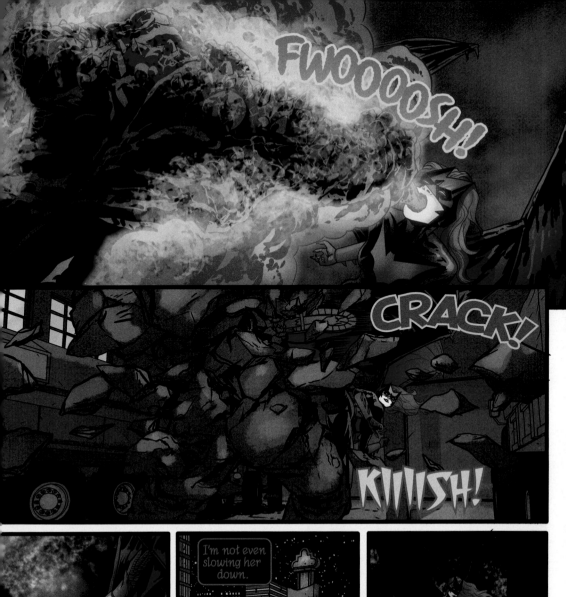

FWOOOOSH!!

CRACK!

KIIIISH!

SHLOP

I'm not even slowing her down.

I need some breathing room. *Badly.*

YOUR BAG OF TRICKS IS RUNNING *LOW,* SISTER.

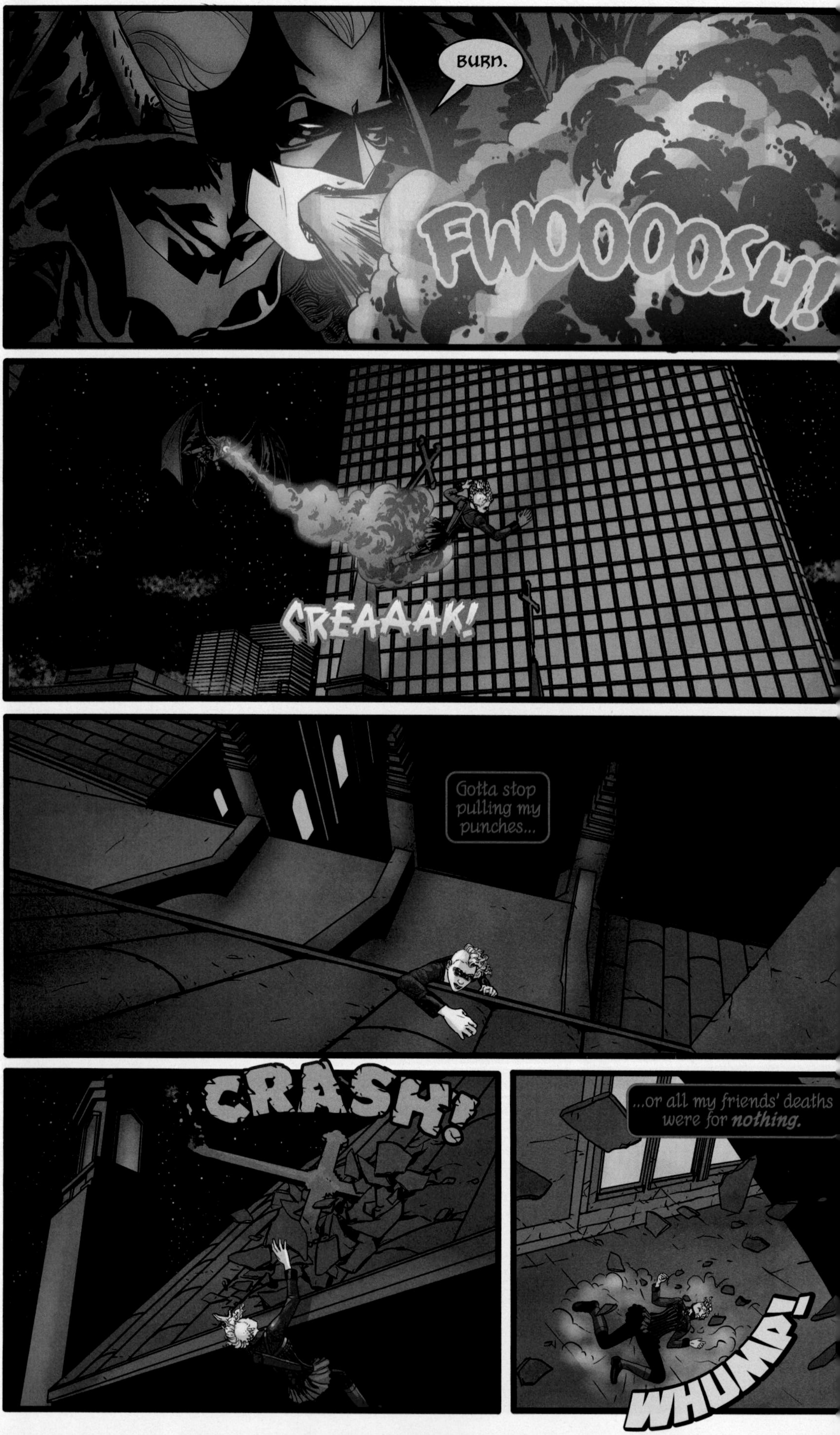
BURN.
FWOOOOSH!
CREAAAK!
Gotta stop pulling my punches...
CRASH!
...or all my friends' deaths were for *nothing.*
WHUMP!

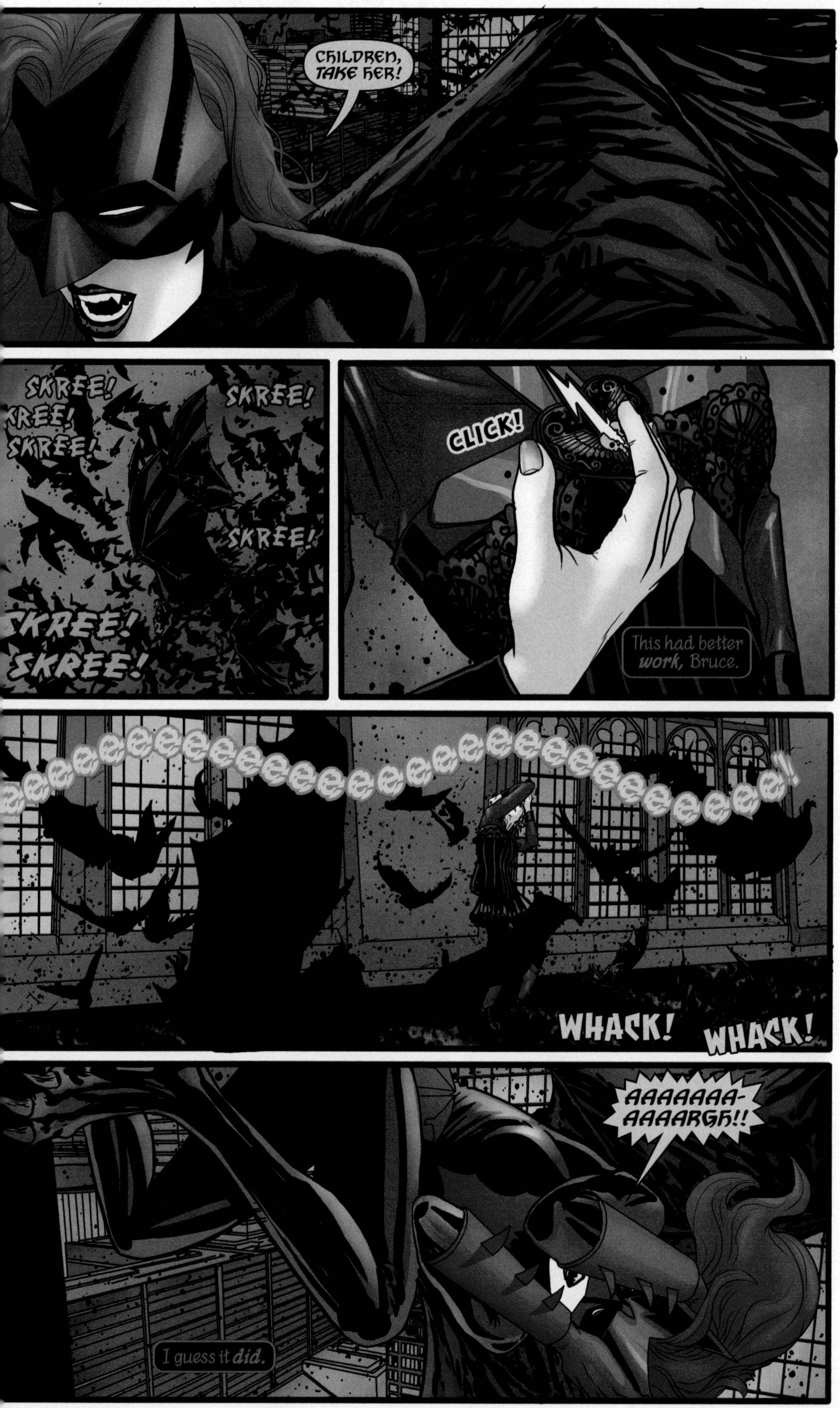
CHILDREN, TAKE HER!
SKREE! SKREE! SKREE! SKREE! SKREE! SKREE! SKREE!
CLICK!
This had better work, Bruce.
EEEEEEEEEEEEEEEEEEEEEEEEEEEEEEEEEEEEEE!!
WHACK! WHACK!
AAAAAAA-AAAARGH!!
I guess it did.

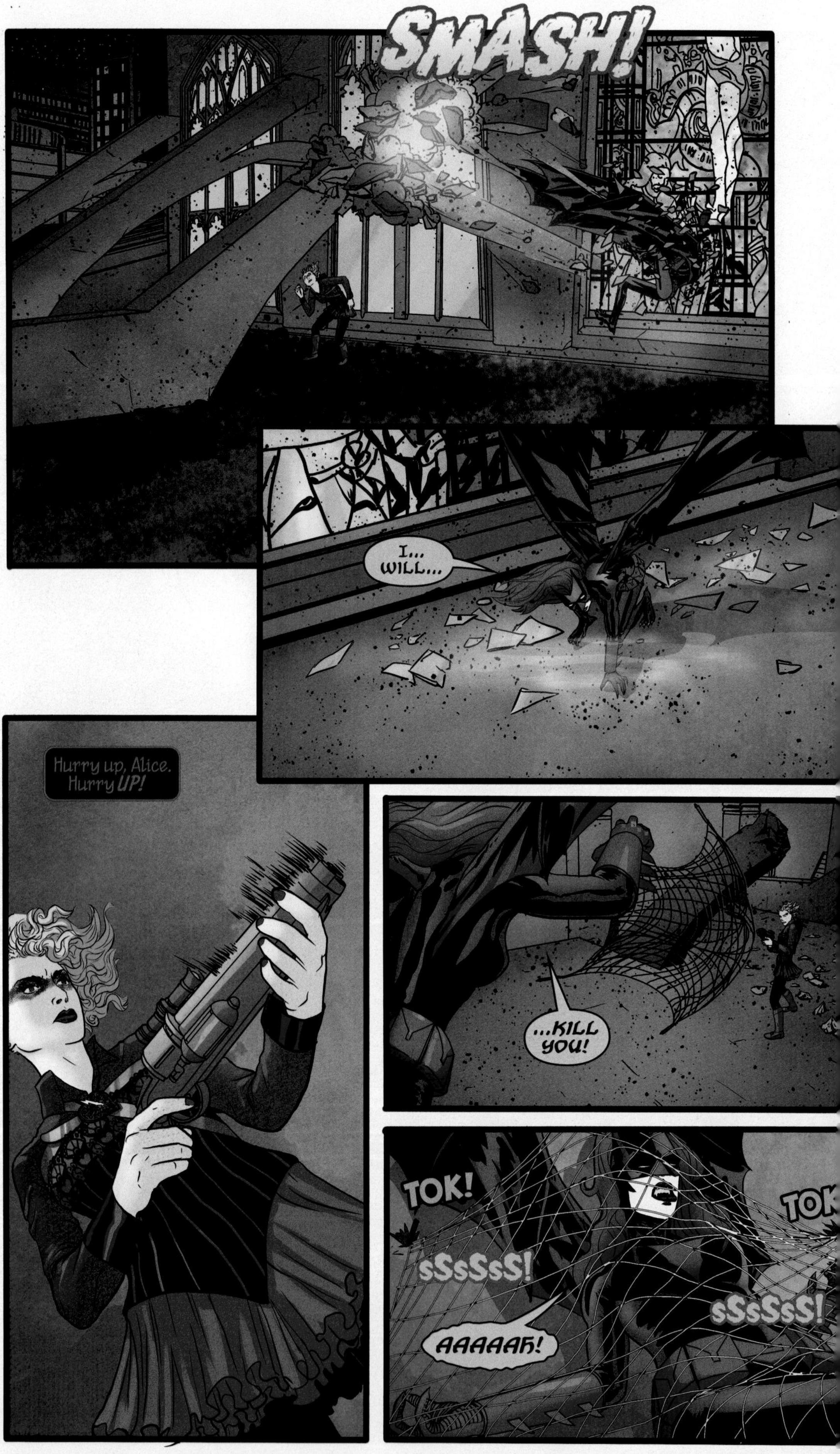

SMASH!
I... WILL...
Hurry up, Alice. Hurry UP!
...KILL YOU!
TOK!
sSsSsS!
AAAAAH!
sSsSsS!

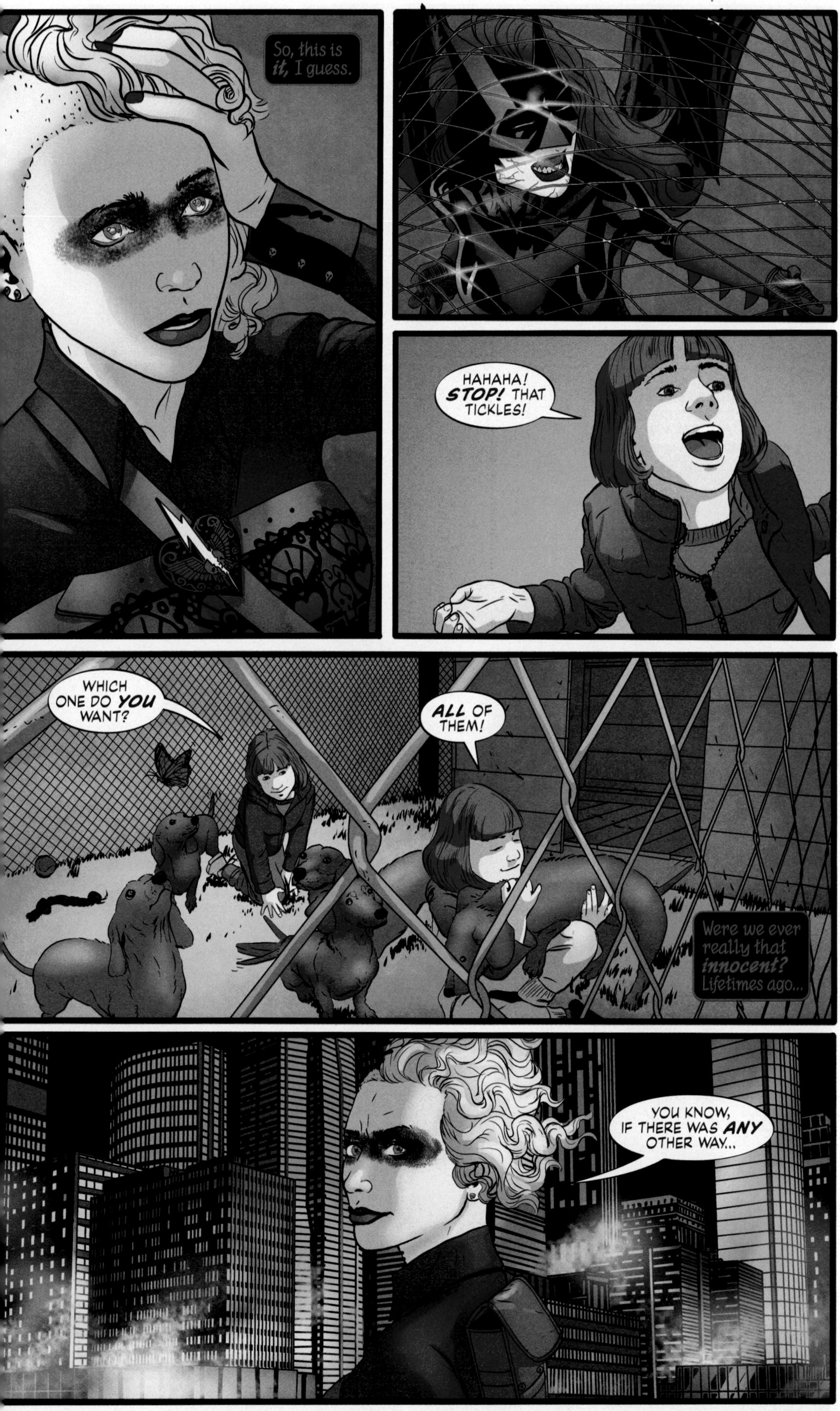
So, this is *it,* I guess.
HAHAHA! **STOP!** THAT TICKLES!
WHICH ONE DO **YOU** WANT?
ALL OF THEM!
Were we ever really that **innocent?** Lifetimes ago...
YOU KNOW, IF THERE WAS **ANY** OTHER WAY...

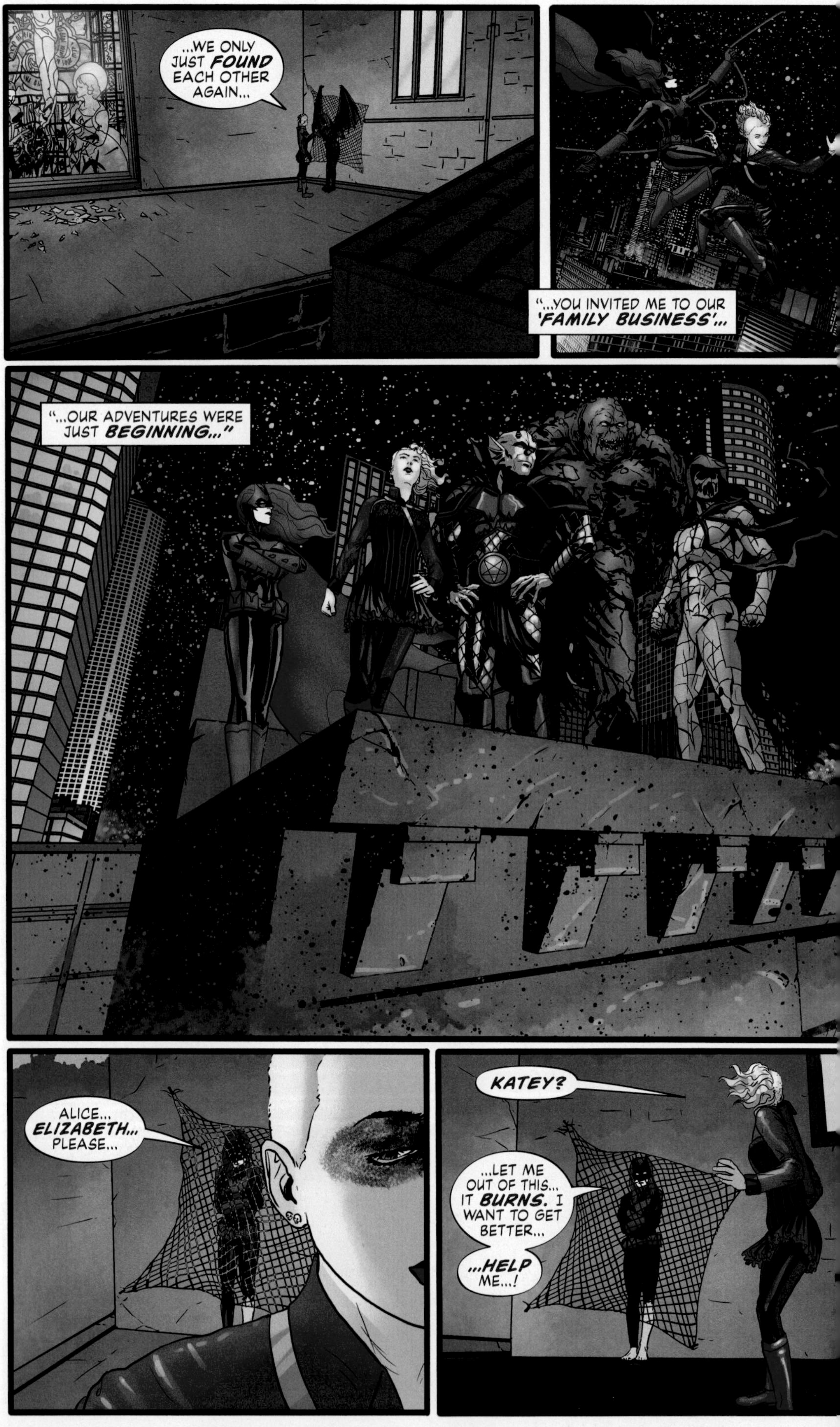
...WE ONLY JUST FOUND EACH OTHER AGAIN...
"...YOU INVITED ME TO OUR 'FAMILY BUSINESS'...
"...OUR ADVENTURES WERE JUST BEGINNING..."
ALICE... ELIZABETH... PLEASE...
KATEY?
...LET ME OUT OF THIS... IT BURNS. I WANT TO GET BETTER...
...HELP ME...!

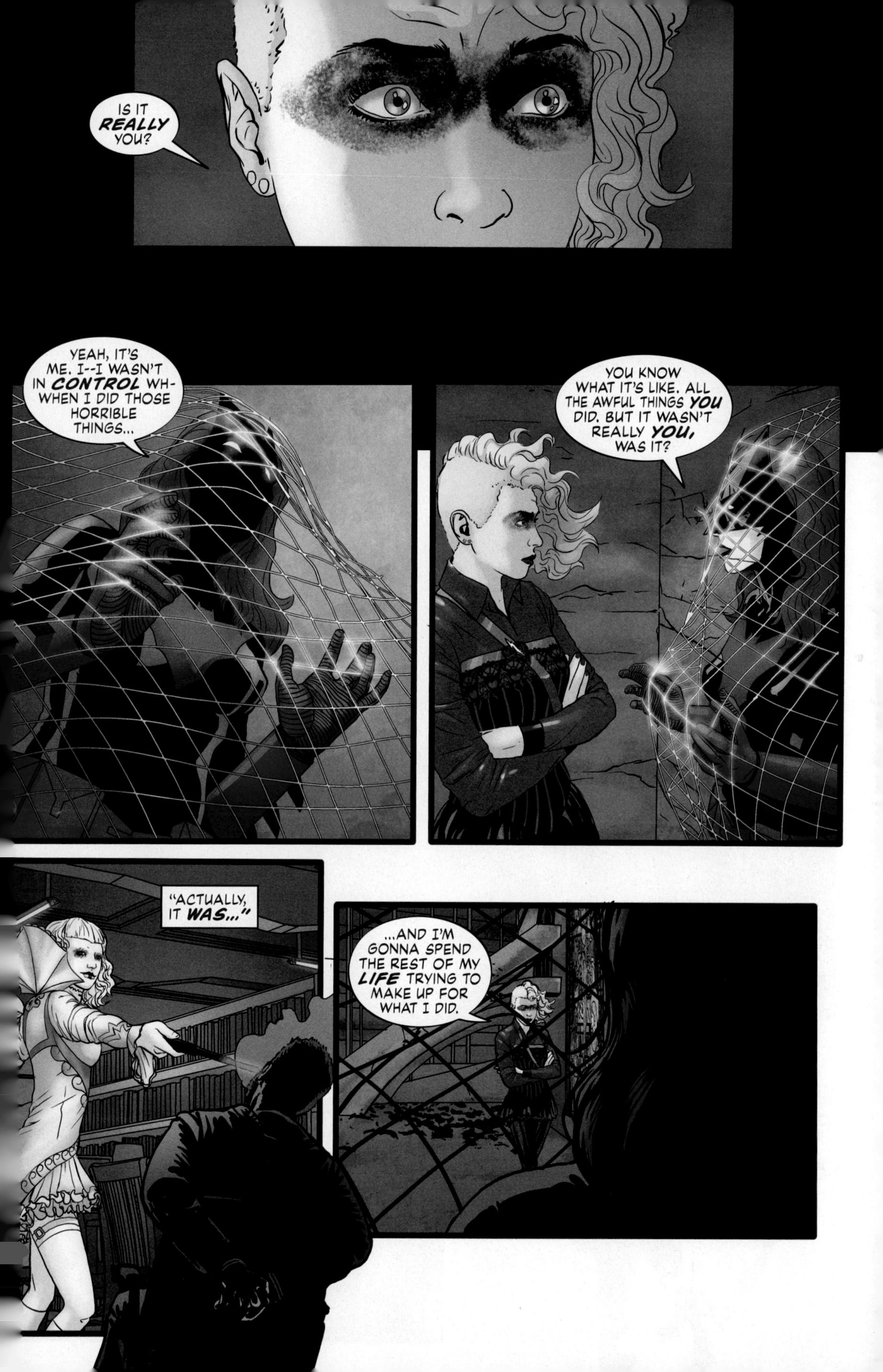
IS IT *REALLY* YOU?
YEAH, IT'S ME. I--I WASN'T IN *CONTROL* WH- WHEN I DID THOSE HORRIBLE THINGS...
YOU KNOW WHAT IT'S LIKE. ALL THE AWFUL THINGS *YOU* DID. BUT IT WASN'T REALLY *YOU,* WAS IT?
"ACTUALLY, IT *WAS*..."
...AND I'M GONNA SPEND THE REST OF MY *LIFE* TRYING TO MAKE UP FOR WHAT I DID.

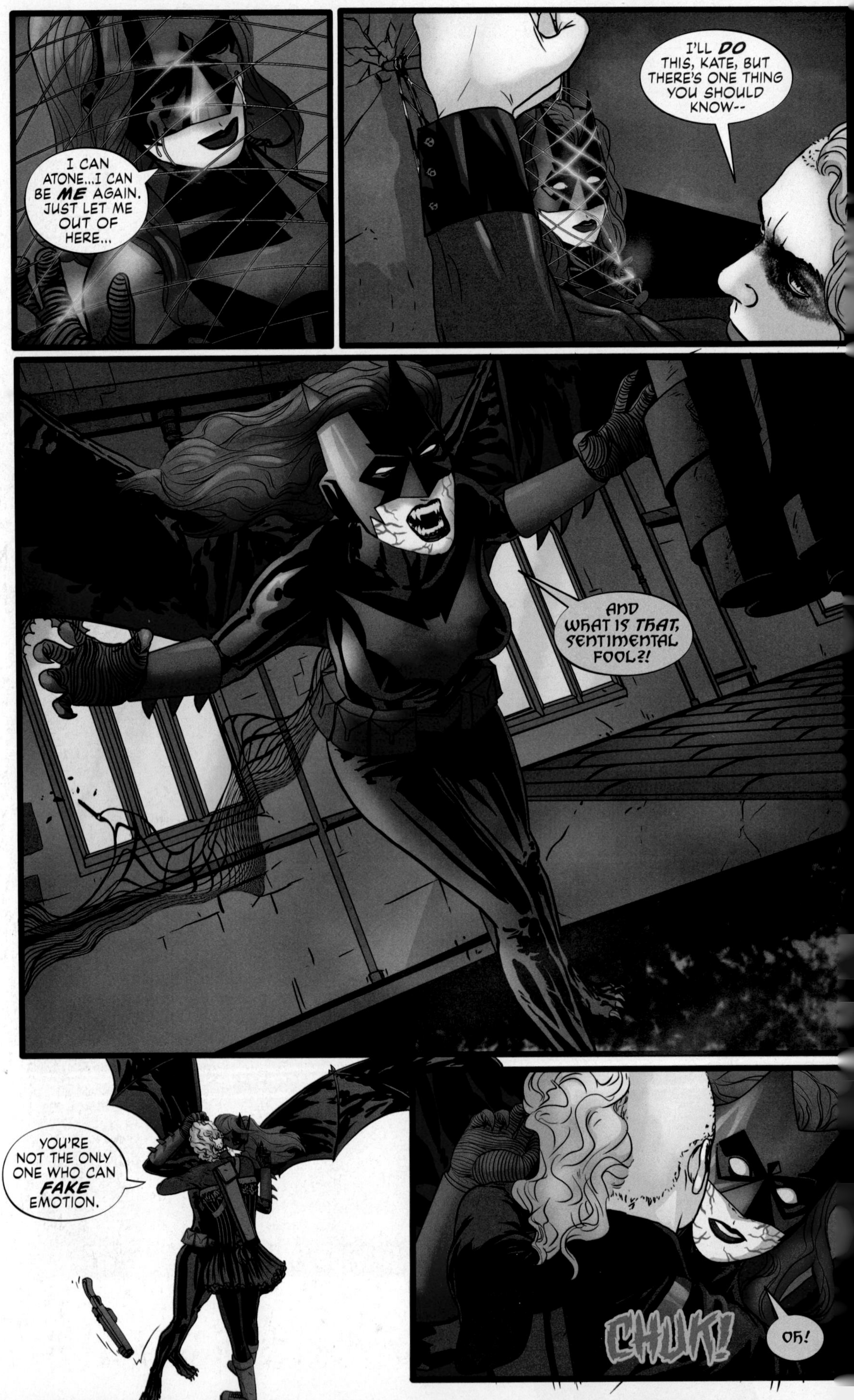
I CAN ATONE...I CAN BE ME AGAIN. JUST LET ME OUT OF HERE...
I'LL DO THIS, KATE, BUT THERE'S ONE THING YOU SHOULD KNOW--
AND WHAT IS THAT, SENTIMENTAL FOOL?!
YOU'RE NOT THE ONLY ONE WHO CAN FAKE EMOTION.
CHUK!
OH!

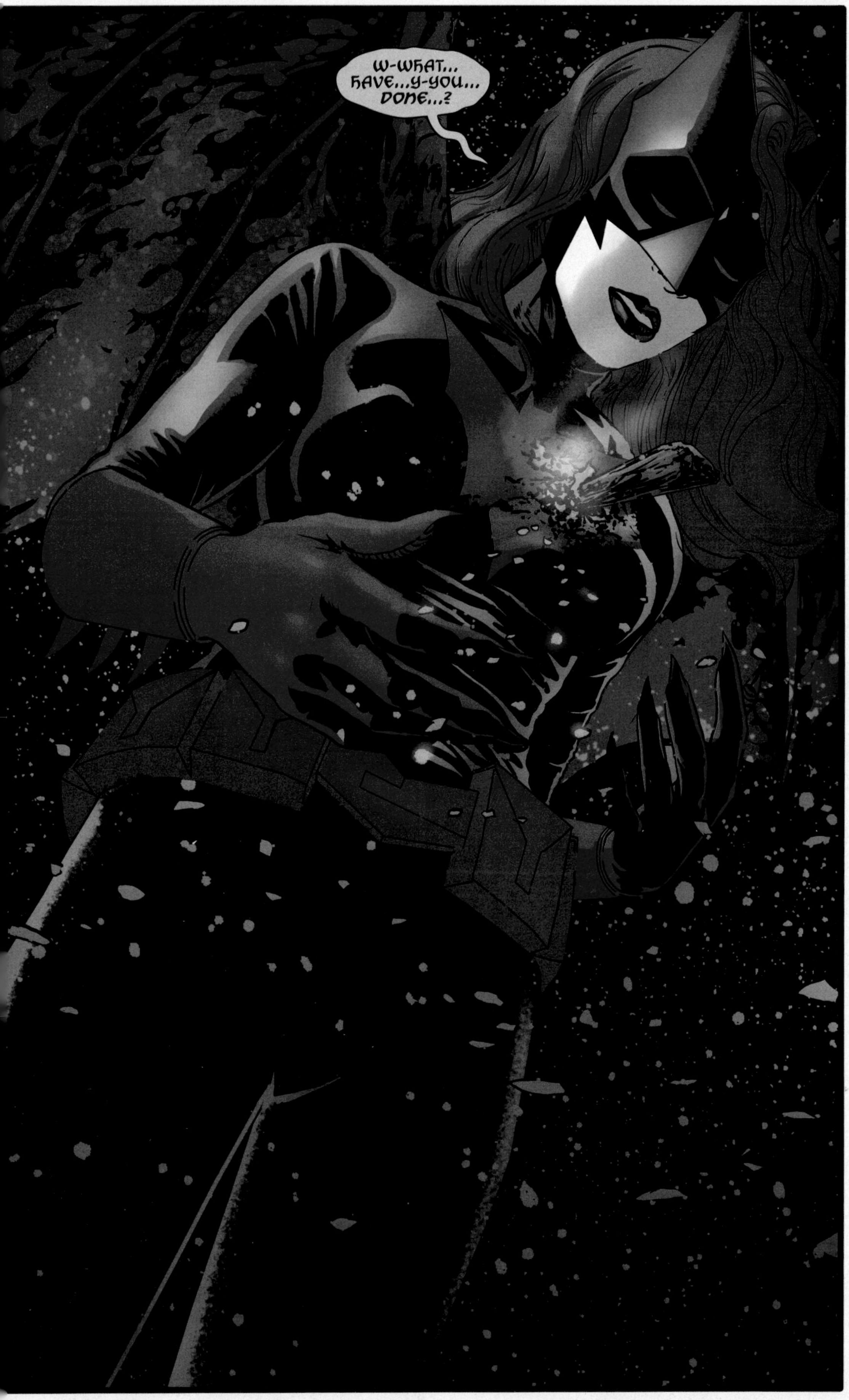
W-WHAT... HAVE...Y-YOU... DONE...?

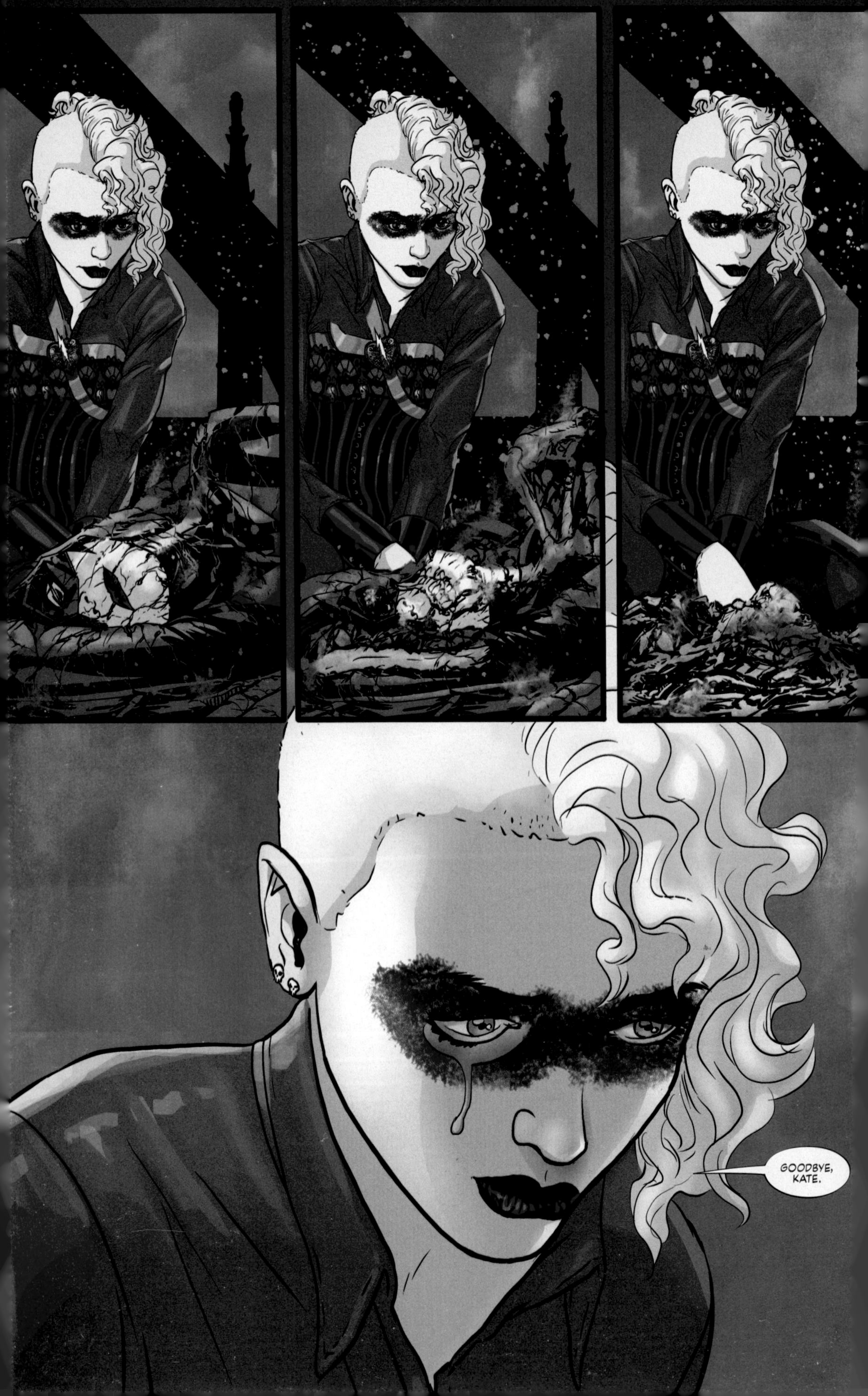
GOODBYE, KATE.